THE MATRIX OF VISUAL CULTURE

Cultural Memory

in

the

Present

Mieke Bal and Hent de Vries, Editors

THE MATRIX OF
VISUAL CULTURE
*Working with Deleuze
in Film Theory*

Patricia Pisters

STANFORD UNIVERSITY PRESS

STANFORD, CALIFORNIA

2003

Stanford University Press
Stanford, California
© 2003 by the Board of Trustees of the
Leland Stanford Junior University.
All rights reserved.

Printed in the United States of America
on acid-free, archival-quality paper.

Library of Congress Cataloging-in-Publication Data

Pisters, Patricia.
  The matrix of visual culture : working with Deleuze in film theory /
Patricia Pisters.
      p. cm. — (Cultural memory in the present)
  Includes bibliographical references and index.
  ISBN 0-8047-4027-5 (cloth : alk. paper) —
  ISBN 0-8047-4028-3 (pbk. : alk. paper)
  1. Motion pictures—Philosophy.   2. Deleuze, Gilles—Contributions
in film theory. I. Title. II. Series.
PN1995 .P53 2003
791.43'01—dc21

                                                    2002015662

Original Printing 2003

Last figure below indicates year of this printing:
12   11   10   09   08   07   06   05   04   03

Typeset by Alan Noyes in 11/13.5 Adobe Garamond

Contents

Acknowledgments

I wish to thank many people for their support: Helen Tartar for her patience and dedication as a publisher; Mieke Bal for her encouragement and support over the last years and for her comments on some chapters; Thomas Elsaesser for his comments on earlier drafts of the chapters; Thomas Poell, another severe but helpful critic; my colleagues and students at the Department of Film and Television Studies of the University of Amsterdam, who have always been most helpful and inspiring; especially Charles Forceville and Janet Taylor for their precise readings of (parts of) the manuscript; my friends for their supporting and enriching friendships; and my parents and sister for their unconditional love. Finally, I thank Gertjan ter Haar for so wonderfully sharing his life with me and our son Rocco for having arrived.

THE MATRIX OF VISUAL CULTURE

Introduction

The material universe, the plane of immanence, is the *machinic assemblage of movement-images*. Here Bergson is startlingly ahead of his time: it is the universe as cinema in itself, a metacinema.
　—*Gilles Deleuze*[1]

The brain is unity. The brain is the screen. . . . We must understand cinema not as language, but as signaletic material.
　—*Gilles Deleuze*[2]

The World as Metacinema: Camera Consciousness and the Plane of Immanence

In 1999 Sam Mendes's film *American Beauty* won five Oscars. One of the awards went to Kevin Spacey for his performance as Lester Burnham, an American man in his forties who wants to free himself from the constraints of his imprisoning and empty suburban life. In discussions about this film with friends, colleagues, and students, I found that many were irritated by the film's story of midlife crisis. Granted, Lester's falling in love with the girlfriend of his daughter Jane, for instance, is not a particularly surprising or original event in the plot; insofar as the story is concerned, I agree with the critics.

Other aspects of this film are interesting, however, for example, the videocentric world view of Ricky, the neighbor boy with a terrorizing military father. Using a video camera, Ricky films everything he sees: his neighbors, a dead bird, a paper bag dancing in the wind—anything that catches his eye. The walls of his bedroom are lined with videotapes, a database of memories and impressions with no (narrative) coherence or logical development. Much like Godard, with his nonlinear presentation of history in and of cinema in *Histoire(s) du Cinéma*, Ricky found a way to liberate the images, the camera, and, as a consequence, his own gaze: "His video camera has freed his gaze, released it from the chain of cause and effect. Tragedy and transience, blood and pain and death, they are all still there; the intensely looking neighbor has not transcended his narrow world in any respect. But his gaze has become detached. He has freed himself from his personal life story. In his eyes shines a mystical astonishment about the world."[3] Ricky has managed to loosen his gaze from what Deleuze calls the segmental lines of the fixed structures of society and representation. By filming, Ricky has discovered a new mode of individuation, a mode that is nonpersonal and not related to him as a transcendental subject ("I see").

Haecceity is the term Deleuze and Guattari borrow from the medieval philosopher Duns Scotus to indicate this type of nonpersonal individuation: "A season, a winter, a summer, an hour, a date have perfect individuality lacking nothing, even though this individuality is different from that of a thing or a subject. They are haecceities in the sense that they consist entirely of relations of movement and rest between molecules or particles, capacities to affect and be affected."[4] Deleuze and Guattari speak of a nonpersonal kind of individuation in terms of molecules, movement, rest, and affects. What is important in *American Beauty* is that this nonpersonal "detachment of the gaze" and the susceptibility to haecceities happen through a camera. As Deleuze argues in *The Movement-Image*, the essence of cinema lies in the mobility of the camera and in emancipation of the viewpoint whereby cinema stops being spatial and has become temporal.[5] According to Deleuze, who follows Bergson in his cinema books, it is through the camera that we have come to live in a universe that is metacinematic. In it, all kinds of virtual (past and future) images are "stored" and actual (present) images are constantly generated, and both types mutually influence one another. In this sense, we come to understand our past, present, and future through a new "camera consciousness" that has entered our perception. In his book *Cinematic Political Thought*, Michael Shapiro argues that experiencing events critically in the present is made possible not "by the exercise of a faculty of judgement that can integrate the domains controlled by disparate cognitive functions, but by a cinematographic apparatus."[6] To understand contemporary culture and its pasts and futures, it is therefore necessary to develop a camera consciousness that makes it easy to jump between layers of time as well as between the actual and the virtual.

Deleuze's cinema books and some of the concepts he developed together with Guattari offer useful tools for such a new critical consciousness. The first aim of this book, therefore, is to investigate this new type of metacinematic consciousness and its nonpersonal forms of individuation with the help of Deleuze's cinema books and the concepts developed by Deleuze and Guattari.

According to Bergson and Deleuze, all images are situated on a plane of immanence where past, present, and future coexist and can be ordered in various ways, including linearly. Images are there; they do not represent some other-worldliness but constantly shape the world and its subjects. With this conception of images, Deleuze developed a film theory that is quite different from traditional film theory, which always sees images as representations of other (transcendental) worlds. One of the questions posed within traditional film theory that loses its usefulness when one works with Deleuze is the question concerning the difference between real and unreal (dream, fiction, memories). As Deleuze has argued, the distinction between virtual and actual offers a more adequate way to think in images. Virtual and actual are not opposed to each other; both are "real," but only the actual is in the (physical) present. In the most recent French edition of *Dialogues*, Deleuze states in an added text called "L'actuel et le virtuel" that every "actual" image is surrounded by a mist of virtual images: "A perception is like a particle: an actual perception wraps itself in a mist of virtual images that distribute themselves in mobile circuits that move further away and grow larger, that construct and deconstruct themselves."[7] Virtual images react to actual images, and actual images belong to the virtual. As Deleuze puts it in *The Time-Image*:

In Bergsonian terms, the real object is reflected in a mirror-image as in the virtual object, which, from its side and simultaneously, envelops or reflects the real: there is "coalescence" between the two. There is a formation of an image with two sides, actual and virtual. It is as if an image in a mirror, a photo or a postcard came to life, assumed independence and passed into the actual, even if this meant that the actual image returned into the mirror and resumed its place in the postcard or photo, following a double movement of liberation and capture.[8]

Madonna's video clip *Don't Tell Me* is a perfect illustration of Deleuze's point about the coalescence between the virtual and the actual. In this clip, the images of dancing and rodeo-riding cowboys "come to life" not on a postcard but on a billboard in the desert, and these images in turn give a virtual quality to the actual images of Madonna in front of a screen showing a desert road. The actual and virtual images start to exchange their specific qualities, in this clip especially through repetition of the movements and gestures of Madonna and the dancing cowboys. The clip is as simple as it is strong, and its strength lies precisely in this play between the virtual and the actual, which thus become interchangeable, like the many facets of a diamond. According to Deleuze, the actual is defined by the present that passes, the virtual by the past that is preserved. A constant process of crystallization is taking place between the two. Both the actual and the virtual are contained on what Deleuze calls "the plane of immanence." The plane of immanence contains not just filmic images but all images relating to "a life." New camera consciousness is fundamentally related to "a life" that is nonpersonal and nonsubjective and yet highly specific and individuated, always part of a concrete assemblage.

In traditional film theory, the cinematographic apparatus (perhaps as an "old" form of camera consciousness) conceives the image as a representation that can function as a (distorted or illusionary) mirror for identity construction and subjectivity. As has been proved by the last fifty years of film theory, representations can profoundly affect identity formation by providing positive or negative role models. Feminism and (post)colonial discourses have shown, often with the help of psychoanalysis, the ways in which representations can have negative consequences for certain groups in society. It seems clear that a different conception of (cinematographic) images and camera consciousness would also have consequences for identity and subjectivity. To discover the ways in which a Deleuzian approach to visual culture differs from a traditional view of images as representations, I start with a comparison between a traditional theoretic approach to film and a Deleuzian way of seeing things.

In Chapter 1, "The Universe as Metacinema," I look specifically at the implications of these two approaches by opening a dialogue between Slavoj Žižek and Deleuze through the work of Alfred Hitchcock: How does Hitchcock's universe look if we consider his world either as a representation of impossible desire or as a network of relations between virtual and actual images? I end this first chapter by discussing the film *Strange Days*, a film that has much in common with Hitchock's *Vertigo*. It presents a universe as metacinema in a Deleuzian sense and illustrates that Hitchcock's premonition seems to have come true: "a camera consciousness which would no longer be defined by the movements it is able to follow or make, but by the mental connections it is able to enter into."[9]

Throughout this book, I return regularly to a comparison between a traditional psychoanalytic approach and a Deleuzian approach to the image. The aim is always to understand what these different approaches enable us to see and feel.

In Chapter 2, "Material Aspects of Subjectivity," I discuss the horror genre and the monstrosities of the flesh, explicit images that have become more frequent and important during the last few decades. Psychoanalysis has demonstrated how these images are connected to the horror and fascination of abject femininity. In this way, images of the monstrous flesh always indicate a border that is necessary for the establishment of identity (borders between human and nonhuman, between life and death, between man and woman). In a Deleuzian approach, these images do not have one fixed meaning, but they always need to be reconsidered and related to their specific assemblages. Thus, they can construct different aspects of subjectivity that are "materialized" in the image. I return to this point of assemblages later in this Introduction when I propose one way of working with Deleuze in film theory.

Sound and music are other aspects of contemporary image culture that have gained greater importance. Again, it is possible to look at sound and music as representations, as an acoustic mirror of sexual difference, in the way that, for instance, a psychoanalytic approach to the sound track proposes. In a Deleuzian conception of music, sound and music do not constitute an acoustic mirror; rather, they provide the means to free oneself from self (mirror) images: music deterritorializes the subject in becoming-music. Nevertheless, music also can have strong territorializing powers. All these points concerning music and "identity" are elaborated in the last chapter.

Before we move on to the second aim of this book, it might be useful to recall briefly what Deleuze said about representational thinking, to clarify why we might want to change our basic "image of thought" and perhaps to try to establish why representation has been, and still very often is, such an attractive way of thinking. In *Difference and Repetition*,

Deleuze discusses the dominant image of thought, which is defined by thinking in terms of representations. Representation is characterized by four aspects: identity, opposition, analogy, and resemblance:

Such is the world of representation in general. We said above that representation was defined by certain elements: identity with regard to concepts, opposition with regard to determination of concepts, analogy with regard to judgement, resemblance with regard to objects. . . . The "I think" is the most general principle of representation—in other words, the source of these elements and of the unity of all these faculties: I conceive, I judge, I imagine / I remember and I perceive—as though these were the four branches of the Caught. On precisely these branches, difference is crucified. They form quadripartite fetters under which only that which is identical, similar, analogous or opposed can be considered different: *difference becomes an object of representation always in relation to a conceived identity, a judged analogy, an imagined opposition or a perceived similitude.*[10]

According to Deleuze, the dominant image of thought is a restrictive one, one that does not allow thinking to occur unless there is something with which we can compare. It does not allow us to think of real difference, the way things differ from themselves, because there is always *a principium comparationis* at work (that is, one is either good or bad, young or old, man or woman). Deleuze proposes a much more open and multiple way of thinking, which he and Guattari later call *rhizomatics*, the type of grassroots thinking that does not acknowledge hierarchies, beginnings and endings, or segmental and oppositional divisions.[11] This rhizomatic thinking is also pertinent with respect to cinema, but I return to that point in a moment. What is important for now is to notice that this rhizomatic way of thinking implies a type of thinking in assemblages, where heterogeneous aspects come together. It also implies thinking in terms that differ from those to which we are accustomed, for instance, territorialization and deterritorialization, speed and slowness, and affect.

At first, this may seem confusing or chaotic compared with the clear and binary logic of the dominant image of thought. At the same time, we encounter the strength and power of the dominant image of thought: it provides stable and recognizable forms that can give the idea of security and stability, for instance, in an identity. As Dorothea Olkowski explains in *Gilles Deleuze: The Ruins of Representation*, "Representations are produced by a certain organization of elements in the assemblage—any collection of molecular or quasi molecular elements. The production of representations is a second-level articulation that establishes functional, compact, and stable forms (objects) that simultaneously actualize in molar compounds or substances. The resultant stable, functional structure is the type that represents differences as different only in relation to identity."[12]

Leaving the "safe" territory of representation therefore entails the adventure of multiplicities and new thoughts, affects, and percepts. It also entails leaving behind the model of the eye, which traditionally has been the most important model for perceiving, conceiving, imagining, and judging representation and difference ("I see," "I think," "I imagine," "I judge," all through the noble sense of sight, which presupposes an "I" that transcends experience) for a model of the brain. In Deleuze's immanent conception of images, the brain itself functions like a screen. It is here that we make assemblages and rhizomatic connections. "The brain is the screen," says Deleuze. If there is a domain that can assess changes in film, aesthetically or otherwise, it would be the biology of the brain:

It's not to psychoanalysis or linguistics but to the biology of the brain that we should look for principles, because it doesn't have the drawback, like the two other disciplines, of applying ready-made concepts. We can consider the brain as a relatively undifferentiated mass and ask what circuits, what kind of circuit, the movement-image or time-image trace out, or invent, because circuits aren't there to begin with.[13]

Moreover, each circuit of movement-image or time-image enters into a rhizomatic assemblage of cinematographic and noncinematographic aspects. This leads me to my second aim in this book.

Working with Deleuze: A Book for Use

Although Deleuze's cinema books of the 1980s were rapidly translated into English, they did not find their way into film theory until the turn of the century. David Rodowick's *Gilles Deleuze's Time Machine* helped to establish both the philosophic and the film theoretic value of Deleuze's cinema books. He convincingly demonstrates that Deleuze's cinema books "continue a deep and complex meditation on time that is one of Deleuze's central contributions to contemporary philosophy."[14] Whereas Rodowick looks at the connections between Deleuze's cinema books and his other philosophic works, such as his books on Bergson, Nietzsche, and

Spinoza, Gregory Flaxman in *The Brain is the Screen* collected a number of interesting metacritical reflections on the implications of *The Movement-Image* and *The Time-Image*, considering, for instance, a Deleuzian geology and ontology of the image or looking at the emergence of cine-thinking.[15] In his *Film Theory: An Introduction*, Robert Stam is first to include Deleuze in the official canon of film theory. He concludes his passage on Deleuze by expressing doubt about the practical relevance of Deleuze's cinema books: "While one can acknowledge the brilliance of Deleuze's analyses, and while one can dialogue with Deleuze, try to philosophize like Deleuze, or do with other philosophers something analogous to what Deleuze does with Bergson, it seems somewhat more problematic to 'apply' Deleuze, to simply 'translate' analysis into a Deleuzian language."[16]

Although both Rodowick's book and Flaxman's collection present some concrete analyses of specific films, the emphasis in these books is indeed on a metadiscursive level.[17] Moreover, the analyses presented in these books concentrate on "minor cinema," films that have the characteristics of, for example, the modern political film as described by Deleuze in *The Time-Image*.[18] This led me to reflect on the possible relevance of Deleuze's work for more popular and commercial cinema. Inspired and challenged by the aforementioned studies, my second aim in this book is therefore to find some answers to a pragmatic question: How can we work with Deleuze in analyzing specific expressions of contemporary popular media culture? Clearly, in his cinema books, Deleuze confined himself strictly to the masterpieces of cinema history. In presenting my encounters with Deleuze's cinematographic and noncinematographic concepts in contemporary cinema and popular culture, however, I do not strictly follow all of Deleuze's approach. In this respect, I concur with Ian Buchanan, whose ambition in his *Deleuzism: A Metacommentary* is to "suggest the possibility of an *other* reading of Deleuze that would enable his work to be systematically applied."[19] As Buchanan admits, this might imply some anti-Deleuzism, which nevertheless should "be taken in the spirit of Deleuze, who rejected all forms of slavishness in favor of (liberating) creativity."[20]

Through Deleuzian concepts, I hope to establish unexpected encounters between avant-garde film, political cinema, and more commercial media expressions. Deleuze's (and Guattari's) toolbox of concepts serve here as virtual guides, accompanying me on my "expedition to unknown territories." The experimental and explorative character of this (re)search may not always be in line with more traditional academic practices. I do not attempt to persuade the reader that Deleuze's ideas are "truer" than, for instance, psychoanalytic concepts or that my reading of Deleuze is the "right" interpretation. I simply try to demonstrate how some of his ideas can work: What new thoughts become possible? What new emotions can I feel? What new sensations and perceptions can be opened in the body?[21] Therefore, my hope is that the open-ended nature of this work will create *a book for use* that contributes to the growing field of "Deleuzism" in cultural analysis.

Indeed, Deleuze's cinema books may seem to be perfect self-contained essays that preclude any room for new experiments; but this impression is incorrect. The books are full of concepts that can be employed as practical tools in the analysis of all kinds of media expressions. Moreover, one of the most challenging aspects of "applying" Deleuze is to highlight the relation of the cinema books to concepts that he developed elsewhere, mostly together with Guattari. In this way, it is possible to avoid making a strict formal and aesthetic analysis of either cinematographic concepts or of purely content matters related to the stories of the films. The concept of assemblages is important in this respect.

In *Anti-Oedipus* and *A Thousand Plateaus*, Deleuze and Guattari introduced the concept of "machinic" assemblages. They are greatly indebted to Hjemslev when they discuss possible ways of conducting analyses of assemblages. Deleuze and Guattari do not consider Hjemslev a linguist but rather as the Danish Spinozist geologist:

Hjemslev was able to weave a net out of the notions *matter, content,* and *expression, form* and *substance.* These were the strata, said Hjemslev. Now this net has the advantage of breaking with the form-content duality, since there was a form of content no less than a form of expression . . . *the first articulation concerns content, the second expression.* The distinction between the two articulations is not between forms and substances but between content and expression, expression having just as much substance as content and content just as much form as expression.[22]

Deleuze and Guattari argue that there is no single Hjemslevian model for analysis because the relation between content and expression can take various forms. Nevertheless, they draw some general conclusions on the nature of assemblages:

On a first, horizontal, axis, an assemblage comprises two segments, one of content, the other of expression. On the one hand it is a *machinic assemblage* of bodies, actions and passions, an intermingling of bodies reacting to each other; on the other hand it is a *collective assemblage of enunciation*, of acts and statements, of incorporeal transformations. On a vertical axis, the assemblage has both *territorial sides*, or reterritorial sides, which stabilize it, and *cutting edges of deterritorialization*, which carry it away.[23]

I develop this *tetravalence of assemblages* as one possible model for conducting a Deleuzian analysis of cinema by looking at both the specific cinematographic forms of *content* and *expression* of specific images and the *territorializing* and *deterritorializing forces* that traverse these images. After the metalevel in *Vertigo* and *Strange Days* in "The Universe as Metacinema" of Chapter 1, I introduce an analytic model of assemblages in Chapter 2, "Material Aspects of Subjectivity." Here I concentrate on material and temporal aspects of subjectivity that thus can be established by different types of cinema, ranging from European art cinema to Hollywood film and African cinema. In Chapter 3, "Cinema's Politics of Violence," I look at more collective enunciations of political cinema. Violence, fabulating the power of film, and schizophrenic strategies are discussed with reference to assemblages of a variety of films: Marguerite Duras's *Nathalie Granger* to Quentin Tarantino's *Pulp Fiction* and David Fincher's *Fight Club*.[24] In Chapters 4 and 5, I take a different approach and "apply" the model of the assemblage more loosely. In Chapter 4, "Conceptual Personae and Aesthetic Figures of Becoming-Woman," I look at the figure of Alice in Wonderland and treat her as a conceptual persona and aesthetic figure that demonstrate in what ways becoming-woman can be a critical, albeit often paradoxic, strategy in cinema and in life. This chapter ends with a discussion of Lars von Trier's *Dancer in the Dark* and the cinematographic and deterritorializing strategies in this film that make it so that becoming-woman here opens up to a becoming-music. In Chapter 5, "Logic of Sensations in Becoming-Animal," I discuss the way in which becoming-animal in cinema is closely related to a logic of sensations and finds its form of expression in affection-images. As indicated earlier, Chapter 6, "(De)Territorializing Forces of the Sound Machine," finally looks at aspects of becoming-music by comparing a traditional approach to sound and music in cinema with a Deleuzian way of establishing the powers of music. Here I argue that it is perhaps possible that, precisely through the depersonalizing force of music, "a people of a new kind" might come into existence.

All chapters present rhizomatic networks of thoughts, sensations, affects, movements, and rest—all fundamentally related to the plane of immanence of images of life. We have come to live in a matrix of visual culture—although not necessarily in the manner presented to us by Larry and Andy Wachowski's film *The Matrix*. To show how the matrix of media culture might be related to the plane of immanence that is so dear to Deleuze, I conclude this Introduction by looking at the way this matrix is presented in *The Matrix*.

The Matrix of Visual Culture

There is probably no other contemporary film that better serves as a kind of Rorschach test for contemporary theory than *The Matrix* (1999). The main character in *The Matrix* is a computer hacker, Neo, who discovers that the world he lives in is actually a matrix constructed by a giant computer that feeds on human energy. He is offered a trip into the real world that lies underneath the matrix and, together with a few other rebels, starts a war against the imprisonment by the illusory world of the matrix. In the film, there is an explicit reference to Baudrillard's *Simulacra and Simulation*, and many debates on postmodernism have centered on this science fiction fantasy. Žižek tells us that his psychoanalysis-oriented friends are convinced that the authors have read Lacan; the Frankfurter School partisans see in *The Matrix* the extrapolated embodiment of an alienating cultural industry; and New Agers recognize how our world is just a mirage generated by a global mind embodied in the World Wide Web.[25] Others have called the film "A High-Tech Plato." *The Matrix* does indeed have some similarities to Plato's cave, in which people are imprisoned until they are released, whereupon they can see the real world. In contrast to Plato's allegory, however, the real world in *The Matrix* is not a bright light and ideal world but a dark and desolate place. In fact, *The Matrix* could very well be compared to Jean-Louis Baudry's formulation of the apparatus theory of cinema, which he develops in analogy to Plato's cave and the Freudian unconscious.[26] *The Matrix* seems to be a paradigmatic film for contemporary audiovisual culture and theory and a blueprint for future cinematography.

Given the gradual but undeniable acknowledgment of the relevance of Deleuze's (and Guattari's) philosophic work to contemporary culture, it may be somewhat disappointing that this work does not seem to pass the Rorschach test of *The Matrix*. Although one could translate *The Matrix* in terms of action-images according to the classification of Deleuze's cinema books, and perhaps even make an argument for *The Matrix*'s bodies without organs, the hypermodern world of this film does not correspond to the conceptual universe of Deleuze and Guattari. Basically, this has to do with the fact that *The Matrix* presents to us two worlds, one virtual and one real, however complexly and perversely they are interwoven.[27] In this way, *The Matrix* presents a techno-transcendental image of the world; but Deleuze's philosophy is one of immanence where the virtual is perfectly real, although not always actual. In one of his last texts, "Immanence: A Life," Deleuze emphasizes this aspect as the heart of his philosophy: "Absolute immanence is in itself: it is not in something, not *to* something; it does not depend on an object and does not belong to a subject. In Spinoza immanence is not immanence *to* substance, but substances and modes are in immanence. . . . Pure immanence is *a life*, and nothing else. . . . A life contains only virtuals."[28]

Deleuze distinguishes between the *transcendental field*, for instance, a subject, an object, consciousness, which is defined by a plane of immanence, and the *transcendent*, which is taken as universal, such as a subject ("I") or an object in general to which immanence is attributed. The transcendental field is a consequence of immanence, a life, and hence is situated within the same world of images but on a different field. Ian Buchanan explains this point further and calls this form of "immanent transcendentalism" transcendental empiricism:

Now, instead of being a Universal, a core "I think" to be sought in all things by transcendental reduction, contemplation is universal, an immanent "it thinks" as the basis of all matter, organic or inorganic. This "it" that thinks Deleuze and Guattari call a "microbrain": "Not every organism has a brain, and not all life is organic, but everywhere there are forces that constitute microbrains, or an inorganic life of things." Yet insofar as this process can be thought philosophy must produce its concepts, at which point it becomes a transcendental term once again. However, it is now of a completely different kind: it is transcendental to immanence, it is a purposefully wrought survey of a vast process, but is not in itself a direct product of that process. This, in an ultra-shorthand way, is what transcendental empiricism actually means.[29]

Because the fundamental idea of two worlds in *The Matrix* presents such a clear transcendental fantasy of the world, I do not think this film corresponds to the immanent or transcendental empiricist philosophy of Deleuze. I have nevertheless discussed this film because it has invited so many theoretic discussions and at the same time proves that the traditional transcendental model of the cinematographic apparatus is still vigorously alive. This is why I keep coming back to this model throughout the book. I also hope to present on the following pages some transcendental empiricist experiments with images and sounds that prove that working with Deleuze's toolbox of concepts, planes, and assemblages reveals some interesting aspects of "our" life and our "subjectivities" in the matrix of visual culture that is defined by immanence and a new nonpersonal but nevertheless individuating camera consciousness.

1

The Universe as Metacinema

Ernie, do you realize what we are doing in this picture? The audience is like a giant organ that you and I are playing. At one moment we play this note and get this reaction, and then we play that chord and they react that way. And someday we won't even have to make a movie—there'll be electrodes implanted in their brains, and we'll just press different buttons and they'll go "oooh" and "aaah" and we'll frighten them, and make them laugh. Won't that be wonderful?
  —*Hitchcock* on the set of *North by Northwest*[1]

Hitchcock's fantasy about directly entering people's brains seemed futuristic and absurd in the 1950s when he expressed these words to his scriptwriter, Ernest Lehman. A few decades later, however, scientific and cinematographic technology has improved to such an extent that Hitchcock's joke no longer seems so far-fetched. In Douglas Trumbull's *Brainstorm* (1983) and Katherine Bigelow's film *Strange Days* (1995), direct recording and playing of brain waves are presented as being possible. Of course, these films belong to the genre of science fiction, and the actual possibilities of such techniques are not as refined as they are portrayed. I am not, however, interested in the exact state of affairs that might be represented in these films. Rather, I am challenged by the implications for the relationship between human beings (subjects), images, and the world—and for the underlying image of thought that Hitchcock's words express, both in respect to his own work and in respect to developments in contemporary cinema and contemporary audiovisual culture. What if we do not consider Hitchcock's words as merely a never-to-be-fulfilled fantasy of having effects on people without representations, bypassing the eyes of the spectators and reaching them directly via the brain, as the psychoanalytic model of thought does? What if we consider Hitchcock a visionary who anticipates contemporary scientific and cinematographic preoccupations, as would a rhizomatic model of thinking, according to which the brain is literally the screen? Would Hitchcock's fantasy then not be a Bergsonian statement about the immanence of body, brain, and images? As Deleuze argues in *The Movement-Image*, Bergson was "startlingly ahead of his time: it is the universe as cinema in itself, a metacinema."[2] After all, Hitchcock's wish seems to entail a revolutionary conception of images that are not representations of something else but that exist in themselves. In *The Time-Image*, Deleuze attributes to Hitchcock explicitly anticipatory insights about the nature of images in contemporary society. When he discusses developments of the image (cinematographic or "real"), he argues, "Hitchcock's premonition will come true: a camera-consciousness which would no longer be defined by the movements it is able to follow or make, but by the mental connections it is able to enter into."[3]

If, however, Hitchcock is not only a visionary and the first of the modern filmmakers, but is indeed also the ultimate classic director who completes the classic action images, his fantasy would be a symptomatic fantasy after all.[4] In any case, his work is a rich source for tracking some of the assumptions of the different images of thought that are presupposed by a classic psychoanalytic and a rhizomatic view of the subject, the world, and cinema.

To bring to the surface some of these presuppositions and implications, I first give a comparative reading of Hitchcock's universe, concentrating on the concept of the subject that is defined by desire. Then I focus on the status of cinema and the cinematographic apparatus by looking at *Rear Window* and especially two other metafilms: Michael Powell's *Peeping Tom* (1960) and *Strange Days*. Although *Strange Days* has much in common with Hitchcock's *Vertigo* (1958), it more often has been compared with *Peeping Tom*. Both *Peeping Tom* and *Strange Days* deal with the (darker) implications of our cinematographic voyeurism. Nevertheless, I argue that by comparing *Strange Days* with *Peeping Tom*, one misses some essential differences between the two films, especially the way in which a new kind of camera consciousness has entered our perception, our experience of the world, and ourselves. I therefore return to Hitchcock, especially *Vertigo*, to explore the ambiguous status of this film: at once a classic picture of an obsessive love affair (a movement-image) and a modern film about the confusing experience of time and virtuality (a time-image) that anticipates *Strange Days*. Contemporary cinema, for which *Strange Days* is paradigmatic, demonstrates that both Bergson's futuristic insights and Hitchcock's premonition have indeed come true: we now live in a metacinematic universe that calls for an immanent conception of audiovisuality and in which a new camera consciousness has entered our perception. In this chapter, I explore various implications and effects of the "universe as metacinema" and the new camera consciousness by considering *Peeping Tom*, *Strange Days*, and Hitchcock's universe as philosophic pamphlets.

Hitchcock's Universe: Žižek and Deleuze

Representations of Guilty Subjects or a Logic of Relations

I begin this exploration by looking again at Hitchcock's work using both the Lacanian ideas of Slavoj Žižek and the Bergsonian film theory of Deleuze. In this comparative way, I try to relate Hitchcock's films both to the psychoanalytic model of the eye and to the rhizomatic model of the brain. This allows me to specify a few of the main differences and similarities between the two models of thought. My aim is not to judge one model over the other. Rather, I try to determine what the different models make possible or impossible to see, think, and feel. I concentrate in this section on the idea of the subject and its relation to images and to the world.

A few remarks about Hitchcock made by Žižek and Deleuze make their respective (presup)positions quite clear. First, both Žižek and Deleuze refer to Rohmer and Chabrol's study of Hitchcock's work.[5] Both recognize the importance of that study and refer to the Catholic interpretation that Rohmer and Chabrol give of the Master's films. Here is the first big difference: Žižek sees Hitchcock's "Catholicism" as an even more profoundly religious form of Jansenism. According to Žižek, both in Jansenism and in Hitchcock, all human subjects are sinful, and for that reason their salvation cannot depend on themselves as persons; it can come only from an outside force, from God, who has decided in advance who will be saved and who will be damned.[6] Deleuze, on the other hand, precisely rejects the Catholic (and by implication Jansenist) dimension of Rohmer and Chabrol's analysis: there is no need to make Hitchcock a

Catholic metaphysician, argues Deleuze. On the contrary, Hitchcock has a sound conception of theoretic and practical relations, which have nothing to do with a guilty subject or a terrible and impossible God.[7]

A second point raised by both Žižek and Deleuze is Hitchcock's own metaphor of "tapestry." Žižek sees this in connection with the impossible Gaze, again the God's-eye view that has caught the subject on the screen in its web of predestination. This subject on screen (the character) represents the subject off screen (the spectator). The spectator can identify with the character's eye / look and at the same time feel his or her guilt and fear of the Gaze of God or the Real, as Žižek calls this impossible entity; the spectator never can identify with the Gaze of God.[8] So, according to Žižek, the cinema of Hitchcock gives an ultimate representation of how subjects outside cinema experience the world: the represented subjects are under the same constraints as the spectators in their own lives. Deleuze, however, sees the tapestry as a network of relations, carefully set up by Hitchcock to implicate the viewer in the (mental) actions. It is not a matter of the look and the eye. At most, we can speak of a mind's eye. The spectator is not looking for representations of his own life but is participating in the game of relations set up by Hitchcock.

A third and final difference in the approaches of Žižek and Deleuze concerns Hitchcock's previously quoted remark about directly influencing the brain. In his expressed wish to reach spectators directly, without mediation, Žižek emphasizes the symptomatic aspect of Hitchcock's fantasy: according to Žižek, it is this urge to function without representation that constitutes the psychotic core in Hitchcock's universe. In "reality," there is always representation as a kind of "umbilical cord" between Hitchcock and the public, between the subjects on screen and the subjects off screen.[9] In representation, subjects off screen constitute their identity by identifying with subjects on screen, taking these subjects as models. Again, it is obvious that Deleuze has a completely different philosophy. Going back to Spinoza and Bergson, Deleuze does not believe in the all-encompassing force of the concept of representation and hence the concept of identification as a means of modeling subjectivity. According to Deleuze, the brain, which is both an intellectual and an emotional entity and functions parallel (not hierarchically) to the body, can give more insights about how we perceive ourselves as subject. So for Deleuze, Hitchcock's remark about the electrodes in the brain is not symptomatic in leaving out the most important thing; rather, it is a philosophic reflection about how images work and about the direct effects of images in themselves. Therefore, even without taking the electrodes in the brain literally, it might be useful to think about images in terms of the effects and affects that are set in motion by a complex interplay between body and brain, perception and memory.

Transcendental or Immanent Desire

Having established these basic presuppositions of the psychoanalytic and rhizomatic models concerning the relationship between the (cinematographic) image, the subject, and the world, it is now necessary to look more closely at the subject and at one of the most important aspects that constitute the subject: desire. Therefore, before returning to Hitchcock, let me briefly recall the concept of the subject in relation to desire in both models. First is the psychoanalytic subject: in early psychoanalysis, according to both Freud and Lacan, desire is based on lack, the absence of an original and imaginary wholeness, which is lost as soon as the subject enters society, the Symbolic order. The subject, marked by this lack, desires an object to find original wholeness, which is always impossible. Needless to say, sexual difference is the crucial difference in this respect (lack is based on castration anxiety, feared by the male subject). Feminist film theory has demonstrated in great detail how the subject, most of whom are male, takes the woman as its object of desire, appropriating or "fetishizing" her at the cost of women's status as a subject. The Gaze often is seen as an all-knowing entity, often assigned to the male patriarchal subject, comparable to the Cartesian eye/I. Sometimes the Gaze refers to a more abstract notion of the other as such. The look, on the other hand, is related to the embodied subject in the diegetic world.

Slavoj Žižek, however, and with him some feminist psychoanalysts like Joan Copjec,[10] puts the Gaze not in the powerful position of the Symbolic order but in what Lacan calls the Real. The Imaginary and the longing for the lost object of desire no longer haunt the late-Lacanian subject; instead, it is increasingly haunted by the Real. The Real is that which the subject cannot understand, cannot see, and cannot be represented in the Symbolic but nevertheless imposes its traces on the subject. It is a third term that goes beyond the Imaginary and the Symbolic. Žižek relates the Gaze to the Real. The Gaze, according to Žižek, is not an instrument of mastery and control; on the contrary, it is that which the subject never can know. It can be defined in several ways: the amorph, the raw and skinless flesh, God, and ultimately death. Sexual difference is still crucial: woman is closer to the Real than man (and therefore an impossible subject: "woman is a symptom of man"). The Real is the "night of the world," the absolute negativity, void, and lack, which is at the basis of the subject. So desire still is based on lack and absence, but now it has become a transcendental notion. Because the subject cannot know the Real, it defines its desire as the desire of the other (the subject desires what it thinks the other desires in the illusion of thinking that the other possesses the Real). According to Žižek, the Lacanian/Hitchcockian subject is a guilty subject, always already guilty of wanting enjoyment, jouissance, which has its impossible origin in the Real. Here we see what Žižek meant by Jansenism based on guilt and God.[11]

If we look at Hitchcock's film in a Žižekian Lacanian-inspired analysis, we could say that the hero of *Rear Window* represents an early Lacan, still tied to the Symbolic order that sometimes is ruptured by symptoms of the Imaginary order; but it is mostly in control, having an overview. Increasingly, the stain of the Real has entered the Hitchcockian image. The hand with a knife in *Psycho*, the birds in *The Birds*, the plane in *North by Northwest* are, according to Žižek, not perceived simply as part of diegetic reality: "It is, rather, experienced as a kind of stain which from outside,— more precisely: from an intermediate space between diegetic reality and our 'true' reality—invades the diegetic reality."[12] It is precisely the Real that stains the Symbolic and therefore threatens not only the subjects on the screen but also the spectator's sense of security: his or her position of safe distance, bridged by the eye, is suddenly threatened by something out of control. In short, the Lacanian subject, which according to Žižek is a Hitchcockian subject, is philosophically subjected to an a-historical transcendental principle that is always mediated by representations (the umbilical cord). Its guilty (Jansenist) desire is based on a fundamental lack related not so much to the Imaginary but to the impossible and horrible Real, which imposes its gaze like a dangerous imprisoning web (the tapestry, according to Žižek).

In a Deleuzian/Guattarian rhizomatic philosophy, Hitchcock's universe presents us with a completely different image of the subject. Desire, first of all, is an important notion; but, according to Deleuze, it is not based on lack and the absence of an original perfect but on an impossible whole or dangerous void-like negativity. Moreover, desire never is related to an object (that obscure object of desire).[13] Rather, desire is a fundamental wish to live and to preserve life by connecting with and relating to those things and persons that give us joy, that is, that increase our power to act. This does not mean there is no sadness or hatred or fear, but they are all reactions to this fundamental drive to preserve life: what is bad for us inspires sadness and other sad passions. Joy should not be confused with *jouissance*, the Lacanian enjoyment, which, as we saw, is a guilty pleasure related to fearful death and the negativity of the Real. As is well known, Deleuze is in this respect much influenced by Spinoza.

According to Spinoza, joy is related to the power to form adequate thoughts and to act.[14] To be active is to enjoy life; to be joyful is to desire connections that are related to affirmative powers, not to the negative ones, as "prescribed" by psychoanalysis. The subject is not by definition a guilty subject controlled by a transcendental notion, although of course the subject can do bad things and become guilty. Nor does this mean that the subject controls everything because in Spinozian / Deleuzian terms the self is or can be confused by the immanent forces of time. The subject in this perspective is not so much challenged by the Real, or God as an external force, or *Das-Ding-an-Sich*, but rather by time and memory. Genevieve Lloyd explains in her work on Spinoza how this influences the idea of the subject or the self:

The Spinozistic self is both the idea of an actually existing body, moving into a future, and the idea of all that has been retained of that body's past. The mind struggles to make itself a unity—a well-functioning temporal as well as spatial whole. In the context of this view of the self as a constant effort to articulate itself, and to maintain itself in being amidst the wider wholes on which it depends, borders become unstable.[15]

This description of the Spinozistic self demonstrates clearly how the subject changes in time, how it becomes in time and therefore cannot always be the same. Deleuze is very Spinozian and Bergsonian when he talks about concepts of becoming in time and duration and unstable selfhood. In any case, according to Deleuze, the subject is not a fixed and transcendentally controlled entity but an immanent singular body whose borders of selfhood (or subjectivity) are challenged in time and by time. The indetermination and insecurity that time brings to the subject are not the negative limits of desire and knowledge but are precisely that which brings about ongoing movements of thought: the gaps in our knowledge are needed to continue living and thinking.

Looking at Hitchcock, then, Deleuze sees the hero of *Rear Window* not as someone possessing the (Symbolic) Gaze, but as someone who, forced into immobility by his accident, becomes a seer, someone who starts making mental relations (mental relations start when the action—temporarily—stops and the subject opens up to time). Where Žižek sees the Real introduced into the Hitchcockian universe (the knife, the birds, the plane), Deleuze stresses the fact that these "things" do not come from beyond. On the contrary, they have a natural relation with the rest of the image. The birds must be ordinary birds, the plane is an ordinary plane, the key in *Dial M for Murder* is an ordinary key; it belongs to the world of the image, and it becomes a sign (a relational indication) when it does not fit the lock. Deleuze distinguishes different signs ("demarks" and symbols) that together form the network of what he calls the *mental image* or the *relation image* that puzzles the subject on screen as well as the subject off screen but not always in the same way: Hitchcock plays with all minds in different ways. In short, Deleuze sees the Hitchcock universe as a network of relations (the tapestry). There is no *a priori* guilt (no Catholicism or Jansenism); there is only an attempt to reason and to establish adequate relations that could improve life and increase the power to act. The subject's desire is not based on negativity and lack (and hence not primarily based on sexual difference and castration), but it is a positive desire to make connections. The image is not seen as a representation, an umbilical cord, but as a thought-provoking encounter.

Hitchcock's universe thus can be interpreted according to two different philosophic traditions: a transcendental Cartesian/Kantian/Lacanian tradition, which is represented by Žižek, and an immanent Spinozian/Bergsonian/(Nietzschean) tradition, which is elaborated by Deleuze. As I explained in the Introduction, in the transcendental tradition, the eye is important because it collects all the impressions that are necessarily unified by an *a priori* "I": "I see, I think, I feel" is what synthesizes all "my" experiences. Hence the subject finds itself before and beyond perception and experience; it is a transcendental subject.[16] In an immanent tradition, the subject is not *a priori* given, but perception and experience form it. It is by the multiplicity of perceptions that the "I" is formed, the brain being the nervous center of all connections and constructive subject formations. Desire, as one of the most constituting elements according to both psychoanalysis and rhizomatics, is equally conceived as either a transcendental imposing category or an immanent constructing force. From the Žižekian and Deleuzian analyses of Hitchcock's work, the implications for the subject become clear if we conceive images, subjects, and the world according to these different traditions. A transcendental philosophy gives a stable concept of the world, the subject, and images: although there is always something unknown haunting the subject, it is also the only thing that gives our experiences a solid basis from which we can compare and identify ourselves. In an immanent philosophy, the subject is in constant formation, always changing through multiple encounters. It is a concept of the subject that is much less sure that can create unwanted uncertainties but perhaps also unexpected possibilities. In subsequent chapters, the implications of such an immanent model for truth, ethics, and politics are elaborated more extensively in relation to specific audiovisual encounters. Here I focus on the metalevel of the audiovisual universe, on the status of the cinematographic apparatus, and on the (cinematographic) image.

Metacinema and the Cinematographic Apparatus: *Peeping Tom* and *Strange Days*

Opening Sequences: Displaying the Cinematographic Apparatus

In the 1950s, the critics of Cahiers du Cinema considered Hitchock's *Rear Window* the prototype of a film about film: James Stewart's immobile position, voyeuristically directed toward the scenes in front of him, spying on his neighbors, was considered the position of the film viewer.[17] When *Strange Days*, a modern or even futuristic metafilm, came out, it was not compared much with *Rear Window*. Bigelow's film was more often compared with yet another metafilm, *Peeping Tom*. More explicitly than *Rear Window* and like *Strange Days*, *Peeping Tom* shows the negative implications of (cinematographic) voyeurism. Before returning to Hitchcock and other aspects of transcendental and immanent conceptions of the (Hitchcockian) universe and finally the new camera consciousness, it is necessary to take a closer look at the different conceptions of the cinematographic apparatus. I do this by investigating the ways these are displayed in *Peeping Tom* and *Strange Days*.

The story (form of content) of *Strange Days* takes place in Los Angeles at the eve of the third millennium. Lenny Nero is an ex-cop who deals in digital recordings of real-life experiences for vicarious adventures. When he receives a digital clip of the real murder of Iris, a prostitute who delivers recordings for him, Lenny is drawn into a dangerous world of crime, racism, power, and paranoia. Still in love with his ex-girlfriend, Faith, he tries to protect her from a fate similar to that of his murdered associate. He is assisted by his two friends, personal security expert Mace and ex-cop and former colleague Max. In terms of the form of content, this film is an action image with a milieu in which characters act and react, the type of image that is typical of classic and commercial Hollywood cinema, as Deleuze explains in *The Movement-Image*.[18] As for the form of expression, *Strange Days*' overloaded visual style is overwhelming: the images stretch far beyond the frames, seemingly without spatial beginning or end. In fact, the images are so overloaded that they seem "out of joint" and have a special relation to time.[19] I return to this point in a later section. Let me first mention something of the critical reception of the film and the apparent links with *Peeping Tom*.

When *Strange Days* first came out, it received strong critiques. In the BBC's cultural program, "Late Review," the three male critics did not like Bigelow's work, whereas the only female critic, despite some reservations, defended the film for its thought-provoking images.[20] In the same program, *Strange Days*' voyeurism and subjective camera movements were compared with Michael Powell's *Peeping Tom*. In particular, the scene of the brutal killing of a prostitute in both films was taken as an example. Are the voyeurism and subjectivity in the two films really that similar? *Peeping Tom* is the story of a psychopathic murderer, Mark Lewis, who films his victims when he kills them. He also films the police investigations of the murders he has committed. His insane behavior is caused by a trauma in his childhood, when his father did all kinds of "scientific" experiments on the boy. His neighbor, Helen, and her blind mother unmask him. Except for the scene where a prostitute is killed, the two films have few similarities in terms of content, mainly because the points of view from which the stories are told and the kinds of subjectivity they aim to establish seem very different: although they are both drawn to the power of images and visual technology, hustler Lenny Nero is a very different character from murderer Mark Lewis. Also on the level of the form of expression, *Peeping Tom* differs from *Strange Days*: *Peeping Tom* follows a much more chrono-logic and spatially coherent logic than the out-of-joint nature of the world of *Strange Days*.

Comparison of the opening sequences of the two films, however, shows some striking similarities. In both films, the first image is an extreme close-up of an eye, clearly an indication of the voyeuristic inclinations of the protagonists. This close-up is followed in both films by subjective cam-era images, presumably from the point of view of the beholder of the eye in close-up, who at that point is still unknown to the audience. In *Peeping Tom*, we follow a prostitute through the viewfinder of a film camera until she has a frightened expression on her face and stares in agony into the camera, and we understand that she is being murdered by the man filming her. We know it is a film camera that has been recording the images be-cause, in a short sequence between the close-up of the eye and the subjec-tive camera images, we have seen in a more "objective" establishing shot the street where the woman is waiting for a client, the person who is film-ing seen from behind, and a close-up of the camera's eye. We also see a hand throwing away a Kodak film box, and we constantly see the crosshairs of the viewfinder in front of the images. After this scene ends with the woman's frightened face, we see a projector that places the same images onto a screen while someone (the man with the camera, protago-nist Mark Lewis, as we will understand later) watches. Then the credits come up. So in this way the whole cinematic apparatus is staged before the actual film starts: from the very beginning, it is clear that *Peeping Tom* is a film about film.

In the opening sequence of *Strange Days*, the only clue we get that the images following the close-up of the eye are technically mediated is the fact that the first image after this close-up is obviously digitized (it takes some time before the pixels constitute a sharp, clear image). Then we are immediately, again via subjective camera movement, in the middle of a robbery; the robbery goes wrong, there is a flight to a rooftop to escape from the police, and finally we experience that the person via whose senses we have lived through all the previous events falls from the roof: "we" fall from the rooftop. With a little nausea, we discover that this was a virtual-reality experience of the film's main character, Lenny Nero. He had his brain connected to a SQUID (Superconducting QUantum Interference Device), a futuristic device that can record experiences and play them back immediately (other people's experiences or personal experiences from the past).[21] Lenny buys and sells these digital drugs, but he is infuriated by this tape: it is a "blackjack," a recording of death. When he pulls the playback rig from his head, he exclaims to his dealer that he does not deal in "snuff." In contrast to *Peeping Tom*, the opening sequence of *Strange Days* makes clear that there is no longer the distance of the camera and the projector but a direct physical involvement of body and brain.

How can we account for this difference on a theoretic level? *Peeping Tom* seems paradigmatic for the so-called apparatus theory, developed in the 1970s by Jean-Louis Baudry, Jean-Louis Commoli, and Christian Metz.[22] The film also can be read as a commentary on psychoanalytic interpretations and feminist gender implications of the apparatus theory. Baudry saw the cinematic apparatus as similar to Plato's cave: the cinematic apparatus "offers the subject perceptions which are really representations mistaken for perceptions."[23] *Peeping Tom*, because it displays the cinematic apparatus, demonstrates how the representation model conceives the world and by extension art: the image that we eventually see is a representation, a copy of the original reality. Philosophy of representation is based on the idea of a model and a copy (the original and the image, the essence and its reflection). Furthermore, *Peeping Tom* demonstrates that in representation there is also a clear distinction between the one who is looking (the subject, Mark, the photographer, the peeping Tom) and that being looked at (the object, the prostitute, the object of desire). Related to the mobility of the camera, the subject in the cinematographic apparatus is conceived as a transcendental subject:

[The] eye-subject, the invisible base of artificial perspective (which in fact only represents a larger effort to produce an ordering, a regulated transcendence) becomes absorbed in, "elevated" to a vaster function, proportional to the movement which it can perform. . . . The mobility of the camera seems to fulfill the most favorable conditions for the manifestation of the "transcendental subject."[24]

Baudry argues that cinema provides the subject with a fantasy of an objective reality that can be controlled by the subject's intentional consciousness. Baudry is a phenomenologist when he argues that this consciousness is a consciousness of something, which then he relates to the status and the operation of the cinematographic image: "For it to be an image of something, it has to constitute this something as meaning." The image seems to reflect the world but solely in the naïve inversion of a founding hierarchy: "The domain of natural existence thus has only an authority of the second order, and always presupposes the transcendental."[25] Clearly, the way in which the cinematographic apparatus is conceived relates film theory to representational thinking, as defined by Deleuze in *Difference and Repetition*. As I explained in the Introduction, this model of thinking is based on a *principium comparationis* of a conceived identity, judged analogy, imagined opposition, or perceived similitude. In *Peeping Tom*, we are always aware of the distance between the model (that which is filmed) and the copy (the represented image). We also notice a distance between the subject who perceives and the object that is perceived.

On the laser disc edition of *Peeping Tom*, Laura Mulvey, who gave her comments on the film on a separate soundtrack, demonstrates how *Peeping Tom* is not only a film about film and filmic representation, but it also refers to the history of the cinematic apparatus (at least to the origins of the cinematic apparatus as it has been conceived traditionally). At the end of the film, we see that Mark Lewis has rebuilt a sort of Muybridgean installation of photo cameras that, in quick succession, take pictures of him while he commits suicide by throwing himself onto a spear that is hidden in the tripod of his camera. According to Mulvey, by relating the tragic end of the film's hero to the origins of the cinematic apparatus, *Peeping Tom* also makes a statement about the death of this apparatus. Therefore, it is not surprising that in *Strange Days*, we do not find the same kind of apparatus: we find ourselves drawn into a frantic world of images and sounds where there is no boundary between self and other. There is also no longer a distance between perceiver and perceived (there is no distancing camera). The virtual experience is a real experience: body and mind receive intensive energy at the same time. It is through diminished distance between who is seeing and what is seen, through the physical and intensive implication of the spectator, that we have an encounter with another world that at the same time forces us to think differently about images that are no longer representation. The cinematographic apparatus that is displayed in *Strange Days* is a Bergsonian one, where matter, body, and brain are the image:

An atom is an image, which extends to the point to which its actions and reactions extend. My body is an image, hence a set of actions and reactions. My eyes, my brain, are images, parts of my body. How could my brain contain images since it is one image amongst others? External images act on me, transmit movement to me, and I return movement: how could images be in my consciousness since I am myself image, that is, movement? . . . This infinite set of images constitutes a kind of plane of immanence. The image exists in itself, on this plane. This in-itself of the image is matter: not something behind the image, but on the contrary the absolute identity of the image and movement. . . . All consciousness is something, it is indistinguishable from the thing, that is from the image of light.[26]

We see here a kind of cinematographic apparatus that differs from that in traditional philosophy and film theory. It is a cinematographic apparatus in which the brain is the screen and in which "subjects" are formed by acting and reacting to various images on a plane of immanence.

Gender Implications: Differently Voyeuristic

Apart from the fact that the cinematographic apparatus in *Peeping Tom* is related to the idea of images as representations in a transcendental logic, the film also relates the cinematic apparatus explicitly to a Freudian discourse. Director Michael Powell first intended to make a film about Freud, but because John Huston had this idea slightly earlier (he made *Freud, the Secret Passion*), Powell decided to make instead "a film about a man with a camera who kills the women he films." This obviously says something about the relation between the cinematographic apparatus and psychoanalysis, and it is not surprising that feminists have demonstrated how cinema has often been misogynistic. Of course, in her commentary on *Peeping Tom*, Laura Mulvey, who was one of the initiators of these feminist critiques, comes back to this question. *Peeping Tom* presents a classic oedipal anxiety drama in which a young man suffers from childhood traumas inspired by his father, which are displaced onto the women he encounters. The women he films and kills are all sexually active (prostitutes) because they represent the greatest threat. It is not for nothing that only Helen, the innocent, decent, and nonsexual girl next door who refuses to be filmed, can reach him (but, of course, too late to offer any cure).

In the opening sequence of *Peeping Tom*, the man is the subject of the look and the woman is "to-be-looked-at," using Mulvey's famous words from her "Visual Pleasure and Narrative Cinema."[27] Because we are in the realm of representation, we can either identify sadistically with the masculine subject or masochistically with the female object. In psychoanalytic terms, voyeurism is related to sadistic distance and the pleasure of imposing punishment (on the woman because she inspires castration anxiety); subjectivity is related to identification and appropriation of the other to gain fullness; and difference is based on gender opposition between male and female. Desire, the key word of psychoanalysis, is also negatively defined on the basis of a lack and the longing for an object that can be appropriated to be integrated into the self-same system. *Peeping Tom* exposes the relationship between the cinematographic apparatus as theorized in the apparatus theory, psychoanalysis, and gender binaries, all of which follow the logic of representational philosophy that underlies these paradigms in film theory.

Strange Days also has been read following this representational model of the voyeuristic eye: Laura Rascaroli, for instance, considers Bigelow's film paradigmatic for the cinematographic apparatus and the Lacanian mirror.[28] In this logic, *Strange Days* also follows the gender opposition that is so strongly at work in psychoanalytic models. Although this view of the film is certainly defendable, I would argue that things are in fact more complicated. Already in the opening sequence, it is clear that we are dealing with a similar yet also different scopic regime, perhaps even a different philosophic model. During the film, gender relations are equally presented differently. Although the hero of the film is rather "weak" and the main female characters are strong women, it is not a matter of a simple role reversal (the woman having the look and the man the to-be-looked-at), which would keep us in the same paradigm. The difference is due not solely to the fact that in *Strange Days*, there are no more oedipal families, although that certainly has some significance. More importantly, in this film, the look is connected to all other senses and is completely embodied. No longer is there a clearly defined subject filming, watching, and appropriating an image/filmed object. A real virtual experience is presented that involves the protagonist and the spectator both physically and mentally. The relation between subject and object becomes a two-way process, an encounter between different forces (different in all its variations, not only in terms of opposition). On the basis of this idea of encounters, the nature of desire also needs to be redefined. Here we can see a more Deleuzian conception of desire. For Deleuze and Guattari, desire is just as unconscious and just as important as it is in psychoanalysis; but, as indicated in the previous section, it is conceived positively as a connection with something or somebody else. This positive definition of desire, then, again has great implications for gender theory. We can no longer speak of a (male) subject desiring/filming a (female) object.

In *Strange Days*, Lenny considers himself a "shrink," someone who helps people to fulfill their desires; but his version of a shrink is related to his capability of connecting (wiring) people to all kinds of experiences (as a "switchboard of the soul"), which makes him quite the opposite of traditional psychoanalysts, whose task is to eliminate all desire that goes beyond the oedipal norm. In the beginning of the film, he says to a client, "What would you like to experience? Would you like to make love with a girl, with two girls may? Would you like to do it with a boy? Or would you like to be a girl maybe?" Of course, there is a utopian element in this presentation of sexual relationships. Nevertheless, it indicates a different and positive attitude toward gender relations, one of multiplicities and becoming (a becoming other instead of having and possessing the other), one of unstable identities and changing relations, in short one of differences and repetitions in many encounters.

Unfortunately, this does not mean that all the abuses have disappeared. Like in *Peeping Tom*, one of the central scenes in *Strange Days* is a rape/murder scene of a hooker, which is absolutely unpleasant to watch. It is to this scene that the male critics of "Late Review" were indignantly referring. There is a difference between the rape/murder scenes in the two films, however. In *Peeping Tom* (and many other similar scenes in the history of cinema, such as in Hitchcock's *Frenzy*), the voyeurism and sadism of these rape scenes are related to the distance between the subject of the crime and his object, the female victim, who is literally appropriated in death. In *Peeping Tom*, however, there is also a sort of identification of the murderer with his victims. While he murders the women with a knife from the tripod of his camera, he also holds a mirror before their faces; so the victims can see the terror of their own death in their eyes, which he again films. It is with this terror that Mark ultimately identifies; however, the identification takes place after the fact, when Mark watches (again at a safe distance) the representations on the screen. It is through this distance that he can continue to be a subject. Nevertheless, in the end, identification with the psychoanalytic female position is complete, and the only possible solution for the man who identifies too much with his victims is death. He comes to his tragic end by killing himself while being photographed.

One could therefore say that in *Peeping Tom* this moment of masochistic identification with the victims brings the peeping Tom into a position that is normally "reserved" for women. This does not challenge the basic opposition between object and subject, however, because Mark now becomes his own object. Although a shift is possible between subject position and object position, there is no solution for the full subject except in death. One must choose either the distance (voyeurism, power) or the proximity (masochism, death). *Peeping Tom* is a strong but sad film that demonstrates in a critical way the (hidden) implications of psychoanalysis and the cinematographic apparatus.

In *Strange Days*, there is also a shift between subject and object, but in a different way and with different implications. Both the victim and the murderer are wired to the same SQUID, and both experiences are transmitted simultaneously, which implies that the one who puts on this playback and receives the images also experiences both perspectives at the same time. There is no longer a distance between *having* the image and being the image. As I said, this does not make the event less harmful or painful, but because of the degree of involvement in voyeuristic experiences, *Strange Days* gives us another critical perspective on voyeurism and the hunger for images, a perspective that implicates the audience to the point where we ourselves become the rapist and the victim. As Joan Smith quotes from James Cameron's screenplay in her article "Speaking Up for Corpses," "We put the knife up to her throat, and she whimpers, afraid to cry out, and then we draw the flat side of the blade down across her body as if to tease her with the prospect of her death." Even more dramatically, Lenny Nero, who has been sent the tape anonymously, is forced when he plays it to feel the killer's excitement and the woman's terror: "Lenny is feeling the stalker's exhilaration, pounding heart, flushed skin, panting breath, overlaid with her own senses . . . so the excitement and terror merge into one thing, one overwhelming wave of dread sensation. Lenny goes to pieces as the tape rolls."[29] It is the worst thing he has ever experienced; to make this clear, unlike in *Peeping Tom*, close-ups of Lenny's horrified face frequently interrupt the rape scene. He literally gets sick and throws up. This immediate physical reaction "contaminates" the spectator as well, without leaving any room for safe distance.

Joan Smith also refers to the violent reactions of mainly male critics to this film and explains why they are so furious. After explaining that prostitutes in cinema often are coded in a stereotypical way and seldom become "real" persons because we know through the codes that they will die soon, Smith continues:

What is different about *Strange Days* is that Iris, although her character is coded in exactly this way—tight, low-cut dresses, wildly unstable behavior—becomes a real person for Lenny Nero and, for the audience, at the moment of her death. Male viewers are not permitted to maintain the customary safe distance from which they observe the process, which turns these women into corpses: instead, they are forced through Lenny's reaction to realize what Iris is suffering. . . . It is hardly a coincidence that [the film] has prompted furious reactions, specifically the accusation that women should not be dirtying their hands like this. There is something illogical about this response, for it is precisely these women—the victims of serial rapists and killers—whose voices are silenced first in real life and second by the authors and directors who find their attackers endlessly fascinating. Men, it seems, can bump off as many women as they like in novels and on screen. What will not be tolerated is women speaking up for corpses.[30]

The violent reactions of the male critics on the BBC's "Late Review" seem related to the shock of the experience of female terror for male viewers (which by the same token is no longer female terror) and to the fact that women "speak up for corpses." ("You would have been furious if a man had made this picture," one critic told his female colleague—"but men wouldn't," seems to be the tacit implication.)

Of course, one also could argue that it is again the Lacanian Real that enters the picture here. This could indeed be one explanation of the rape/murder scene in *Strange Days* (the hooker becomes a subject only at the moment of her death). Whereas the subject in *Peeping Tom* seems to tell us (like psychoanalysis) that actually men are just as much tragic victims as women and cannot help being sadistic voyeurs, the message in *Strange Days* seems different. In creating an experience of becoming both rapist and victim, a critique is given on the whole traditional subject–object opposition. *Strange Days* does not say that "men can't help it, we are all victims," but rather "do something, change your concept of what it means to be a subject."

Another important aspect of the rape scene in *Strange Days* is the place it has among other (SQUID) experiences that are presented: the rape is one of the many other things that happen at the same time. *Strange Days* cannot be judged on the basis of only this one scene. Unlike in *Peeping Tom*, this scene is not paradigmatic for the whole film. One of the other most important aspects raised in *Strange Days* is the execution of a black rapper, *Jerrico One*, by Los Angeles police officers. Of course, this reminds us of Rodney King and other dramas caused by ethnic and racial differences. The Los Angeles presented in this film is slightly exaggerated, but the atmosphere of an overpopulated, crazy, and intolerant city certainly "makes a rhizome" with the actual situation.[31] *Strange Days* presents a critical attitude to our intolerance of other people in a multicultural society. That intolerance, clearly, is still based on the desperate quest for a self-same model of delineated identity at the cost of the oppositional "other," black people being considered as much "other" as women. At least to the same extent as any gender problematic, the film presents questions of race and ethnicity as basic problems that we must face as we enter the third millennium. It is therefore also significant that the strongest character in the film is a black woman, Mace, played by Angela Bassett.

Because of its overwhelming visual style and catchy soundtrack, *Strange Days* can be seen as pure, even excessive entertainment. Through its intensity (both in images and sound) and physical involvement (both of the protagonists and the spectators), the film implicitly also calls for new strategies of analyzing and understanding contemporary cinema and society. Explicitly, *Strange Days* scrutinizes voyeurism and subjectivity, both of which can no more be conceived in terms of subject, object, and distance; the Gaze has become embodied and intimately connected to an energetic way of experiencing the world. All these questions can no longer be dealt with in terms of representation; rather, they must be conceived in terms of multiple differences and repetition and in terms of encounters that agitate both our bodies and our minds.

By looking at the cinematographic apparatus that is displayed in *Peeping Tom* and *Strange Days*, it is possible to conclude that a different type of camera consciousness is implied as well. In the psychoanalytic apparatus theory, the camera gives the spectator (the illusion of) transcendental control and the ability to distinguish between what is objective and what is subjective, which according to Žižek is in fact always an imprisoning illusion. In a rhizomatic model, this distinction cannot be made clearly. There are, of course, more subjective and more objective images, but they seem to oscillate in what Deleuze, following Pasolini, calls a semisubjective or "a free indirect discourse." In his exposition of the perception-image, a type of image that is "presupposed" by all other images, Deleuze argues that a camera consciousness as free, indirect discourse is the essence of cinema: "We are no longer faced with subjective or objective images; we are caught between a correlation between a perception-image and a camera-consciousness which transforms it."[32]

Although Deleuze recognizes the possibility of subjectively and objectively attributed images, he claims that the mobile camera ultimately led to "the emancipation of the viewpoint. . . . The shot would then stop being a spatial category and has become a temporal one."[33] Because Hitchcock is the director who, according to Deleuze, ultimately introduced this type of camera consciousness into the image and into perception, both of which are becoming more temporal, I turn once more to his work before finally returning to *Strange Days*.

Camera Consciousness and Temporal Confusion: *Strange Days* and *Vertigo*

Indiscernibility of Subjective and Objective, Virtual and Actual

Vertigo is the Hitchcock film that most clearly permits both a transcendental and an immanent reading of the subject. Let me elaborate. *Vertigo*'s story is well known: the film is situated in San Francisco, where John "Scottie" Ferguson leaves the police force because of his fear of heights. When an old friend asks him to shadow his wife, Madeleine, Scottie follows her, saves her from drowning, and falls in love with her. Nevertheless, Scottie cannot prevent her suicide. Believing Madeleine is dead, he meets Judy, the living image of Madeleine, and he becomes obsessed by the idea of recreating the image of the dead woman.

If we look at *Vertigo* in a psychoanalytic way, obviously a lot of feminist criticism comes to mind. In early psychoanalytic critiques, Hitchcock's male protagonists are seen as sadistic bearers of the Gaze, trying to appropriate their object of desire: the woman. Clearly, the scene in Ernie's Restaurant, when Scottie sees Madeleine for the first time, could be read in this way: he (the male subject) looks at the object of his desire (the woman). During the first half of the film, he tries to save her from a strange possession (she thinks she is her great-grandmother, Carlotta Valdes) and tries to make her his ("I have you, I have you," Scottie exclaims at some point). When he does not succeed in this, he becomes obsessed with bringing his ideal object back to life at the cost of female subjectivity: Judy first becomes Madeleine again and then dies for the second time, punished for her by definition "guilty femaleness." As Laura Mulvey demonstrated, identification—a prime indicator for spectatorial pleasure and subject positioning—is extremely difficult for a female audience, unless by masochism, transvestitism, narcissism, or bisexuality (all psychoanalytic terms that do not create a powerful subject).

Other feminist psychoanalytic positions present a more complex structure of male and female subject positions. Tania Modleski, for instance, demonstrates that, although women are explicitly "designed" by Hitchcock, *Vertigo* is not as one-dimensional as is often thought in the first instance.[34] The male protagonist does not just master the guilty female object; he also identifies with her. In Vertigo, Scottie identifies with Madeleine. According to Modleski, woman thus becomes the identification for all the film's spectators as well. Modleski places her arguments in a Freudian framework and demonstrates how masculinity is unable to control femininity; femininity is "the unconsciousness of patriarchy."

Žižek would argue differently but nevertheless not too far from Modleski that both men and women, on screen and off screen, are under the constraints of the Real (but women are closer to it than men, hence their enigmatic nature). In this light, Scottie's acrophobia could be seen as fear of an encounter with the Real. In *Everything You Always Wanted to Know about Lacan but Were Afraid to Ask Hitchcock,* Žižek states that Scottie does indeed have such frightening encounters, especially in the nightmare in which he sees his own decapitated head transfixed while the "world" around it is moving very fast. This is the Gaze of the Thing (of the Real), which is the most frightening encounter one can have. After this dream, Scottie becomes mad, but when he recovers, he starts searching for his desired but fearsome object. Whatever the differences may be in a psychoanalytic explanation of the film, the questions always center on subject positioning and identification strategies through desire. Increasingly, it becomes clear that none of the subjects in the film is in control, either because there is an overall identification with the fragile feminine position or because of a (common) encounter with the Real.

What happens when we consider the image not as a representation but as an expression of mental relations? What happens when we consider the dimension of time that is clearly present in *Vertigo*? What happens to the subject on screen? What happens to the spectators? Deleuze already stated that Hitchcock brings the spectator into an active relation to the film. This remark becomes clearer when we consider Hitchcock's answer to the question of why he revealed so early in *Vertigo* that Judy is actually Madeleine:

> Though Stewart isn't aware of it yet, the viewers already know that Judy is not just a girl who looks like Madeleine, but that she is Madeleine! Everyone around me was against this change [in respect to the original novel]; they all felt that the revelation should be saved for the end of the picture. I put myself in the place of a child whose mother is telling him a story. Where there is a pause in her narration, the child always says, "What comes next, Mommy?" Well, I felt that the second part of the novel was written as if nothing came next, whereas in my formula, the little boy, knowing that Madeleine and Judy is the same person, would then ask, "And Stewart does not know it, does he? What will he do when he finds out?"[35]

Modleski reads this quote as indicative of the power of the mother/woman and the female point of view that undermines the male positions in Hitchcock, even though the female character is always punished for that. I would say that Hitchcock's strategy undermines processes of identification: the viewer does not identify with Stewart/Scottie because he or she (the reader) knows more. Instead, Hitchcock gives the spectator a special place. Knowing more than the protagonist involves a different kind of relation and subjectivity for which to aim. As I try to demonstrate, this is entirely because of the experience of time. As Deleuze made clear in *The Movement-Image* and *The Time-Image*, cinema is Bergsonian in its conceptualization of time. Bergson's major thesis about time is known:

> The past co-exists with the present that it has been; the past is preserved in itself, as past in general (non-chronological); at each moment time splits itself into present and past, present that passes and past which is preserved. . . . The only subjectivity is in time grasped in its foundation, and it is we who are internal to time, not the other way around. That we are in time looks like a commonplace, yet it is the highest paradox. Time is not the interior in us, but just the opposite, [time is] the interiority in which we are, in which we move, live, and change.[36]

Deleuze mentions *Vertigo* as one of the films that show how we inhabit time. In his film *Sunless* (1982), Chris Marker emphasizes the complex layers of time in *Vertigo*. Jean-Pierre Esquenazi, in his work *Une idée du cinéma*, elaborates this point in a Deleuzian perspective.[37] According to Esquenazi, the scene in Ernie's Restaurant is a scene that contains everything that will follow. In *Vertigo*, there are three women: Carlotta, Madeleine, and Judy. These three women are the same, but they do not inhabit the same time. It is up to Scottie to distinguish between the different levels of time, which is sometimes impossible because they conflate. Scottie is confused by experiencing several layers of time (the virtuality of the past, the actuality of the present) at the same moment. In a detailed and beautiful analysis, Esquenazi demonstrates how Madeleine's face in profile in the restaurant scene is a crystal image: it is at the same time in the past and the present, virtual and actual. It is quite possible to relate Scottie's look to Madeleine's profile, and hence to identify with Scottie, as psychoanalytic readings have done. In doing so, however, one fails to notice that the relation between the two looks is not a classic shot/countershot, imposing a look from a subject to an object. Before Madeleine enters the bar, Scottie has turned his back. He even looks in the same direction as Madeleine and therefore cannot see her in the same way as we, the spectators, see her breathtaking profile, which means we have to conclude that the image of Madeleine is a virtual image actually presented.[38]

In this first profile, the different layers of time germinate; also, the doubling of Madeleine in the mirror, when she leaves the restaurant, is an indication of the temporal doubling that will follow. Because it is sometimes unclear whether what the spectator sees is an actual or virtual image (Madeleine's profile could be actual to the spectator but virtual to Scottie), the question of the point of view is raised: from which point of view is the story told? The confusion, and at the same time the beauty of this scene, is due to the fact that this question becomes difficult to answer. We can understand now when Deleuze says that a camera consciousness starts to make mental connections in time:

The camera is no longer content sometimes to follow the character's movement, sometimes itself to undertake movements of which they are merely the object, but in every case it subordinates descriptions of a space to the functions of thought. This is not a simple distinction between the subjective and the objective, the real and the imaginary, it is on the contrary their indiscernibility which will endow the camera with a rich array of functions . . .) Hitchcock's premonition will come true: a camera-consciousness which would no longer be defined by the movements it is able to follow or make, but by the mental connections it is able to enter into.[39]

In the profile of Madeleine, the actual and the virtual conflate. From this crystal image, Madeleine will multiply (Carlotta, Madeleine, Judy), occupying each time a different layer in time. Following Madeleine/Carlotta, Scottie starts to wander and wonder. Deleuze stresses the importance of Scottie's real (ordinary) vertigo: it does not so much have a symbolic meaning (although in terms of style it is an important recurrent structure), nor does it relate to any concepts like the Real (or the Big Void), as noted earlier. Rather, Scottie's inability to climb stairs and to master spatial relations puts him in a state of contemplation. It is useful to recall here some of the characteristics that Deleuze establishes for the time-image: instead of performing actors, characters become more like seers and wanderers, confused by the experience of time. In Vertigo, both Scottie and Madeleine are wanderers. In that capacity, they become visionary, capable of seeing the crystals of time. They even decide to wander off together in the forest. In this scene, we can see how Scottie is fascinated by the virtuality of Carlotta in Madeleine, just as later he will be absorbed by the virtuality of Madeleine in Judy.

Jean-Pierre Esquenazi gives a much more elaborate analysis of the crystal-image in *Vertigo*. Here I try to draw some conclusions for the concept of the subject in such an image. As I said earlier, the concept of time makes the notion of selfhood and the subject unstable: one could say, like Tania Modleski, that all identification boils down to the woman, which makes the male subject's position unstable. In a Spinozian/Deleuzian perspective of time, there is not so much to identify with: both Scottie and Madeleine lose their identity, are confused about their identity; they live in the past and in the present at the same time. The notion of the subject is obscured by a desire to connect with virtual worlds of the past, and the spectator is a third term, sometimes consciously addressed by the camera, sometimes presented with a point of view of one of the protagonists, but clearly part of the network of relations, more than just by identification. The spectator starts wondering and wandering on his or her own terms.

To conclude about Hitchcock, one can say that his work demonstrates, as Žižek has shown, that the subject can be seen as a concept that depends on the transcendental notion of the Real. The subject's fundamental desire ultimately is based on this nothingness of the impossible Real. When Scottie sees his own decapitated head in his dream, he has a maddening encounter with the Real. The spectator constitutes him or herself as a subject by identifying with the character(s) on the screen, feeling the same constraints (of the Real or otherwise) as the protagonists. Like the protagonist, however, the subject off screen never can identify with the Gaze of the Real, which is unrepresentable. The Eye and the unrepresentable Gaze are important models for understanding subjectivity.

According to Deleuze, however, Hitchcock saturates the representing movement-image by introducing mental relations into the image. The spectator is no longer invited to identify but to think and make connections between the different images. It is now the model of the brain, the rhizomatic mental connections that it can make and the way it conceives time, that are important. The sense of self is still important, but it is confused, loosened, and made more flexible. Because Scottie literally loses the ground under his feet, the space of the look (his vertigo), he opens up to time and to the confusion between virtual and actual. One can even wonder whether the second part of the movie, after Scottie's nightmare and mental breakdown, is not taking place completely in his mind (we never actually see him leaving the hospital, nor do we see his loyal girlfriend Midge again). In any case, Hitchock's *Vertigo* certainly displays a new kind of camera consciousness.

Brain Waves and Time: Strange Days' "Vertigo"

Comparing now the opening scene of Vertigo with the opening scene of *Strange Days*, we notice another striking case of repetition and difference. In terms of form of content, in both films, the first image of the eye is followed by a chase sequence on a rooftop, ending in a vertiginous image of a dissipating deep space. In *Vertigo*, it is still up to the viewer to relate the eye of the opening sequence to the mind's eye: one can easily forget this because the film's opening is classic. Scottie/Stewart is following a thief on a rooftop, and the spectator is in the first instance invited to identify with him. He is first represented objectively: we see Scottie climbing up some stairs to a roof, followed later by a subjective point of view: we see *his* vertigo when he looks down. Stylistically (form of expression), subjective and objective points of view are displayed carefully to be sure with whom the spectator should identify. Only gradually does the problem of time emerge in the image and subjectivity and objectivity become more and more blurred. The ambiguity of the film lies in the fact that the time layers are centered on a psychoanalytic theme of sexual difference—hence the two possible readings of the film.

Strange Days has a different form of expression: in this film, the spectator is confronted immediately with what seems to be a subjective point of view. The only problem is that we do not know who is the subject in this scene: there is nobody to identify with (in *Peeping Tom*, there was still an indication of the subject holding the camera through which the images are recorded); so, as remarked previously, the spectator is drawn immediately into the image without any distance. What is also implied is that this could be anyone's brain wave. Immediately, this raises the question of what happens to the sense of self if we can connect to anyone's memory or experience.[40] In a futuristic context, *Strange Days* plays with the idea of direct brain stimulation and what this could mean for human beings.[41]

If direct brain stimulation became possible (as is clear by now, a philosophic basis for this is not new and scientifically it is becoming ever more plausible), the question of time and memory would become increasingly relevant. In contemporary cinema, time and memory in relation to subjectivity and selfhood are indeed already frequent themes. Not only in the time-image as described by Deleuze, but even in the Hollywood action-image, time has made its dazzling entrance, which apparently was set off by *Vertigo*. Time and memory are central preoccupations in films like *Blade Runner*, *Total Recall*, and *Twelve Monkeys*.[42] In *Blade Runner*, memories are no longer conditions of authentic selfhood because they can be implanted.[43] In *Total Recall*, the past is equally not guaranteed to be personal, and in *Twelve Monkeys*, the hero lives at the same time in the past, present, and future. Is it possible to become more Bergsonian in thinking time? In *Twelve Monkeys*, there is even a reference to *Vertigo* (the film is being shown in a theater where the protagonists of the film are hiding), and when the heroine Kathryn dyes her hair blonde, how can we not think of Madeleine, the woman from the past in the present?[44] It is striking, though, that all these contemporary films that deal explicitly with time are set in the future (one can add to this list the *Back to the Future* and *Terminator* films and as the non–science fiction film, *Peggy Sue Got Married*). Maybe this is to keep the problem of time at a distance, as if it does not really concern us now and is only an entertaining fantasy. At the same time, the preoccupation with time and memory indicates that it concerns us now more than ever and that in the future it will become an even greater preoccupation; it clearly indicates that time and the world are "out of joint." These films, like *Strange Days*, present themselves as classic movement-images in terms of their form of content. In their form of expression (albeit through excessive spatiality or through time-travel narratives), they cannot escape *Vertigo*-like confusions of the subjective and objective, the virtual and the actual.[45]

Although *Strange Days* is also presented as science fiction, it speaks about what is already the past, the last day of the second millennium. The scientific tool that it presents is not so far-fetched either. Neuroscientists work with SQUIDs and brain stimulations to induce memories or at least neurologic actions and feelings. It is inconceivable only on one crucial point, namely, that it is still improbable to recall other people's memories. This indicates again the importance of time for the concept of selfhood. In *Face Off*, the two protagonists (John Travolta and Nicolas Cage) literally swap faces; so the face, the look, and the visible appearance are no longer the guarantees of identity and selfhood. The only way that Travolta's wife recognizes her husband is through a blood tissue type (a code) and . . . a personal memory. So before tackling the question of whose memory or brain this is, let me look at the way *Strange Days* plays with personal memories.

Like Scottie, Lenny Nero in *Strange Days* is a former police officer who, after quitting his job, becomes obsessed with a woman from the past: by replaying the tapes of his experiences in the past with his girlfriend at that time, Faith, he keeps returning to the past. What was virtual (enclosed in the actual image) in *Vertigo* is made actual, presented as a memory-image in *Strange Days*. As Bergson demonstrated in *Matter and Memory*, there is a profound relation between memory, body, and perception. Every perception is related to a certain memory, which makes it possible for the body to move and to act. We are simultaneously childhood, adolescence, maturity, and old age. At every moment in the present, we jump between these different regions of nonchronologic time in which we live. Someone who lives in pure presence, reacting immediately to every excitement of the body, is impulsive, not able to react properly. On the other hand, it is also possible to give too much preference to memory and memory-images; such a person Bergson calls a *dreamer*. Between these two extremes, Bergson places a memory that is willing to follow the demands of the present moment but that can resist irrelevant demands.[46]

If we consider *Strange Days* now from a Bergsonian perspective of time, we can see that Lenny's addiction to his own memories makes him unable to act, in a similar way (although in a totally different context) to Scottie being unable to act in *Vertigo*. The fact that Lenny can recall his memories whenever he wants by plugging in his brain only makes it worse. The memorized women in both films are unable to break the spell of the past: Judy in *Vertigo* because she consents to becoming Madeleine again, and Faith because Lenny cannot see (because of his recollection-images) that she has become somebody different from who she was. The only person in *Strange Days* who seems to have a sound balance between past and present, between mind and body, is Mace. Placed in a Bergsonian perspective, her remark to Lenny that "memories are designed to fade away" is relevant. Memories are necessary and link up automatically with perceptions, but they should not always be actualized. They should be recalled only insofar as necessary for the present moment.

It is also significant that Mace's memories do not come from a SQUID but are recalled by a present situation of her body. Her first memory is actually presented as a flashback when she remembers how she met Lenny (this is what Deleuze calls the movement-image's way of actualizing the past). Interestingly, this flashback is not just a subjective point of view. In the mind, we conceive ourselves as both other and I as Mace sees herself as another person in her flashback.[47] It is also Mace who encourages Lenny to search his memory for relevant information that Iris, the prostitute who has been murdered, has tried to give him just before her death. These images of the past are the other actualized flashbacks that are necessary for the present moment.

Mace's second recollection is a more direct presentation of a crystal-image, which encloses time virtually in an actual image. It happens when Mace looks at her son, who is not aware that his mother is looking at him; but in the relation between the image of the boy and Mace's look, the mind's eye brings in time: when the boy was little, how one day he will be big—and the only occasion when Mace consents to playing back a SQUID is when she realizes that Iris has given Lenny a crucial playback tape, which holds evidence of the brutal murder of the black singer Jerrico One and some friends. Although these images resemble the Rodney King beatings, which did not really change the world, *Strange Days* expresses the hope that through an opening up of the mind, there eventually will be some kind of tolerance. Despite the film's high degree of action-images, in terms of the role of memories, *Strange Days* presents us with a Bergsonian ethics of time.[48]

New images like digital images and contemporary high-tech cinema are said by Deleuze to present chaotic spatial relations without beginning or end, going in all directions.[49] The spaces in *Strange Days* are like that: no room seems to end; there is always an opening to another connecting space, and the characters always find themselves in the middle of all this spatial abundance. Because of this, *Strange Days* opens up to time. As the brain experiments with memories and different time layers also indicate, time and memory do not need to be personal. Related to this, the film also asks questions about the sense of self. As already indicated, the fact that the SQUID experiences seem to be subjective points of view means that the spectator is not given many assurances about whose point of view it is. Moreover, it has been demonstrated (for instance, by Robert Montgomery's subjective camera experiment *Lady in the Lake*) that a subjective point of view alone does not increase the experience of identification in the spectator.[50] What *Strange Days* adds to this is not only that identification does not work by purely subjective camera movement but also that the sense of self becomes very unstable when we can experience anybody's memory. This can provide new possibilities once the concept of desire is seen as a Spinozian/Deleuzian wish to make multiple connections (creating Bodies without Organs, as Deleuze would say), but it also has its dangerous sides. We have already seen this in Lenny presenting himself as a new kind of psychiatrist: "I am your shrink, your priest, I am the magic man, the Santa Claus of the soul." The combination of shrink/priest and magic man/Santa Claus of the soul is interesting in the sense that again a transition is indicated. The shrink/priest, seen as the traditional psychoanalyst, forgiving the subject its guilty enjoyment, has become the magic man/Santa Claus of the soul. He has a very different way to "cure," namely, by stimulating new connections without being afraid to lose the self-same, knowing that desire is an affirmative and creative element to construct the subject. If one thinks of the horrible rape scene analyzed in the foregoing, or the racial murders, there is still enough to feel guilty about (the danger of microfascism, internal in ourselves, is always present, according to Deleuze).

At the same time, *Strange Days* expresses very clearly the wish for more flexible nomadic visions on concepts of the self and desire, which are necessary to survive in a jungle-like world. The self-subject no longer depends on the supposed desire of the other (although the other remains important for connections). Desire is no longer connected to sexual difference only ("we have to liberate desire" and "a thousand tiny sexes—that can be on every part of the body" are famous words from Deleuze and Guattari). Spectators no longer can confirm their identity by identifying with subjects on screen but have to negotiate between the images presented to their minds and the memories induced by their own bodies. Body, brain, and perception work together to establish a sense of self in each point of time, which differs according to the demands of specific situations. *Strange Days* demonstrates an ethics of Bergsonian memory; it also takes scientific possibilities one step further in asking us what would happen if we could induce other people's memories. Maybe the shock of this mental possibility is necessary to change our ideas about the self-same subject in the first place. In his article "The Imagination of Immanence: An Ethics of Cinema," Peter Canning explains why this change is necessary in the first place. He speaks of a war against the delusional signifier (which is the classic apparatus):

A struggle for liberation, not for annihilation, even of an enemy. . . . To survive the end of mediation, we should learn to *think without Law*, without the Father, to develop an absolute ethics that begins where symbolic-moral mediation leaves off and an aesthetic experience of nonrelation appears. It remains an ethical experiment, however, in that it is always a question of discovering and inventing new relations, new powers, without falling into the nostalgia or perverse denial that never *seems* to tire of killing the father (in reality it lives and dies in despair)—but never risks a step beyond it.[51]

Although I did not explicitly discuss the Law of the Father nor of the signifier, clearly the transcendental apparatus, the representational image of thought and the psychoanalytic model are part of that discourse.

As a metafilm, *Strange Days* demonstrates how the cinematographic apparatus of *Peeping Tom* has become only one aspect of contemporary image culture and that the apparatus has changed. From a transcendental apparatus, designed to give the subject the illusion of control but actually controlling the subject, the apparatus has become an immanent one, to the point where the whole universe becomes cinematic. As Hitchcock already anticipated in *Vertigo*, we have entered an age where a new camera consciousness makes clear distinction between the subjective and the objective impossible; the past and the present, the virtual and the actual have become indistinguishable. *Strange Days* tells us in what ways the brain has literally become the screen and how this necessitates an immanent conception of the image. Better still, *Strange Days* invites us to a plane of "cinemance"[52] where it is necessary to have immanent conceptual tools for looking at images in themselves and for understanding the ethical and political implications of such a philosophy. Moving from the metalevel of the cinematographic apparatus, in the next chapter, I work with some of the conceptual tools that Deleuze presented in his cinema books and elsewhere to determine how aspects of subjectivity can be constructed on the plane of images.

2

Material Aspects of Subjectivity

> The plane of immanence or the plane of matter is a set of movement-images; a collection of lines or figures of light; a series of blocs of space-time.
> —*Gilles Deleuze*[1]

The body often has been considered to be the most material thing of all. Traditionally, body/matter has been opposed to mind/spirit. In the dominant traditions of Western philosophy, the image has been considered a representation of matter, the mind as the faculty to understand and give meaning to representations. Cinema, as the most "complete" form of representation, often has centered on images of the body as opposed to the more spiritual and rational aspirations of the written word. The bodies of the divas and stars from classic Hollywood and contemporary media stars are obvious examples. The 1970s seem to have introduced a whole new emphasis on the body and the materialism of the cinematographic image. In horror film, science fiction, action cinema, and special-effects movies but also in art cinema, we find bodies of all extreme kinds: screaming bodies and quivering flesh, running and fighting bodies, beautiful bodies, sexual bodies, bodies in pain and agony, invincible bodies, (living) dead bodies, and masochistic bodies. Many of these bodies have been usefully explained and interpreted in psychoanalytic frameworks. As I argued in the previous chapter, this psychoanalytic framework is related to traditional representational thinking and hence to the idea of a separation between body and mind. I begin this chapter by briefly investigating the consequences for the perception and understanding of the image of the body and especially of subjectivity. The next step is to investigate how Deleuze assigns a different place to the body in relation to thinking and to questions of subjectivity. It is therefore necessary to turn to Spinoza, the philosopher of the body who inspired Deleuze enormously.

The ultimate aim of this chapter is to situate the body on the plane of immanence, the plane of images, and to ask in what ways the tool box of Deleuzian concepts can be used and what differences these tools can make perceptible. According to Deleuze, following Bergson, image, matter, brain, and body are one. In his book *Gilles Deleuze's Time Machine*, David Rodowick elucidates how in this way Bergson challenges Western philosophy's dualism between realism and idealism. For both realism and idealism, perception is tied to knowledge: to see is to know. "But for the former," Rodowick explains, "one represents to oneself what actually is according to the presumed laws of nature; for the latter, one represents to oneself what is according to the presumed laws of thought. In both cases, the speculative interest of pure knowledge requires divorcing of mind from both matter and time."[2] Contrary to the traditions of Western philosophy, Bergson not only equates matter and image but also sees the body and the brain as special images in the sense that they are "receptive surfaces acting and reacting to the propagation of energy and the force of matter."[3] In this way, Bergson overcomes the dualism of matter and mind. Obviously, this has consequences for the image and for the way perception is thought.

If the image is no longer a *representation* of matter but is matter, what then is perception? In the previous chapter, I argued that the subject in a cinematic universe is no longer a transcendental one whose eye gives access to the representations in front of it; rather, it is an immanent one that is itself an image among other images and that is slowly constructed by its different perceptions and experiences. How, then, is subjectivity constructed in perception according to Bergson? In his cinema books, Deleuze develops Bergson's categories of perception: the different types of movement-images (such as the perception-image, action-image, affection-image) and time-images (such as the recollection-image and the crystal-image). I look at four films from the 1970s and early 1980s in which a central place is occupied by the body, but especially the flesh, which is even more material: Michael Critchton's *Coma* (1978), Paul Verhoeven's *The Fourth Man* (1983), Rainer Werner Fassbinder's *In a Year with Thirteen Moons* (1978), and Djibril Diop Mambety's *Touki Bouki* (1973). The body and the images of the flesh in these films are nevertheless very different; they constitute quite different subjectivities. With the help of Deleuze's image categories, I attempt to establish these differences. I propose a model for analyzing in a Deleuzian spirit by looking at the different assemblages formed by these films. On the horizontal axis of the assemblages, I look at the forms of content and forms of expression, for which I will refer to the immanent concepts of images of the cinema books. On the vertical axis, I look at the (re)territorial and deterritorial lines of the different films, for which I will refer to Deleuze and Guattari's A *Thousand Plateaus*.

Psychoanalysis and the Monstrous Flesh

Abject Femininity

Flesh is the most obvious sign of the physical body. In contemporary cinema, images of flesh have become more and more explicit and recurrent. The horror genre ("splash and splatter") has become ever more explicit in presenting images of raw flesh, bloody bones, and other monstrous bodily forms. The word *flesh* in German or in Dutch ("Fleish" or "vlees") has a double meaning: it means both the living flesh of the body and dead flesh, or meat. This double meaning, between flesh and meat, life and death, indicates a borderline, a zone where things are ambiguous and therefore can be disturbing for the subject. To describe this zone of ambiguity, in her book *Pouvoirs de l'horreur*, Julia Kristeva introduces the concept of abjection.[4] The abject is neither subject nor object; it is, according to Kristeva, that which disturbs the system. Kristeva's frame of reference is psychoanalysis, and although she never mentions it, abjection or the abject is close to what Slavoj Žižek calls the Real. One of Žižek's descriptions of the Lacanian Real is "the flayed body, the palpitation of the raw, skinless red flesh."[5] It is what constantly threatens life and at the same time makes life possible. In *The Monstrous Feminine*, a feminist study on horror cinema, Barbara Creed explains the notion of the abject in a way that comes close to Žižek's idea of the Real:

The place of the abject is the place where meaning collapses, the place where "I" am not. The abject threatens life: it must be "radically excluded" from the place of the living subject, propelled away from the body and deposited on the other side of an imaginary border which separates the self from that which threatens the self.

Although the subject must exclude the abject, the abject must, nevertheless, be tolerated, for that which threatens to destroy life also helps to define life. Further, the activity of exclusion is necessary to guarantee that the subject take up his/her proper place in relation to the symbolic.[6]

Although we do not like it, the abject is necessary to define us as subjects. Like the Real, it is threatening and, at the same time, necessary for our identity, precisely because it indicates a border.

Creed relates the notion of abjection to the horror film in three ways. First, horror cinema is full of images of abjection: corpses (whole, mutilated, or living dead zombies) and bodily waste like blood, vomit, sweat, tears, saliva, and putrefying flesh are frequently depicted on the "screaming screen." All these images refer to the border between the inside and the outside of the body. The concept of the boundary, in all kinds of variations, is a second element of abjection in horror cinema. Here many boundaries are undermined: the boundary between human and nonhuman; man and beast; natural and supernatural; normal and abnormal sexual desire and gender roles; the clean, proper, and dirty abject body. According to Creed, following Kristeva, the full symbolic body does not bear any signs of its debts to nature; the woman's body, because of its maternal functions, acknowledges its debt to nature and is therefore more likely to signify the abject. The maternal figure as abject is therefore the third element of abjection to be found in horror cinema. Kristeva talks in this respect about the platonic concept of *chora*, a receptacle: the child struggles to break away from the motherly chora. To create distance, it has to make it (the mother's body) abject. In any case, the mother has a double role. On the one hand, she gives toilet training to the child (the difference between proper and improper is taught by her). At the same time, the mother's body is considered impure (menstrual blood, deformations during pregnancy). This ambiguity of the motherly authority is in itself already abject.

Creed mentions different aspects of this maternal abjection that are evident in horror film. Many images of horror relate to procreative functions of the female body. In *Alien(s)*, it is the idea of an archaic (parthenogenetic) mother, the Ur-mother (Gaia, Mother Earth) that is present everywhere, a terrible omnipotent force. Creed also mentions the blood of the female (often lesbian) vampire and the monstrous womb; images of possessed and abject women are presented in *The Exorcist* and *Carrie* (which Creed calls "the woman as witch"). In some horror films, the witch's supernatural powers are linked to the female reproductive system—especially the monthly (lunar) cycle of menstruation. This is the case in *The Exorcist*, where Regan, the girl, is about to have her first menstruation when she is possessed, and, of course, in *Carrie*. In this film, we find the traditional fears of witchcraft explicitly related to all kinds of blood (menstrual blood, pig's blood, birth blood, the blood of sin, the blood of death). Carrie acquires her telekinetic powers at the same time that her menstrual blood flows. Throughout history, witchcraft has been related to "monstrous femininity" (especially midwifery) that threatens the full symbolic male body. Especially the authorities of the Catholic Church have been notorious in persecuting these abject women (think of the *Malleus Maleficarum*, the inquisitor's manual for witch prosecution commissioned by the Catholic Church).

In *Carrie*, the most extreme representative of the Church is here not a priest but another woman: Carrie's mother, who also believes Carrie is a witch (abjecting herself, this woman thinks according to the same sexist religious principles of the Church and patriarchy). Yet Carrie is not represented as a traditional witch; she is not only the spirit of evil that sleeps with the devil, has a third nipple, and has an insensitive spot on her back. Rather, her extreme force and fury are reactions to the sadistic treatment she receives from her classmates and insane mother. Carrie is also a sympathetic figure. Actually, what the film shows is how fear and abjection of feminine corporeality, combined with an extreme attachment to an unwise mother, can lead to destructive results. Seen in this light, we could say that *Carrie* is not so much about witchcraft as it is about a completely suffocating mother–daughter relationship that is influenced by ideas about witchcraft related to the female body. *Carrie* could be seen as a maternal melodrama, skinned to the body and the abject flesh.

In this psychoanalytic reading, the flesh and all kinds of other bodily material always represent what is outside the subject but nevertheless also constitutes the subject. It is fascinating and threatening at the same time. The images are seen as representations that help the subject in its search for a stable place where it can distinguish itself from objects/others. Similar to the metalevel of the cinematographic apparatus, also on the level of particular images, here images of the flesh, gender binaries are strong elements in establishing subjectivity and subject positions.

Dangerous Femininity

In the previous chapter, the horrible rape scenes in *Peeping Tom* and *Strange Days* were connected to the Freudian implications of the classic cinematographic apparatus. It was argued that *Strange Days* certainly can also be connected to this psychoanalytic frame of thinking but that there is also something else at stake. In *Strange Days*, the subject and object of the look become one and the same, which makes the self difficult to distinguish from the other and calls for a Bergsonian ethics of time. There the confusion of subject and object is not an abject representation but an encounter that forces us to rethink the implications of the apparatus in a metacinematic universe. In both *Peeping Tom* and *Strange Days*, however, the prostitute is killed, no matter what kind of "apparatus" is involved. It is not surprising that with the influence of women's liberation, a new subgenre in horror cinema came into existence, with an angry woman at the center: the rape–revenge film. Here, too, psychoanalysis is an obvious reference for understanding these types of films.[7]

Barbara Creed relates the rape–revenge story to the myth—overlooked or repressed by Freud—of the vagina dentata: the woman as castrating instead of castrated. Creed rereads Freud's case on Little Hans and discovers many moments where Freud represses the power of the castrating woman. According to Freud, Hans' fear of horses represents his fear of the castrating father. The black bit on the horse's mouth that fills Hans with anxiety, for instance, is interpreted as father's moustache. Creed, however, argues that the black thing is much more easily linked with the mother: "the black hair near her widdle" or even mother's black underwear. In this way, Creed argues that it is the castrating power of the mother that inspires Hans' real fear. It is also this myth of the dangerous castrating woman that Creed uses to explain the success of the rape–revenge movie. I return to Little Hans and Creed's interpretation in a moment. Let me first summarize the way in which Creed connects this myth to the rape–revenge story.

Creed argues that woman is slashed or raped because she is blamed for the human condition (an attitude we also saw in the behavior of Carrie's mother and other religious and patriarchal ideas). The sadistic nature of the attack can be seen only as an attempt to rob woman of her terrifying—even if merely imaginary—powers before she can use them. Her revenge confirms that she does indeed possess such powers. What Creed finds disturbing about films like *I Spit on Your Grave* and *Ms. 45* is that the woman uses her seductive charms to get men killed. In other words, Creed is disturbed by the fact that women are raped without any seduction or pleasure, whereas men can die in masochistic pleasure. Both sexes bring out their repressed parts (women become sadistic, men become masochistic). Nevertheless, Creed's conclusion about the rape–revenge story is clear: "Man must be ever on the alert, poised in phallic anticipation whenever signs of the deadly femme castratrice are present."[8] The rape–revenge film is an ultimate expression of the infamous battle of the sexes: bringing out the worst in man (rape) and woman (revenge), the flesh of both sexes is torn to pieces.

Slavoj Žižek argues in *The Metastases of Enjoyment* that woman is closest to the Real, the "raw, skinless flesh" or "the night of the world." Therefore, she seems to possess *jouissance*, which man wants to possess, even if this means raping her (in a *marriage de jouissance*). In a chapter on David Lynch and feminine depression, Žižek argues that violence against (Lynchian) women is not the cause of their depression but that this violence is actually "therapeutic," caused by their "transcendental" state of depression; the violence functions as a sort of shock therapy to prevent women from slipping into the absolute depression of the Real: "The status of depression is thus strictly 'transcendental': depression provides the a priori frame within which causes can act as they do. . . . The philosophical name for this 'depression' is absolute negativity—what Hegel called 'the night of the world,' the subject's withdrawal into itself. In short, woman, not man is the subject par excellence."[9] Žižek does not mention any revenge, but implicitly woman's ultimate revenge would of course be the idea that she is a subject *par excellence* anyway. According to Žižek's reading of Lacan and popular cinema, the war between the sexes is irresolvable, except maybe in death/murder.[10]

From these psychoanalytic interpretations of different images of mutilated bodies and the flesh, we can conclude that although psychoanalysis certainly can explain many of the problematic relations between subject (especially men and women), images, and the world, it also functions as an imprisoning matrix of thinking,[11] seeing, and feeling, even if it is in a reversal of cause and effect, as Žižek so often brilliantly argues—as indeed he did for *The Matrix* (see Introduction) and for feminine depression as mentioned in the previous paragraph. Or, if subject positions are reversed, as

Barbara Creed does with Little Hans' story, by turning Hans' fear into a fear of his mother instead of his father, by replacing father's black moustache by mother's black underwear, we are kept in the same oedipal triangle and impasses. What is ignored in these frames of thought is the fact that the relationship between subjects, images, and the world consists of multiple connections (of which the family is but one).

Deleuze and Guattari refer to Little Hans in *A Thousand Plateaus* and reproach psychoanalysts for blocking his rhizomatic desire to make all kinds of connections: "They barred him from the rhizome of the building, then from the rhizome of the street, they rooted him in his parents' bed."[12] No account is given of the impressions from the horses, carriages, and events of the street, no account of the affective and machinistic assemblages: "horse-omnibus-street" and "having eyes blocked by blinders, having a bit and a bridle, being proud, having a peepee maker, pulling heavy loads, being whipped, falling, making a din with its legs, biting etc."[13] Little Hans's horse is not representative but affective, conclude Deleuze and Guattari. Multiplicity and affect (other than neurosis and psychosis) seem to be important aspects of subjectivity that cannot be taken into account by psychoanalysis. In the next section, I return to the question of affect. Now I first look at another reading of the horror genre, which allows more room for multiplicities.

Multiplicities: Rezoning Bodies

In her book *Men, Women and Chainsaws*, Carol Clover also analyzes the horror genre and its bodies. Clover discusses many of the same films as Creed, but whereas Creed sees Carrie, for instance, as a sort of purification ritual, connected to the concept of the abject, for Clover the concept of the abject is not so important. Although she does refer to Carrie's menstruation and all the other "dirty blood" in the film, she is more interested in possibilities of identification for especially the male audience (the story is written by a man, Stephen King; filmed by a man, Brian de Palma; and a large proportion of its audiences is men). The introduction of her book is therefore called "Carrie and the Boys." Clover here quotes Stephen King:

Carrie is largely about how women find their own channels of power, and what men fear about women and women's sexuality. . . . For me, Carrie White is a sadly misused teenager, an example of the sort of person whose spirit is so often broken for good in that pit of man—and woman-eaters that is your normal suburban high school. But she is also Woman, feeling her powers for the first time and, like Samson, pulling down the temple on everyone in sight at the end of the book. . . . And one of the reasons for the success of the story in both print and film, I think, lies in this: Carrie's revenge is something that any student who has ever had his gym shorts pulled down in Phys Ed or his glasses thumb-rubbed in study hall could approve of.[14]

As Clover explains King's words, a boy so threatened and so humiliated is a boy who recognizes himself in a girl who finds herself bleeding in the gym shower, pelted with tampons, and sloshed with pig's blood at the senior prom. This is the general and basic idea that Clover develops in her book: the possibility that male viewers are quite prepared to identify not just with screen females but with screen females in fear and pain. Although some studies on male masochism refer to this identification strategy,[15] this aspect has not often been related to horror cinema, which often is considered a rather macho-male experience at the expense of women. Clover demonstrates that possession films like *Carrie, The Exorcist, The Serpent and the Rainbow, Witchboard, Poltergeist,* and *Angel Heart* can be considered as "opening-up" films. In such films, two stories are usually told: one of the possessed woman (abject in Creed's terms) and one of the man in crisis. Parallel to these stories are mostly two competing systems of explanation: white (male) science and black (female) magic. The possessed girl in *The Exorcist* is confronted with Father Damien Karras, who finds himself in crisis. In *Witchboard*, it is the possessed woman Linda who forces her very closed boyfriend to "open up" to emotions. In *Carrie*, the concentration is more on the story of the possessed woman, but as I just indicated, men also are implicitly concerned in this film.[16] What Clover actually argues is that the female story of bodily possession is similar to the male story of redefining himself. Moreover, this bodily possession and extremities are necessary for the "new man" to change: to have an "open mind" (and body), to gulp things in like a woman does, to be open to emotions, to be open to the more irrational and magical aspects of life. According to Clover, it is only by referring to the woman's body that this can be done. As she expresses it:

Crudely put, for a space to be created in which men can weep without being labeled "feminine," women must be relocated to a space where they will be made to wail uncontrollably; for men to be able to relinquish emotional rigidity, control, women must be relocated to a space in which they will undergo a flamboyant psychotic break. Mostly the woman comes back from her crazy trip, and then in the mean time the man has changed so that they can meet each other halfway (as the genre requires).[17]

So, according to Clover, the body horror in possession films is mostly a re-zoning project, and the masculine can be redefined only by relocating the feminine. I return to this point in Chapter 4 when I discuss images of be-coming-woman. For now, I want to emphasize that Clover's analysis of dif-ferent story lines that constitute the subject allows more room for multiple connections that constitute the subject. Also in the rape–revenge movies, there are mostly (at least) two stories: one about women versus men and another about country versus city life. In *I Spit on Your Grave*, for instance, the woman comes from the city of New York to a rural, backward country place; city people are rich, soft, and therefore "rapeable" seems to be the underlying assumption (Clover speaks about "urbanoia"). The attention to issues of class and social background adds a dimension to the gender op-position in this kind of film.

Another point where Clover's analysis differs from Creed's is her con-sideration of male identification strategies in rape–revenge movies. For this, she refers to one of the first rape–revenge films of the 1970s: *Deliver-ance*. Again in this film, the difference between the city and the country is exploited, but the rape is a male rape (two country "uglies" rape one of four city men spending a weekend in the country). This demonstrates that men, too, can be brought into a (traditional feminine) position in which their body is assaulted. Clover concludes that "even the most body-based of genres manages to complicate the sex/gender system, especially on the side of the victim–hero, whose gender is clearly coded feminine but whose sex, it seems, is up for grabs. . . . These films are predicated on cross-gender identification of the most extreme, corporeal sort."[18] Again, according to Clover, the horror cinema presents possibilities for rezoning the male sub-ject. The possibility of cross-gender identification makes all bodies vulner-able. In her view, horror cinema is not so obviously monstrously feminine. Rather, body horror allows for cross-gender identifications and can be seen as an important tool for rezoning the borders of the subject. Both men and women have tender bodies; ultimately, they are made out of soft flesh, and their subject positions are related not only to sexual difference but also to multiple other aspects, such as social background and religion—and they are open to change and becoming. In fact, Clover demonstrates in non-

Deleuzian terms a philosophic teratology as proposed by Rosi Braidotti when she discusses the relevance of Deleuze's work for feminism:

> The challenge that the monstrous throws in our direction is a dissociation of the sensibility we have inherited from the previous end of the century. We need to learn to think of the anomalous, the monstrously different not as a sign of pejoration but as the unfolding of virtual possibilities that point to positive alternatives for us all. As Deleuze would put it: the pattern of becoming cuts across the experiential field of all that phallogocentrism did not program us to become. In that sense, the phantasmagoric diversity of monstrous beings points the way to the kind of line of becoming which our crisis-afflicted culture badly needs.[19]

In Chapter 5, I return to "monstrous" becoming-animals. Here I focus on the Spinozian conception of the body that such a different conception of teratologic bodies would allow.

Affects and Politics of the Spinozian Body

Body and Brain, Power and Affect

It could be argued that horror cinema has drawn attention to the bodily aspects of the subject. As is well known, Western philosophy never has shown much interest in the body. Except for the strong and important notion of the abject and Freud's infamous belief that "anatomy is destiny," psychoanalysis never has taken the body very seriously either.[20] Before moving to Deleuze's Bergsonian inspired analysis of (cinematographic) images and the different forms of subjectivities that can be constructed from it, it is therefore useful to rethink the body. So I now turn briefly to Spinoza, another philosopher who is of great importance for Deleuze's own concepts. I already mentioned the affective dimension in Deleuze and Guattari's commentary on Little Hans. The affect, to which I will return in a moment, is part of the physical dimension that Spinoza gave to philosophy. Spinoza's philosophic formula is "we don't know what a body can do." It should be recalled that in Spinoza body and mind are fundamentally connected. As he says in *Ethics*: "Very often it happens that while we are enjoying a thing we wanted, the body acquires from this enjoyment a new constitution, by which it is differently determined, and other images of things are aroused in it; and at the same time the mind begins to imagine other things and desire other things."[21]

Thought and extension are related to mind and body. As Edwin Curley explains in the introduction to his translation of Spinoza's work, a mind's capacity for thought is strictly correlated with its body's capacity for interaction with its environment. Spinoza believes furthermore that just as extension is determined by no (*a priori*) limits, so also thought has no limits:

Therefore, just as the human body is not extension absolutely, but only an extension determined in a certain way, according to the laws of extended nature, by motion and rest, so also the human mind, or soul, is not thought absolutely, but only a thought determined in a certain way, according to the laws of thinking nature, by ideas, a thought which, one infers, must exist when a human body begins to exist.[22]

The inconscience of the mind is strictly related to the unknown of the body. There is no transcendental preestablished framework of the human subject: it will change according to its relations with its environment and other beings.[23] In any case, Spinoza's *Ethics* offers an alternative theory for looking at the bodily dimension of the subject. It also explains why the strong bodily affects of horror or other physical cinema can cause a change in attitude, or a *rezoning*. What affects the body has an effect in the mind. We can conclude from this that Carol Clover's work on body horror is closer to Spinoza than to Barbara Creed's concept of the abject and the vagina dentata.[24]

A body, according to Spinoza, consists of powers and affects (dynamic axis) and of movements and rest (kinetic axis). There are three "primitive" affects that constitute human behavior: desire, joy, and sadness. Whenever the mind considers itself and its power of acting, it passes to a greater state of activity and hence "rejoices." Sadness, however, involves a diminishing or restraining of the mind's power of acting. The affects of joy and desire, arising from the activity of the mind in adequate ideas, "give rise in turn to strength of character, to tenacity—the desire by which we strive 'solely from the dictates of reason' to preserve our being—and to nobility—the desire by which we strive to aid others and join with them in friendship."[25] Spinoza moreover conceives the affect of love in terms of joy: not the union with the loved object, but joy, accompanied by the idea of an external cause. Spinoza gives a whole list of possible affects that follow from these basic ones. Ultimately, however, the subject's desire is the striving to persist in being (*conatus*). This striving is closely related to Deleuze's idea of body politics, which is elaborated in the next section. Clearly, Spinoza's body philosophy also implies an ethics that differs from traditional morality. In this, Spinoza is close to Nietzsche, as is made clear in Chapter 3.

The Body's Striving to Persist

The strength of reason is, for Spinoza, the strength of human desire and human joy. According to Spinoza, desire is our striving to persist in being. It is our only essence. As Genevieve Lloyd explains, this striving to persist, in which virtue and happiness reside, necessarily involves our dealings with "things outside us." The virtuous life does not demand isolation; rather, it involves engagement with the rest of the world, especially with other minds that are also intent on virtuous striving to persist.[26] Connections can increase joy (bondage of passions) and the activity of the mind (freedom of reason). In this respect, it is also useful to remember Spinoza's famous evocation of the wise life as a joyous one: "The part of a wise man is to refresh and restore himself with pleasant food and drink, with scents, with the beauty of green plants, with decoration, music, sports and the theatre."[27] This is not to say that Spinoza is an epicurean who only strives for momentary pleasures. Again, it is the interconnection between body and mind that is important: "Indeed, the human body is composed of a great many parts of different natures, which require continuous and varied food, so that the whole body may be equally capable of doing everything which can follow from its nature, and consequently, so that the mind may also be equally capable of conceiving many things."[28]

Now it could seem that Spinoza recognizes no sorrow or sadness. This is not true, however, as becomes clear in his reflections on suicide. Suicide, in his view, is never rational and never free. For every finite thing, the human mind included, there is something more powerful that can destroy it, but those forces lie outside us. Those who kill themselves, according to Spinoza, are conquered by external causes. Now, as Lloyd explains, the point is not that the self will remain in existence as long as it manages to keep external to it all those forces that can destroy it. The point is, on the contrary, that it needs to join forces with other things that can enhance its *conatus*. Once more, it becomes clear that, for Spinoza, to protect oneself does not mean to withdraw behind the secure borders of a stable identity. It is by opening out to the rest of nature that we become ourselves. As we already saw in the previous chapter, the borders of the Spinozian self are rather fluid (influenced by time). What is important, however, is to see how each body and mind are taken up in a network of forces and influences.

Body Politics: Territorializations and Deterritorializations

At this point, it is useful to recall briefly the ideas of Deleuze and Guattari on politics. In the next section, I discuss these politics with respect to four films in each of which the main character, confronted with a danger that can destroy his or her body (and hence mind), "strives to persist." The confrontation in these films is always related to an image of flesh that is about to become meat. All these films present us with "bodies in a slaughterhouse," but the kind of "subjectivity" that these similar images create depends entirely on the network of political lines and on the different immanent action–reactions as expressed in the different image-types. To see what forces are external, and how each character tries to join other forces, it is useful to draw a rhizomatic map of territorial and deterritorial forces that constitute the vertical axis of assemblages. The horizontal axis of form and content of the image types constitutes the horizontal axis to be discussed.

In *A Thousand Plateaus*, Deleuze and Guattari explain their ideas of rhizomatic politics.[29] Each group or individual consists of several political lines: first, the *hard* or *segmental line*, which frames the individual into social groups, family structures, classes, sex and gender, and professional structures. Everybody must deal with this molar line. In connection to the films to be discussed, I take this line mostly as extracinematic: these are the political, historical, sociologic, economic segments that are virtually present in the different filmic universes. Sometimes it is referred to in the film, but mostly it is just an implied fact (the film as an open totality). This is the territorializing line of the vertical line of the assemblage.

The second line that Deleuze and Guattari distinguish is the *molecular line*, the line where small changes (within the individual or within the group) take place, the line where resistance or deferral takes place but still remains within the segmental law and order. This line is discussed with respect to the main character of each film. To clarify the different reactions of these characters (their "schizzes or breakflows") and to explain the different ways in which they give form to this molecular line, it is necessary to look at the whole film and the type of image that each film presents. This is where the categories action-image, relation-image, affection-image, and time-image come in as well. Here form of content (corporeal modifications) and form of expression (incorporeal transformations, the expressed attributed to bodies) constitute the horizontal axis of the assemblage.

Before discussing the third line and its relation to the assemblage, a few words about the particular way subjectivity is constructed in Bergsonian image theory are needed. Deleuze explains in *The Movement-Image* that there are three basic forms or material aspects of subjectivity. The first way to define a material moment of subjectivity is subtractive; it subtracts from the thing whatever does not interest it. Deleuze states:

In short, things and perception of things are *prehensions*, but things are total objective prehensions, and perceptions of things are incomplete and prejudiced, partial, subjective prehensions. An image that thus goes from objective to subjective prehensions is the first avatar of the movement-image: the *perception-image*. However, when the universe of the movement-image is related to one of these special images which forms a center in it (a body), we move towards the *action-image* where "perception is master of space in the exact measure in which action is master of time" and the operation is no longer selecting or framing but "the incurving of the universe, which simultaneously causes the virtual action of things on us and our possible action on things." This is the second material aspect of subjectivity. The third aspect is related to the final avatar of the movement-image, *the affection-image*. Here the subject is between "perception which is troubling in some respects and a hesitant action" and feels itself "from the inside."[30]

Deleuze concludes by saying that each of us is nothing but an assemblage of three images, a consolidate of perception-images, action-images, and affection-images. In some moments, however, the movement-image ceases to function, and a different type of image, with different aspects of subjectivities, comes into existence. This is what happens with the *relation-image*, which exhausts the movement-image and gives way to the *time-image*. These categories and aspects are explained in the next section when the films are discussed.

Back to the assemblage. Deleuze finally distinguishes a third line, which is the *nomad line* or *line of flight*, the line that draws one into new unknown domains and constitutes a real break with the segmental line. It is this line that has the most direct consequences for the flesh, and it is also the most dangerous line (in all films, the characters run great risks in following their line of flight, even though this line may be inspired by a striving to persist). This is the deterritorializing line of the vertical axis of the assemblage.

On this axis, one could also look at generic deterritorializations and the way in which one image type starts to blend into another. Assemblages can be constructed in other ways, such as that proposed by Ian Buchanan with his analysis of *Blade Runner*.[31] I concentrate my reading of rhizomatic assemblages around one particular image (of the flesh) and the particular subjectivities that act and react on that image; therefore, I have chosen to look at assemblages that are constructed around these rhizomatic lines.

Let me summarize the steps in my reading of the assemblages. The vertical axis of the assemblage has territorializing and deterritorializing sides: it comprises *molar lines* (the film as open totality to the structures and institutions of the world) and *lines of flight* (moments when characters break with the structure, or generic deterritorialization). The horizontal axis contains form of content and form of expression. Here we are situated at the plane of composition of the film, where subjective "schizzes" (molecular lines) are constituted in different image categories. The following diagram is elaborated in the next section:

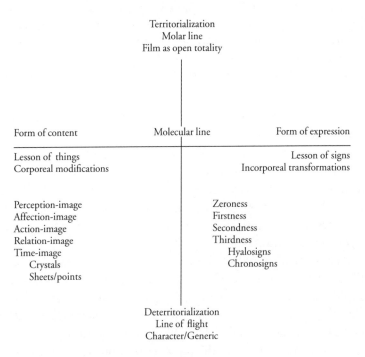

FIGURE 1.   Tetravalence of Assemblages

The Plane of Immanence: Subjectivity and Images of the Flesh

Material Aspect of Subjectivity in Action-Images

The first film I want to read with Deleuze belongs to the Hollywood action-image. The scene around which I center my analysis is situated in a sort of "human slaughterhouse" where comatose bodies are stored for further handling. *Coma* was made in 1978 by Michael Crichton. Crichton's work (such as *The Andromeda Strain, Westworld, Jurassic Park*, and *Disclosure*) always focuses on technology and its dangers, be it molecular biology, robots, information technology, nuclear physics, or, as in *Coma*, organ transplantation and modern surgery techniques. *Coma's* story centers around a doctor in the Boston Memorial Hospital, Susan Wheeler. She has a relationship with Mark, also a doctor at the same hospital. One day a friend of Susan, Nancy, is taken in for a simple operation, but she never awakens from it. Susan, who does not understand how this could happen, investigates what went wrong and discovers that other young and healthy people have gone into coma, which she finds suspicious. Of course, no one wants her to investigate, which leads to some suspenseful moments; in the end, her suspicions are proved correct and the villain (the hospital's chief) is arrested.

What are the assemblages and different lines that the film constitutes? First are the segmental or hard lines implied in the film. The most basic and hardest line is capitalist moneymaking, the use of bodies as pure labor power, or even as sheer products: human organs are sold for a great deal of money, patients are even killed for this purpose. This is the hardest underlying segment on which the film is built and that becomes clear only at the end. It is obvious from the beginning, however, that the questions of money and power (power over the flesh, as we could call it) are also part of the hospital politics: which position goes to which person and how power is distributed. Mark and Susan have a quarrel about this issue when Susan reproaches Mark for having eyes only for this aspect of his profession.

Another hard line of the film is therefore the gender structures displayed in the film (Susan being a woman in "a man's world"). Elizabeth Cowie wrote an interesting article in which she explains how Susan is conditioned by her femininity. Even though she is not the stereotypical

Hollywood woman (she is not a nurse or a patient but a doctor; she is not glossy or fancily dressed), her femininity nevertheless labels her in another segment.[32] All these molar segments (money/nonprofit; doctor/patients; power/powerless; men/women) are territorial forces that keep the system running.

So how does the segmental system start to crack, especially around Susan's subjectivity? For this, we first must look at the film as a whole and at the several categories of images that Deleuze distinguishes. Deleuze has characterized (classic) Hollywood cinema as Bergsonian action-images. This means that at the center of the image there is always someone, a character, who finds himself or herself in a certain situation and reacts to that situation by undertaking some kind of action according to the sensory-motor scheme. Without going into details, it is easy to recognize in *Coma* an action-image of the large form (Situation–Action–New Solution, or SAS) where we go from one situation via the intermediary of the action to another final situation. The main character discovers something strange, undertakes action, and changes the situation.[33] After the death of her friend, Susan is first puzzled; something happens inside her, her intuition tells her something is wrong, but she cannot say what.[34] This marks the first crack in the hard line. She goes out to investigate and discovers that there are too many young patients going into a coma. They were all tissue typed, and in the pathological laboratory, she discovers that this could be done by giving them carbon dioxide (instead of oxygen) during surgery in operating room (OR) 8.

She still undertakes her actions in the open, however, and tries to join forces that can help her: she tells Mark and her boss, Dr. Harris, about her intuitions and what she has discovered. Dr. Harris tries to put Susan back into the molar system, first by sending her off for the weekend (here is the work-holiday segmentation at work) and by labeling her as having an oversensitive feminine reaction to the death of her friend. Dr. Harris plays his "femininity" first by saying to Susan, "Emotion is what makes us human," and as soon as she has left, he sighs, "Women, Christ!" (a clear case of man–woman segmentation). When this does not work, he sends a hired killer after her, from whom Susan manages to escape in a quite spectacular way. So we see here a molecular line, immediately transformed into action. All these actions in action-images are forms of content, the "lesson of things," where we see the actions and passions of bodies.

For the correlating form of expression, we have to move to the "lesson of signs." In his cinema books, Deleuze relates the Bergsonian image categories to a Peircian semiotics. In *The Movement-Image*, those different categories are related to Peirce's firstness, secondness, and thirdness, modes of signs that Peirce uses to describe reality: *firstness* indicates the possibilities and potentiality of the image in itself, that which can be felt rather than thought; *secondness* refers to actual facts, actions, and states of affairs; and *thirdness* refers to conventions and laws of symbols and language. The action-image is governed by secondness. The actions and passions of the bodies we see undergo incorporeal transformations. In this way, *Coma* can be related to the signs of secondness: to concentrate on Susan—she changes from a loyal doctor into a suspicious investigator, which takes place in a "real milieu," a "situation in relation to a subject."[35] We see here what Deleuze called a "second material aspect of subjectivity": "the incurving of the universe, which simultaneously causes the virtual action of things on us and our possible action on things."[36]

The final aspect of the assemblages, the deterritorializing forces, already started on the molecular line. But Susan's real breakflow, her line of flight, starts when she has become suspicious of everybody; escapes from Mark's place, where she was sent to rest; and goes to the Jefferson Institute, where she discovers what actually happens with all the coma patients. In a large purple-lit space, their bodies are hanging on large hooks, kept warm for most efficient organ removal when the demand is most urgent and the price is best. When Susan's presence is discovered, she cleverly escapes from the human slaughterhouse. Again, we see here how much these images are action-images; the center of the actions remain around Susan, the human "flesh for slaughter" belonging to the milieu. Still not knowing that her boss is not to be trusted, she goes to Dr. Harris, which is, of course, the worst thing she could have done. This is when the line of flight manifests itself as a real rupture: Dr. Harris sees he can no longer control her, that she knows too much and is not going to take his side. Susan realizes that she has ventured into the lion's den. Dr. Harris gives her a poison that causes symptoms of appendicitis and takes her into OR 8 for an operation from which she is not supposed to awaken. So here we see the risk (of which we are carefully warned by Deleuze and Guattari) involved in following a line of flight: the risk of having the living body, with its intuition and power to act, turned into dead flesh. Trying to prevent more "slaughters," Susan almost became a piece of meat, useful and expensive organs, hanging in the Jefferson Institute—"almost" because she is saved at the last minute, because Mark realizes that she has not been paranoid at all, and that her life is now at stake. He has to undertake action, and finally the flesh is saved. A new situation where the doctor is arrested and patients no longer risk their lives is established.

Material Aspects of Subjectivity in Relation-Images

In the next film, images of the flesh are also quite prominent, but here they are related to a different type of image and consequently a different aspect of subjectivity. *The Fourth Man* is one of the Dutch films made by Paul Verhoeven before he went to Hollywood. The main character in *The Fourth Man* is a writer, Gerard Reve (the name of an actual Dutch writer), who goes to a Dutch seaside town to give a lecture. At the railway station, he encounters a man with whom he immediately falls in love but who disappears. At the lecture, he meets a woman who asks whether he would like to stay with her. Gerard discovers that she is the mistress of the man he saw at the station, whose name is Herman, and he decides to stay; but he constantly has dreams and visions that scare him and seem to be warning of some danger.

First the lines. The main territorial segment of the film is the professional world because all the characters are prominently defined by their profession: Gerard is a writer, and this "profession" gives him a different status than the other, more down-to-earth characters: Herman, the man he falls in love with, is an opportunistic plumber; Christine, the *femme fatale*, has a beauty parlor, which she inherited from one of her husbands. All Christine's other husbands also are shown (on home-movie material) in relation to their profession (a pet-shop owner and a soldier). Everyone has his or her place, and it is the writer who has the privileged status of moving between those worlds. Another hard segment is again the opposition men–women: the film centers around sexual attraction of women, and the writer can play with this because he is actually more attracted to men. A last hard segment is the segment of religion: the writer is Catholic and has faith (albeit in an anarchistic way; at some point, he imagines that Herman is hanging on the cross and he is making love to him like that). Profession, sex, and religion are thus the territorial markers of the characters in this film.

It is clear that from the beginning and in all respects the writer translates the cracks into these segmental systems: his imagination as a writer, his desire as a homosexual, and his anarchistic faith as a Catholic make him suspicious of all hard segments, especially of the intriguing rich woman he encounters. From the start, this woman is marked as dangerous by associating her with a spider, a (literal) black widow. It is also amusing to notice that, as a real *femme fatale* who has phallic power, she plays with the cinematic convention of the camera as a deadly weapon, an instrument of power that usually is held only by men (she films all her husbands, all of whom will die). She could be seen as a female *Peeping Tom*. Of course, she also represents the *femme castratrice* as described by Barbara Creed. So one could say that the segmental in this film conflates with the molecular line because of the extraordinary position of the main character.

In some respects, this film is still an action-image that centers around the actions of the main character. More precisely, this film centers not so much around his action but around thoughts and visions. The writer has visions and dreams all the time, and because of his sensitivity to imagination, desire for men, and Catholicism, he takes seriously the signs he receives. At the beginning of the film, he explains that writer's imagination, desire, and Catholicism are actually one, when he says "being Catholic means: being ready to accept imagination and the fantastic." These visions must be interpreted; they must be related to other things to understand them. It is in this sense that the film is not an action-image but a relation-image in Deleuzian terminology[37]: cues and inferences of the metaphoric images constitute the overall organization and content of the images. Every symbol or convention is explained explicitly within the context of the film. There is, for instance, an obvious dream scene in the film: Gerard goes to bed with Christine and falls asleep: in the dream, he sees a woman in a blue cape (obviously representing Mary) who is carrying a bunch of red roses and a huge key. With this key, she opens a door that gives access to a place where three slaughtered cows are dripping with blood. A fourth hook is waiting; "Mary" places the red roses under it and looks at Gerard. Then Gerard feels Christine's hands caressing him; before he knows it, she literally castrates him. He wakes up screaming. Obviously, the Freudian and Christian symbolisms speak for themselves, but later the film explains the dream once more. This time, Gerard and Herman are driving in a car. Suddenly, Gerard sees the woman from his dream. He follows her to a graveyard, whereupon it starts to thunder and rain, and Gerard and Herman seek shelter in a burial vault: it is the place of Gerard's dream. This time, there are no cows but three urns with the ashes of Christine's deceased husbands. The three slaughtered cows in the dream are the three deceased husbands of Christine, and the fourth will be either Gerard or Herman.

Admittedly, mental relations of this type are not so sophisticated as those made in the work of Hitchcock, the filmmaker whom Deleuze describes as the inventor of the relation-image. Hitchcock plays a much more refined game with symbols and marks that involve the spectator more actively. Nevertheless, *The Fourth Man* is governed by thirdness, the level of signs that are governed by laws, habits, and conventions. This film is based entirely on symbolic and cinematographic convention, to the point that it completely exhausts the possibilities of the movement-image. So the meat we see in this film is symbolic or metaphoric flesh (although it also entails the actual death of the bodies; thirdness implies secondness as well). Here we do not have action in the slaughterhouse, but we have symbolism. The material aspect of subjectivity presented here is related to the mental states of the main characters.

As already noted, Gerard's position as a writer made him wary of segmental organization from the very beginning; but it is at the moment when he sees the three urns of ashes, which he connects to the slaughtered cows, that his deterritorial breakpoint occurs: he realizes his life is in danger and that he has to get away from this woman. The message of the film seems to be that one has to listen to the signs one receives. Herman does not believe Gerard, does not listen to the signs, and therefore becomes the fourth man: he dies in a horrible car accident (right after the scene just described), with Gerard sitting next to him. Gerard survives, thanks to his line of flight. One might wonder, however, whether he is really saved because at the end of the film he is regarded as paranoid and mad, and he is put into another hard segment ("mad" as opposed to "sane"). Again, it is clear that following the line of flight, which always starts with an intuition or a certain affective sensitivity, is a dangerous undertaking. Whereas Susan is rescued at the last moment, Gerard is saved but may be mad forever.

Material Aspects of Subjectivity in Affection-Images

Yet another aspect of material subjectivity is related to the affection-image. I now consider this aspect by looking at *In a Year of 13 Moons* by

Rainer Werner Fassbinder. *In a Year of 13 Moons* was made in 1978, right after the suicide of Fassbinder's partner, Armin Meir. The film is certainly strongly autobiographical; I do not elaborate on this point, but it is one of the reasons the film is so (almost unbearably) intense. The main character is Elvira, who was Erwin before she underwent a sex-change operation. The film shows the last days of her life, in which she is left by her current partner, Kristoff, and searches for some knowledge about the past; finally, she visits the man for whom she once went to Casablanca, Anton Saitz, a Jewish camp survivor who became rich and powerful after the war. Anton, however, has forgotten Erwin/Elvira completely. Elvira is more or less rejected by everybody: his wife and daughter cannot live with her anymore, her friend Zora makes love to Anton, Kristoff has left her, and the journalist who interviewed Elvira has no more time to listen to her. At the end, she commits suicide.

The first segmental line to which Fassbinder's film opens up is the historical, long, painful relation between Germans and Jews, the past of the war and the concentration camps. Another hard segment is that of family structures (parents–child), and the last hard segment I distinguish is that of fixed sexual identity (man–woman or neither). The past of the war and the impossible relation between Germans and Jews may not be apparent in the film. In fact, there are never explicit cues to this aspect of the film: the strongest direct indication is a code word that Elvira has to give to see Anton Saitz. This code word is Bergen–Belsen (also in other films Fassbinder makes this allusion to concentration camps, for instance, in *Veronica Voss*, where there is a Jewish couple who survived Treblinka). The family structure is present in the fact that Elvira is married to Irene, and they have a daughter, Marianne. Then, of course, there is once more the hard segment of the men–women opposition, this time in the form of the sexual identity of the main character.[38] All these issues reach beyond the film and are larger territorial segments in the world and in history.

Again, all kinds of molecular lines are present as well, again carried out by the protagonist. Elvira creates such a line by trying to escape all these categories: an attempt is made to bridge the difficult relation between Germans and Jews with Erwin's desire for the Jewish Anton Saitz (I am not saying these are conscious, deliberate acts but might be an unconscious effect of the collective past that slips into the individual life). On the one hand, the family structure is retained, albeit also cracked and messed up: Elvira is still the father of Marianne (she goes to see Anton Saitz out of responsibility to their daughter—to present excuses for an interview she has given). On the other hand, they do not form a family; Elvira does not live with them anymore. Erwin tries to overcome the sexual boundaries by having a sex-change operation and becoming Elvira. At one point in the film, it is said that Erwin did not always already have a "feminine soul," which would have been a motivation for undergoing this operation. As a man, she was not homosexual. The fact that she nevertheless fell in love with a man, and that if necessary would change her sex for this man, proves that to her sexual identity should not be important. More important is that the man she falls in love with is Jewish: desire is constituted by more than just sexuality. One could say that Elvira's desire, as a German, is to connect with the Jewishness of Anton Saitz. One could also conclude that Elvira's molecular line, the cracks in the system, are carried out literally and in the open. Before looking at the affection-image, its forms of expression, and the aspects of subjectivity it creates, let me go straight to the deterritorializing line of flight of the assemblages of *In a Year of 13 Moons*.

The most deterritorializing force in this film is Elvira's masochism. Deleuze and Guattari see masochism as a line of flight. It is therefore less dependent on Freudian sexuality (caused by the death drive and the pleasure-out-of-pain principle, which is a punishment for forbidden desire for one of the parents) in that it is related to the creation of a Body without Organs (BwO) and a becoming-animal. The BwO does not necessarily mean that we have to create bodies that no longer have any organs at all, although Elvira does take this literally by having her sexual organ removed. The BwO is desire, a process of a body that does not want to depend on the functions and places that the organs traditionally have. Creating a BwO is creating a body that is full of intensities on an immanent, microlevel: "There is a distribution of intensive principles of organs, with their positive indefinite articles, within a collectivity or multiplicity, inside an assemblage, and according to machinic connections operating on a BwO."[39]

The BwO makes new connections that are not limited to the self-same organism. A BwO is a field of intensities that works purely on the sensitive, the invasion of the affect, that constitutes an "I feel." Masochism is a way of creating a BwO (but again a dangerous one, a body that easily can be missed, like the body of a drug addict, an anorexic, an alcoholic):

What is certain is that the masochist has made himself a BwO under such conditions that the BwO no longer can be populated by anything but intensities of pain, *pain waves*. It is false to say that the masochist is looking for pain just as it is false to say that he is looking for pleasure in a particular suspenseful or roundabout way. The masochist is looking for a type of BwO that only pain can fill, or travel over, due to the very conditions under which that BwO was constituted.[40]

A BwO feels intensities everywhere in the body, as if sexual organs are everywhere. One actually could say that Fassbinder's cinema is full of people who try to create BwOs, who try to open up their entire system to new connections (Veronica Voss by drugs, Elvira and Martha and many other characters by masochism, the alcoholic in the *Merchant of Four Seasons* by alcohol). Even Fassbinder himself tried to reach this state by his intensive lifestyle, and also for him it became fatal. In my view, this constitutes the attraction and fascination of Fassbinder's films and characters: they all try to reach a BwO, which is a difficult and dangerous but also passionate enterprise. In general, the BwO is not in opposition to the flesh; it even takes place in the sensitive flesh. It is on the level of sensitivity and affects that the BwO is constructed. This becomes clear if we look at how masochism and the BwO also are connected to the concept of becoming-animal.

In fact, masochism and the BwO are closely related to becoming-animal. In Chapter 5, I elaborate on becoming-animal in cinema in more detail. Here it is important to see that becoming-animal takes place in a BwO because it tries to connect different/new elements with one another, which takes place on the level of internal energies (movement and speed) and affect. "Becoming" is never an imitation but always an entering into a zone of proximity, an in-between status on a microlevel. Therefore, the pain and humiliation of the masochist are driven by a becoming-animal; they do not—metaphorically—lead to becoming an animal. In the beginning of the film, Elvira explains to her friend Zora that slaughtering cows is not against life. On the contrary, "The cows scream to be slaughtered," she explains. This "masochism of the cow," which is a passive affect, is something that Elvira senses as well. This is her becoming-animal. Affects can be either passive or active; cinema is also full of active becoming-animals, as I argue in Chapter 5. Here, however, we are dealing with extremely passive affects.

Moving to the form of content and the form of expression of the assemblage, it is now logical to see that *In a Year of 13 Moons* is an affection-image: it works directly on the nervous system, creating immediate sensations. In his book on the painter Bacon, Gilles Deleuze explains how he paints sensations, affects that are related to the becoming-animal. Some of Bacon's paintings express the same idea of becoming-animal as the affects that are evoked by the slaughterhouse scene in Fassbinder's film. In this scene, near the beginning of *In a Year of 13 Moons*, Elvira takes her friend Zora to the slaughterhouse where she used to work when she was still Erwin. Although the images present us with the whole process of slaughtering cows in a terribly slow and crude way, Elvira's voiceover tells about her life. At some points, her voice becomes like a scream and is unbearable in connection with the images: it is through this special combination of image and sound that Fassbinder creates affect. Here it becomes clear how the affection-image works: it does not work on our sensory-motor schema that leads to action, and it does not work in the first instance on our cognitive or mental ability. Rather, it works directly on the affective nervous system that has its sensors everywhere in the flesh. This scene in the slaughterhouse is not just a metaphor for victimhood or masochism, but it is also an expression of the becoming-animal of Elvira and her masochism. Affection, where subject and object (Elvira and the cows) coincide, is the way the subject feels itself "from the inside" and is a third material aspect of subjectivity.

It is also possible to read other moments of affection (passive affects in this case) throughout the film. Fassbinder uses various cinematographic means to express these affects. According to Deleuze, the affection-image often is composed of close-ups and through the expressive use of colors. The close-ups in *In a Year of 13 Moons* are reserved mainly for Elvira, and the colors and lighting are mainly red and cold blue, like in Bacon's paintings. In the video-arcade scene, for instance, Fassbinder, through cinematographic tools, creates the same passive and sad affects as in the slaughterhouse scene. The colors of the images are mainly red and blue, and Elvira's crying face in close-up is heartbreaking. Again, sensations are reached on the level of the sound: the noises of the arcade machines and Brian Ferry's voice singing his sad song, which echoes the words that a man throws at Elvira: "If you look any longer at me I will slaughter you, stupid cow." Parallel to and in connection with the colors and the framing of the images, a world of sad affects is created.

In his article on Godard and Deleuze, Joseph Vogl demonstrates how in Godard's film *Le Mépris* the affective and potential qualities of the colors force the expression of the spiritual choice the characters have to make between yes and no, between sadness and happiness.[41] In a similar way, one could say that in the video-arcade scene, Elvira is confronted with a choice between red and blue, life and death. Her tears make clear that her "choice" already has been made. With these moments of choice between life and death, we already have moved into the form of expression and the incorporeal transformations of the affection-image. Speaking with Peirce, Deleuze relates the affection-image to firstness, the level of all possibilities, where all becomings and all affects are possible but not (yet) an action or a thought. It is the virtuality of the possible that governs these types of images. It brings the subject into a state of suspension, incapable of acting or thinking, just before something (new) is about to happen. For Elvira, the past is what is revisited to find possibilities for the future. When she does not find these possibilities, there is no reason left to live. In Spinozian terms, Elvira is too full of passive affects, incapable of making the necessary connections to persist in her being. Unable to find joy and active affects, she is forced to commit suicide. In Deleuzian terminology, Elvira's fate could be seen as the black hole of self-destruction that is the danger of the line of flight. Becoming-animal and the BwO are the intensive expressions of the line of flight; but the becoming-animal of her sensitive flesh stops at the moment when it turns into meat.

Temporal Aspects of Subjectivity in Time-Images

So far, I have discussed all kinds of movement-images and the different aspects of subjectivity they construct and express. They all presuppose some kind of center around which the images are grouped and from which some aspects of subjectivity can be constructed. The perception-image, going from the most objective to the most subjective, is thereby a sort of "condition," a "zeroness" as Deleuze calls it,[42] for all other movement-images. As Deleuze argues at the end of *The Movement-Image*, the movement-image, and especially the action-image, has come to the end of its possibilities. This does not mean that there are no more movement-images, but that a new type of images, which in new ways tries to create a new thought, feeling, or perception, also has come into existence. Deleuze situates this crisis around the Second World War, which creates a break between the movement-image and the time-image.[43] The time-image is also a Bergsonian image category, which he relates to persons whose sensory-motor system no longer functions, such as a sick person, someone who no longer knows to orient himself, no longer knows to speak spontaneously, no longer has a goal or knows how to act.[44] In a cinematographic universe, starting with Italian Neo-Realism, we find in a similar way such "sick" images and subjects where the world and time are "out of joint." As Deleuze argues in *The Time-Image*: "Subjectivity, then, takes on a new sense, which is no longer motor or material, but temporal and spiritual: that which 'is added' to matter, not what distends it; recollection-image, not movement-image."[45]

Already in the affection-image, where the action temporarily stops, we find that the image opens up to the fourth dimension of time and the fifth dimension of spirit. In the time-image, time and mental confusions between the virtual and the actual, the past and the present, become predominant. Deleuze gives many different forms and signs of the time-image (see appendices), and it is not my intention to repeat all these variations. Rather, I want to look at one last film in which images of the flesh, again slaughtered cows, form an assemblage within a film that could be classified as a time-image, Djibril Diop Mambety's *Touki Bouki*.

Mambety, who died in 1998, was one of Senegal's most famous filmmakers.[46] In 1972, he made *Touki Bouki*, a film that does not fit into the realistic tradition of many African films but has more in common with Neo-Realist or Nouvelle Vague films, especially the early films of Godard, or with American road movies, influenced by the "new wave" of time-images, such as *Easy Rider*. Like all of Mambety's films, *Touki Bouki* is set in Dakar, where Mory, a former shepherd meets a university student, Anta. They share a dream of leaving Senegal and go through all kinds of misadventures to find money for the journey. At the end of the film, they can board a ship to Europe, but then Mory cannot bring himself to leave Senegal after all.

To summarize the plot in this way does not say anything about the out-of-joint way the film deals with spatial and temporal continuity. Like all time-images, *Touki Bouki* is characterized by almost imperceptible shifts between what is actual and what is virtual, between the past and the present, and especially between the real and the dream or lyrical fantasies. In the first instance and throughout the film, this is achieved by what Deleuze calls a "heautonomous" use of sound, where the visual and the sound are dissociated but at the same time in an incommensurable or "irrational" or "free indirect" relation are connected to each other.[47] At the beginning of the film, we see a shepherd boy with his herd of zebus. The sound of soft African flutes accompanies the images, but gradually we also hear the sound of a motorbike over the images: through the sound, another time layer is placed over the images. In the next scene, we see the handlebars of a motorbike with zebu horns attached to them while the flutes are still audible. This scene is followed by the sound and images of screaming zebus being slaughtered in the slaughterhouse. Most probably, these slaughters have happened between the time the young boy was a shepherd and the time he rides a motorbike with zebu horns, although we have no direct clues that it is the boy who is now riding the motorbike because we have not yet seen the rider of the horned bike.

In itself, the beginning of the film already shows the way in which time layers are mixed and confused, and we have not yet seen a "central image," a subject that would clearly connect all these images. Although later in the film Mory and Anta are clearly the main characters, the sheets of the past between which they move never are explicitly connected to their subjectivities. It is as if they speak about more general, indefinite layers of time: "a childhood in Senegal," "a new time in which technology slowly replaces nature." One of the characteristics of the time-image is that it is no longer tied to a central image of subjectivity but becomes more loosely connected to characters who themselves are wanderers, not knowing anymore how to act and react. Precisely because of this status of paralysis, they open up to the virtual (time, dreams, hallucinations).[48]

Although the symbolism in *Touki Bouki* is sometimes obvious (the sea and boat on the sea for the desire to leave, the zebu horns for the connection to the Senegalese land, the Dogon cross—a symbol of fertility—for the love scene between Mory and Anta), dream sequences and actual sequences are mixed. So, if we can speak here of aspects of subjectivity, it is a temporally confused subjectivity, a subjectivity in time: "the affection of self by self as definition of time."[49] As for the signs, they range from "hyalosigns," where the real and imaginary become blurred, to "chronosigns" of sheets of the past.[50] At the end of the film, when Mory (unlike Anta) leaves the boat and returns to Dakar, the image of the slaughtered zebus returns. On a symbolic level, one could say that Mory offers his love (Anta) like the zebus are sacrificed or killed for Senegal. Certainly, this is not so obvious as the symbolism of the cows in *The Fourth Man*, however. One could conclude rather that these images of suffering flesh now can be assembled only in a temporal perspective that gives Mory his definition in time: even though his herd no longer exists, he cannot be a distance from them—and hence from his land.

Looking now at the territorial and deterritorial forces of *Touki Bouki*, again many different movements are visible. One of the segmental forces is of course the colonial past and influences in Senegal, a former French colony. The film contains many references to the postcolonial heritage: the university students speak French, there are references to the World Bank and to the devaluation of the the common African franc (CFA), on the boat we hear colonial discourse expressed by two white tourists, and so on. The opposition Senegal–France also is marked by Mory and Anta's desire to leave for France, which in the film is frequently evoked by the voice-over of Josephine Baker singing "Paris, Paris, Paris." At the same time, this desire is their line of flight to break with the poverty of the living conditions in Dakar. Contrary to the breakflows in movement-images, the line of flight in the time-image does not really offer a solution: at the end of the film, nothing is resolved, not even for Anta, who is on the boat to France, but who will face a very uncertain future. Nothing, not even the postcolonial segmental line, is divided into clear oppositions. The characters remain wanderers in a world that is out of joint.

I have looked at these four films separately and distinguished different image types and signs. Obviously, not many films consist of really one type of image. Although there are famous examples, for instance, Dreyer's *The Passion of Joan of Arc*, which consists uniquely of affection-images, most films combine different images and aspects of subjectivity. As Peirce argued, every thirdness also implies secondness and firstness. In the images of the flesh in the slaughterhouse in *The Fourth Man*, it is clear that the symbolic cows (thirdness) also refer to the actual dead meat (secondness). The human flesh hanging in the Jefferson Institute in *Coma* and the cows representing the dead husbands in *The Fourth Man* also have some affective qualities of firstness within them. Like in *In a Year of 13 Moons*, this is done mostly by color effects. In *Coma*, the bodies are hanging in a purple/blue light, charging the action-images with a dimension that immediately affects the nervous system. In *The Fourth Man*, the same colors of warm red and cold blue are predominant in the image. *Touki Bouki* equally has many affective color moments, such as the close-up of blue and green water buckets, made slightly transparent by the sunlight. They have no narrative or logical function in the film; they are pure affect, countering the desire to leave Africa with just a simple but powerful image of beauty that cannot be found elsewhere. It also should be noted that all assemblages could be elaborated with more lines or with, for instance, generic deterritorializations (the road movie in Africa, *In a Year of Thirteen Moons* as a melodrama, *Coma* as a surrealist movie, *The Fourth Man* as camp).

With the preceding analysis, I hope to have demonstrated that in any case the flesh, as the most material aspect of subjectivity, is not just a matter of body horror and abjection. In horror cinema, the flesh certainly can sometimes be interpreted this way—and it is also possible to relate the slaughtered cows in *In a Year of Thirteen Moons*, for instance, to the Lacanian Real, anticipating the transcendental "night of the world" that Elvira is approaching, first by turning herself into a woman, then by killing herself. As I argued before, this is also a rather narrow view on the effects and affects of the multiple images on the plane of immanence. Even in horror cinema, the body can be the source of (political) rezoning projects. In a Spinozian/Deleuzian perspective, the body constitutes our being. The body forces one to strive for persistence as well as to think and act or even to wonder and wander in the virtual and actual layers of time.[51]

In this last section, I tried to experiment with body politics in four different films and have demonstrated how we can map different aspects of the flesh in relation to the different political territorial and deterritorial lines that constitute it. The paths that are followed are different in the various types of images that relate in turn to different aspects of the world and different aspects of subjectivity: the action-image produces action and actual bodies, which has an effect of excitement; the relation-image calls for interpretation of the metaphors that are displayed and produces symbolic meat; the affection-image works directly on our sensitivity, in this case on (our) passive and sad affects; and the flesh expresses the affects of a becoming-animal; the time-image produces a subjectivity in time. Although cinema does not give us the literal presence of bodies, it nevertheless produces the "genesis of an 'unknown body' which we have in the back of our heads, like the unthought in thought, the birth of the visible which is still hidden from view."[52] The four films together constitute a rhizomatic network of heterogeneous lines, thoughts, and affects that meet each other in the slaughterhouse. I hope thus to have demonstrated that the subject's basis is grounded in a Spinozian body of actions and passions and constructed according to the image selections and assemblages it makes. Although we do not know what a body can do (what it can make us do, think, feel, or become, how flexible and changeable it is), it clearly has its limits in that zone where the flesh runs the risk of turning into meat.

3

Cinema's Politics of Violence

In the previous chapter, I presented material and temporal aspects of subjectivity as they are constructed and manifested in different image types. I worked with the political lines around certain "images of the flesh" to look at the different assemblages that constitute subjectivities. Now I move to a more collective level of political cinema and the creation of a people, although this also involves actions, sensations, and thoughts on an individual scale. In *The Time-Image*, Deleuze distinguishes a classic form of political cinema in movement-images from a modern form of political cinema in time-images. In classic political cinema, we find representations of the people and political ideals. They are presented as transcendental ideals that are related to life in an indirect way. As David Rodowick puts it, "Constrained by sensorimotor situations and organic narration, cinema excels in projecting self-contained possible worlds. . . . These are transcendent worlds that demand to be judged in opposition to life."[1]

In the time-image, however, representing a people has become impossible for various reasons that will be discussed later. In any case, there is a change in the relation between the image and life, and one of the consequences is that the time-image no longer can be judged in opposition to life. On the contrary, it restores our belief in the world, our belief in life: "To believe, not in a different world, but in a link between man and the world, in love or life, to believe in this as the impossible, the unthinkable, which none the less cannot but be thought: 'something possible, otherwise

I will suffocate.' It is this belief that makes the unthought the specific power of thought, through the absurd, by virtue of the absurd."[2] This "belief in the world" makes many time-images inherently political.[3] Deleuze discusses the modern political cinema in relation to a "cinema of the body," a "cinema of the brain," and the "fabulation of a missing people." In this chapter, I work mainly with these ideas of Deleuze from *The Time-Image*.[4]

I begin with an investigation of violence in cinema, which, according to Deleuze, can be both an original impulse and a political option. Focusing on a film by Claire Denis, *I Can't Sleep* (1994), I attempt to investigate how violence is connected to the time-image of a cinema of the body. When discussing a cinema of the body, it is useful to keep in mind that the distinction from a cinema of the brain is no more than a question of style:

> There are then two different styles, where the difference itself is constantly varying, cinema of the body in Godard and cinema of the brain in Resnais, cinema of the body in Cassavetes and cinema of the brain in Kubrick. There is as much thought in the body as there is shock and violence in the brain. There is an equal amount of feeling in both of them. The brain gives orders to the body which is just an outgrowth of it, but the body also gives orders to the brain which is just a part of it: in both cases, these will not be the same bodily attitudes nor the same cerebral geste. Hence the specificity of a cinema of the brain, in relation to that of a cinema of bodies.[5]

In this first section, I focus on a cinema of the body, but this does not exclude a similar analysis of a cinema of the brain, which I sometimes refer to as well. I also look in this section at the question of ethics in relation to violence. Finally, I attempt to relate all these issues of violence to Marguerite Duras's concept of "the class of violence" and the type of political options this "class" chooses, which is the politics of a line of flight.

In the next section, I concentrate on the fabulating constructing powers of modern political cinema: the creation of a people through cinematographic storytelling. In particular, I look at the French *banlieu* film *Brothers* (1994), which I consider an example of modern political cinema.

In the last section, I inquire into the ways in which some contemporary Hollywood films, often defined as pure action-images, can be seen as modern political films. As also the case with *Strange Days*, which I discussed in Chapter 1, I argue that many contemporary Hollywood films, like *Fight*

Club and *Pulp Fiction*, are time-images "disguised" as action-images or action-images that take on characteristics of the time-image. This often makes the violence in these films ambiguous and even "schizophrenic" in a Deleuzian sense.

While working with the ideas of Deleuze around the questions of politics, violence, and fabulation, I also turn to Nietzsche and Spinoza. These two philosophers inspired Deleuze in developing "the power of the false," which is so important in the time-image and with respect to the question of fabulation (Nietzsche). It is also important in the development of an "ethics without morality" (Spinoza), which is necessary for evaluating the violence of many contemporary films and their political implications.

Violence and Cinema of the Body

Over the last decade, the topic of violence in cinema has evoked a huge discussion. Terms like *nouvelle violence* are raised, roundtable discussions about the moral limits of violent images are arranged, articles and books are published, and conferences are held on the theme of violence.[6] It seems there are two camps in the discussion of violence in films: either the films are rejected on moral grounds because images of violence as such are considered bad and immoral, or the violence is seen as merely a formal-genre aspect of the film, comparable to dance in the musical, nothing to bother about.

The first position is expressed by Michael Medved, for example, in his article "Hollywood's Four Big Lies" and by John Grisham's argument in his famous polemic with Oliver Stone in "Natural Bred Killers." Grisham accuses Stone of inciting two teenagers to follow the example of Mickey and Mallory in *Natural Born Killers* in real life. Stone answers with "Don't Sue the Messenger," arguing that his films reflect (and critique) society's perverse preoccupations (which is, according to Medved, precisely one of Hollywood's big lies). Moreover, Stone claims artistic freedom: "It is only a small step from silencing art to silencing artists, and then to silencing those who support them and so on until, while we may one day live in a lawyer's paradise, we will surely find ourselves in a human hell."[7] This argument of artistic freedom aligns with the second camp in the debates about violence: that it is nothing more than colors and sounds, which are part of the artistic undertaking and that it is certainly not worth discussing as a new phenomenon. The poetry of violence has always been part of artistic expressions.

Neither option is satisfying. There is indeed nothing new about violence, although since the 1970s, violence in the cinema has become more explicit (just as images of the flesh have become more explicit); violence always has been part of the cinematographic image as it has been part of the world. This does not mean, however, that violence is simply a conventional-genre aspect or something to reject morally in advance and by all means. Violence raises many questions that cannot be dealt with in purely formalistic or moralistic models.

In this chapter, I investigate some possible ways to think of violence, with the help of some of the tools offered by Deleuze (and Guattari). Again, this must be done in the form of looking at assemblages, or, as I propose more loosely here, in the form of a rhizomatic network around this concept. This rhizomatic network is of course incomplete because the complexity of everything forces us to make selections. Another reason the rhizomatic network is always incomplete is that every singularity (in this case, every singular film) is, as we saw before, composed of multiple and heterogeneous lines. Those lines are again in a constant dynamic interaction with one another. Nevertheless, I think it is possible to raise and relate some common notions that can provide some clarification.[8]

Violence: Impulses and Political Options

Deleuze does not discuss violence in detail in his two cinema books. Although he recognizes active violence of the action-image (violence as a reaction to a concrete situation, against others to defend one's identity), only the impulse-image appears to contain and express original violence. The impulse-image is situated between the affection-image (which it is no longer) and the action-image (which it is not yet). It should not be seen as a transition between the two categories of images, however. Impulse-images have a consistency of their own; they present original worlds that exist and operate in the depths of a real milieu, whose violence and cruelty they reveal. It is the world of naturalism, describing a real milieu that exhausts and is restored to the original world of the impulses. Deleuze distinguishes three great directors of the impulse-image: Eric Von Stroheim, Luis Buñuel, and Joseph Losey.[9] According to Deleuze, these directors all deserve the Nietzschean name "physicians of civilization." They diagnose civilization in all its violence and cruelty.

Also in the impulse-image, Deleuze recognizes signs that are fundamental concepts in psychoanalysis. The impulse-image is full of symptoms and fetishes. Symptoms are the presence of impulses in the derived world, fetishes the representation of fragments, the "partial objects" of the impulses (like the notorious shoe fetishism of Buñuel). In the impulse-image, Deleuze sees perverse modes of behavior such as sadomasochism, cannibalism, necrophilia, and such. Characters are in constant predator–prey relationships; they are human animals (hyenas and vultures). Impulses are violently exhaustive; they exhaust the milieu in which they arise, driven by the ultimate death-impulse. Characters regress to the bottom line in the desert in Von Stroheim's *Greed*. In Buñuel's *The Discreet Charm of the Bourgeoisie* or in *The Fantome of Liberty*, it is the bourgeois and Catholic milieu that is exhausted. Joseph Losey mostly shows a Victorian milieu being preyed on, like in *The Servant*, where the Victorian house is taken over by the servant. Clearly, Deleuze recognizes this impulsive behavior that is also at the basis of psychoanalytic theory; however, he does not take it as a general model from which all images originate. Rather, certain images express impulses in symptoms and fetishistic signs.

Without going into detail about the differences between the naturalist directors mentioned by Deleuze, it is important to consider one other characteristic of the impulse-image. With naturalism, states Deleuze, time makes a prominent appearance in the cinematographic image. Just as Buñuel plays havoc with the order of periodizations of time, the impulse-image destroys Chronos. Consequently, the impulse-image only grasps the negative effects of time: attrition, degradation, wastage, destruction, loss, or simply oblivion by implosion (Von Stroheim) or cyclic repetition (Buñuel). Nevertheless, Deleuze also sees an opening to more positive repetition and more positive effects of time, especially in respect to the work of Buñuel:

To reach a repetition which saves, or which changes life, beyond good and evil, would it not be necessary to break with the order of impulses, to undo the cycles of time, reach an element which would be like a true "desire," or like a choice capable of constantly beginning again . . . ? Buñuel nevertheless gained something by making repetition, rather than entropy, the law of the world. *He injects the power of repetition into the cinematographic image.* In this way he is already going beyond the world of impulses, to knock on the doors of time and free it from the slope of the cycles which still subjugated it to a content. Buñuel does not cling to symptoms and to fetishes, . . . which perhaps gives us a time-image. . . . But it is from inside that Buñuel goes beyond naturalism, without ever renouncing it.[10]

As is clear from the preceding, the impulse-image—and the violence it contains—has a certain relation (albeit mostly a negative one) to the time-image. Because I concentrate in my case studies on contemporary cinema, which at least has knowledge of the changed status of the image after the Second World War (although not all contemporary films are time-images), I elaborate some aspects of the time-image that can be related to the concept of violence. In doing so, I am assuming that original violent impulses sometimes can be visible in the time-image; but I also want to introduce another dimension of impulses that Deleuze and Guattari put forward in *A Thousand Plateaus*: "Drives and part-objects are neither stages on a genetic axis nor positions in a deep structure; they are political options for problems, they are entryways and exits, impasses the child lives out politically, in other words, with all the force of his or her desire."[11]

For Deleuze and Guattari, drives and impulses are nothing more than political options. So, although they use these psychoanalytic terms, they put them in a political perspective. This move can be understood only by considering Nietzschean and Spinozian conceptions of the body and of ethics, as Deleuze describes them in the second part of *The Time-Image*. Claire Denis's film *I Can't Sleep* (1994) expresses, in my view, what Deleuze means when he speaks about these Nietzschean and Spinozian aspects of the time-image. So I first look at this film to clarify some implications of these aspects before returning to the question of violence.

Nietzschean and Spinozian Aspects of the Time-Image

Powers of the False and Powers of the Body.   *I Can't Sleep* is based on a real event: in the early 1990s, a Parisian neighborhood was haunted by a serial killer of old ladies. The film could have been presented as an exciting action-image thriller centered on a duel between the investigator and the murderer like, for instance, *The Silence of the Lambs*. The story also could have been filmed as haunted by original impulses, presenting the characters as predators and prey, governed by their impulses and drives. Although some aspects of *I Can't Sleep*, such as the brutal killings, could be related to the negative series of impulses, I argue that *I Can't*

Sleep connects to the series of time, especially as it is manifested in and through the body.

Denis offers a cross-section through this Parisian neighborhood during this period when everyone was afraid of the "granny killer." We meet many different people who live in that neighborhood, including the murderer Camille and his boyfriend. We observe mainly from the outside, on a surface level without psychological insights, bits and pieces of the lives of all these characters. *I Can't Sleep* consists of purely optical and sound situations, which is characteristic of the time-image. The title suggests the state in which the characters find themselves: because of various anxieties, the characters become insomniacs—and therefore their normal sensory-motor functions also become somehow distorted; sleeping awake, the characters become seers, hearers, and wanderers and therefore open up to the notion of time, where the imaginary and real, virtual and actual start to blur.

The way in which this film describes the world it wants to evoke is quite different from the descriptions in the sensory-motor situation of the movement-image. In the sensory-motor situation (the action-image), there is mostly a clear distance and a difference between objective and subjective descriptions. In the time-image, this distance is eliminated. As Deleuze states, here the description conflates with its object, even effaces its object and takes its place. Free, indirect discourse, in which the act of describing and the object of description become indistinguishable, replaces objective and subjective descriptions.[12]

In *I Can't Sleep*, there is not one main character with whom we could identify subjectively or from whom we could take objective distance. The film opens with Daiga, a Lithuanian girl who comes to visit her aunt in Paris, and ends when she leaves town; we do not, however, see everything from her point of view. The film presents a free, indirect discourse by sometimes letting the camera follow a character's viewpoint and at other times wander off on its own. Many possible worlds are presented in this way: the street cleaners in the beginning of the film are given as much emphasis as the characters we observe more closely later in the film. Attention and intuition might be needed to make and to understand such images, to see the possible worlds that are presented, and to see that the actual images open up to the virtual (of the past) and the possible (of the future).

Another aspect related to the time-image concerns the veracity of the narration:[13] when the virtuality and possibility of time become part of the actual image, when the present becomes at the same time past and future, it is more difficult to say what distinguishes the real from the imaginary or to tell the difference between true and false. Whereas the classic movement-image does everything possible to avoid fooling the spectator, this is not the case with the time-image: false cuts, aberrant movements, never-explained gaps in the narration, they all make the actual open up to the virtual (and the possible) and at the same time make truth impossible to grasp: we can only guess what happens between, before, and after. In the movement-image, truthful narration is developed organically according to reliable connections in space and chronologic connections in time. It always refers to a system of judgment. In the time-image, the duration of time, which implies change and becoming, provokes undecidable alternatives and inexplicable differences between true and false. Real and imaginary become undecidable alternatives, and differences between true and false become unexplainable. Falsifying narration frees itself from the system of judgment: "It shatters the system because the power of the false (not error or doubt) affects the investigator and the witness as much as the person presumed guilty."[14] Orson Welles (*F for Fake*) was, according to Deleuze, first to introduce both falsifying narration and forgers, which are now determining the image.

In *I Can't Sleep*, Camille and his friend could be considered forgers: they are called "very nice guys" by the owner of the hotel where they live; we see them at a family party, dancing in nightclubs, and being generous with friends. We see Camille in a hospital waiting to see a doctor because he has AIDS. In the end, he and his friend also turn out to be the criminals who the whole time have been startling the neighborhood (and haunting the images). The entire time, we have been unable to determine their "true nature," and even when Camille is arrested, he has not just turned unambiguously into a ruthless killer. Deleuze argues that with time that puts truth into crisis, cinema has become Nietzschean. According to Nietzsche, even the veracious and righteous man finally has to discover that he never stops lying. Everything is in perpetual movement of becoming and metamorphosis, and the forger is exemplary of this movement. The truth is impossible to grasp, and that is what creates "the power of the false": because truth and falsehood are undecidable, falsehood can be true, and truth can be false. Deleuze asks, if the true world no longer exists, and the world is not what it appears to be (in the present), what is there left to believe in? The Nietzschean answer he gives is: "bodies." Bodies are forces, nothing but forces.[15] They are forces that express a "will to power." Truth becomes in this sense no longer a question of what is (the absolute) truth. Rather, it becomes a question of forces: Who wants the truth? What are the forces in play? Then an identical phenomenon changes in sense according to the forces that appropriate it. For the hotel owner, Camille is a nice guy, for his mother he is the sweetest son, for his lovers a very attractive man, for the old ladies a brutal killer. This does not mean that Camille should not be punished for his crimes. Rather, it means only that he is not purely good or evil; but this is a matter of ethics, to which I turn in the next section.

Let me first discuss the bodies and their forces as one of the last things we can still believe in. In *The Time-Image*, Deleuze explains:

"Give me a body then": this is the formula of philosophical reversal. The body is no longer the obstacle that separates thought from itself, that which it has to overcome to reach thinking. It is on the contrary that which it plunges into or must plunge into, in order to reach the unthought, that is life. Not that the body thinks, but, obstinate and stubborn, it forces us to think, and forces us to think what is concealed from thought, life . . .) "give me a body then" is first to mount the camera on an everyday body. . . . The daily attitude is what puts the before and the after into the body, time into the body, the body as a revealer of a deadline.[16]

Claire Denis can be considered a filmmaker who makes a "cinema of the body." Very often, she films her characters close to the body or observes their bodily gestures and postures with silent distance. In *I Can't Sleep*, Camille especially is emphasized as a bodily force: he has a strong and beautiful body, which he uses and misuses in several ways (walking, making love, dancing, but also for killing old, fragile grannies). His body also reveals, quite literally, a deadline: he has AIDS, and time will deteriorate his body, even though the only sign of his condition is a small blemish on his skin. It is this body under time pressure that seems to explode into the most extreme and paradoxic attitudes and gestures of love and death, that forces us to think about life, about the limits of life, and about its ethical borders. The violence in *I Can't Sleep* is therefore not only an original impulse but also a bodily attitude and force that forces a shock in the brain.[17]

Ethics Without Morality.   The power of the body is not just physical force; when Deleuze starts talking about power, Spinoza enters the rhizomatic network to give more insights about power and the body.[18] According to Spinoza, power is the ability to affect or to be affected, the relation between one force and another. I already discussed in the previous chapter how Spinoza gives a new model to philosophy, namely, the model of the body.[19] All we experience are infinite effects of different encounters or relations between bodies: existing bodies meet, all relations can be combined endlessly, but not all combinations work. Bodies may agree or disagree: they can cause both sad and harmful or joyful and useful affects. So all we can have are good or bad encounters; and bad encounters, encounters with bodies that do not agree with our nature, are like poison: they make us sick, sad, and unable to act.[20]

The consequence of this conception of the body is that evil in itself does not exist. As Deleuze explains Spinoza's view: "There is no Good or Evil in Nature in general, but there is goodness and badness, useful and harmful, for each existing mode."[21] So this does not mean that there are no more values, that everything is indifferent. Evil exists, but it is not an absolute (God-imposed) entity. Evil is a bad encounter, a poisoning. As Deleuze puts it in *The Time-Image*: "It is not a matter of judging life in the name of a higher authority which would be the good, the true; it is a matter, on the contrary, of evaluating every being, every action and passion, even every value, in relation to the life which they involve. Affect as immanent evaluation, instead of judgement as transcendent value: 'I love' or 'I hate' instead of 'I judge.'"[22]

We find here a similar critique of morality as in Nietzsche's ideas on beyond good and bad. Nietzsche also insists on the fact that values still exist. He speaks of the noble and the base that are to be evaluated instead of judged. It is in this respect that both Spinoza and Nietzsche propose an ethics without morality for which they have both often been incorrectly accused of immoralism. Spinoza and Nietzsche indeed do not believe in an absolute goodness or badness, but they do propose ethics. This ethics consists of the attempt to create as many joyful encounters as possible, which will increase the power to act and to live intensively without harming others.[23] Let others live, provided they let you live, seems to be the simple but strong Spinozian message. This refusal (and inability) to judge has become an aspect of the time-image that is also present in *I Can't Sleep*: nowhere is any judgment given of any of the actions of the characters. They are observed from the outside in the several encounters they have. As already indicated, the murderers are not just evil (judged as bad), the nice girl is not just the nice girl (judged as good): in the end she runs away with the murderer's stolen money.

This brings me back to the central notion of this chapter: violence. Seen in the light of Spinozian (and Nietzschean and Deleuzian) wisdom, violence *as such* cannot be judged; it is beyond judgment. Violence is born out of bad encounters that have the affect of sadness; and, as Deleuze explains in *Expressionism in Philosophy*: "Out of sadness is born a desire, which is hate. This desire is linked with other desires, other passions: antipathy, derision, contempt, and envy, anger and so on."[24] So violence is a way of getting rid of the object that causes sad passions. To quote Deleuze again, "We are always determined to seek the destruction of an object that makes us sad . . . ; we experience then a joy that increases again our power of action. (But this is, of course, a partial joy, which does not sufficiently disrupt the chain of sorrows and hatred)."[25]

Violence of the War Machine: The Class of Violence

Violence in this way could be seen as a defense mechanism or as a refusal to accept the sad affects that are caused by certain bad encounters. Violence often is associated with impulses and drives, as Deleuze explains in relation to the impulse-image. As already noted, impulses or drives also can be seen as political options to get out of a certain dead end, a certain blockage on the way to joyful passions. In *A Thousand Plateaus*, Deleuze and Guattari distinguish four regimes of violence: *struggle*, the ritual violence of (primitive) fight; *state policing*, the legalized violence of the police; *crime*, the illegal violence of taking possession of something to which one has no "right"; and *war*, the nomadic violence of the war machine against the state apparatus. It is this last type of violence on which I concentrate.[26]

Deleuze and Guattari dedicated an entire plateau to the war machine, which I cannot discuss here in all its details and consequences. What is important to know is that the war machine is a force against and outside the state apparatus (a form of the hard segmental line). As Paul Patton demonstrates in *Deleuze and the Political*, the war machine does not have war or violence as its aim.[27] Rather, the war machine is related to the deterritorializing forces of the line of flight that aims at change and becomings. Patton prefers to speak of a "machine of metamorphosis" instead of a war machine. Nevertheless, the war machine can engage a kind of violence, that of refusal.

If we go back once again to *I Can't Sleep*, it will become clear that the violence that haunts the film is a violence of the war machine or the line of flight (even though it is also violence related to crime). To clarify this point, I make a brief sidestep and compare *I Can't Sleep* with *Nathalie Granger*, a film by Marguerite Duras from 1972, which presents a portrait of two women, Isabelle Granger and her friend and two daughters, Nathalie and Laurence, in their house (Duras's own house) during an ordinary weekday.[28] Of course, on the level of the form of content, this film is very different from *I Can't Sleep*, but on the almost invisible, incorporeal level of the form of expression, Duras's and Denis's films are really similar: both films are haunted by a kind of violence that runs silently under the images and only sometimes comes to the surface, through audio indications or other signs in the image. In the beginning of *I Can't Sleep*, the violent murders are present in radio announcements; later, we see a newspaper with an article about a new murder; and the self-defense lessons of the old ladies are another indication of the threatening violence. The same thing happens in *Nathalie Granger*. On the surface level, the women do nothing but normal household tasks: setting the table, doing the dishes, ironing, burning trash in the garden. In the same way as in *I Can't Sleep*, the images are penetrated by violence. Here, too, a voice on the radio talks about murderers (*les petits tueurs des Yvelines*), and the newspaper makes similar announcements. In *Nathalie Granger*, we never get to see or know the young killers, unlike in *I Can't Sleep*, but the basic presence of violence is similar.

There is another striking similarity: the presence in both films of a girl (Nathalie Granger and Daiga) who is silently associated with the violence of the killers. Both girls are rather taciturn, but sudden ruptures of a violent movement show their original violence (their attitude of refusal). The only actual violent moment in *Nathalie Granger* is when the little girl suddenly throws her doll's pram on the ground. In *I Can't Sleep*, the big girl, Daiga, is also a silent observer most of the time. There is one scene where her anger is revealed: when she is trying to sell her car, and she suddenly sees the man who has treated her badly earlier in the film (with whom she had a bad encounter), she bumps into his car. He must have gotten the message because to the police he "admits" that it is his own fault that he has to write off his car.

In the video interview that was released together with *Nathalie Granger*, Duras explains that she wanted to establish this line between Nathalie Granger and the young killers to show that they constitute a *classe de la violence*. This "class of violence" is not the violence of a (social) class. On the contrary, it is the violence experienced by people from different backgrounds who constitute a class of their own. It is a violence based on "a refusal that is felt by young people in their confrontation with modern society," as Marguerite Duras puts it. It is something everyone can recognize (this kind of violence is not learned; it is an original refusal or an original impulse as Deleuze would say). The class of violence is driven by the political option of the line of flight that undercuts all hard segments (all social classes, as Duras puts it). In the class of violence, all hard segmental society is seen as a bad encounter.

In the same way that Nathalie Granger and the criminals of the Yvelines constitute a class of violence, in *I Can't Sleep* there is an affinity between Daiga and Camille. This is made clear in a subtle and beautiful way, near the end of the film: Daiga follows Camille into a café (she knows what he has done because she has observed his moves) and orders a cup of coffee, standing next to him. They do not speak, they do not really look at each other, but in passing the sugar, their hands touch briefly. Then Camille pays for both their drinks and continues his own way, as does Daiga. One could say that here there was a moment of silent recognition between "members" of the class of violence and of the mutual becoming between the girl and the murderer. He will be picked up by the police and confess all the murders; she will take all the stolen money from Camille's hotel room and leave Paris. Without judgment, both Duras and Denis have shown a kind of violence that is part of all of us, which of course does not mean that it is good and that everybody should be like that (it is not for nothing that the old ladies in *I Can't Sleep* take lessons in self-defense).

Duras insists on the conviction that there is not violence of a class but rather a class of violence and, in this respect, drives are regarded as political options, a line of flight. These facts also indicate a different conception of politics and the political film. In a way, according to Deleuze, modern cinema has become completely political (without always having politics as a specific aim). Therefore, *I Can't Sleep* and *Nathalie Granger* can be seen as modern political films. In *The Time-Image*, Deleuze speaks about the modern political film. The notion of "missing people" is central in this respect.

Missing People and Fabulation

Deleuze distinguishes the classic political film from the modern political film in several ways. First, in the classic political film, such as *Birth of a Nation* or the Russian Revolution films of Eisenstein and Pudovkin, there is always a nation, the people, the common good. In the modern political cinema, the people no longer exist or do not yet exist: "The people is missing," says Deleuze.[29] "The people" has become a multiplicity of people; there is no unity. At best, "the people" is a "becoming" when it is inventing itself in the suburbs and the ghettos. All the political film can do is contribute to this becoming of the people. In any case, it is clear that there is no self-evident unity. "Ours is becoming the age of minorities," say Deleuze and Guattari in *A Thousand Plateaus*.[30] These minorities are proliferating and multiplying. Fragmentation and disintegration, the explosion of all unity, are therefore other characteristics of the modern political film (and contemporary political reality).[31]

This nonunity is clear in *I Can't Sleep*: the world Denis depicts is a multicultural society that consists of many different people, often of different minorities. Even more explicitly, this idea of missing people is central in another recent French *banlieu* film, *Brothers*, made by Olivier Dahan. *Brothers* was made as the last part of a series for French cinema and television that consisted of nine films by nine filmmakers about their adolescence in different periods over the last century.[32] *Brothers* deals with the last period, the beginning of the 1990s, and it does not present a happy picture of the contemporary world. In one of the Parisian suburbs, a 15-year-old boy, Zakari, accidentally kills another boy in the back of a car. His sister, brother, and girlfriend try to find him to help him while the brother of the murdered boy tries to find him to take vengeance. It is clear in the first place that there is no unified "people" in this film, but many different groups with many tensions between them. That people are missing in this film is evident: the feeling of loneliness and of individuals who seem to have bad encounters within their own "group" is dominant throughout. This feeling of nonunity is expressed explicitly in one of the interviews with suburban youngsters that are cut through the whole "fictional" story. One of them (Ablo) says: "C'est entre nous, les Arabes, les Noirs, qu'on va s'éclater" ("We, Arabs and Blacks, will destroy ourselves"). So one could say that the class of violence, which acts aggressively from a kind of refusal of society (a society that is not friendly to minorities of any kind), implodes and is directed inward (within the minority groups).

The feeling of intolerance and impossibility (it is impossible to live under such conditions) is very strong—and this brings me to the second difference between classic and modern political film that Deleuze distinguishes, which concerns the distinction between private and political. In the classic political film, there is still a border between private and political life. In the modern political cinema, the private is immediately politically engaged. Connected to this is the fact that revolution (the change from one political belief to another, mediated by a private consciousness) seems no longer possible: the modern political film is based on a feeling of the impossible and the intolerable. It is impossible to live under the conditions of being immediately politically implicated. All the characters in *Brothers* are fed up, angry, sick, and completely exhausted. In vain, they try everything to get out of their situation: Zak's sister is addicted to drugs (which is a dangerous line of flight); his brother plays a dangerous game, "la roulette rouge," to win money to leave town (which will become his death); and Zak wanders around completely exhausted and in a state of shock, not knowing where to go or what to do.

In *The Exhausted*, Deleuze defines the exhausted as follows: "Nothing is 'possible' anymore: a grim spinozism."[33] Although Deleuze is referring to the television plays of Becket, and I do not want to compare *Brothers* with Becket's work, I think it is legitimate to say that *Brothers* clearly expresses this same kind of exhaustion and end of the possible. This is not only because the characters look worn out and tired to death; also, the way things are presented visually adds to this exhaustion of all possibilities. One way of expressing this exhaustion in the image, on the level of the form of expression, is, according to Deleuze, by dissipating the power of the image.

In *Brothers*, there are several instances where the movement of the image literally dissipates by slowing down, as though all power and vitality are fading away both from the image and from the bodies that are in the image: three times a body falls down during these dissipating scenes (Zak's sister, the mother of the killed boy, and Zak himself). In any case, the whole film reflects this feeling of impossibility, the impossibility of a political revolution both in terms of form of content and in terms of form of expression.

A last characteristic of the modern political film again is related to the free, indirect discourse, as we also saw in *I Can't Sleep*. For the modern political film, Deleuze describes the free, indirect discourse as follows: "The author takes a step towards his characters, but the characters take a step towards the author: double becoming. Story telling is not an impersonal myth, but neither is it a personal fiction: it is a word in act, a speech act through which the character continually crosses the boundary which would separate his private business from politics, and which *itself produces collective utterances*."[34]

The modern political film is a free, indirect discourse in which the people are given space for their fabulation, their becoming taking place in the stories and myths that are told by the filmmaker, who in turn becomes part of the people as well. A narration or fabulation, David Rodowick explains further:

> . . . is neither a psychological memory where the individual recalls a repressed history, nor simply a historical memory as the representation of the occluded story of a people. Rather, it entails a serialism that transforms the individual at the same time as the collective. This double becoming intertwines two discursive series in a free indirect relation: communication between the world and the I in a fragmented world, and communication of the world and the I in a fragmented I, which must find common points of articulation.[35]

Rodowick explains how this fabulation works as a power of the false; images and sounds become separate forces where "the utterable invokes what cannot be seen and the invisible evokes what cannot be said."[36] For Deleuze, adds Rodowick, cinema in this way becomes a performative act that has an expressly political dimension: "The pure speech-act is the basis for 'fabulation' wherein the serial form of narration becomes a political cinema. Here the powers of the false created by the direct time-image require not only an overcoming of the model of the true, but also a new conceptualization of the subject as a 'realizing fabrication' creative of an event: the constitution of a people."[37]

Rodowick analyzes how this fabulation takes place in Third World cinema by looking specifically at one of the first African films *Borom Sarret* (1963) by Ousmane Sembene. Together with Djibril Diop Mambety, whose film *Touki Bouki* was discussed in the previous chapter as a time-image, Sembene is among the most important filmmakers of Senegal and Africa as a whole. *Borom Sarret* presents the life of a Dakar cart driver, moving through Senegal's working poor. Rodowick analyzes how through the use of neorealist postsynchronized sound that moves freely in relation to the images, Sembene creates an act of storytelling where he lends his voice to the principal characters, and the characters lend their voices to the filmmaker. They present a power of the false as follows:

An attempt to break the repetition of the past in the present and to expose the limits of an identity that resists change because of a nostalgia for the past and a refusal to recognize the emerging, collective voice of the Senegalese people. Each character of the film acts out of his or her interest. In this manner, the episodic structure of the film traces the serialization of the Senegalese people; but while the people are still missing, the passage of the free indirect style from voice to voice and of the image from episode to episode demonstrates how they are all connected, in equally serial fashion, to a collective situation.[38]

Indeed, Third World cinema does seem important for these acts of fabulation and the creation of the people that is still missing. It is not difficult to recognize in *Touki Bouki* similar fabulating powers of the false. Here, too, the relation between image and sound is a free, indirect one. Between the main characters, Mory and Anta, and the filmmaker Mambety, there is a double becoming of their voices and bodies. Although no solution is offered and no new people come into existence, *Touki Bouki* presents a series of commentaries on and fantasies about the collective situation of the people in Dakar, where precolonialism and neocolonialism are important forces. I argue that these collective fabulations are presented not only in Third World cinema but also in many European and American films. In *Brothers*, for instance, we can speak clearly of a double becoming of the filmmaker and the filmed people, of a free, indirect discourse, and of a fabulation of missing people. In that film, there are two different layers (forms) of content and expression. The "fictional" story in color is regularly interrupted with black and white "documentary" speech acts by young people. Nevertheless, the fictional elements look real and the documentary parts could have been staged. It is difficult to distinguish between what is "real" and what is "invented." The border between fiction and reality, as in all modern time-images, is vague. In both cases, the filmmaker gives his voice to the characters, and the characters give their voices to the filmmaker. The power of the false works and brings a message, the fabulation of the people.[39] It does not matter what is exactly true or false; the important thing is the effect and function of the film, that is, to give a collective utterance as the prefiguration of the people who are missing, capable of the invention of a people.

To conclude, let me briefly return to the question of violence. Like *I Can't Sleep*, *Brothers* expresses a violence of a class of violence, a line of flight. Whereas in *I Can't Sleep* the violence was still rather hidden, only emerging sometimes like an original (yet political) impulse, in *Brothers* the hatred is directed inward, directed at the interior of the missing people. The feeling of impossibility prevails in these images. Everything is exhausted; the violence is like a last convulsion of worn-out bodies. As in *I Can't Sleep*, there is no absolute good or bad, no absolute judgment. What is shown are aggression and violence in a particular situation, in a particular encounter between bodies that are at the end of their forces (even though they are all young). In *Brothers*, there is no moralism but only a demonstration of bad encounters and sad passions. The aim of the modern political film is not to judge and to blame the bad guys. Violence is not related to a certain group or class that is more violent than others but is related to a shared feeling of refusal, intolerance, and impossibility (the class of violence). The aim of the modern political film is to give a fabulation space for the people who are missing but nevertheless are connected to a collective situation and in this way to aid in their becoming.

Other films similarly present this kind of violence related to this question of missing people. Mathieu Kassovitz's film *La Haine* (1994) is another French example of the problems of postcolonial multicultural society. It should be noted that in this film the missing and fragmented people have a common enemy: the police. Here, too, there is an "accidental" shooting (by a police officer), which brings all the tensions to an explosion at the end of the film. In the United States, and even in Hollywood, films that present this kind of what I would call serious or sad violence also are being made. In Chapter 1, I discussed *Strange Days* as a metafilm that displays a new kind of camera consciousness. With respect to the question of violence, one can say that *Strange Days* is certainly also a modern political film. There is not just one kind of violence in this film. Clearly, the violence we see in the streets of Los Angeles, where all kinds of minorities are fighting, is a violence of the class of violence that consists of many different ethnic groups. The violence of the policemen against the rapper Jerrico One is a form of state violence, even though the police officers cross the borders of what is legal. The violence of the murderer against the prostitute is a psychoanalytically explainable impulse. Finally, the fight between Mace and the police officers could be seen as a classic instant of violence of the action-image, where in a duel two opposing forces fight as a reaction to a concrete situation and to defend their territory. As I argued in Chapter 1, despite the appearance of being an action-image, *Strange Days* has nevertheless many characteristics of a time-image where time, the virtual, and the actual play confusing roles. Now I can add that also in terms of fabulation and the creation of a people, *Strange Days* follows the strategies of the time-image and the modern political film.[40] Many other contemporary Hollywood films belong to this type of modern political film as well. Think of *Boy'z'n the Hood* (John Singleton, 1992), *Menace II Society* (Allen and Albert Hughes, 1993), *Fresh* (Boaz Yakin, 1995), *Do the Right Thing* (Spike Lee, 1989) and even *Falling Down* (Joel Schoemacher, 1993), which show the "impossibilities" of the middle-class white man, confronted for the first time (ever) with the feeling of becoming a minority. Of course, these films are never exactly the same: each film consists of multiple lines that constitute different assemblages, even though they share the feeling of the class of violence and the missing people. In any case, the violence in these films has the effect of sadness on the viewer, sadness about the impossibility of living joyful affects and having power to act.

Schizophrenia in Contemporary Hollywood

Another kind of violence in contemporary filmmaking has many exponents in both Hollywood and Europe. The violence in the "nouvelle violence" is often (though not always) funny and makes us laugh. Sometimes violence seems to give a feeling of relief and liberation. *Pulp Fiction* and *Fight Club* are two films that raised particularly "violent" discussions around this topic. Both films have been accused of being fascist or socially irresponsible films.[41] In any case, they raise ambiguous feelings, in particular with regard to the violent scenes. In this last section, I discuss this ambiguity of the modern political film as it presents itself within the context of Hollywood. To do this, it is necessary to turn to a few of Deleuze and Guattari's ideas on capitalism and schizophrenia, as presented in *Anti-Oedipus* and *A Thousand Plateaus*, and to their relation with cinema.

Following Marx, Deleuze and Guattari propose an immanent analysis of capitalism.[42] Considering capitalism as an immanent system entails that the system carries all the dangers and possibilities in itself. The notion of surplus, for instance, is a concept that is at work in an immanent analysis of capitalism. In *Anti-Oedipus*, Deleuze and Guattari describe surplus value as follows: "Instead of simply representing the relations of commodities, it enters now, so to say, into relations with itself. It differentiates itself as original value from itself as surplus value."[43] Furthermore, they state that surplus value always is absorbed into the system again but also constantly injects antiproduction, which they call *schizophrenization*. I think that schizophrenization producing and "antiproducing" is an important concept for looking at contemporary image culture as well, especially because capitalism seems to be coming to realize itself increasingly as cinema (in the broad sense of audiovisual culture). In his article "Capital/Cinema," Jonathan Beller considers Deleuze's cinema books of equal importance for the twentieth century (and perhaps the twenty-first) as Marx's *Capital* was for the nineteenth century. Beller explains:

The experiences of events in the cinema are, from the standpoint of capital, experiments about what can be done with the body by machines and by the circulation of capital. . . . If capital realizes itself as cinema, that is, if industrial capital gives way to the society of the spectacle, one might well imagine cinema, with respect to the body, geography, labor, raw material, and time, to have become the most radical deterritorializing force of capital itself. As production itself moves into the visual, the visceral, the sensual, the cultural, cinema emerges as a higher form of capital.[44]

It is clear that with his cinema books, Deleuze has proposed an immanent analysis of images. If we now link cinema to capitalism, we find a schizophrenic dimension as well. It must be noted that with schizophrenia, Deleuze and Guattari distinguish a clinical schizophrenia as a mental illness from schizophrenia as a process that operates on a broad sociohistorical field rather than on a narrow psychological scale.[45]

Fight Club's Schizzo-flows

Looking now at *Fight Club*, for instance, we can see clearly that this film is permeated with "schizzo-flows."[46] If we analyze the film along the lines of the vertical axis of the assemblage it constitutes (see previous chapter), we can see that in the beginning of the film, the main character and narrator, Jack, is completely territorialized by capitalist consumption and what in the film is called "Ikea nesting instincts." His deterritorialization begins when he meets Tyler Durden, who invites him to fight with him. Soon, many men join Jack and Tyler in secret meetings in hidden cellars, car parks, and backyards. Of course, the violence of the fights is a literal attack on the beauty and glamour of consumption culture. Tyler and Jack look with contempt at Calvin Klein underwear ads and cherish their self-mutilations as a resistant act against capitalism and its (surplus) values. There is one scene in the film where the schizo-movements of cinema/capitalism become very clear. It is the moment when Tyler teaches Jack how to make soap and bombs. To do this, they take the ultimate residual element of glamour culture as the basic material for their products: they go to a liposuction clinic and steal liposuction fat. From that body fat, they skim the glycerin from which they make both glycerin soap and nitroglycerin bombs. The soaps they sell to large department stores ("It was beautiful, we sold rich ladies their own fat asses."). The explosives are used to explode credit card company buildings and other symbols of capitalism. In a powerful and concrete way, we see here an immanent system of capitalism at work: the residual (fat) is turned into a consumption good (soap, which in itself produces beauty and glamour as its surplus value) and into the ultimate destructive weapon against the whole system, nitroglycerin bombs.

Looking at the kind of territorializations (consumption culture) and deterritorializations (the fight clubs, Tyler's rebellious actions) in *Fight Club*, we also have to add that reterritorializing forces are in play as well. By the end of the film, the fight clubs have turned into a sort of terrorist organization, Project Mayhem. All members wear the same black shirts, they give up their names, except in death, when they ritually start singing "His name is Robert Paulusen," and they blindly follow Tyler's orders. These are the instances when the deterritorializing moments of freedom turn again into a problem of unfreedom that is also addressed in *Anti-Oedipus*: "How could the masses be made to desire their own repression"[47] and to which Deleuze and Guattari return frequently. This problem of unfreedom can be seen as a negative effect of the abundance of freedom and the difficulty of affirming and sustaining freedom.[48]

On the horizontal axis of the assemblage of *Fight Club*, the film seems to be determined by action-images. Quite literally, the film consists of a series of duels, the fights that seem to be primitive ritual fights. The sensory-motor function rules the action and reaction of both the narrator and Tyler. In this sense, the film seems to be a classic "cinema of the body." At the beginning of the film, however, we have literally moved into the narrator's brain, and this film is certainly also a "cinema of the brain." At the end of the film, the narrator is Tyler, or Tyler is the narrator. Instead of considering this ending as a forced narrative twist or a frustrating gimmick, as was the disappointed reaction of many,[49] it is also possible to see this ending as the logical outcome of a schizo-strategy, where the actual and the virtual images of thought fold into each other. As Jennifer Heuson puts it, the film shows the following:

> The process of becoming of the self-image, where the narrator and Tyler Durden are "folded" into each other. The action of the film, then, is to unfold the two and refold them into a single image. The fight scenes show this process best. The narrator and Tyler begin fighting as two images, one folded "against" the other. As the film progresses, however, this fold opens, and the spectator sees fight scenes not *between* the narrator and Tyler but with others. But, the crucial scene in this process of unfolding is the fight the narrator has with himself in his boss' office. This indicates the virtual refolding of the narrator and Tyler that will be actualized in the final scenes. The folds in the flesh of the brain, then, become folds in the film screen. They are completely spatial and active.[50]

Because of the continuous slip between the actual and the virtual, between the narrator and Tyler, and because of the fact that they ultimately fold into one, this contemporary movement-image has characteristics of the time-image (just as *Strange Days* has in a different way, as I argued in Chapter 1): the fact that at the beginning of the film we have seen that the narrator suffers from insomnia, and hence his sensory-motor action has become distorted, that he has become susceptible to time and the powers of the false. As for the violence, it is now possible to conclude that this physical violence equals the shocks in the brain and is connected to a strategy of deterritorialization. Again, we can see here members of the class of violence fighting their fights. The schizophrenic dimension of *Fight Club* is determined not only by the fact that the violence is directed toward symbols of capitalism, which produces its own antiproduction, but also by the fact that Jack produces his own "counterimage," with whom he fights and forms a class of violence.[51]

Laughing Lions: The Tarantino Effect

Quentin Tarantino's films are also notorious for their violence; and, as I argue, many discussions about his films also have to do with the fact that he too plays with the movements between movement-images and time-images, albeit in his own characteristic way. The violence in Tarantino's films is judged primarily according to the criteria I mentioned at the beginning of this chapter: it is seen either as immoral or as no issue for discussion at all.[52] As Dana Polan remarks, "Those who like the film do so because it doesn't seem to have anything to say and renders the cinematic experience as pure play. Those who dislike the film dislike it for the very same reasons, seeing the deliberate cool superficiality of *Pulp Fiction* as a symptom of the empty post-modernity of our age."[53] In *Pulp Fiction*, both reactions are actually cleverly built in within the film itself. The moral strategy is represented by the gangster Jules, who in the end rejects violence in the name of the Lord (Ezekiel 25:17). On the other hand, Tarantino gives his audience the possibility for complete cult-genre appropriation, a strategy one can adopt for enjoying the film's violence. Cult audiences consider horror, violence, and shocking moments more as a Bakhtinian carnival; the blood is considered purely makeup and masks. For a cult audience, it is the exaggeration of violence that transgresses its moral impacts. A clear example of a cult element in *Pulp Fiction* is the "gimp," the black leather sadomasochistic figure that is awakened from a trunk by the two creeps that rape Marsellus Wallace.[54]

It is clear that Tarantino has built in both the moralist reaction and the cult appropriation in his film, but *Pulp Fiction* is actually too ambiguous to adopt easily either of the positions. The moralistic view is undermined because the Ezekiel passage is first used to kill in the name of the Lord, and when Jules finally rejects violence in the name of that same Lord, he does not speak in terms of good and bad, but in terms of weak and strong (the shepherd has to lead the weak). Neither is the cult option easy to adopt because reality keeps knocking on the door. For instance, the choice of Christopher Walken as the Vietnam veteran brings back in a mediated way (*The Deer Hunter*) the cruel reality of the Vietnam War. When Mia overdoses on heroin, it is hard to forget that this also happens in reality. The ambiguity of *Pulp Fiction* is present on all levels. One could even speak of a "Tarantino effect" (meaning the uncomfortable pleasure to which his films, especially *Pulp Fiction*, give rise).[55] My hypothesis is that Tarantino's film is difficult to grasp because he cleverly plays with the status of the time-image while at the same time maintaining the characteristics of the action-image. To conclude this chapter, I therefore discuss briefly the status of the image (and the violence) in *Pulp Fiction* before trying to determine why it is so funny and why we laugh at the presentation of violence in this film.

On the Borders: Action, Impulses, and Time

In many respects, *Pulp Fiction* is an ordinary Hollywood movement-image, more specifically an action-image, as Deleuze defines it. Although there are at least three different stories, all the stories have one or two central characters that are goal oriented (Vincent and Jules getting even with cheating little drug dealers and getting rid of a corpse, Vincent going on a date with his boss's girlfriend while remaining loyal, Butch getting back his father's watch). They find themselves in a certain situation and react to it.[56] The characters are far from seers, hearers, and wanderers: they are active, sharp, and "cool." The foot massage dialogue between Vincent and Jules could be seen as verbal fetishism, however. "Don't be telling me about the foot massages. I'm the foot fucking master!"—although we never see Mia's notoriously big feet in this scene, they are certainly the partial object here. Also, the fact that the chronological order of the sequences is shuffled around indicates a preoccupation with time that is characteristic of the impulse-image. Although the characters are busy and actively involved in their milieu, the action-image has tendencies to become serial impulse-image.

To complicate matters, Tarantino also plays with the powers of the false and the new status of the image as a time-image. The difficulties in the reactions to the film often are related to the problem of distinguishing between real and fiction. Moreover, the characters are considered pure bodily forces and seem to act and react only to the encounters they make. The characters are driven by Spinozian affects of love and hate. The character of Butch is exemplary of this attitude. He is a hard-boiled guy, a boxer who literally plays a hard game with all the men he encounters (he kills his opponent in a boxing game, shoots Vincent, and crashes into Marsellus). As soon as he is with his girlfriend, Fabian, though, he is sweet and caring: depending on the different bodily forces he encounters, he is affected by either hate (or contempt) or love. He saves Marsellus only because they both encountered a pair of even bigger scums, not because he suddenly judges Marsellus to be good.

Tarantino is certainly also influenced by Godard (one of the exponents of the time-image and the power of the body preferred by Deleuze). The famous dance scene of Mia and Vince is a homage to Godard's *Bande à Part*. Godard's statement "it's no blood, it's red" in *Weekend* is clearly taken up by Tarantino. He is also influenced by Godard's use of cartoons. Instead of using cartoons as a sort of commentary on the other images, Tarantino turns his characters into paper dolls: cartoon characters are cool, like Tarantino's characters are cool. They are what Deleuze calls "pure speech acts," characteristic of new images.[57] But Godard's films, however, always seem to be aware of the metadiscourse that is referred to in the film; the power of the false is always indicated (and even theorized and analyzed in the images and sounds). In Godard's cinema of the body, it is clear that bodies are pure forces, that everything is nothing but affect and effect (in body and brain) created by a (false) filmic device. Tarantino also creates a cinema of the body, full of bodily forces; however, he combines the color "red" and the "cartoon characters" with realistic conventions. As I said, even though the chronological time structure is mixed up, the film is carefully constructed to maintain the credibility of an action-image. Also, most of the settings are realistic. The bodies are like paper dolls, but at the same time they are extremely physical (they eat, go the toilet, and so on). Another aspect that brings the paper dolls to life is their language: streetwise dialogues give the characters a natural and funny twist but also reinforce their status as speech acts. In this sense, Tarantino plays with the power of the false in a masterly fashion. He completely denies the classic distance not only between reality and fiction (as is normal for the time-image) but also (even more so) between fiction and metafiction. Because he also draws on realistic conventions, one cannot completely forget reality—hence the difficulty in either adopting the film as cult or rejecting it as immoral garbage.

Another point where Tarantino shows his awareness of the modern time-image is in its political implications. Again in *Pulp Fiction*, in a way the people are missing; but in presenting, in his own way, a multicultural world, Tarantino is accused of appropriating the "cool" aspects of black culture (which includes violence as a refusal-strategy). He is also accused of misusing words like "nigga" and "bitch" and adopting a minority language.[58] In politically correct terms, this is undeniable, but on the other hand one could say that Tarantino shows that actually there is no difference between black and white when they form a "class of violence." Of course, one could argue that this class of violence is criminal, but as is clear from *I Can't Sleep* and *Nathalie Granger*, criminal violence is not that far from line-of-flight violence (which again does not mean that it is essentially good). As we have seen, the time-image makes judgment impossible. Here is another aspect where Tarantino is a modern filmmaker who is aware of the implications of the time-image: he does not judge his characters. It is all a play of forces.[59] In any case, the status of the image, between a time-image and an action-image, means that we sometimes feel confused by the violence Tarantino presents in his images. Should we judge it as immoral, or is it possible to develop another strategy? This brings me to the last point I want to make: why do we (at least many of us) laugh when we see Tarantino's violent images?

Zarathustra's Laughter

In various instances, Deleuze emphasizes the importance of humor. In *Dialogues*, for instance, he states that humor (as opposed to more moralistic irony) has to do with the becoming-minority of language. One of the aspects that makes Tarantino's films so funny is precisely the language, which is indeed a minority language, the street language, and the rap of African Americans. Language in this way becomes an event invaded by humor. Another way in which Deleuze defines humor in *Dialogues* is by seeing it as "the art of consequences and effects." *Pulp Fiction* certainly demonstrates such an "art of consequences." Think, for instance, of the consequences of the importance of Butch's watch, of the consequences of a dirty car, or of the consequences of an overdose. According to bell hooks, the laughter that *Pulp Fiction* provokes is precisely dangerous: "The fun thing about Tarantino's films is that he makes that shit look so ridiculous you think everybody's gonna get it and see how absurd it all is. Well, that's when we enter the danger zone. Folks be laughing at the absurdity and clinging to it nevertheless."[60] Although taking hooks's objection seriously, I look for a more positive view on the film's humor. Maybe it is possible to laugh but not forget about the absurdity, in other words, to have a more schizophrenic attitude toward the film. Being implicated in the laughter, the spectator, too, is "caught with his pants down," caught in a double consciousness of the laughter of a child and the seriousness of the adult world.

We can extend reflections of Spinoza and Nietzsche on this matter.[61] According to Spinoza, the ethics of life consists of creating as many joyful affects as possible because only joy can lead to actions and to adequate ideas, to a better way of living. In *Brothers*, we see how bad encounters can only make us sad. Hence the violence in this film (this kind of film) also has a sad effect on us. In *I Can't Sleep*, it is the class of violence, the unexpected refusal of social conditions and the compensation it finds in aggression, that already turns a sad affect into more a joyful experience. At the beginning of *I Can't Sleep*, there is an almost enigmatic image of two people in a helicopter who are really "laughing their heads off." There is no explanation whatsoever for this image in the rest of the film; but one could say that it is a literal expression of a "laughing of the height" of Nietzsche's Zarathustra.[62] In an article on Nietzsche and laughter, John Lippitt explains that Zarathustra comes to realize "that the highest affirmation of life possible is to say a joyous 'Yes' to life despite its negative side, despite its horrors and suffering, despite life's absurdity."[63] Except for this first shot, which is really explicit, *I Can't Sleep* expresses a "happy despair" in a subtle way. The notion of happy despair again brings Marguerite Duras to mind: *le gai desespoir* is also Duras's basic attitude toward life.[64]

As for *Pulp Fiction*, I would say that, less subtly than in Duras's vision, a similar process of happy despair is going on. Lippitt states that Zarathustra, by embracing eternal recurrence, is bringing to life itself that spirit of childlike playfulness, which is so common an element in humor.[65] As Dana Polan argues: "Much of the fascination of *Pulp Fiction* is *infantile*, intending this term less as a judgement than as a description of the world it depicts and the appeal to the spectator it generates."[66] Polan says that on the one hand, even as the film deals with an adult world of sex, crime, and moral decision, it maintains a tone of wide-eyed innocence (Butch and Fabienne as "big babies"), obsession with scabrous anality (characters on toilets, the "hiding place" of the father's watch), and regressive orality (food like french fries with mayonnaise, milkshakes, and pancakes). On the other hand, the flip side of this wide-eyed innocence is sadistic cruelty, which is also part of children's behavior when they want to master their own inadequacies. Bad taste and childlike obsession with smearing ("blood and puke") are all part of this infantile world depicted by Tarantino.

Tarantino as a director is also a child who plays with images, picking a heterogeneous selection of images from film history's cookie box, affirming a joyful eternal recurrence. Tarantino's laughing—and the laughing to which his version of the world gives rise—is a playful laughing, not because serious reality is excluded but because reality is so impossible and absurd. It is the laughter of Zarathustra, who states that "laughing lions must come!" Tarantino is a "laughing lion, his laughter is a 'laughter of the height' as an expression of individual (and maybe collective) liberation and creation." It is (to quote Lippitt again) "a praising laughter of a surfer on successfully riding a dangerous breaker over the mocking laughter of the crowd who take malicious pleasure in seeing him take a fall," which is more the Bergsonian version of laughter, the laughter of the herd as opposed to the laughter of the height; it is "the laughter of a child playing with a new toy over the laughter of a group of children at a particular child who does not fit in."[67]

Like Zarathustra, Tarantino confronts and destroys the "spirit of gravity" by laughter of the free individual, not the social corrective. This redeeming laughter involves nevertheless a consciousness of suffering and emphasizes a vitally important point: "that the tragic and the comic are not polar opposites, or mutually exclusive, but subtly and sometimes almost paradoxically interrelated modes of experience."[68] This paradoxic link is a schizoanalytic experience.

In *Pulp Fiction*, there is a scene that in terms of violence greatly resembles the scene in *Brothers*. In both films, there is an accidental fatal shooting in a car. As is clear from the preceding, this accidental shooting is sad and shocking in *Brothers*. In *Pulp Fiction*, however, this scene mostly provokes laughter. The way it is presented, embedded in really funny dialogue (between "Le Big Mac" and "Oh man, I shot Marvin in the face") and followed up by an art-of-consequences scene (how to clean a blood-smeared car) provokes a completely different reaction. Because the realism of the action-image is so ambiguously related to "the powers of the false, this is also the scene where people feel guilty for having laughed." Tarantino certainly knows how to confuse people.[69]

Both Fincher and Tarantino present images that play with the status of the movement-image that has become "contaminated" with characteristics of the time-image. Their styles are different, one presenting a cinema of the brain, the other presenting a cinema of the body. In different ways, the violence in their films presents forms of schizophrenic movements of deterritorialization of the constraints or absurdities of life. Because Tarantino's humor is an act of happy despair that is inspired by the absurdity of life, when we laugh about the violence he presents, we are perhaps becoming "laughing lions" ourselves. It is an attitude to get out of the impasse of the seriousness of life, as also shown in a less explicit way in *I Can't Sleep*. *Brothers* demonstrates that it is not always possible to get out of this seriousness of life. It is not a matter of saying that one is more politically correct or morally acceptable than the other or that one is more real than the other. Sad and happy despair, expressed in violence, are both expressions of the complexity and absurdity of life, which can be full of bad encounters. Deleuze's rhizomatic toolbox of concepts can help to explain why some violent images make us sad and others make us cheerful. Both are sides of the same coin of the contemporary condition where missing people and the class of violence express the absurdity or impossibility of life. One is powerless and sad, the other is powerful and joyful, but both redefine goodness and badness and both are beyond good and evil. This also redefines the subject from a moral being who judges into an ethical individual who loves or hates. In any case, without a revolution to expect, politics has become something that concerns everyone; and cinema can make us think about these matters through images of the body, images of the brain, or fabulations.

Conceptual Personae and Aesthetic Figures of Becoming-Woman

> Why are there so many becomings of man, but no becoming-man? First because man is majoritarian par excellence, whereas becomings are minoritarian; all becoming is a becoming-minoritarian. . . . In this sense women, children, but also animals, plants, and molecules, are minoritarian. It is perhaps the special situation of women in relation to the man-standard that accounts for the fact that becomings, being minoritarian, always pass through a becoming-woman.[1]

It is well known that for Deleuze and Guattari "becoming," as opposed to "being," is important in the philosophy of Deleuze and Guattari. In *A Thousand Plateaus*, they discuss many types of becoming: "becoming-intense, becoming-animal, becoming-imperceptible. . . ."[2] Becoming is always a molecular process that involves a becoming-minoritarian. All becomings seem to be initiated by a becoming-woman. As recent feminists have discussed, however, this becoming-woman should not be seen as a molar becoming a woman or as an end in itself.[3] Every becoming is a process and an attempt to think differently, to see or feel something new in experience by entering into a zone of proximity with somebody or something else: "[Becoming] constitutes a zone of proximity and indiscernibility, a no-man's land, a nonlocalizable relation sweeping up the two distant or contiguous points, carrying one into the proximity of the other."[4]

In his book *Deleuzism*, Ian Buchanan discusses becoming-woman in relation to the world-historical. He sees Deleuze and Guattari's concept of becoming-woman as part of the utopian vocation of their concepts:

From a certain point of view, the most deeply utopian texts are not those that propose or depict a better society, but those that carry out the most thoroughgoing destruction of the present society. For Deleuze, however, simply seeing/transgressing the limit is not enough to release us from perceptibility because it preserves the idea of a limit. One must do more, but what? The answer is becoming-woman, where becoming-woman is the basis of a total critique.[5]

Buchanan then refers to Deleuze's *Essays Critical and Clinical*, in which he shows that becoming-woman is in the first instance a procedure that allows one to live freely; otherwise one is paralyzed. "This freedom to live is not of course the same freedom enjoyed by people mercifully free of psychosis, it is rather the freedom of someone who has moved into an alternate universe where things are measured differently, valued differently and generally held together by an entirely fresh set of rules."[6] Becoming-woman, like schizophrenia, can have its clinical psychotic form (like schizophrenia, becoming-woman is taken from psychoanalysis; Freud diagnoses his patient Schreber as suffering from becoming-woman), but it also has a critical/artistic form in which becoming-woman becomes something capable of inducing an effect (on readers or spectators). It is in this latter form that becoming-woman is no longer a diagnosis but an indictment, as Buchanan argues.

To look at some forms of artistic becoming-woman that have an effect, I use a "conceptual persona" that will shift gradually from the plane of immanence of philosophy to the plane of composition (no less immanent) of art and thus become an aesthetic figure. As Deleuze and Guattari argue in *What is Philosophy?*, philosophy and art need intercessors:

The conceptual persona is not the philosopher's representative but, rather, the reverse: the philosopher is only the envelope of his principal conceptual persona and of all the other personae who are intercessors, the real subject of his philosophy. . . . The difference between the conceptual personae and aesthetic figures consists first of all in this: the former are the powers of concepts, and the latter are the powers of affects and percepts. The former take effect on a plane of immanence that is an image of Thought-Being (noumenon), and the latter take effect on a plane of composition as image of a Universe (phenomenon). . . . Art thinks no less than philosophy, but it thinks through affects and percepts.[7]

Now, what conceptual persona/aesthetic figure other than Alice in Wonderland could be "someone who has moved into an alternate universe where things are measured differently?" Therefore, in this chapter, I take Lewis Carroll's figure as my guide through the world of becoming-woman.

First, I investigate in what way Alice in Wonderland could be seen as a conceptual persona of becoming in general and becoming-woman in particular: What happens when Alice grows smaller and larger? What does her body tell? Does she have a Body without Organs (BwO)? Is she becoming-woman? Then I look at the possible significance of this little girl as a conceptual persona for feminism. "Only recently and reluctantly have feminists taken a positive turn in the direction of Gilles Deleuze," writes Verena Conley in her article "Becoming-Woman Now."[8] Indeed, especially the concept of becoming-woman has met with serious critiques from female theorists. Is Alice indeed naive and a poor example for women, or could she be seen differently? Is she a cyborg *avant-la-lettre*? To find some answers to these questions, I finally look at Alice as an aesthetic figure in modern cinema. In films like Marguerite Duras's *Aurélia Steiner* (1979), Sally Potter's *Orlando* (1992), and Jean Pierre Jeunet and Marc Caro's *The City of Lost Children* (1995), Alice appears to have many contemporary avatars as powerful film figures. I end by looking at Lars von Trier's "Goldenheart Trilogy" of *Breaking the Waves* (1996), *The Idiots* (1998), and *Dancer in the Dark* (2000). When focusing on *Dancer in the Dark*, I argue that von Trier's heroines too can be seen as aesthetic figures of becoming-woman.[9]

The Philosopher Meets Alice in Wonderland

Alice's Growing Larger and Smaller: Which Way?

In *The Logic of Sense*, Gilles Deleuze has many encounters with Lewis Carroll's *Alice's Adventures in Wonderland* and *Through the Looking-Glass*.[10] According to Deleuze, Alice's growing smaller and larger are events of pure becoming. The concept of becoming is central to Deleuze's philosophy: it is related to many other ideas, such as the uncertainty about fixed identities, the BwO, and a concept of time and duration that is always invaded by the past and the future, which is particularly important for his cinema books, especially *The Time-Image*. The paradox of becoming is that there are always two things happening at the same time: when Alice grows larger, she simultaneously becomes larger than she was and smaller than she will be (when she grows smaller, she is simultaneously smaller than she was and larger than she will be). As Deleuze concludes, all movements of becoming move and pull in both directions at once: Alice does not grow without shrinking and vice versa. This affirmation of both senses and directions at the same time is a paradox. It is a logic of sense that counters good sense in which there is always a determinable sense or direction. Alice demonstrates her confusion about, and fascination for, these adventurous becomings. As Deleuze puts it:

The paradox of this pure becoming, with its capacity to elude the present, is the paradox of infinite identity (the infinite identity of both directions or senses at the same time—of future and past, of the day before and the day after, of more and less, of too much and not enough, of active and passive, and of cause and effect). . . . "Which way, which way?" asks Alice, sensing that it is always in both directions at the same time, so that for once she stays the same, through an optical illusion; the reversal of the day before and the day after, the present always being eluded—"jam tomorrow and jam yesterday, but never jam *to-day*"; the reversal of more and less: five nights are five times hotter than a single one, "but they must be five times colder for the same reason"; the reversal of active and passive: "do cats eat bats?" is as good as "do bats eat cats?"; the reversal of cause and effect: to be punished before having committed a fault, to cry before having pricked oneself, to serve before having divided up the servings.[11]

All these paradoxic movements of becoming also undermine the fixed personal identity—hence Alice's doubts about her own name. Paradox not only destroys good sense as the only direction; it also destroys common sense as the assignation of fixed identities. A subject in the paradoxic situation of becoming is a subject that questions its identity. It is a subject with a Spinozistic body. In *Expressionism in Philosophy: Spinoza*, Deleuze describes the elasticity of the body in the following way: "One may almost say that a mode changes its body or relation in leaving behind childhood, or entering old age. Growth, aging, and illness: we can hardly recognize the same individual. And is it really indeed the same individual?"[12] In the previous chapters, I discussed how Spinoza defines bodies in terms of what they are capable of instead of what they are. It now can be understood that his claim that "we do not know what a body can do" relates to the process of becomings in which the subject constantly finds himself or herself. It also implies that its meaning and capacities will vary according to context. This elastic conception of the body also provides useful new perspectives in feminist debates, as I discuss in the following section. A "Deleuzian feminism" seems to be gaining territory, going beyond the often-heard feminist critiques on the concept of becoming-woman that are due to an implicit traditional concept of the body (including the mind–body split).

Molar and Molecular Levels of the Subject

Like the Spinozian body, Deleuze and Guattari's concept of the BwO is a body that challenges or resists single and fixed identities. In Chapter 2, I discussed the BwO in relation to Fassbinder's BwOs and how in *A Thousand Plateaus* Deleuze and Guattari define the full BwO as a body populated with intensities (life) and multiplicities. The BwO does not oppose the organs: it opposes the *limits* of the organism and makes multiple connections that go beyond the organism's organization as it is traditionally defined. The organism is one of the great organizing principles, situated on the molar or segmental level of the world, which Deleuze and Guattari call the strata. Deleuze and Guattari are concerned with three great strata: the organism, significance, and subjectification: "You will be organized, you will be an organism, you will articulate your body—otherwise you're just depraved. You will be signifier and signified, interpreter and interpreted—otherwise you're just deviant. You will be a subject, nailed down as one, a subject of the enunciation recoiled into a subject of the statement—otherwise you are just a tramp."[13]

The BwO opposes the strata and is part of the political lines as distinguished by Deleuze and Guattari, which also were discussed in Chapters 2 and 3. All becomings and the BwOs are lines of flight situated on a molecular level. One could say that the BwO is the zero degree of the body, where every body part has its potential: "a thousand tiny sexes" that on a molecular level can make infinite connections and combinations. These combinations can be made not only between different human bodies but also in relation to plants, animals, and other "bodies": becoming-plant, becoming-animal, becoming-wind, becoming-music. The BwO is not an easy thing to achieve, and Deleuze and Guattari see the dangers of this creative act. In Fassbinder's *In a Year of 13 Moons*, for instance, the BwO is missed. Instead of a full and rich BwO through which many intensities can pass, an emptied BwO is also possible: the body of the drug addict, the masochist, and the hypochondriac are such bodies that cannot produce any intensities and flows but disappear in a black hole. This is also the reason it is necessary to keep some elements of the organism, some forms of the strata. "You do not reach the BwO, and its plane of consistency, by wildly destratifying," say Deleuze and Guattari. One must keep enough (small) rations of subjectivity to respond to dominant reality. Because dominant categories in reality probably will never disappear, it is important to confront those categories and to deal with them; but processes of becoming happen in that same reality: they slip through and in-between the categories. It is therefore important to consider construction of the subject both on the molar level of strata (identities, segments, and categories) and the molecular level of becomings (the "breaking" or "opening up" of the subject).

Alice's Becoming-Woman

After explaining that all becomings take place at a molecular level, Deleuze and Guattari state that all becomings start with becoming-woman. This is an intriguing remark, one that has given rise to many questions. I will look again at some of these questions that have been asked by feminists through the figure of Alice. Apart from the notion of pure becoming, Alice also shows us more specifically what becoming-woman could mean. Deleuze and Guattari see becoming-woman as a process of microfemininity that can take place in both female and male bodies (as well as in all other sorts of bodies). Becoming-woman is basically a question of the body: the body that is stolen in order to give it a fixed organization of the organs. Because it is first of all the body of the *girl* (Alice is seven years and six months old) that is stolen, it is also through her body that it has to be regained:

The question is not, or not only, that of the organism, history, and subject of enunciation that opposes masculine to feminine in the great dualism machines. The question is fundamentally that of the body—the body they steal from us in order to fabricate opposable organisms. This body is stolen first from a girl: stop behaving like that, you're not a girl anymore, you're not a tomboy, etc. The girl's becoming is stolen first in order to impose a history, or prehistory upon her. The boy's turn comes next, but it is by using the girl as an example, by pointing to the girl as the object of his desire, that an opposed organism, a dominant history is fabricated for him too. The girl is the first victim, but she must also serve as an example and a trap. That is why, conversely, the reconstruction of the body as a Body without Organs, the anorganism of the body, is inseparable from a becoming-woman, or the production of a molecular woman.[14]

Deleuze and Guattari see becoming-woman not as the growing of the girl into a woman, the apprehension of the girl about what it is to be a "woman" according to the segmental categories that are imposed. On the contrary, it is not the girl who becomes woman, but it is "the becoming-woman that produces the universal girl." Besides, Alice's in-between status (between a child and a woman, no longer a little girl, not yet a woman) makes her the perfect figure to reveal the possibilities of becoming.[15] Becoming-woman is fundamentally a question of transforming and liberating the body and desire in multiple ways; it is the beginning of the creation of BwOs.

Félix Guattari explains in an interview the concept of becoming-woman as a struggle in relation to their bodies that women share with male homosexuals and transvestites. He says about the relation to the body that woman has preserved the surfaces of the body, a bodily pleasure much greater than that of man, who has concentrated on his phallic libido:

[Man] has concentrated his libido on—one can't even say his penis—on domination, on rupture of ejaculation: "I possessed you," "I had you." Look at all the expressions like these used by men: "I screwed you," "I made her." It is no longer the totality of the body's surfaces that counts, it's just this sign of power: "I dominated you," "I marked you." This obsession with power is such that man ultimately denies himself all sexuality. On the other hand, in order to exist as body he is obliged to beg his sexual partner to transform him a bit into a woman or a homosexual.[16]

Guattari does not want to say that homosexuals are women. He wants to indicate a common situation in respect to the body, which he (and Deleuze) indicates with the term *becoming-woman*. Seen in this way, becoming-woman means something very different from Simone de Beauvoir's famous claim that one is not born a woman but becomes a woman.

Becoming-Woman in Feminism: Alice Doesn't?

Molar Anxiety

The becoming of woman in a Beauvoirian sense means the construction of woman according to social, patriarchal standards. In this respect, de Beauvoir represents the constructionist pole in feminism, which states that all differences between men and women are socially imposed, even though they are basically equal and neutral at birth. The opposite position in feminism is to argue that one is born as a woman, which often, although not necessarily, leads to essentialist views. This binary distinction between essential femaleness and constructed femininity also is formulated as the distinction between sex and gender, which also has been discussed at length in feminism. Although the current debates are complex and contain many nuances, these two poles still represent traps that feminism finds hard to avoid. Segmental and binary thought is difficult to give up, but because most feminist struggles take place on the segmental lines of the strata, it is sensible and even necessary to confront binaries and inequalities. Another reason binary ideas about the body persist is that, despite their molar *political* struggles for the female body, as Moira Gatens argues in her book *Imaginary Bodies*, feminists have not done much work on a conceptual level: "In the absence of such theory it is culturally dominant conceptions of the body that, unconsciously, many feminists work with."[17] Gatens, too, suggests going back to Spinoza to start this conceptual work on the body. Before looking at some of her proposals, it is useful to address a recurrent feminist suspicion about the concept of becoming-woman, as also expressed by Dorothea Olkowski in *Gilles Deleuze and the Ruin of Representation*.[18]

Rosi Braidotti and Elisabeth Grosz, two of the first feminists to show interest in Deleuze, demonstrate that rhizomatics, cartographies, and other Deleuzian strategies are useful to feminists; but the concept of becoming-woman often is seen as a masculine appropriation of the feminist struggle. As Braidotti states, "Deleuze gets caught in the contradiction of postulating a general 'becoming-woman' that fails to take into account the historical and epistemological specificity of the female feminist standpoint. A theory of difference that fails to take into account sexual difference leaves me, as a feminist critic, in a state of skeptical perplexity."[19] The greatest anxiety expressed by these feminists concerning the notion of becoming-woman is fear of the disappearance of "woman" in favor of the larger category, "man." In the conclusion of her article on becoming-woman, Elisabeth Grosz is particularly wary of the masculine appropriation of the feminist cause. This suspicion is due to the culturally dominant conceptions of the body mentioned by Moira Gatens. When Rosi Braidotti says, "I am not willing to relinquish the signifier," and when Elisabeth Grosz sees the becoming-woman as "merely a stage or stepping stone in a broader struggle" that would obliterate woman's struggle, they are reasoning within the culturally dominant theories of the body that indeed have proved to be unfriendly to women or to any other minority.[20] It is now recognized, however, that Deleuze fully supports women's struggle on the level of molar politics; that is, he does not want to erase "woman" as a segmental category (after all, small portions of segments are quite necessary).[21] On the segmental line, difference can be conceived only in binary oppositions (to which sexual difference belongs as well), which is precisely the kind of difference beyond which Deleuze wants to go. To liberate desire, and to liberate the whole body, sexual difference should be overcome and desire should not be conceived in terms of lack and objects of desire (like in psychoanalysis) but in terms of positive connections that can be made with every part of the body.

Deleuze does stress the importance of creating the basic conditions for a positive desire: "Those whose lack is real have no possible plane of consistence which would allow them to desire. . . . Even individually, the construction of the plane is a politics, it necessarily involves a 'collective,' collective assemblages, a set of social becomings."[22] Clearly, the segmental political feminist struggle is necessary to create conditions for the creation of desire, for actualizations of becomings. Nevertheless, when Deleuze speaks about becoming-woman, he does not think about bodies in terms of signifier and signified, nor does he speak about stages that follow in succession. Rather, Deleuze's Spinozian concept of the body allows more fluid adaptations and encounters of forces that differ from context to context. At every moment, multiple political lines are in play. Becoming-woman is situated on a molecular level, which allows many connections and encounters that go beyond any sexual, racial, or other distinction and that slip through segmental categories:

Thus girls do not belong to an age, group, sex, order, or kingdom: they slip in everywhere, between orders, acts, ages, sexes: they produce *n* molecular sexes on the line of flight in relation to the dualism machines they cross right through. The only way to get outside dualism is to be between, to pass between, the intermezzo. . . . The girl is like a block of becoming that remains contemporaneous to each opposable term, man, woman, child, adult. . . . It is thus necessary to conceive of a molecular woman's politics that slips into molar confrontations, and passes under or through them.[23]

One could say that Deleuze wants to prevent feminists from getting blocked in a "new" (albeit more positively or powerfully evaluated) segment, for segments impose "fixities" and do not allow flexible intensities and flows. Constructionism and essentialism seem to be precisely such (unconscious) blockings.

Teresa de Lauretis is one of the feminists who have defended the constructionist paradigm.[24] In her book *Alice Doesn't*, she argues against the power of the paternalistic master language, which she sees as represented by the figure of Humpty Dumpty in *Through the Looking-Glass*. On a molecular level of becomings (which is the level where Alice's adventures take place), however, when Alice meets grumpy Humpty Dumpty, she does not meet her master, as de Lauretis suggests. Would a master look like an egg ("The egg got larger and larger, and more and more human . . . Alice saw clearly that it was Humpty Dumpty himself.")? Would a master take seriously playful words like "Jabberwocky," "'twas brillig" and "borogove"? Would he propose playful ideas like "un-birthday presents"? Rather, Humpty Dumpty is a BwO. His remark that, if he were Alice, he would have left off at the age of seven, is an "invitation" to her becoming-woman as Deleuze understands it, not an erasure of femininity as a category.[25] On a molar political level, de Lauretis is right to struggle against "the master's language," and in that sense Alice's refusal to accept dominant language is necessary. Humpty Dumpty, however, does not represent this language. De Lauretis also presents an interesting strategy for undertaking this refusal of dominant language. Her proposal to look at lived experience and Peircian semiotics, thus providing room for concepts such as *habitas* and dynamic changes in those habits mediated through the body, is useful. First, it is necessary to reconsider the body itself. De Lauretis's strategy in *Technologies of Gender* of distinguishing sex and gender is based on a dualistic conception of the body: the body seen as a neutral surface that can be inscribed with all kinds of historically different discourses presupposes an ahistorical mind/body split.

Imaginary Bodies: Spinoza's Situated Bodies

In *Imaginary Bodies*, Moira Gatens criticizes the sex/gender distinction in feminist discourse; however, she does not fall back into an essentialism that sees the human subject determined by biology, nor does she want to efface the influence of social and political environments. Instead, Gatens argues for recognition of at least two kinds of bodies: the male and the female.[26] Different bodies have quite different personal and social significance when acted out by the male subject on the one hand and the female on the other, says Gatens. With this statement, however, Gatens is not claiming any commitment to a fixity or essence of the social significance of bodily functions. To understand this apparent paradox, Gatens, inspired by Foucault, proposes the concept of the lived body situated in a network of specific and historical discourses about the body: the "imaginary body." It is not a question of either/or but of a simultaneous understanding of the biological and the imaginary and historical body: "I would suggest that 'masculinity' and 'femininity' correspond at the level of the imaginary body to 'male' and 'female' at the level of biology. It bears repetition that this statement does not imply a fixed essence to 'masculine' and 'feminine' but rather a historical specificity."[27] It is important to see that historical specificity is not regarded as a determining factor (as in constructionist feminism, which also found inspiration in Foucault), but as a set of conditions for certain ideas about the body to be actualized.

On a conceptual level, Gatens argues for a Spinozian account of the body and its relation to social life, politics, and ethics that does not depend on the dualism that has dominated traditional modern Western philosophy. Because this Spinozian body is in constant interchange with its environment and is radically open to its surroundings, it never can be viewed as a finished product. With the help of Spinoza, Gatens creates a conceptual framework for the body that looks differently at bodies and human subjects on a segmental level. It should be clear that, if Gatens has "updated" Spinoza to understand the political and ethical situation of the (female) body in a nondualistic manner, Deleuze proposes in a different way a contemporary Spinozistic view: the BwO as a resisting body, a body that escapes from any segmental politics.

Thus, there is a shifting of attention from macro/molar bodies (Gatens's sexed and situated bodies) to more micro/molecular bodies (Deleuze's BwOs). The two bodies thus are located on different political lines. One could say that the macrobody creates the conditions for the microbody to become. The one cannot do without the other, although Deleuze does argue that the microbody and molecular politics will be increasingly important.[28] Gatens emphasizes a double strategy. In her article "Through a Spinozist Lens: Ethology, Difference, Power" she states: "We need to engage with the sexual norms of our culture on two fronts: the macropolitical *and* the micropolitical. We need to address both the plane which organizes our possibilities into molar political realities *and* experiment with micropolitical possibilities that may be created on the plane of immanence. We do not have to choose between either this or that: we may say feminist politics is this *and* that."[29]

Gatens uses the term *ethology* for the ethics of the molecular, the micropolitics concerned with the "in-between" of subjects, manifesting itself in a range of becomings. Ethology, according to Spinoza, is the study of the relations of speed and slowness, of the capacities for affecting and being affected that characterize each thing. Seen from an ethologic perspective, (molar) political questions can be put in a different light. Gatens gives the example of the violence of rape. "On an ethological reading, no individual is *essentially* penetrable or *essentially* impenetrable. The power of one body to dominate another through penetration is dependent on the total context of both. . . . Masculinity and femininity may be read as clusters of specific affects and powers of bodies which are organized around an exclusive binary form (male/female) through various complex assemblages: legal, medical, linguistic and so on."[30] In Chapter 2, I mentioned how Gatens creates, for instance, an ethologic analysis of rape where rape can be seen as a specific "technique" whereby sexual difference is created and maintained through violence and through a sexualized female body defined as "wound." "Rape script" does not need to be an eternal prescription, however. It would be possible to "rewrite the script" perhaps by refusing to take it seriously and treating it as a farce, perhaps by resisting the physical passivity that it directs us to adopt.[31]

Cyborg Alice's Body Without Organs

The increasingly technologic and audiovisual environment of the late twentieth century certainly has its effects on the human body. To understand better why Deleuze thinks that microbodies and politics will become increasingly important, it is useful to look at the work of Donna Haraway, who deals specifically with the "new world order": issues of a technoscientific nature.[32] Her work displays considerable insight into how science and technology serve as cultural discourses that are strongly related to both our lived and imaginary bodies. Although Haraway does not philosophize the body (nor desire) as such, and looks from a scientific and feminist perspective on the human body in contemporary culture, her ideas could be defined as Spinozian, and the image of the hybrid cyborg she proposes is close to Deleuze's BwO in its denial of traditional borders of the subject (between man/woman, culture/nature, human/animal, human/machine, and visible/invisible).[33] One could consider the cyborg as a critical pair of eyes (or should we say a rhizomatic brain?) that looks in many directions at the same time, trying to negotiate between multiplicities and to live with paradoxes.

One of these paradoxes is raised by Haraway's own concept of the cyborg in respect to sexual difference. The fact that Haraway has a feminist agenda seems to be in contradiction to the very idea of the cyborg, which defies all traditional boundaries, including the boundaries between the sexes. Toward the end of her manifesto, she states that "cyborgs might consider more seriously the partial, fluid, sometimes aspect of sex and sexual embodiment. Gender might not be global identity after all, even if it has profound historical breadth and depth." On the other hand, Haraway declares on several occasions that the cyborg is clearly feminine: "My cyborg is a girl."[34] Now that we have learned from Alice's adventurous becomings in Wonderland that paradoxes are always both directions at the same time, it is also possible to understand the paradox of the cyborg. The cyborg is situated precisely at the point where Gatens's imaginary sexed body and Deleuze's BwO meet and are both true simultaneously.

Haraway's cyborg is a girl, not a woman, and this of course reminds us again of Alice. Haraway herself raises the figure of "cyborg Alice" when she talks about the boundary-transgression between the physical and nonphysical, the visible and the invisible in respect to technology and machines that have become so small we hardly notice them:

The new machines are so clean and light. Their engineers are sun worshippers mediating a new scientific revolution associated with the night dream of postindustrial society. The diseases evoked by these clean machines are "no more" than the minuscule coding changes of an antigen in the immune system, "no more" than the experience of stress. The nimble fingers of "Oriental" women, the old fascination of little Anglo-Saxon Victorian girls with doll's houses, women's enforced attention to the small take on quite new dimensions in this world. There might be a cyborg Alice taking account of these new dimensions.[35]

Microscopic images, nanotechnology, and the molecular are, for Haraway, increasingly important. The renewed interest in women's traditional attention to the micro and invisible dimensions of the world is in her view an important strategy to develop for grasping the possible dangers of new machines and techniques of segmentation and domination. Like Alice, the cyborg is situated on a molecular level, creating becomings, connections, and affinity groups (the cyborg chooses on the basis of affinity, not on the basis of identity and origin, which is anyway undermined in politics of becomings). On the other hand, the cyborg also can act at a segmental political level as a tool in concrete political situations, creating a "war machine" or a "line of flight." Haraway gives the example of the spiral dancing in Santa Rita jail (linking guards and arrested antinuclear demonstrators in the Alameda County jail in California in the early 1980s).

On a segmental political level, however, both Haraway and Deleuze show an extreme wariness of modern technoscientific society. On the one hand, this society makes molecular and minority movements increasingly possible, concrete, and even necessary. On the other hand, both thinkers see the spectral return of old molar structures that are (re)gaining more and more power. Therefore, Haraway distinguishes two types of cyborgs: first, the cyborgs that act in the name of universal defense and peace, impose a final grid of control on the planet ("the Star Wars apocalypse"), and lead to the final appropriation of women's bodies; from another perspective, cyborgs can create a world of lived social and bodily reality "in which people are not afraid of their joint kinship with animals and machines, not afraid of permanently partial identities and contradictory standpoints."[36] Haraway's informatics of domination and Deleuze's control society are concepts that indicate how, within these molecular environments, information and control form the "new" molar systems, boundaries, and hierarchies of our society.[37] The cyborg (on the molar and molecular levels) and the BwO (on the line of flight but not unaware of the molar segments) are tools for resisting too much control, too singular and dogmatic visions. They are concepts that allow negotiation between old and new possibilities and old and new dangers in respect to a late capitalist technoscientific world order.

In any case, Deleuze's concept of becoming-woman and Haraway's cyborgs are full of paradoxes. As Jerry Aline Flieger argues in her article "Becoming-Woman: Deleuze, Schreber and Molecular Identification," thinking in paradoxes, or perhaps schizophrenia, as I called it in a different context in the previous chapter, may be precisely the strategy in which feminism and Deleuze can meet: "Deleuze and feminism may seem to be at odds, from the perspective of the concerns of real women. Like the orchid and the wasp, the relation of Deleuzian thought and feminist thought may be 'mapped' or interwoven in a kind of productive disjunction. It is perhaps neither a matter of window-dressing, masquerade and cosmetic solutions, nor of conflict and irreconcilable differences, but a matter of paradox."[38]

In Chapter 2, I discussed Carol Clover's observations of how in horror cinema (the bodies of) men "open-up" and change in a rezoning process where both men and women move toward each other, both changing and moving to a zone of proximity at the end. Clover also demonstrated that it is through the extreme behavior of the female body that men can rezone their own bodies. It is now possible to conclude that this can be related to the concept of becoming-woman. Clover's occult and slasher heroines perhaps could be considered "Alices" in cinematic horror land. Shifting now from Alice as a conceptual persona of becoming-woman to an aesthetic figure, my next question is whether it is possible to find any other paradoxic "cyborg Alices" in modern cinema?

Alice in Cinematic Wonderland

Aurélia's Becoming-Imperceptible

As I mentioned at the beginning of this chapter, BwOs and processes of becoming are related to a concept of time that is invaded by both past and future at once. So to find cyborg Alices in cinema, I must return to the concept of time. It is known that in his cinema books Deleuze distinguishes two ways of expressing time: *indirectly* as a representation, through the movement-image, and directly as a presentation, through the time-image. Another way to define these two concepts of time can be found in *The Logic of Sense*, where Deleuze also conceptualizes two forms of time: Chronos and Aion. The movement-image constitutes time in its empiric form, the course of time: "a successive present in an extrinsic relation of before and after, so that the past is a former present, and the future a present to come."[39] This time coincides exactly with Deleuze's description of Chronos, the time of interlocking presents of past, present, and future. Time also can be "out of joint," as in the time-image of modern cinema and in the time described as Aion. In Aion, and in the time-image, Chronos is sick: the present is constantly invaded and eclipsed by other layers of time, past or future. It is a time of becoming, which does not so much follow empiric reality as have a profound connection with thought: the time-image forces one to think the unthinkable, the impossible, the illogical, and the irrational. Deleuze demonstrated at length how these time-images have come about and what different shapes these images can take. Because Alice's body is a body of becoming confused by the experience of time, it is logical that an encounter with her audiovisual sisters is likely to take place in a modern time-image.

As I mentioned before, one of the characteristics indicating a crisis of the movement-image is that the characters no longer respond to their situations according to sensorimotor schemata. Instead, they become more like spectators themselves, seers and observers that wander about, not wanting or unable to be fixed in a certain place. In this sense, Wim Wender's *Alice in the Cities* (1974) presents us clearly with a time-image in which journalist Philip Winter is helped in his "becoming-woman" by the little girl Alice, with whom he travels through Holland and Germany to find the girl's grandmother. The entire film is invaded by a fear of losing one's identity (and by the "fear of this fear"). Alice, who has not found her identity yet, and the journalist, who has lost his identity, are in the process of "becoming-woman," opening up to new experiences through traveling. The film has an open ending (the man and the girl lean happily out of the open window of a fast-moving train), and there is some hope of (re)finding their identity (finding again one's mother or home country). It remains ambiguous whether this (re)found identity would put a hold on the liberating process of "becoming-woman." We cannot be sure whether this Alice will stay an "eternal girl" or nevertheless will grow up as a woman. In fact, emphasis on the importance of (molar) identity and the fear of losing it entail that we probably should see *Alice in the Cities* as a temporary sickness of Chronos. Different visions on the time of becoming and becoming-woman are presented in Marguerite Duras's *Aurélia Steiner* films and in Sally Potter's cinematic version of Virginia Woolf's *Orlando*.

The most extreme expression of the time-image in respect to absolute and pure becoming is perhaps Duras's *Aurélia Steiner* films. All the films of Marguerite Duras are time-images full of becomings where no character seems to be sure of its own identity. In her films, image and sound autonomously invade each other's space, making everything undecidable and moving in many directions at the same time. Duras thus achieves the characteristic undecidability of the time-image (between actual and virtual, real and imaginary, true and false) by separating sound and image, giving them a free, indirect relationship. Deleuze indicates that in the beginning of her cinematic work Duras was a great filmmaker of the house, "not simply because women 'inhabit' houses in every sense, but because passions 'inhabit' women."[40] Clearly, Deleuze is referring here to woman's relationship to her body, which in her own house she can experience more freely than in public and society life.

Nathalie Granger, discussed in the previous chapter in relation to the class of violence, is certainly one of the most beautiful examples of Duras's "house-ground" films. Duras, however, leaves the relative safety of the house and goes to the beach and the sea to find other dimensions of becomings: the personal becomes increasingly impersonal and universal in Duras's "any-space-whatevers." Starting with *La Femme du Gange* (1973) and *India Song* (1974), her films also become less and less inhabited by visible and recognizable characters.[41] Aurélia Steiner is no more than a shadow on a bridge over the Seine or just a rock in the ocean. She is an aesthetic figure that expresses a becoming-woman to the point of becoming-imperceptible.

Aurélia Steiner has three written versions: *Aurélia Steiner (Melbourne)*, *Aurélia Steiner (Vancouver)*, and *Aurélia Steiner (Paris)*.[42] The first two versions have been made into films. Aurélia Steiner is a fictive (but ever so real) Jewish girl who has a diasporic body (living in Melbourne, Vancouver, and Paris). She is always the same age: eighteen years old (still a girl), although Aurélia Paris is seven years old (like Alice). Aurélia Steiner could be seen as the sad sister of Alice in Wonderland. Whereas *Alice in Wonderland* marks a beginning of new ways of conceiving the world (love and life) and of making connections, Aurélia Steiner reaches pure impossibility (love and death). The film *Aurélia Steiner (Vancouver)* reaches the limits of expressing becomings. Here it is clear how the becoming-woman can lead to becoming-imperceptible: the images contain no more bodies; they have all evaporated into empty spaces of rocks, sand, and water. Although Duras's voice-over reads her written texts, the writer/filmmaker becomes Aurélia, and Aurélia becomes imperceptible and impersonal, which is precisely the point of becoming. As Jerry Aline Flieger explains:

For Deleuze, it is a change in ways of being and thinking that will effect a true "becoming," rather than perpetuating habits of thought that support "majoritarian" business as usual. Deleuze asserts that "Man constitutes himself as a gigantic memory, through the position of a central point," a monument to his own centrality, while the minoritarian or molecular is anti-memory. Thus the point of any becoming is, in a sense, to lose face, to become imperceptible, in order to counteract the very notion of individual stature.[43]

With the figure of Aurélia Steiner, Duras presents a molecular counter-memory. She creates and at the same time "effaces" Aurélia by describing the sea: its movements, its play with the changing light and colors evoke the image, the name and the "H/history" of Aurélia. Through visionary observing and describing, she (Duras/Aurélia) expresses the incomprehensible pain of wars (the horror of the holocaust: Aurélia's parents died in a camp) and at the same time pays a deep respect to life and love (Aurélia was born; Aurélia has an anonymous lover whom she desires with all her body). Because Aurélia Steiner has this capacity of becoming other than herself, she can be granted cyborg *avant-la-lettre* quality. Aurélia Steiner's "body" is certainly a BwO, but Aurélia Steiner also shows the way in which becoming-woman is "world-historical" and not so much a case of individual psychology. *Aurélia Steiner* is therefore also an example of fabulation in the modern political film: through her stories, Aurélia Steiner/Marguerite Duras helps to invent a people (in this case the Jewish people that are "missing" because of the diaspora), paradoxically by becoming-imperceptible.[44] *Aurélia Steiner* demonstrates that the point of molecular becoming-woman is to open up and to "lose face" in favor of an impersonal counter-memory. The feeling of impossibility prevails in *Aurélia Steiner*. As Duras herself states: "The film *Aurélia Steiner Vancouver* was impossible. It was made. The film is admirable because it does not even try to correct that impossibility. It accompanies that impossibility, it walks by its side."[45] Again, we see here a paradox: centered on the aesthetic figure of Aurélia Steiner, the film was impossible, and yet it was possible—it was made.

Duras's film is a limit-image expressing the limits of becoming and perhaps even the limits of expressing in images, words, and sounds. Many contemporary films negotiate much more between movement, and time-images, between Chronos and Aion, between being woman or man and becoming (woman or other). Sally Potter's *Orlando* is an extremely beautiful negotiating voyage, which in a way is driven by forces opposite those displayed in *Alice in the Cities*: it is not the fear of losing a fixed identity and the longing to refind home but the desire to lose identity and to leave the home/house.

Orlando's Becoming-Woman

In her article "The Woman in Process," Catherine Driscoll considers the way in which both Deleuze and Kristeva discuss "the girl" in the work of Virginia Woolf:

Woolf produces this "girl" as an escape from Oedipalised territories and, as *Orlando* (1928) exemplifies, from any other fixing of the girl in relation to sexual difference concretized as a binary opposition located in either the body or identity. There is no girl in *Orlando*, only a boy who becomes a woman. While Kristeva would see this as symptomatic of the girl's traumatic struggle with the paternal symbolic, the girl might otherwise be seen, as Deleuze and Guattari infer in *A Thousand Plateaus*, as a name for *Orlando's* process of becoming-woman. . . . Gender entraps desire or, rather, claims to trap desire: a territorialisation shaping desire into a signifying and signifiable field. Becoming-woman is a deterritorialisation of the organised body precisely because it uses gender against that organising signification.[46]

The film *Orlando* is interesting because it makes clear that to experience the liberating forces of becoming-woman and the ways in which gender identity might escape from the codes that constitute the subject, Chronos must be confused and give way to Aion.[47] In cinematic terms, the movement-image must be invaded by a time-image. Because Orlando lives for such a long time (four centuries), a whole range of real and imaginary bodies are presented before she reaches her BwO, her cyborg body. In the beginning of the film, we see Orlando as a sixteen-year-old boy walking under an oak tree, and we hear a voice-over saying, "It wasn't privilege he sought, but company." Immediately, we know that Orlando wants to connect, that he is full of positive desire, that he wants to love—in short, that he wants to become. We are in the year 1610, however, and imaginary bodies are strongly divided between (male) subjects and (female) objects. So when he falls in love with the Russian Sasha, he tells her, "You are mine." When she asks why, he answers, "Because I adore you!" not knowing that this is not the best way to connect, to love, and to become. When she leaves him, he feels betrayed and has his first disappointment. In the following centuries, he will be disappointed further by poetry and by politics. He is not able to find the right connections, heavily influenced as he is by historical circumstances that force him, as a man, to reduce his body to phallic power and to seek an object for his desire.

Then, sometime in the eighteenth century, Orlando changes his sex. For him/her, it does not make any difference: "Same person, no difference at all, just a different sex." Orlando has literally become a woman, which in this case is a first step to her "becoming-woman." Before she can really become-woman, however, some time will pass. First, Orlando will be disappointed again when she discovers that in society it makes a lot of difference whether you have a male or a female body. In the literary salon of 1750, the poets (Dryden, Swift, and Pope) give Orlando "poetic compliments," like "I consider woman to be a romantic animal who should be adorned in furs and feathers, pearls and diamonds" and "Woman is at best a contradiction, and frankly most women have no character at all." Furthermore, she faces lawsuits because as a woman she has no right to her property. The Archduke Harry offers to marry her (to save her property), but when she kindly refuses he shouts, "But I am England and you are mine. I adore you!" It is clear that in all the historical episodes of Orlando, Moira Gatens's remark about the relation between bodies and imaginary bodies is very important. Chronos imposes his weight on embodied subjects in their present, always determined by past and future. In the time of Chronos, Orlando first has to change sex to understand what it means when your body is stolen from you ("You are mine!").

Time changes, not only chronologically, but also in nature: Chronos becomes Aion, the molecular time of becoming. The film expresses this change. When Archduke Harry claims possession of Orlando as "Pink, Pearl, Perfection of her sex," she goes on the run: this literal "line of flight" leads her straight into the labyrinth in her garden. Here time also gets labyrinthically confused ("out of joint") and becomes more a time of becoming. As Deleuze remarks: "Aion is the eternal truth of time: *pure empty form of time*, which has freed itself of its present corporeal content. . . . It is perhaps all the more dangerous, more labyrinthine, and more tortuous for that reason."[48] Because Aion and the time-image are so related to modernity, it makes perfect sense that, after escaping from the garden, Orlando literally falls into modern times: the nineteenth century, with its modern technologies and means of transport (Orlando is astonished by the railways). It is now that Orlando finds her company, her connection: Shelmerdine. Out of the blue, he enters her life as a prince on a black horse. And "Within two seconds at the utmost, they had guessed everything of any importance about each other."[49] The (molecular) vibrations between the two are so strong that they themselves are surprised; it even makes them wonder about each other's "real" sex. Virginia Woolf puts it in her novel in the following way: "'You are a woman, Shel!,' she cried. 'You are a man, Orlando!,' he cried. . . . For each was so surprised at the quickness of the other's sympathy, and it was to each such a revelation that a woman could be as tolerant and free-spoken as a man, and a man as strange and subtle as a woman, that they had to put that matter to the proof at once."[50]

In the film, the dialogue is slightly different but boils down to the same surprise about the discovery of the nonfixity of (imaginary) bodies. Clearly, the encounter with Shelmerdine signifies for both lovers the liberation of desire and of their bodies, the escape from coded gender patterns. Sexuality is one of the ways in which molecular becomings take place, as Deleuze and Guattari stated in *A Thousand Plateaus*. Also, the image itself will slowly change from a movement-image into a time-image; from representing time and historical bodies into the capturing of something more powerful, escaping the presence of Chronos in the breathtaking last image of the film. Before coming to that, Virginia Woolf's ideas about time are worth considering as well.

Virginia Woolf's book ends in 1928, the time when she finished her novel. Throughout her work, time plays an important role. Like Deleuze she sees two different times. What she calls the "time of Big Ben" (in *Mrs. Dalloway*) is comparable to the chronologic, measurable time of Chronos. Besides that time, she experiences what she calls "the other clock"—immeasurable, undifferential time in which the passage of years seems to occupy merely a few seconds: Aion. It is this time that is always already virtually present in *Orlando* but only actualized by the end of both the book and the film. In the book Virginia Woolf writes:

. . . In that moment of darkness, when her eyelids flickered, she was relieved of the pressure of the present. There was something strange in the shadow that the flicker of her eyes cast, something which . . . is always absent from the present—whence its terror, its nondescript character—something one trembles to pin through the body with a name and call beauty, for it has no body, is as a shadow without substance or quality of its own, yet has the power to change whatever it adds itself to.[51]

This is clearly an experience of Aion, an experience of pure becoming. In the film, the present has been updated. First we see a pregnant Orlando walking through the battlefields of the Second World War. Given the significance of this historical fact for our experiencing and expressing of time in cinema, this is not insignificant, even though this particular image is still a representing movement-image. This image is a long way from expressing the becoming-imperceptible of Duras's *Aurélia Steiner*. Here the image of war and battlefields demonstrates an important historical circumstance that nonetheless has had profound influences. Then we see Orlando in the 1990s. She has lost her house; her former property has become a museum where guided tours are given. Orlando visits the house but shows no regret about this loss. Instead, she rides a motorcycle, becomes a wanderer, a seer. She also has a little daughter. In the novel, Orlando's child is a boy, but Sally Potter made this character a girl. Of course, this girl reminds us again of Alice and emphasizes the importance of becoming-woman in *Orlando*. Finally, in the last images of the film, the time-image, the time of becoming and Aion, is reached. Again, we see Orlando sitting under the oak tree, now filmed by a video camera held by her daughter. The images the girl makes are shaky and irregular; they capture first some grass and then the face of Orlando. It is like stammering, not in language but in images . . . "Why are you sad?" asks the little girl. "I am not, I am happy," answers Orlando, directing her daughter's attention to an angel in the sky, who starts singing.[52] Then we see Orlando's face in close-up, we hear the angel singing: "Neither woman nor a man. We are joined, we are one, with a human face. I am free of the past and the future that beckons me. I am being born and I am dying. At last I am free."

It is Aion's time that is sung, free from the past and future that beckon the present of Chronos. And the close-up of the face is an affection-image that opens up to the possibility of becoming: eternal, without feeling or expressing the burden of any codes or strata like gender, class, or race. The presence of the angel is perfectly logical given the sense of becoming of this performance, the molecular quality of the music, the voice and the images. Orlando is thirty-six years old and finally free, finding the eternal girl in herself. The history of her body is a Spinozian history, the changes in time go from Chronos to Aion, and the images turn from representation to direct presentation of what it means to become-woman and hence to become free in a Spinozian sense of the word. As Deleuze explains in *Spinoza: Philosophie Pratique*, being free, according to Spinoza, is being able to accept all the changes that occur during one's lifetime, seeing that they are necessary according to an internal logic (but not strictly according to a fixed identity). Furthermore, freedom means coming into possession of our "power of acting." It is a matter of our *conatus* being determined by adequate ideas from which active affects follow. It is having a desire that relates to what we know to be most important in life. Human beings are not born free. According to Spinoza, the way to understanding (understanding the causes of sadness) and the way to freedom are ethical undertakings, a process that is inherently incomplete.[53] Orlando's story is not finished; she will continue to strive for her persistence and continue to learn, but she has discovered how to increase her power to act and to creating joyful affects. Orlando is Alice's wise sister.

Lost Children or Lost Innocence?

Aurélia and Orlando could be seen as cyborg Alices *avant-la-lettre*; however, with the increasing technologic dimensions of our environment, as hinted by Haraway's remark, the appeal of Alice in Wonderland in a cybernetic and technoscientific context seems to be growing. Not only Deleuze has been challenged by her adventures. Neurologists talk about the "Red Queen" effect in the brain and explain paradoxes through the work of Lewis Carroll. In Robert Gilmore's *Alice in Quantumland*, Alice passes not through the looking glass but through the television screen and becomes as small as a particle. Here she learns the uncertainty principle and many other aspects of quantum physics. Also in cyberspace, Alice regularly appears on Web sites or in discussions about the digital revolution; recently, Alice met her robot sister, Celia. In Jeff Noon's novel *Automated Alice*, nineteenth-century Alice time traveled to the end of the twentieth century and discovers how the world has changed and become increasingly impregnated with technology.[54] Apart from the useful knowledge that cyborg Alice can pass on to us (creating more understanding, for instance, about the invisible dimensions of the world, as Haraway saw her relevance), what else is to be learned from cyborg Alice, especially for women?

In *The City of Lost Children*, we encounter yet another contemporary sister of Alice. This time, she is called Miette (the French word for crumb, indicating again the microdimension). Miette lives in a technologic world, full of dangerous cyborgs (the kind of cyborgs that form the informatics of domination or the society of control). They are the kind of cyborgs that appear regularly in popular science fiction films: fighting machines that act on command. These cyborgs are cyclopes with one mechanical eye. They act on the order of Master Krank (significantly the German word for sick), who kidnaps little children to steal their dreams. This is because Krank himself cannot dream and therefore is aging very fast; unfortunately for him, he scares all the children so much that they only have nightmares. Miette has organized herself with some other children (cyborgs are needy for connections) to escape from the cyclopes. She also becomes friends with One (meaning in English at the same time one singular person and many in general), the man whose little brother has been kidnapped by Krank and his cyclopes.[55] Together, they will fight the enemy and free the lost children of the city. The entire film is like a modern fairy tale, combining elements from both the nineteenth and twentieth centuries and also from Carroll's Alice world and the world of cyborgs.

On the level of the presentation of technology, this combination is quite clear. On the one hand, the city seems to be a nineteenth-century city marked by the industrial revolution: all machines are still heavy and large (no nanotechnology yet), and everything squeaks and cracks. There is also the atmosphere of the fair, with attractions like the flea circus, the Siamese twins, the strong man, and One, who can break heavy chains with his chest. On the other hand, hypermodern technology is everywhere: Krank turns out to be a product of a mad scientist and was created in a test tube. This scientist has cloned himself, so seven younger specimens are running around. Furthermore, there is a brain in a sort of aquarium that functions as a real character, and there are many references to molecular biology and genetic engineering. Also, on the level of the film production itself, *The City of Lost Children* combines old and new technology. On the one hand, the film seems to belong to the "cinema of attractions" from the early film period, full of visual spectacle.[56] On the other hand, the images are created largely by modern digital technologies, like microscopic enlarged images (a flea, a teardrop) and morphing techniques that create distortions and changes within the image (without montage).

Miette also seems to shift between the world of *Alice in Wonderland* and the cyborg world; the film makes many references to the book. When Miette has entered the strange world of Krank by crawling through a tiny hole (comparable to a rabbit hole), for instance, she does not know where to go: "Which way?" she asks. The main reference, however, is the reference to becoming smaller and larger. Miette often refers to the fact that children are not so small as they may seem. And vice versa: One, the big strong man, is actually still a child. The smaller–larger pair of becoming in *The City of Lost*

Children actually is replaced by a becoming younger–older. This kind of becoming is beautifully expressed in a scene where Miette enters the dream of Krank. After placing a neurotransmitter on her head, she encounters Krank in his virtual world. Very slowly, through morphing, the image itself changes: at first, almost invisibly, Miette grows and becomes older while Krank grows smaller and younger.[57] Here we can see a literal process of becoming, beautifully presented through a new visual technology. Finally, she is an old woman, and he is a toddler who is afraid of her. He now realizes what he does to the children and dies from this horrible insight. Miette has defeated him with his own means.

Miette's implication and participation in the technoscientific world make her a cyborg. All types of cyborgs use the same technologies, either to dominate or to resist. This also means that cyborg Alice has lost her nineteenth-century innocence. In feminist debates, this innocence often has been related to the moral superiority of the victim and the idea that the world would be a better place if it were populated only by women. This is a strategy that is radically rejected by cyborg feminism in the spirit of Haraway. Cyborgs are not innocent; they are formed by the same historical, technological, scientific, and social developments as everybody else. No one transcends this world with the possibility of moral judgment. We recognize here again the ideas on ethics beyond good and evil as expressed by Nietzsche and Spinoza. In a cyborg perspective, this ethics consists of taking responsibilities for the social connections made and the technologic tools used. Alice's Victorian context and the rules she has learned in her upbringing still suggest the possibility of moralism.[58]

What is liberating about *Alice in Wonderland* is that Alice discovers that the rules and good manners she has learned do not serve her at all in a world full of paradoxic becomings; but she remains at a distance from that world, observing everything in wonder. Miette learned a long time ago that she is part of the world, and to survive she steals and bribes. She has become "the leader of the pack," the children who have found clever ways to stay out of the hands of cyclopes, which cause nothing but sad affects. In the next chapter, more will be said about packs and lines of flight in becoming-animal. For now, it is important to see that cyborg Alice has changed in certain respects from her nineteenth-century version. Aurélia and Orlando have demonstrated that Alice has learned a lot during the last century. With Miette, she has definitely lost her innocence. It therefore comes as no surprise that Alice's twentieth-century robot sister, Celia, in Jeff Noon's novel *Automated Alice* takes a gun from her mechanical leg and shoots at an enemy that was about to destroy both Alice and Celia. Alice's time travel has changed her undeniably.[59]

Humans have always used technologic tools. Tools were formerly extensions of our bodies. Today's technologies enter our bodies and therefore also our minds. With his books on cinema, Deleuze demonstrates how technologically mediated images force us to think, how they penetrate our bodies and minds. The time-image shows that we can think time as Aion: although there are still molar strata, and chronologic time of Chronos certainly has not disappeared, time as becoming (implying multiplicities and BwOs) will be increasingly important. As Deleuze and Gatens demonstrated, Spinoza is the philosopher who can provide us with a powerful conceptual framework for these "new" bodies of becoming. Haraway's work indicates the relevance of these new perspectives in respect of our technoscientific culture. Deleuze once compared becomings, starting with the becoming-woman, to enchanting winds (*vents de sorcière*). Spinoza and Deleuze, Haraway, Woolf, Duras, and Jeunet and Caro are perhaps witches. They have given witch's brooms to Alices, Aurélias, Orlandos, and Miettes to show the contemporary cyborg subject (both man and woman) how to become-woman and fly/flee whenever possible or necessary. They are powerful film figures that have real effects on spectators. As Michelle Langford, in her article on female film figures in New German cinema, quotes from an Alexander Kluge film, "Roswitha feels an enormous power within her, and films have taught her that this power really exists."[60]

I want to conclude this chapter by looking at three other paradoxically powerful contemporary film heroines who can be seen as Alice-figures: Bess, Karen, and Selma from Lars von Trier's *Breaking the Waves, The Idiots*, and *Dancer in the Dark*. In focusing on *Dancer in the Dark*, in this final section, I again make an analysis of the assemblages around the aesthetic figure of Selma/Björk, arguing that Selma's becoming-woman is part of a world-historical assemblage.

Resisting Bodies Without Organs in Dogma Films: From Becoming-Woman to Becoming-Music

When he was a small boy, Lars von Trier read in a picture book the story of Goldenheart, an uncommonly kindhearted little girl who goes out in the woods on her own.[61] Along the road, she gives away everything she has. At the end of the story, she leaves the woods, completely naked and destitute. Nevertheless, she concludes that she managed all right anyway. Since von Trier read this story, it haunted him and led to what he calls his "Goldenheart Triology" of *Breaking the Waves*, *The Idiots*, and *Dancer in the Dark*. In all three films, the heroine is not so much an Alice in Wonderland as a modern Jeanne d'Arc who, with a strong belief in the voice of her heart, has the courage to go against the grain of common sense. In this respect, the heroines are becoming-woman (trying to free themselves from the existing codes) and again resemble Alice. von Trier's films are a sort of fairy tale in which woman has the role of martyr. Thus, in the first instance, his films seem to confirm all the stereotypes of feminine passivity and female sacrifice that feminists have been fighting for decades. If one considers these films as molar representations that invite women to identify with their suffering heroines, this is indeed true.

I would argue, however, that von Trier's films do not invite identification with their heroines, nor can they be seen as representations and role models. Von Trier's films are paradoxic events in which a complex assemblage of many elements together forms the strong effect of *pathos*. Possibly, von Trier draws his inspiration from Kierkegaard's concept of pathos as "suffering in favor of the idea of finiteness."[62] In any case, the capacities of von Trier's heroines to be affected and to affect, make them very powerful Spinozian and Nietzschean film figures. In this way, they become intercessors, true aesthetic figures of becoming-woman who have moved into a universe where things are valued differently and in this way criticize the order of things. As Bodil Marie Thomsen argues in her article on *The Idiots*, Danish (and International) artists are (with or without inspiration from Kierkegaard's concepts of pathos) currently concerned with an "entire way of sensing and confronting the world. The work becomes an expression of this confrontation and thus must also influence the viewer."[63]

So, instead of seeing Bess in *Breaking the Waves* merely as an awful cliché of the woman who gives up her life for her husband (she literally dies because she believes she can save her husband in that way, which in the end is what actually happens), we can also consider her a BwO. Through her actions, Bess resists the severe and ascetic morals of her village and through her passions affects the viewer in his or her own moral judgments. In this sense, Bess is a film figure with enormous paradoxic power that delivers a critique on what Buchanan calls "the world-historical." Frans-Willem Korsten argues in his article "Is Bess a Bike?" that by the end of the film, Bess's face has become an image of combat.[64] As Deleuze stated in *Essays Critical and Clinical*, "Combat is not a judgement of God, but the way to have done with God and with judgement. . . . Combat is a powerful, nonorganic vitality that supplements force with force, and enriches whatever it takes hold of."[65] The paradox in *Breaking the Waves* and in Bess as an aesthetic figure is that old values are sentimentalized while at the same time new ones are brought into existence. And "Bringing new things into existence requires a faith to break away from old ones, and a love that replaces the restrictions of judgement."[66] In other words, it requires a becoming-woman.

Karen in *The Idiots* is also a figure full of pathos. She is in a state of shock over the death of her child, and even though we know this only at the end of the film, from the beginning, it is clear that she is greatly affected. She joins a group of people who act like idiots, and the moment in which she "finds the idiot in herself" is one of the most powerful moments of the film. Here it becomes clear that not only will she act like an idiot, but she actually is a true idiot who is unable to pretend. So she is the only one of the group who dares to act like an idiot, breaking the codes in front of people they know in daily life, in her case, her family, who react to her in a very cold way. Bess and Karen are both aesthetic figures who demonstrate the power of "becoming-woman" through pathos. The same is the case with Selma in *Dancer in the Dark*.

Dancer in the Dark's form of content tells the melodramatic story of Selma, performed by Björk, a poor Czech immigrant in America in the 1960s who works in a metal factory. She suffers from a hereditary eye disease that gradually blinds her. To give her son an eye operation that will save him from a fate similar to hers, Selma saves all her money and takes on all kinds of extra jobs. Things take a grim turn when her neighbor Bill steals her money and she is forced to kill him. In the end, Selma even dies for her son, again the ultimate melodramatic female sacrifice. Looking at the form of content, *Dancer in the Dark* is a pure melodrama; however, von Trier mixed the form of content of the melodrama with a form of expression of the musical. In my view, it is because of this paradoxic mix that the strongest effect of pathos is created in the assemblages of the film. Let me elaborate.

A video clip by Björk, *It's Oh so Quiet,* will function as a starting point for my analysis of the musical scenes. In this clip, Björk pays homage to the classic Hollywood musicals of Fred Astair and Gene Kelly. An umbrella scene filmed from above also refers to the kaleidoscopic movements of Busby Berkeley movies. In the décor (the gas station/garage) and the props (the umbrellas) also can be sensed one of the few European musicals from the 1960s, Jacques Demy's *Les Parapluies de Cherbourg.* This self-reference of the musical is typical of the genre: many musicals are backstage stories or refer in other ways in a self-aware way to their production process. Although this video clearly has Björk's touches (particularly her "Alice-like" performance and the simplicity of her dress, which is less glamorous than in the Hollywood musical), the "feeling" of this clip also corresponds with the musical genre. "It's Oh so quiet and peaceful—until . . . you fall in love, zing boom," Björk sings. It is all about love, even though there is not one particular couple like in the boy-meets-girl stories of most musicals; and it is ecstatic and happy, entertaining and utopian, as Richard Dyer once described the musical in his article "Entertainment and Utopia."[67] The clip has musical-like energy and intensity in its song-and-dance routines and also the camerawork is "classic": the camera dances with the characters, using mainly (back)tracking or crane shots.

Slow and Fast: From Motor-Action into Optical and Sound Situation

What is special about this clip is the cinematography, especially the slow motions when Björk sings, "It's Oh so Quiet." One could see the alternations between the slow and fast rhythms of the music and the images as a compressed reference to the alternation between the story and the song-and-dance routines in normal musicals. To grasp this typical musical alternation, we have to look at what Deleuze calls the "zero degree" that is typical of musicals. In *The Time-Image,* Deleuze discusses the musical as a genre in a chapter about recollections and dreams.[68] In musicals, there is always a moment where the normal sensory-motor actions stop (the typical action of classical cinema—the movement-image—where characters find themselves in situations to which they will respond through their actions) and where the image transforms into what Deleuze calls a purely optical and sound situation. This change takes place progressively (or can be discovered only slowly in the depths of the image). Characters' actions change accordingly. As Deleuze puts it, "Their personal actions and movements are transformed by dance into movement of world which goes beyond the motor situation, only to return to it, etc."[69] The normal motor step becomes, sometimes imperceptibly, a dance step that goes beyond the personal action and touches on something bigger. I return to this "something bigger" in a moment, when I move from an aesthetic level to the conceptual level of *Dancer in the Dark*. The imperceptible moment between motor and dance step is what Deleuze calls a "zero degree," like "a hesitation, a discrepancy, a making late,"[70] before entering into another world, a dream world in the case of the musical. In these optical and sound situations of the musical scenes, the colors, sound, and forms become intense, and the dance becomes a part of the moving elements that have a dreamlike power and open up into another world.

The clip starts with what one could call a motor situation, a rather poor and sleazy-looking washroom where Björk is washing her face and the sound of the opening of the tap and the running water sounds hollow. As soon as she enters the garage, the image slows and the volume of the sound lowers. Here we get a zero degree before we enter the optical and sound situation of the dreamlike musical set, where the colors, sounds, and movements become intense. Because this is a video clip, not a feature-length musical, after the brief first scene, the sensory-motor situations are simply skipped altogether. We witness a quick series of zero degrees and dream worlds that alternate. In this video, between the slow and the fast, we go from zero to the *nth* degree of intensity and other worldliness that absorbs us (as spectators) as well. So, even without a story and normal motor situations, in a compact way, we see and feel how a traditional musical song-and-dance routine pull us into another world. This means that the clip has very much a "musical feeling" to it. It also has a happy feeling to it, which, as I said before, is typical of the musical. Having now had, through a video clip from Björk, this impression of the "traditional" musical, the next question is, then, what does Lars von Trier do with this cinematic form and what effects/affects does that create?

Hot and Cold: Musical and Melodrama

As we saw, with *Dancer in the Dark*, von Trier transferred the musical form into the genre of melodrama, which is a genre that centers on excessive emotions ("weepies," "tearjerkers"), family drama, forced marriages, motherly love, and impossible loves.[71] In melodrama, often a woman is the main character and the setting is a small town or the home. Although it is certainly not new to mix genres since postmodernism and television, the happiness of the musical and the drama of the melodrama are not an evident combination. Only *West Side Story* is perhaps another example, although here tragedy—not melodrama—is combined with the musical, but there is no room to elaborate on this film here.

Before looking at the melodramatic scenes and the contrast they form with the musical scenes, let me first discuss the musical scenes of this film. The first musical scene is forty-five minutes into the film, almost when you have stopped expecting it. It happens when Selma takes on a night shift at the factory and is really tired. All musical scenes start when Selma is either exhausted or terribly upset and paralyzed by the her situation, for instance, when she has killed her neighbor Bill, who stole all her savings, or when she finds herself powerless in a courtroom or prison cell. This is significant, for, as Deleuze demonstrated elaborately in *The Time-Image*, it is only when one is exhausted or "paralyzed" that the sensory-motor action gives way to pure optical and sound situations that one enters into a dream-world or a visionary otherworldliness (in the previous chapter, I argued similarly in respect to the main characters in *I Can't Sleep*, *Fight Club*, and, albeit in a different way, *Brothers*). Like in the video clip, each musical scene starts with a kind of zero degree, where environment sounds start to deviate from their normal functioning, where they start to group together in harmonic rhythms, and where the colors seem to become more intense and absorbent, as if a very fine layer of Technicolor sprinkles the images. The musical scenes themselves then are characterized by a subtle intensity of the colors and a rapid cutting between many camera positions (in fact, von Trier used a hundred cameras for these shots). Whereas in the video clip *It's Oh So Quiet*, traditional musical movement is used (the camera "dances" with the characters or sees them from above), in these musical scenes, a typical MTV video-clip style of fast cutting is used. This moment of intertextual translation is of course enforced because it is Björk who is Selma and who does the performing. It reinforces the effect of some kind of supra-personalization that moves Selma/Björk into "a movement of world," as Deleuze calls this effect, a movement that goes beyond the normal sensory-motor situation and carries these scenes into a different world.

So far, the musical scenes seem pretty much similar to traditional musical scenes. Each scene starts with a moment of "zero-degree" in which the rhythm and nature of the images start to change. These musical scenes have a completely different effect, however. Whereas in traditional musicals the song-and-dance scenes make you cheerful and happy, in *Dancer in the Dark* these scenes provoke precisely the strongest emotions, even more than the (melo)dramatic scenes. This has to do with the fact that within the series of alternations between the melodramatic and the musical scene, the contrast is emphasized not only by the rhythm of the images but also by the difference in "temperature" of the images: in terms of color effect, they go from cold to hot and back again. Therefore, the contrast becomes significant. Let me explain first how the contrast becomes so sharp that it creates such a strong effect.

The melodramatic part of the film is realistic in style, although it is not at all "glossy" Hollywood realism but more "raw" European realism, shot in dogma-style: shaking handheld (digital) camera, natural light, not a lot of cuts but panning and long shots. Because of the natural light, the colors are rather cold. The difference in "temperature" and style is quite significant. The contrast between the melodramatic scenes and the musical scenes, mediated by "zero-degree" moments, makes the structure of the film as a whole almost dialectic. In this way, von Trier becomes a strange heir of Eisenstein's "theory of attractions." Pathos was something Eisenstein reached through montage of oppositions; pathos can be reached only when there is a contrast or change in both form and content.

In a different way (not so much between shots as between sequences), in von Trier's film, there is a pathetic passage of oppositions into their contrary. As Deleuze says of Eisenstein's pathetic jumps: "From sadness to anger, from doubt to certainty, from resignation to revolt. . . . The pathetic implies a change not merely in the content of the image, but also in the form. The image must, effectively, change its power, pass to a higher power."[72] Von Trier experimented with transferring and translating two different genres into each other. The effect is pathos, a new experience of both the melodrama that goes beyond its ordinary sense of tragedy and the musical that goes beyond its ordinary sense of utopian entertainment. In other words, by taking certain image types into new territories (by "deterritorializing"), images and sounds take on new dimensions. On an internal aesthetic formal level, one could conclude that without these movements of deterritorialization of forms of expression, nothing new would ever be felt or thought.

Territorialization and Deterritorialization: Becoming-Music

So far, I have been speaking about the formal/aesthetic aspects of *Dancer in the Dark*. I conclude by also addressing another level of the film, where art and philosophy mutually illuminate each other. How can we translate what we hear, see, and feel (especially when it is something new) into concepts that make sense, that help us to see more, deeper, and better? In *What is Philosophy?* Deleuze and Guattari argue that philosophy needs a nonphilosophy that comprehends it, just as art needs nonart (and science needs nonscience).[73] Art (cinema and music, in my example) thinks in percepts and affect, whereas philosophy thinks in concepts. Having seen and felt the percepts and affects that are raised by *Dancer in the Dark* and the effects that these images and sounds (of movement and time) can have, what would be the corresponding concept that establishes a greater understanding between art and nonart, philosophy and nonphilosophy? What does this concept do? How does it function? Clearly, what we witness in the musical scenes is a "becoming-music" of Selma and of the world. Thus, Selma's becoming-woman changes into a becoming-music. In singing, one can become, for instance, child, bird, insect, or sea.

As I argue more elaborately in the last chapter of this book, music and its content the refrain *(ritournelle)* has tremendous power: "Flags can do nothing without trumpets," Deleuze and Guattari argue.[74] The power of music and the refrain is a territorial and deterritorial power: a child that sings softly in the dark creates a safe territory for itself; we create sound walls to create our environments. The difference between noise and sound is the labor of (and sensitivity to) the refrain. Music is also a deterritorialization of the voice, which becomes less and less tied to language (although it can still be part of it). Music also can open up territories, like the voices of opera singers in the movie *The Shawshank Redemption* that open up the prison walls and give the prisoners an overwhelming feeling of freedom (see Chapter 6). This is exactly what happens to Selma when groups of sounds pack together on the zero degree of aesthetic change from motor situation into optical and sound situation: here she creates a refrain, she hears music, she becomes-music; and she opens up a new world, a new territory that is much safer and much vaster than the small town she lives in, even though it features the same people. This force is tremendously powerful and liberating.

I will give another example. In one of the most beautiful musical scenes, Selma's boyfriend, Jeff, has just discovered that she is almost blind. They are standing on a railway, and Selma does not see a train coming. Selma throws her glasses in the water, and while the colors warm, she hesitantly starts to sing, "I've seen it all—I've seen water, it's water that's all" (zero degree). Jeff answers—entering slowly into a refrain as well: "Have you seen the Chinese wall, the Niagara Falls" and "the house you will share, your grandson's hand as he plays with your hair?" The images suggest some of the words in *The Sound of Music*–like scenes that Selma and Jeff see from a train while singing; but the becoming-music of the world has an almost all-embracing cosmic effect, deterritorializing the words and images, carrying them to a suprapersonal/transpersonal level that is overwhelming. Having this strong effect of territorializing and deterritorializing, the becoming-music of the images (dance) and sounds (voices and instruments) is the most powerful characteristic of *Dancer in the Dark*. In this way, the aesthetic and the philosophic translation work together in reinforcing mutual understanding rather than philosophy claiming the right to think about art, which in itself cannot think. In terms of the assemblage, we can say that on the vertical line of the assemblage, we find here territorial and deterritorial forces of crossing genre boundaries and of becoming-music that work together to create a powerful effect of pathos and a critique on injustice of the capitalist system and poverty and the system of the law.[75] On the horizontal axis, pathos is created in the moments where the movement-image (melodramatic scenes) passes into pure optical sound situations of the time-image (musical scenes).

I started with the quiet (silent) images of *It's Oh so Quiet* and the zero degree of the musical, where the motor action passes into the optical and sound situation of song and dance. *Dancer in the Dark* starts with an overture, a musical composition without voices, of almost four minutes over a completely dark screen with no images. Of course, this refers to Selma's blindness and the importance of music to her, but one could also say that here we have a zero degree of the image and sound in general. From here, a territory (the film) will be created and opened up (deterritorialized) on different levels. On an aesthetic level, both melodrama and the musical will be deterritorialized with the effect of pathos. On a conceptual level, the overture could be seen as an ultimate becoming-music, with the effect of cosmic power, "Quiet" and "Dark" as zero degrees of aesthetic and conceptual translations. These translations can never be fixed but are always moving because out of the vast virtuality of "a life" (the world), it is in the ongoing movements of translations, between the incorporeal of the concepts and the corporeal of the actual images and sounds (percepts and affects), that new sensations and thoughts will keep coming into existence.

With these analyses of von Trier's heroines, I conclude my survey of different kinds of "modern Alices" as conceptual personae and aesthetic figures in cinema. I hope to have indicated that they are all paradoxic figures in various ways. They are all examples of the effects and affects of becoming-woman. They share the paradoxic fact that they all initiate a process of becoming by entering a zone of proximity of the historically defined subject position of women, with the effect of precisely criticizing and breaking away from traditionally defined segments and molar systems. In this respect, I agree with Donna Haraway and with Jerry Aline Flieger that paradox is what we will have to come to terms with if we want to make a rhizomatic connection between feminism and Deleuze, feminism and many contemporary films, and feminism and contemporary society.

Logic of Sensations in Becoming-Animal

Bryan Singer's *X-Men* (2000), based on the comic strip by Stan Lee, is populated with mutants: Sabretooth has the teeth of a tiger, Mystique is a human chameleon, Wolverine is a man with steel claws who can heal himself, Rogue is a girl who can absorb the memory and power of somebody else, Xavier can read minds, and Magneto is a human magnet. Contemporary audiovisual culture is flooded with a teratologic imaginary. Horror and science fiction genres in cinema have gained in popularity and moved from more obscure B-genres to mainstream cinema: vampires, replicants, zombies, and mutants of all sorts have become common features.

In her article "Teratologies," Rosi Braidotti argues that a culture that is in the grip of such a techno-teratologic imaginary is in need of Deleuze's philosophy: "The proliferation of a monstrous social imaginary calls for adequate forms of analysis. More particularly, it calls for a form of philosophical teratology which Deleuze is in a unique position to provide."[1] Braidotti argues that Deleuze's philosophy can explain the fascination for monstrous images. Also, it can provide an antidote against the nostalgic and nihilistic position that the inflation of monstrous images is a sign of cultural decadence of our times and the decline of "master narratives" or the loss of the great canon of "high culture." Like in *X-Men*, the humans consider the mutants dangerous and to be protected from, and monstrosity in general is seen as something terrifying and threating to human identity. Deleuze provides the tools to construct more flexible forms of identity and subjectivity, grounded in "matter" and "memory" but never fixed.

In Chapter 2, I discussed the monstrous image of the flesh and how in psychoanalysis this is connected to the feminine and the abject as a borderline concept, between self and other, inside and outside, man and woman, human and machine, human and animal. I also discussed how images of the flesh can be conceived differently, as material or temporal aspects of subjectivity in movement-images or time-images, depending on the assemblages of which the image is part. In this chapter, I look at another way to conceive subjectivity through the imagination that is at work in audiovisual culture. As Braidotti argues, imagination is "a transformative force that propels multiple, heterogeneous 'becomings' or repositioning of the subject. The process of becoming is collectively driven, that is to say, relational and external; it is also framed by affectivity or desire and is thus eccentric to rational control. The notion of 'figures' [term modified]—in contrast to the representational function of 'metaphors'—emerges as crucial to Deleuze's notion of a conceptually charged use of imagination."[2] I look specifically at all kinds of narratives and figures of becoming-animal to find out how Deleuze's concepts and those he developed together with Guattari can provide an adequate analysis of contemporary audiovisual culture inasmuch as it is occupied with a teratologic imaginary. I also attempt to discover how these concepts can form and transform our self-image, which seems to be in need of a "becoming-minoritarian" of everybody. A "logic of sensations" and affection-images seem important to express and sense the passive and active affects that are involved in becoming-animal.

Stories, Sensations, and Affection-Images

Animals: Series, Structures, and Beyond

To discover how becoming-animal might be understood, it is useful to have a look at some old stories about the relation between humankind and animals. I limit myself to some nineteenth-century novels and some of their (many) cinematic versions.[3] A general characteristic of all horror creatures that "become-animal" is that they are always considered monsters. As I argued in Chapter 2, the incapacity of the traditional subject to think in terms of the in-between status (characteristic of all becomings) has evoked a feeling of those monsters' abjection. In addition, almost all traditional monsters are seen mostly seen as metaphors or archetypes for certain forms of human behavior.

Long before any written accounts existed, the vampire occupied the imagination of humankind. In old traditions, vampires were known to be dead humans who returned from the grave and attacked and sucked blood from the living as a means of sustaining themselves. They were associated with demonic beings, black magic, and other supernatural powers. It was Bram Stoker, in his 1897 novel *Dracula*, who presented the modern version of the vampire.[4] Drawing on Transylvanian and Romanian myths and the history of Count Vlad Dracul, Stoker charged his vampire, Count Dracula, with symbolism. The vampire is equipped with a pair of fangs to symbolize its bloodsucking instinct, the coffin as its bed symbolizes its relationship with death, and finally the vampire also becomes associated with the bat (the cape and Dracula's capacity to transform into a bat: the only flying and bloodsucking animal that is, like humans, a mammal).[5] It is an impossible task to give an account of all the variations of the vampire myth. Hundreds of books, comics, films, fan clubs, and Internet news groups share a fascination for vampires. Stoker's book has been visualized many times. The best-known films are *Nosferatu, Eine Symphonie des Grauens* (Murnau, 1922), *Dracula* (Browning, 1931), *Nosferatu, Phantom der Nacht* (Herzog, 1979), and *Bram Stoker's Dracula* (Coppola, 1992).[6]

Because of their high degree of symbolism and metaphor, these stories and films serve an important purpose in representing a collective imaginary. Deleuze and Guattari explain in *A Thousand Plateaus* that there are two methods of natural history to classify the relations between animals and between man and animal (man and woman, man and child, in short: man and "inappropriate/other").[7] According to Deleuze and Guattari, classification occurs either through series or through structures but mostly through a combination of the two (much to the annoyance of Lévi-Strauss, who preferred pure structures). Series work with Jungian archetypes, with each term representing a transformation of the libido, the unconscious lust principle. They operate on the level of dreams and imaginations and are metamorphoses. In this way, a human can turn into a bat because there is a resemblance between the vampire bat (which lives by night, can fly, and sucks blood) and the human vampire (who lives by night, can fly, sucks blood, and can transform into a bat). Bela Lugosi, with his strong sexual attraction to his victims, is the ultimate example of this serial vampire. The structural relations between human and animal work on a conceptual level and are represented by metaphors: the vampire is to humans as the bat is to animals. All these kinds of relations are based on resemblance, imitation, or maybe even identification.

Whatever the importance of these serial and structural relations between man and animal, there is yet another relation between the two: that of becoming-animal. Becoming-animal has its own reality, which is not based on resemblance or affiliation but on alliance, symbiosis, affection, and infection. Deleuze and Guattari say it in the following way:

> Does it not seem that . . . there is still room for something else, something more secret, more subterranean: the sorcerer and becomings (expressed in tales instead of myths or rites)? . . . Becomings-animal are neither dreams nor fantasies. They are perfectly real. . . . What is real is the becoming itself, the block of becoming, not the supposed fixed terms through which that becoming passes. . . . The becoming-animal of the human being is real, even if the animal the human being becomes is not; and the becoming-other of the animal is real, even if that something other it becomes is not. . . . Becoming is always of a different order than filiation. It concerns alliance . . . in the domain of *symbioses* that bring into play beings of totally different scales and kingdoms, with no possible filiation.[8]

According to Deleuze and Guattari, there exists a reality of becoming-animal that consists of a proximity between man and animal on the level of affects, movements, and speeds. This means that becoming-animal is based on the affinity of certain affects. In other words, becoming-animal is a way of creating a Body without Organs (BwO). It is on the level of intensities that the assemblage animal-human is made. It is not evoked by blood ties or heritage but by contagion and infection. From this point of view, vampires also can express a reality of becoming because they can pick and choose any other person to make a vampire as well. More specifically about vampires and werewolves, Deleuze and Guattari say:

> Man does not become wolf, or vampire, as if he changed molar species; the vampire and werewolf are becomings of man, in other words, proximities between molecules in composition, relations of movement and rest, speed and slowness between emitted particles. Of course there are werewolves and vampires, we say this with all our heart; but do not look for a resemblance or analogy to the animal, for this is becoming-animal in action, the production of molecular animal (whereas the "real" animal is trapped in its molar form and subjectivity).[9]

Deleuze and Guattari thus acknowledge the existence of real becoming-animals in vampires and other monstrous figures. In the history of cinema, however, Dracula and his mates often rely on heavy sexual symbolism and metaphors (and changing of molar species) and therefore belong more to the serial and structural relations between man and animal. Maybe Dracula's popular successors Lestat de Lioncourt and the sensitive vampire Louis from Ann Rice's novel *Interview with the Vampire* get closer to the becoming-animal.[10] In the first instance, this could be due to the fact that in Rice's version much of the symbolism is no longer valuable for these vampires: they can stand garlic, they do not need to sleep in coffins, and they can even tolerate light, albeit artificial light such as a sunset on celluloid. They are still nocturnal creatures and depend on blood, but they do not metamorphose into a bat. They are in a constant status of becoming (they are closer to a wolf than to a bat); Lestat and Louis have their own dynamics and affections. Out of affinity and affection, Louis makes a little girl Claudia into a vampire. Neil Jordan filmed Rice's book, but I will not go into details of this film here.

Neil Jordan did, however, make another film, *The Company of Wolves*, based on a novel by Angela Carter, which will be discussed in one of the next sections. What vampires share with werewolves is that they "procreate" by contamination. Stories and legends of werewolves are also old and have been told over and again. I believe that, at least in some cinematic versions, these stories are closer to the becoming-animal than most of the vampire stories, but I return to this point later in this chapter.

Becoming-Animal in Affection-Images

Not all monsters of the nineteenth century (as well as before and after) are created by the mysterious, dark forces of nature. Another way to create new species or in-between species ("monsters") is via the illuminated path of science and technology. Of the many stories of mad scientists and monsters, such as Mary Shelley's *Frankenstein* and H. G. Wells's *The Island of Dr. Moreau*, I will look more closely at the story of Dr. Jekyll. Stevenson's novel *Dr. Jekyll and Mr. Hyde* takes place in the prudish, narrow-minded Victorian era.[11] It is the tragic story of a man, a doctor, who cannot cope with the tension between his hidden feelings of lust and sexual energy and the rules and regulations of society to which he, as a distinguished person, is confined. He thinks he has found the solution to this problem by discovering a chemical that can separate good and bad. Of course, the bad takes over and must be destroyed: with the bad, the good then dies, too. The novel presents the events as a search after his death, which is different from most cinematic versions, which show what happens before our eyes. To get closer to the cinematic experience, I limit myself here to Rouben Mamoulian's version *Dr. Jekyll and Mr. Hyde* (1931).[12]

The first sequence of the film consists solely of the viewpoint of Dr. Jekyll. The only moment we get to see him is when he sees himself in the mirror while getting dressed. The rest of the images are rather shaky, with a lot of movement (the movements of Jekyll) and with vague black borders that end before the frame of the whole image ends. The movement of the images makes the viewer feel a bit dizzy, and the fact that the borders of the image are within the frame evokes a claustrophobic feeling: one has the impression that vision is seriously constrained and limited. In this purely visual way, Mamoulian expresses exactly Dr. Jekyll's struggle, which he makes explicit in the next scene during one of his classes. The point of view has changed, and we see and hear Jekyll lecturing: " . . . We have set boundaries for our vision. As men of science we should be curious and bold enough to peel beyond them. . . . " In a Cartesian way, he goes on explicitly to separate body and soul/psyche by proclaiming that man is not one, but two: "One strives for nobility and is good, the other seeks the expression of life impulses that bind him to some animal relation with the earth, and is bad." So he invents a chemical that allows him to separate his two internal forces.

In the visualizations of the transformations, there is one striking aspect: they all take place in close-ups or in Deleuzian terms in affection-images. One of the possible affection-images is the face (or the face-like).[13] The close-up has the power to express a pure affect without any spatiotemporal relations, but the close-up paradoxically presents at the same time a face and its effacement: the individuation of each person/thing is diminished or even ended by a close-up.[14] Now it seems to me that all these processes are at work in the expression of the becoming Mr. Hyde of Dr. Jekyll. There are many close-ups throughout the film. The first striking set of close-ups is near the beginning of the film, when Dr. Jekyll begs his fiancée, Muriel, to marry him soon because he can wait no longer (to have sexual intercourse). The sequence consists of several shots/countershots, which become closer and closer. In the end, we see only Muriel's eyes, and we hear her voice saying, "I love you, I love you," and Jekyll's eyes while we hear his words, "Who shall ever separate us then?" The answer to this question is given immediately in the next image when a shadow falls on the two lovers, now in embrace. They are requested to behave and go back to the party that is going on. Later we see a similar close-up of the eyes, this time of Mr. Hyde, who is saying, "I love you, I love you" to the prostitute Ivy. This shows the complete fusion and confusion of both Jekyll and Hyde and Muriel and Ivy: there is no more space, no more distance, a real conflation of body and space means that the individuation ends and a process of becoming can start.

The face, which expresses affects in quality or power, is tangible in the images of transformation. For instance, the second transformation consists of five close-ups that show first the still wondering face of Jekyll and then a close-up of his hand, expressing a first change, and back to the face, which is on its way from quality to power. The next shot is another close-up of the hand, which by now has started to grow hair; finally, we see the powerful (but hideous because it is in binary opposition) face of Mr. Hyde. Here the different close-ups are linked together (or interrupted) by the editing process. Later in the film, on three occasions, in one close-up shot, we see the change from quality to power (which can be positive, but here is negative), from Jekyll to Hyde happening before our eyes. This is morphing *avant-la-lettre* and shows the quality and power of cinema to make the invisible visible, even if in an exaggerated way. In any case, this film shows what is meant by the affection-image and how it can be employed for expressing the sensations of becoming-animal.

As is well known, it all ends disastrously. Dr. Jekyll cannot resist the evil power of Mr. Hyde; he becomes a killer and has to be killed himself. Jekyll shares with all his contemporaries the binary opposition that is believed to be fundamental for humankind: good–bad; man–woman (woman is subdivided into virgin–whore); rich–poor. He is, however, one of the few to admit that there is good and bad in everyone. He does not want to repress the bad (here the animal); he wants to set it free (to get rid of it) so that the good can be pure. The chemical he invents for doing this works like a drug. At the end of this chapter, I elaborate on the relation between drugs and the becoming-animal. Now I will just remark that the "drug" makes him feel good, but it makes him look bad and behave badly.

The final message of the film seems to be that one should repress "animal instincts" and stick to the rules and conventions; but the countermessage would be that rules and conventions should allow more room for free expression and affection, more room for becoming instead of being animal. The binary organization of Jekyll's world does not allow for such becomings, however. Although the film shows some moments of becoming-animal, especially in the "depersonalizing" affection-image, in the end, Hyde is seen in a structural way, as a metaphor for the beast in man. If we discuss the film in terms of the tetravalence of the assemblage, it is obvious that the affection-image (form of content) gives us (literally) a corporeal modification. At the same time, something new happens on the level (form) of expression; an incorporeal transformation takes place in Dr. Jekyll's mind. Mr. Hyde is Dr. Jekyll's deterritorializing "line of flight," but in the end, the territorializing forces and binary oppositions of Victorian society are much stronger. Here is no place for becomings.

Becoming-Animal in Painting: Senses and Color

One of the most important aspects of becoming, and certainly of becoming-animal, is the sensation through which this becoming is felt: becoming creates new sensitivities. This also explains why it is precisely the affection-image that can take account of such becomings. The French writer Paul Valéry defined sensation as "that which is directly transmitted, without the 'detour' or the 'boredom' of a story to tell." More positively, the painter Francis Bacon defines sensation as "that which shifts from one order to another, from one level to another."[15] This still rather vague definition might become clearer when we look at Bacon's paintings, in which there is always some kind of deformation, mainly of bodies, going on. In other words, his painted figures and their surroundings do not belong to one specific level (neither "realistic" representation nor pure mental conceptualization). Because becoming-animal is so strongly expressed in Bacon's work, it is useful to look at this artistic domain first, before we return to the cinematographic image.

In his book about Bacon, *Francis Bacon, Logique de la Sensation*, Gilles Deleuze explains how Bacon expresses sensation through the use of figures instead of figurations.[16] *Figuration* (representative and narrative) and its absolute counterpart *abstraction*, work through mental operations rather than directly on the nervous system; therefore, they do not operate through sensation. I would like to add that if sensation is felt in figurative and abstract works, this does not occur on the level of figuration or abstraction. Sensation works on an instinctual level; it is felt rather than thought.[17] Because we have multiple senses, and because every sense questions each object in its own way, sensation (*le sentir*) is always an intersensorial and synesthetic experience.[18] Deleuze formulates this synthetic and synesthetic combination of sensations as follows: "Between a color, a taste, a touch, a smell, a noise, a weight, there would be an existential communication that would constitute the 'pathic' (nonrepresentative) moment of the sensation."[19]

Deleuze mentions the painting of Isabel Rawsthorne to explain how Bacon makes this multisensoriality visible: it presents a head with ovals and lines that enlarge the eyes and also the nose and the mouth; the whole face is mobilized, all the senses are exercised at once. At the same time, all our senses as spectators are addressed at once. This power of the multisensual figure is a power (vital and affective) that Deleuze equally refers to as rhythm: "This force is Rhythm and is more profound than vision, audition, etc. Rhythm manifests itself as music when the auditory level is invested, as painting when the visual level is invested. A 'logic of the senses' that is not rational, not cerebral, said Cézanne."[20] Rhythm is not visible as such; sensation is vibration on a molecular level, and it can only be felt. One is *moved* by invisible forces, by invisible movement brought to the surface by an artist. Of course, the question of rhythm can be related to the concept of becoming-music. This will be elaborated in the next chapter. Returning now to the "portrait" of Isabel Rawsthorne, one has the feeling that it is not the face of a woman but rather more like the head of some animal-like creature: a becoming-animal, which takes on some "monstrous" proportions. Animals have extremely well-developed (instinctual) senses, and it will be no surprise to discover that becoming-animal is closely related to the microperceptions of sensations.

Like every phenomenal body, every figure needs a space in which to be situated. Bacon always creates a flat surface and a contour (a ring, a circle, a rectangle, or a line) that encloses the figure. At the same time, the figure also transmits its invisible forces to the space.[21] Every figure has its own place in relation to its environment (the surface and the contour); they are interrelated, influence each other, and together form an image. Because every sense has its own effects, it is quite possible that a space is not limited to just one dimension: this experience is expressed, made perceptible by Bacon's paintings. Another well-known example is what happens to space when you listen with closed eyes to a concert: if you open your eyes after a while, you feel that the visible space is much smaller in relation to that other space that was created by the music.[22] Even with open eyes, the clearly perceived space can be doubled with another, more mysterious space. From this example, it is clear that space is an experience, a construction of the senses, either in "real life" or as expressed by works of art.

In fact, this is precisely the function of works of art (be they avant-garde or popular): to enclose spaces that would otherwise remain unknown, to which no one would have direct access. The interrelation between bodies (figures) and spaces takes place on the level of the surface. This does not mean that there is no depth. It only means that depth is not necessarily three dimensional. Rather, it is a reversibility of dimensions, a bidimensional proximity of figures and spaces. Deleuze says that both Cézanne and Bacon show this coexistence or proximity of dimensions: "Bacon remains faithful to Cézanne . . . especially in his treatment of colors, . . . in a coexistence or proximity modulated by color. And through the membrane of the contour, a double movement is made: a flat extension towards the frame and a voluminous contraction towards the body."[23] According to Deleuze, the major difference between Cézanne and Bacon seems to be the way their figures are deformed.[24] This difference is due to the dissimilar forces that act on them (Cézanne's world being open, Bacon's world being closed). I will not elaborate this point further, however. Most important is the fact that both painters try to express directly what is at the source of sensations and what is perceptible only at the surface, which could be described as a contact surface, through a bundling together of different senses.[25]

As Deleuze already indicated, one of the most important means to achieve this sensational effect is through colors. Again, it is not a matter of resemblance or copying colors of nature. Each color has its own dimension, its own materiality and quality.[26] Bacon and other colorists, such as Van Gogh and Gauguin, render space in pure colors. They can use black and white, light and dark as well, but in that case they use black and white as colors by opposing their tonality. Everything becomes dependent on the space–color distribution, which demands a haptic view rather than an optic one. Colors are pure affect: they have their own independent quality and invisible movement.

From painting, we now to move back to cinema. As Deleuze argued in *The Movement-Image* and discussed in Chapter 2, the qualities and potentialities of the affection-image are related not only to the close-up but also to the use of colors (shadows and light included) and to "any-space-whatevers." Because the becoming-animal is closely related to the sensation of (mostly) invisible forces, it must be situated at the level of Peircian firstness, which is the form of expression of the affection-image. As mentioned in Chapter 2, firstness is the level that expresses something new in the experience; one could say that it is comparable to a first (instinctive) impression or, indeed, a sensation. Like sensation, firstness is difficult to define because it is felt rather than thought. It expresses qualities or powers that have value on their own merits (like the colors mentioned already) without as yet any question of actualization. On this level, a possibility is expressed, and all is virtually contained in the affection-image. Therefore, I argue that becoming-animal as a deterritorializing force of the human subject finds its form of content and expression in the affection-image and Peircian firstness.

Becoming-Child Before Becoming-Animal

Children Are Spinozists

For children, every experience is new. Maybe it is for that reason that children have a conception of the world that is closer to the idea of becoming-animal. It might therefore be interesting to have another look at two stories that deal with children and animals to determine whether these provide additional insights. Rudyard Kipling's *Jungle Book* has been told over and again, and "real" stories about wolf-children also have existed for ages. I analyze two cinematic wolf-children in this section, but first it might be useful to philosophize a little about the world of children. In the previous chapter, I took Alice in Wonderland as a figure of becoming-woman that expresses a "logic of sense" through paradoxes and nonsense. Now I want to see whether children are also close to a "logic of sensation" and a becoming-animal.

"Children are Spinozists," say Deleuze and Guattari in *A Thousand Plateaus*. To understand this expression, it is necessary to go back to what was said before about Spinoza's ethology. To recall briefly, it asserts that everything is essentially situated on the plane of immanence, on which "everything is given, upon which unformed elements and materials dance that are distinguished from one another only by their speed and that enter into this or that individuated assemblage depending on their connections, their relations of movement."[27] This means that what distinguishes one thing or body from another is the different ways they distribute movements of speed and rest. I have discussed Deleuze's example of Freud's little Hans, who speaks about a *fait-pipi* (a "make wee-wee"). If you were to ask a boy whether a girl has a "make wee-wee," he would answer "yes" because effectively girls do make wee-wee. What is important is not so much the organic function as the mechanical function. The difference is one of movement and rest (a girl does not have a pee standing, nor does she do this from a distance). A locomotive also has a "make wee-wee" in yet another mechanical agency. For children, an organ can take changeable forms, although these have nothing to do with psychoanalytic partial objects but everything to do with different relations of movement and rest, which Spinoza called "longitude." The other axis of the body, the "latitude," consists of powers and affects that are related to the longitude. Children have the natural instinct to look at organs in a mechanical, nonorganismic way, which makes them closer to the becoming-animal. We can see again here how greatly such a view on the case of little Hans differs from the Freudian interpretation and from Barbara Creed's revision discussed in Chapter 2. As Deleuze and Guattari put it:

Once again, we turn to children. Note how they talk about animals, and are moved by them. They make lists of affects. Little Hans' horse is not representative but affective. It is not a member of a species but an element or individual in a machinic assemblage: draft horse–omnibus–street. It is defined by a list of active and passive affects in the context of the individuated assemblage it is part of: having eyes blocked by blinders, having a bit and a bridle, being proud, having a big peepee-maker, pulling heavy loads, being whipped, falling, making a din with its legs, biting, etc. These affects circulate and are transformed within the assemblage: what a horse "can do." . . . A horse falls down in the street! It can't get back on its feet with that heavy load on its back, and the excessive whipping; a horse is going to die!—this was an ordinary sight in those days.[28]

Hans is also taken up in an assemblage (the parental element, the house, the street, the right to go out on the street, the horse on the street). Might there be a becoming-horse of Hans, an encounter or assemblage between the two? Certainly, the horse affects Hans, but the question is whether this is because the animal represents either the father or the mother.

Spinoza, on the other hand, considers childhood an unfortunate state of being because in childhood we depend too much on external causes. We suffer much more during childhood; our affects are much more passive because they are largely dependent on others (parents, siblings, friends, teachers). "Childhood," says Spinoza, "is a state of impotence and slavery, a state of foolishness in which we depend in the highest degree on external causes and in which we necessarily have more of sadness than of joy; we are never more cut off from our power of action."[29] To be freed from this slavery, it is necessary to learn and to reason; but reason, according to Spinoza, is closely related to nature. On the one hand, the state of nature is not subject to the laws of reason: reason relates to the proper and true utility of man and tends solely to his preservation, the *conatus* mentioned before. Nature, on the other hand, has no regard for the preservation of man and comprises an infinity of other laws concerning the universe as a whole, of which man is but a small part. Reason, therefore, demands nothing contrary to nature. Reason demands only "that everyone should love themselves, seek what is useful to themselves, and strive to preserve their being by increasing their power of action. . . . Reason proceeds not by artifice, but by a natural combination of relations: it does not so much bring calculation, as a kind of direct recognition of man by man."[30] Even extended into culture, the state, and the city, this natural reason is the kind of reason for which one strives. The city is even the best environment in which a reasonable man can live, according to Spinoza; and this kind of reasoning is the reasoning a child should learn to become more joyful and more active.

Mowgli's Jungle Reasoning

Although there are several film adaptations of Kipling's stories of the *Jungle Book*, I refer only to the first filmed version, the one by Zoltan Korda (1942).[31] What is remarkable in the first place is the film's style. It is a film that evokes affects, not through the close-up of the affection-image, as with Dr. Jekyll and Mr. Hyde, but through its color effects. Most of the shots are long or medium takes. A few close-ups are seen, especially of Mowgli's head and the different animal heads, but they do not dominate the picture. The overall impression is of a colorful painting in beautiful Technicolor. In this respect, Korda's version is close to Disney's animation film. Children love *Jungle Book* not only because a child, a boy, has the lead and not only because children are closer to the world and affects of animals; it is also because children react immediately to the sensations provoked by the colors. The question of realism is in no respect important to the direct effect of the events that we see. The leaves of the bushes are sometimes blue, the water seems like a painter's palette with all the brightly colored water lilies, and the mostly (but not always) real animals run through studio settings that evoke the jungle but do not resemble it. The images are enchanting and exciting, full of a logic of sensations.

Out of this colorful palette of sensations derives a story told by a narrator: an old Indian beggar, who at the end turns out to be Boldeo, Mowgli's human enemy in the village where he was born. As is well known, Mowgli was born of humans but raised by wolves. He learns the laws of the jungle (to which I will return) and learns how to move through the jungle. It is mainly his motor system, the way he moves lightly, and his athleticism (the way his body moves and rests, slows down, and speeds up), that shows he is in the state of becoming-animal. In relation to the other animals and in relation to the jungle, Mowgli develops intensive and extensive capacities that give him power.

In a different way, Bacon's figures are also athletic; but, because Bacon's figures cannot move, their athleticism cannot be translated into an actual movement (jumping, crawling, swinging from liana to liana). Therefore, the athleticism is expressed in a sort of spastic position, which makes Bacon's bodies appear to be struggling with their internal powers; they want to escape from their own bodies. Mowgli does not need to escape from his own body; he is not locked up in it because he has balanced his movements. Nevertheless, he has to escape from the jungle. Although he has many animal friends, Mowgli has one enemy: Shere Khan, the tiger, who chases him away.

It is in the confrontations between Mowgli and Shere Khan that we see the rare close-ups of the film. In the beginning of the film, we see Mowgli's face, expressing fear, in medium close-up. The tiger's head shows anger and aggression. Mowgli is in the position of a child; he has no power to turn his passive affections into active ones. During his stay with the humans, he grows up. At the moment when he gets "a tooth," he is adult and sees the possibility of taking revenge. This "tooth" is a knife, but as a real

Spinozist, for Mowgli it makes no difference whether his tooth is organic (part of his body) or not. As long as he can defend himself with it and it gives him another (in this case, more powerful) dynamic, there is no difference between a knife and a tooth; each has a purely mechanical function. So Mogli can go back to the jungle for a new confrontation with Shere Khan. This time, the heads of both Mowgli and Shere Khan express anger and aggression, and Mowgli is successful in his revenge. Mowgli has learned to reason, which does not exclude him from nature.

In this respect, he is the opposite of the narrator, Boldeo, who started his story with these words: "What is the book of life itself but war with nature, the struggle between jungle and village?" Boldeo and most of the villagers have learned to reason only for their own benefit: they are greedy for what Mowgli calls worthless things (the treasures of the fallen city in the jungle). They kill for the game or the pride, not for food or defense (which is law number one in the jungle), and they do not take care of their interactions with other people (they mistrust everybody) or with their surroundings. This last aspect becomes hilariously clear in the sequence where Boldeo and two other villagers walk through the jungle dressed completely in the fine clothes they found with the treasures and carrying heavy bags of gold through the woods. They totally misfit the environment; indeed, two of them will not survive. Mowgli, on the other hand, has partly learned the reasoning of man. For instance, he has learned the language so that he can communicate with other humans. The scene where he is initiated in language is touchingly simple. Because he is able to make only wolf sounds, Mowgli's (human) mother, who is not sure this wolf-boy is her son, says that he can call her mother. After a few repetitions, he can pronounce the word. Then she asks for his name. When he does not understand her, she makes the sound of a wolf. Apparently, she knows exactly how to speak this animal language because Mowgli understands her and answers her question by saying something that sounds like Mowgli (which means "little frog").

We see here that both children and women are close to the animal world and to becoming-animal. The film does not show the learning process. The narrator just tells us that in a few months Mowgli "learns the ways, language and customs of men." So it is not the learning process itself that is important but what one does with the acquired knowledge. Mowgli uses his knowledge to empower his natural forces: he buys a "tooth" and speaks with the wise snake, who advises him about how to lure Shere Khan to the water, where he can more easily master him. That is all he wants to learn from man because at the end of the film he decides to go back and stay in the jungle: "Man is idle, senseless and cruel. I am of the jungle; their trail is my trail, their fight is my fight," Mowgli concludes, leaving humans behind with their own (non-Spinozian) reasoning.

The Taming of the Wild Child

Mowgli is not the only wolf-child. Both legends ("Romulus and Remus") and true stories abound. Deleuze mentions a study about wolf-children by Schérer and Hocquenghem, which says that those children have not really become wolves. Neither is it true that wolf-children simply imitate the beasts that have raised them; nor is a metaphor in place. The researchers speak about an objective but indeterminate and uncertain zone of something the animal and the human have in common, an *intensive proximity*, that is actually visible in all children, as if each child has room for other becomings. A wolf-child is the reality of a becoming-animal without becoming an animal in reality. In 1969 François Truffaut filmed one of those true stories about wolf-children that took place in 1798 in the surroundings of Paris: *L'Enfant Sauvage*. Interestingly, this film is in many aspects the opposite of Korda's *Jungle Book*.

First, let us look at the style of the film. Like in Korda's film, there are few close-ups. Most of the shots take a considerable distance (medium or long shots), but this time there is no enchanting Technicolor to take care of the sensations and the affects. The images are in black and white (not a coloristic use of black and white, but the black and white of reasoning). This is not in contradiction to the content of the film, however, because this time the aim is not to show the becoming-animal and to let the law of the jungle prevail. This time, a "becoming-human" is the central focus: Doctor Itard (played by Truffaut himself) takes care of the education of a wild child who has been found in the forest. In the first part, until he is entrusted to Dr. Itard and his housekeeper, Madame Guerin, the child is a real wild child. As Schérer and Hocquenghem discovered, the child had not really become an animal, nor equally was he "stupid" or mentally less capable, like an animal (although this is presumed by some of his discoverers). Rather, the child has a way of moving and resting that comes somewhere close to the motoricity of animals. The film is divided into parts that are marked by one image that is captured and isolated in an iris. Each part shows a stage in the development of the child. In the first stage, the child is wild.

Then he is brought to Paris, to a clinic for deaf and mute children. His movements are still close to those of an animal. In the clinic, he is examined: he has a normal human constitution, but he is covered with scars. One of the scars, on his throat, is not from an animal but from a knife: his mother or parents had wanted to get rid of him. The director of the clinic considers the wild child to be mentally diseased, which probably would have been why his parents abandoned him. Dr. Itard has a different opinion: he thinks the child was probably illegitimate and abandoned for that reason. He sees nothing wrong with the child except that he has lived for many years in complete solitude without any human contact: Itard understands that becoming-animal does not mean mental retardation but is a matter of external movements (*longitude*) and instinctual affects (*latitude*).

Itard can take the child with him. The first step to humanity is indeed learning how to walk and how to move as a human being, like the gestures one must make while eating. Note how close this is to all children's learning process: they also have to learn to walk on two feet, to eat with a spoon, and such. At the same time, Dr. Itard works on the child's other immanent axis: he tries to change his sensations so that he can approve emotions. Now the child smells at everything, is rather insensitive to cold or heat, and cannot cry or show any emotions. "I want to make him weaker, I want him to get less physical power, but more emotions," says Itard. This is where humanity starts: a certain way of moving and sensations that can become emotions. In the next nine months, a "human is born." The boy gets a name: Victor. He also gets a crash course in representation, the alphabet, reading, writing, speaking, memory training, a sense of justice, and behavior. All through the punishment–reward method, Itard is a man with a great sense of fairness: he sees that the boy would have been better off in the woods if he does not learn how to "survive" in the human world. Therefore, he has to learn the language, he has to understand what is right and wrong, he has to wear clothes, and he has to try to communicate with other people.

Itard is a severe but good teacher. Significantly, though, it is always Madame Guerin who takes care of comforting Victor when he breaks down (for instance, when he has to learn the alphabet), who hugs him and kisses him, and who speaks kindly to him. Except for his sense of justice, all the emotions that are close to the initial affects are learned by the side of the housekeeper. Itard wants to turn Victor immediately into a man, a reasonable and sensible man (not like the *Jungle Book* villagers), because he knows what the norm is to survive as a man. This is a noble ambition and produces results; but looking at Victor's face, one might wonder what he is thinking. He probably knows there are some limits and constraints (especially from the father and reason that excludes emotions or brings in false reasoning) to being human, which is probably why he flees back to the forest. After a few days, he discovers that in the meantime he has become too accustomed to his new environment: the four walls of a house and the company of other human beings. He has also become too weak for the forest. So he returns to the house and to his teacher (we see again the importance of the interaction between bodies and spaces). When he climbs the stairs, however, he looks at Dr. Itard with mixed emotions: partly grateful for his education and attention, partly suspicious about what is to come—rightly so because not all humans have the same fairness and reasoning to balance the laws of nature and culture as do Dr. Itard and Madame Guerin.

Passive and Active Affects

Suffering Flesh

Up to now I have looked at stories about the relation between humans and animals that have been told over and again. Those stories, as legends and myths, have cultural and philosophic value. Although their adaptations vary against the background of various historical changes, their basic assumptions remain the same: becoming-animal is seen as something monstrous unless a child is involved. A child can make a bridge between humans and animals because the natural motor system and instinctual reactions of children are closer to those of the world of animals. In the next section, I return to some recent variations on some of the old themes when I talk about the active power that the sensation of becoming-animal can provoke. First, I look at passive affects, which are also a possible part of the becoming-animal. As Deleuze states in his book on Bacon, in becoming-animal, human and animal enter in an affective relation of proximity: "A human who suffers is an animal, an animal that suffers is human. This is the reality of becoming."[32] I therefore revisit Fassbinder's *In a Year of 13 Moons*, which I discussed in Chapter 2, and to the paintings of Bacon.

When I saw Bacon's crucifixion paintings (Triptych, *Three Studies for a Crucifixion*, 1962), I thought immediately of Fassbinder's film. The choice of comparing this film with Bacon's work thus is based on this instinctive sensation. I was moved in a similar way by both the painting and the film—hence my search for some reasoning about this initial affect. As a preliminary remark, I must say that this film is not part of a larger "mythology" around humans and animals, as are the films discussed previously in this chapter.[33] Rather, it is a specific story at a specific moment with specific references to history. It is also the story of the creation of a specific BwO through a becoming-animal. In Chapter 2, I already discussed some of those specificities.[34] Here I concentrate on everything that is related to becoming-animal. Fassbinder's film works directly on the nervous system; it is full of the affect of becoming-animals. Not all becoming-animals are the same, however. *In a Year of 13 Moons* presents us with a becoming-animal through passive affects that make us sad.

As indicated, the main character in *In a Year of 13 Moons* is the transsexual woman Elvira (formerly Erwin). Her becoming-animal certainly could be seen as a becoming-pet: a dog that is being beaten by its master(s), a child being beaten by its father (or mother). For Freud, masochism is part of sadomasochism; however, this need not always be the case. In his study on masochism, Deleuze finds another way of talking about masochism.[35] He goes back to the literary sources that have given their name to these "basic perversions": Marquis de Sade and Sacher-Masoch. Like a doctor giving his name to a disease for which he described a set of symptoms (like in the case of Parkinson's disease), de Sade and Masoch provide the symptoms and essential characteristics of sadism and masochism. According to Deleuze, as soon as one reads Masoch, one finds that his (Masoch's) universe has nothing to do with that of de Sade. They not only have different techniques but also very different problems and projects. This does not mean that some transformations between sadism and masochism are not possible. What Deleuze is arguing against is the sadomasochistic unity.

I want to raise two points about Deleuze's study of Masoch.[36] First, I must stress again that Deleuze does not deny that there can exist oedipal structures in human relations; but they are not always the basic and only relations between people, animals, or other things. Deleuze distinguishes three types of women in the universe of Masoch; these types correspond to three images of the mother: the primitive mother (the real "womb" mother), the *oedipal* mother (the lover), and the oral mother (the earth-mother, giving life and death).[37] The oral mother plays the most important role in masochism, and I will return to the oral mother.

The second point about Deleuze's interpretation of masochism concerns the principal masculine characters that Masoch distinguishes: Cain and Christ. Cain is the child preferred by the mother; he even commits a crime (killing his brother and breaking with his father) to make of Eve a mother–goddess. This crime is not a symbol of sadomasochism but belongs completely to the masochistic world. Christ also breaks the pact with his father ("Why hast thou forsaken me?"), and it is the mother who puts him on the cross. Like a real oral mother, says Deleuze, she assures the son of a resurrection like a second parthenogenetic birth.[38]

If we look again at Bacon's painting "Crucifixion" and relate this to Deleuze's remark on masochism and the figure of Christ, masochism is related not only to crucifixion but also to becoming-animal. The slaughter-house scene in *In a Year of 13 Moons*, which was the central image in the last section of Chapter 2, evokes the same sad affects as Bacon's crucifixion paintings. One could read this scene metaphorically: the cows are slaughtered like Elvira is "slaughtered." Right at the beginning, Elvira is beaten by two homosexuals who discover that she has no penis. When she comes home, she sinks onto the floor, bending her head down, like the crucified figure of Bacon's painting. Right after that, she is beaten up again by her boyfriend Kristoff, who will then leave her. It was also noted earlier that in the video-arcade scene Elvira is insulted by one of the customers of the arcade, who tells her that he will slaughter her if she looks at him once more (". . . und Ich schlachte dich ab!"). The slaughtered animals are not just a metaphor for Elvira's condition.

Throughout the film, there are visual and discursive signs that point toward a real becoming-animal of Elvira. As argued before, almost all the close-ups in Fassbinder's film are reserved for Elvira, expressing her sad affects. None of the other persons gets closer than medium-close, and if they are so close in the image, it is to express an affect that is similar to Elvira's (for instance, Elvira's friend Zora or the nun, Sister Gudrun). In the slaughterhouse, there is also a medium close-up of the head of a cow, which has been skinned. Under it are not bones, but red flesh. "Pity the flesh," says Deleuze about Bacon's crucifixion paintings. The flesh in his paintings is not dead flesh but still contains all the sufferings and the colors of life (red blood). Bacon is not saying, "Pity the animals"; rather, he is saying that every man who suffers is "fleshy," and the flesh is the indiscernible zone between humans and animals. Bacon himself comments, "I have always been very touched by images that are related to the slaughterhouse and to the flesh, and for me they are all strongly connected to the crucifiction. . . . It's certain that we are powerful carcasses. When I go to a butcher shop, I am always surprised not to be there, in the place of the animal. . . ."[39] So it is in the flesh that the becoming-animal of humans finds its expression.

In the flesh, humans become animal, the body becomes a figure, and the face becomes a head. In this way, the close-ups of Elvira's face gain something akin to a "head-like" quality, which expresses passive affects. This effect is reinforced by Fassbinder's frequent and dominant use of red and blue light, which gives some scenes a painterly quality (in contrast to other scenes filmed in harsh realistic light). Bacon also uses a lot of red and blue for his crucifixion paintings. Not only on the image-track of *In a Year of 13 Moons* are there numerous references to the becoming-animal of the flesh; the soundtrack, too, includes many references to the flesh. Elvira's head and body are rather "fleshy." We can see that, but more often we are told that she is, For instance, Kristoff, who forces Elvira to look at her face in the mirror ("*Ekelhaft*," he shouts) and then throws her on the bed in disgust: "*All dieses überflüssiges Fleisch!—Weil du keinen Willen hast, du bist nur passiv.*"[40]

Here flesh is here associated with passiveness (passive affects), which is one kind of becoming-animal. Anton Saitz, the man for whom Erwin had himself operated into Elvira (taking away some "superfluous flesh"?), was a "meat dealer" (*Er handelte in Fleisch*). When Elvira visits him after many years, one of the first remarks he makes about her is that she has become fat. Finally, there are a few remarks about mothers who try to "stuff" their children: Erwin as a child was stuffed with food by the nuns in the nunnery; so they did not see "the happy child becoming a sad child." and Elvira's ex-wife insists that their daughter Marianne should eat. "All right then, for your sake, I'll get as round as a ball," the girl replies.[41] This is where the oral mother enters the masochistic scene again: the fattened child becomes dependent and passive and eventually returns to mother earth what it has taken: the cycle of becoming-human and becoming-animal.

Finally, I want to remark on three instances where Fassbinder uses "disembodied" voices. These disembodied voices have, in the first instance, a narrative function, namely, to narrate Elvira's life story. This first happens in the slaughterhouse scene. Although we know that Elvira is in the slaughterhouse of which we see the images (so the voice is not completely disembodied), her voice sounds far away, as if it has escaped from her body and is now floating around trying to find that body again. In combination with the screaming voice at a certain moment and the images of the poor, bloody, and fleshy cows, this scene expresses exactly the same as Bacon's crucifixion painting, discussed previously. The scream painted by Bacon is now displaced to the soundtrack; it is "glued" against the images of the descending flesh of the animals. It is almost too sad to endure watching and listening. So a second function of the disembodiment of the voice is to give it a "painterly" effect / affect.

Another half-disembodied voice in the film is the voice of Sister Gudrun (played by Fassbinder's mother), who speaks about Erwin's youth. Again, the voice sounds like a voice-over: the body is actually in the image but seems nevertheless absent from that voice. In this way, we learn that Erwin is a bastard child, and his real mother did not want her husband to find out about his existence, which meant that the child could never have any foster parents either. His "primitive mother" threw him away; his "oral mothers" (the nuns) first made him a fatty, and then they also took their distance. Actually, Elvira is like the wolf-children who are abandoned by their real mother and raised by surrogate mothers. Only nuns are not wolves, and instead of developing a sense for active affects, Elvira has developed a sense for passive affects. Finally, Erwin tries himself to become an "oedipal mother," a mistress for her "father" (Anton, Kristoff), all related to becoming-animal and masochism. Actually, the whole film is a tour of all Masoch's mothers; when the tour is finished, Elvira commits suicide, which is the final spasm of the body (comparable to Bacon's paintings).

The last disembodied voice is then Elvira's voice again, this time recorded on tape for an interview in a magazine. Again, this is a reflection on her life, which is heard while her dead body is discovered. Not all the words can be discerned because the scene goes on, and other people enter the house, talk, and cry while Elvira's recorded voice continues. One of the things that can be heard is that she was not sure she wanted to die. "Maybe there were still a few words that played a role: consolation, (melancholic) desire and maybe I wanted to live those ideas," is one of the last sentences. Bitterly, we may conclude that consolation and desire were now worn out, completely consumed, and there was nothing left to live for anymore. Fassbinder's *In a Year of 13 Moons* is a sad, bloody, and cruel film. Through the camerawork and the colors, through the dialogues and monologues, and through the very effective use of the soundtrack, the film evokes strong sensations that are similar to the sensations evoked by Bacon's paintings. Passivity, pity, and sorrow are the affects attained by experiencing this kind of BwO in becoming-animal.

Contamination: The Pack of Animals

Besides passive affects, there are also a possibility and wish for active affects. Cows, pigs, and sheep in general are led more by passive affects than, for instance, wolves. A human being that is more inclined to active affects (it is clear that transformations from passive to active are possible and even necessary for the persistence of being) will likely become an active animal. In this section, I look at such becoming-animal. As I already said, stories and myths about wolves and werewolves have a long tradition and easily could be read as metaphoric or archetypical. Nevertheless, I think stories about werewolves are more than that, especially in some modern adaptations, such as Neil Jordan's film *The Company of Wolves* (1984) and Mike Nichols's *Wolf* (1994). Wolves are wild, flesh-eating animals of the dog family, which hunt in packs. The "flesh-eating" indicates the active (and dangerously wild) part of the wolf. This could be seen as the sadistic pendant of the passive masochistic affects just discussed. It will become clear, however, that a completely different economy at stake.

According to Deleuze and Guattari, becoming-animal has always involved "a pack, a gang, a population, a peopling, in short multiplicity. We sorcerers have always known that."[42] Animals are fundamentally a band, a pack, say Deleuze and Guattari. Hence, a becoming-animal should entail the multiplicity of the pack. Deleuze and Guattari argue that the problem with Freud is precisely that he does not recognize this multiplicity. In "One or Several Wolves" in *A Thousand Plateaus*, they comment on Freud's Wolf-Man, demonstrating how Freud manages to make the singular from the multiple. Although Freud had just discovered that the unconscious often has to do with multiplicities, he nevertheless reduces the dreams of the wolf-man to *the* father. Because they put it so eloquently, I quote the passage where they describe Freud's free association on the level of representation:

The wolves will have to be purged of their multiplicity. This operation is accomplished by associating the dream with the tale, "The Wolf and the Seven Kid-Goats" (only six of which get eaten). We witness Freud's reductive glee; we literally see multiplicity leave the wolves to take the shape of goats that have absolutely nothing to do with the story. Six wolves: the seventh goat (the wolf man himself) is hiding in the clock. Five wolves: he may have seen his parents make love at five o'clock, and the roman numeral V is associated with the erotic spreading of a woman's legs. Three wolves: the parents may have made love three times. Two wolves: the first coupling the child may have seen was the two parents *more ferarum*, or perhaps even two dogs. One wolf: the wolf is the father, as we all knew from the start. Zero wolves: he lost his tail, he is not just a castrator but also castrated. Who is Freud trying to fool? The wolves never had a chance to get away and save their pack: it was already decided from the beginning that animals could serve only to represent coitus between the parents or, conversely, be represented by coitus between parents.[43]

The fact that goats have nothing to do with this story about wolves indicates again the incorrectness of equating masochism to sadism: as noted before, they have their own economies. Deleuze and Guattari see the association of the wolf with goats and then finally with the father as an insult to the wolves and to the fascination of becoming-wolf. As we already learned from Mowgli, children understand more of this fascination than adults; but from the previous chapter, it is also clear that some women, too, at least when they are open to a becoming-woman, are closer to the understanding of this kind of becoming-animal.[44]

Angela Carter is known for her rewriting of myths and fairy tales in which she shows a deep insight into the real fascinations for real becomings. *The Company of Wolves* is one of those rewritten stories. She also collaborated on the script of the film that Neil Jordan made from her stories about wolves.[45] As with all the previous analyses, I concentrate on the film. Jordan made of Carter's short story a film with a complex *mise-en-abîme*[46] structure: there is a girl dreaming; there is the visualization of her dream, and within that dream several stories are told that are also visualized. I do not want concentrate on this narrative structure, although it indicates different levels of "reality." The connecting thread of the film is the tale of

"Little Red Riding Hood." According to the *rereading* of this tale by the psychoanalyst Bruno Bettelheim, the red cape symbolizes her first menstrual blood, the wolf being the dangers of sexual intercourse and the forester being the father, who restores law, order, and innocence, liberating both Riding Hood and her grandmother and killing the wolf.[47] Carter's *rewriting* of "Little Red Riding Hood" contains some elements of Bettelheim's interpretation. In the first instance, Little Red Hiding Hood is the story of the little girl who becomes a woman. Jordan emphasizes this association of the color red, menstrual blood, and sexuality on all levels of the narrative by giving the dreaming girl shining red lips and in the dream indeed a very large red cape, knitted by her grandmother.

The Company of Wolves is not only about becoming a woman in the traditional (psychoanalytic) sense. It is also about becoming-animal by first becoming-woman (Riding Hood is not for nothing a girl, another modern Alice). First, Carter (and with her, Jordan) understands that wolves operate in packs. When we see one wolf, there will soon be two wolves, three wolves, ten wolves, many wolves. When Riding Hood, whose name is Rosaleen in the film, is alone with her wolf-man in the last scene of the film, they suddenly hear the howling of a multitude of wolves: "These are the voices of my brothers, darling," says the wolf-man, "I love the company of wolves." Rosaleen, very pragmatically ("Being afraid wouldn't do me much good, would it?"), is not scared. She is a bit suspicious because her grandmother told her so much idle gossip about werewolves; so she grabs a gun to defend herself. At the same time, she senses that there is something exciting to discover here. Earlier in the film, Rosaleen has witnessed a Freudian scene: she saw and heard her parents making love. Instead of being traumatized, however, she is fascinated and curious. The next morning (when she sees her mother happy and alive working in the house), she asks her mother if he (daddy) hurts her. Rosaleen has a wise mother, who does not give her a slap in the face for such an impolite question, but asks her why she thinks he would hurt her. "Because it sounds like the beast granny told about," answers Rosaleen. Rosaleen's mother replies to this that she should not listen so much to granny's stories and that "if there is a beast in man, it meets its match in woman too." A very wise mother indeed, who demythologizes all (Freudian) binarism between man and woman and who gives her daughter instead a knife to defend herself if necessary and trusts her to make her own judgments about the affinities she has and the alliances she wants to make.

The knife is because not all men/animals match with all women. One must find the one that can make the alliance (but this is a different "one" than the Freudian "One"). As Deleuze and Guattari put it: "Wherever there is multiplicity, you will also find an exceptional individual, and it is with that individual that an alliance must be made in order to become-animal. There may be no such thing as a lone wolf, but there is a leader of the pack."[48]

Rosaleen is the exceptional human who can establish this alliance, but she in turn is also looking for the exceptional animal who can show her this unknown territory of becoming-animal. In the film, Rosaleen has a little neighbor who is clearly in love with her, but she does not want him. She likes him quite well, but he is a rustic clown to her, a playmate, nothing more. In the woods (having left the only safe track), she meets a "fine fellow" to whom she feels immediately attracted, even though she senses that he might be a (were)wolf. This is the "exceptional individual" with whom she can make alliance. Finally, she will burn the symbolic red cape.

Carter's story ends with the girl sleeping in granny's bed (granny is dead and remains dead) between the paws of the tender wolf. Jordan goes one step further. As Laura Mulvey puts it in her essay on Angela Carter, "Cinema Magic and the Old Monsters," "In *The Company of Wolves* Rosaleen comes to terms with the wolf inside the charming hunter, in such a way as to suggest that she is accepting not so much the bestiality of *men* as the presence of her now recognized, but unrepressed sexuality."[49] In the film, Rosaleen actually becomes a wolf, and before her father can shoot her (like the forester in the fairy tale), her mother sees that the wolf is wearing Rosaleen's necklace and prevents him from doing so. The wise mother has seen that her daughter has chosen to become-wolf and lets her go to seek the company of wolves. The last images of the dream are of one wolf (Rosaleen) who joins another (her "prince of darkness"), who joins many others (the pack). Carter and Jordan have transformed a metaphoric myth into a fairy tale of becoming-animal.

It is clear that the becoming-animal as just described has nothing to do with the passive affects and becoming-flesh/meat of Bacon. Becoming-wolf has everything to do with active affects. In *The Company of Wolves*, this activity was always already a part of Rosaleen; she just had to continue on her path of becoming. Another possibility is the transformation of passive affects into active ones. This is clearly the case in the film *Wolf*. Will Randall works at a publishing house that is going to merge. At the beginning of the film, Randall is a tired, passive man who is not able to stop the games that are being played with him. He is given a choice either to quit or to be transferred to Eastern Europe (which in this case boils down to the same thing). At the beginning of the film, when he is stuck near the border of a forest (the border zone where, according to Deleuze and Guattari, alliances get made), he is bitten by a wolf and slowly he senses that something of the spirit of the wolf is becoming part of him. He feels "reborn" and starts to fight back. Slowly, he discovers that he is really becoming a wolf, with all the negative (murderous) consequences as well.

First, it should be noted that Randall, although he seems passive and is overruled all the time, is "exceptional." This becomes clear at a publisher's party, where he does not conform to the rules of polite conversation. When his boss announces to him news of his transfer, he says that "taste and personality" (Randall's qualities) are not the right qualities to have in the publishing business. His boss's daughter Laura is also an outcast. She hates her father's business and does not feel at home at the party. In this respect, she matches Randall perfectly, and it is no coincidence that they meet. We see here again two exceptional beings who will make the alliance.

Second, this alliance is not something hereditary but something that is contagious (as was already remarked about vampires as well). This contamination (for instance, by a bite) is typical of the notion of becoming in general, particularly of the becoming-animal. The difference between contagion and inheritance is that it can connect very heterogeneous elements, such as a human and an animal. It is worthwhile to note how this alliance is related to Donna Haraway's concept of affinity, which characterizes the relations of the cyborg: "Affinity: related not by blood but by choice, the appeal of one chemical nuclear group for another."[50] Although Randall apparently has not chosen to be bitten by a wolf, he has something in him on the plane of immanence that chooses to be inspired by the spirit of the wolf. Laura, however, will at the very end of the film clearly make a choice to become-wolf. In that sense, she is comparable to Rosaleen.

This brings me to the second way of contamination: sexuality (which was also clear in *The Company of Wolves*). Sexuality has the power of alliance, say Deleuze and Guattari. Both Rosaleen and Laura become-wolf through sexual alliance, which they consider not a threat but a liberation. As in *Dr. Jekyll and Mr. Hyde*, it is interesting to see that this alliance, this becoming-animal, is expressed again in the image by close-ups and extreme close-ups of the eyes. In the last image, we see the eyes of Randall-wolf in extreme close-up. Then we see Laura walking alone (but certainly not afraid) in the woods. The next moment, we see her eyes slowly conflating with the wolf's eyes. In this way, the (spatial and other) difference between man, woman, and animal is dissolved and the becoming-animal has become real. Just before that moment, Laura's becoming-animal also was rendered in a different way. Like Randall before, she exhibited an extremely well-developed sense of smell: from a great distance, she can smell that the police inspector had been drinking vodka and tonic. The improvement of the senses (all senses or at least other senses than the normal human ones) is the first sign of becoming-animal.

This relates to the third remark I would like to make about *Wolf*. It is through a better development of the senses that Randall first becomes aware of his changing spirit. It is through the senses that he can change his passive affects into active affects. Randall discovers that he can smell things he could never smell before, that he can hear through the walls of his office, and that he can suddenly read without glasses; he notices that something inside of him is changing (and again these sensations are shown in close-up). His movements also change. First, he becomes very active sexually, but after a while, he can also jump like an animal. In short, it is his "longitude," his movements and rests, that also change his "latitude" axis. Randall's change of perception (through all the senses) is similar to the effects of drugs. Also, in this respect, there is a proximity between Mr. Hyde and Randall-becoming-wolf: they feel like they have taken a drug. In the plateau on becoming-animal, Deleuze and Guattari dedicate several pages to the effects of drugs. They state that drugs change movement and perception:

All drugs fundamentally concern speeds, and modifications of speed. What allows us to describe an overall Drug assemblage in spite of the differences between drugs is a line of perceptive causality that makes it so that (1) the imperceptible is perceived; (2) perception is molecular; (3) desire directly invests the perception and the perceived. . . . It is our belief that the issue of drugs can be understood only at the level where desire directly invests perception, and perception becomes molecular at the same time as the imperceptible is perceived. Drugs then appear as the agent of becoming. . . . The unconscious as such is given in microperceptions. . . . Drugs give the unconscious the immanence and plane that psychoanalysis has consistently botched.[51]

What happens to Randall is like a drug effect: he perceives what he can normally not perceive; it is as if he can see through people, as if he can look at his own plane of immanence and understand what and who is important for him and how he can reach this and them.

With their elaborations on drugs, Deleuze and Guattari do not want to romanticize drugs (a reproach they often received) or want to make us all junkies. The great danger of drugs is that, instead of giving you more power and rapidity in movement and perception, they make you no longer master of movements and perceptions. The "black hole" of addiction leads to destruction instead of enrichment of one's life. According to Deleuze and Guattari, we should arrive at a point where the question is no longer "to take drugs or not to take them" (I paraphrase) but rather that the drug has changed the general conditions of perception to such an extent that also without drugs we reach the plane of immanence: in order not to be fooled by the drugs, the aim is to become "drugged" by water, by music, by anything but drugs. Randall has not taken drugs, but the effects are the same. In the end, however, he is not destroyed; he has found his line of flight by becoming-animal, as will his matching alliance Laura.

New Experiments—New Images—New "Manimals"

Despite all the intrinsic dangers of all kinds of becoming, of all kinds of rhizomatic experiences, Deleuze and Guattari nevertheless advocate experimenting: "Make a rhizome. But you don't know what you can make a rhizome with, you don't know which subterranean stem is effectively going to make a rhizome, or enter a becoming, people your desert. So experiment."[52]

As is clear from the foregoing, certain kinds of becoming-animal always have already played a role in human imagination, in mythology and fairy tales. Since the modernization of science, certainly since the nineteenth century, these becomings have become more specific and more related to scientific experiments. Often these experiments still have been rooted in archetypical and binary models of thinking: Dr. Frankenstein, Dr. Moreau, Dr. Jekyll, they all suffer from it and provide us with our traditional monsters. In the twentieth century, science developed enormously and is changing our perception on all levels. Slowly but surely, some new perceptions are becoming possible. Many experiments are ongoing, and although they do not always have happy endings, these are developments we cannot stop. Some recent films show experiments that try to change our perception, which also implies that we leave the "familiar" becoming-animals (be they passive or active), our familiar monsters, and step into the unknown zones between human and insect, human and ram, and human and kangaroo. In other words, we are entering a cyborg world of techno-teratologic imaginations.

If there is one filmmaker who has always shown an interest in experimenting with the possibilities of new science, it is David Cronenberg. Perhaps by now not surprisingly, his colleague and friend Martin Scorsese compared Cronenberg's work with the paintings of Francis Bacon.[53] Although Cronenberg has made several films that show becoming-animals, for example, *Shivers* (1975), *Rabid* (1976), and, of course, *The Fly* (1986), on which I concentrate in this section, his films show a very different becoming-animal from Fassbinder's *In a Year of 13 Moons*, which was close to Bacon's paintings.[54] Unlike Fassbinder's, Cronenberg's films always have been associated with the horror genre, but the way he films the horror of becoming is how he is close to Bacon. This actually means they do not so much show the horror as visible spectacle. Rather, they show the horror of invisible forces that come from inside. Bacon himself refers to this as "painting the cry, more than painting horror."[55] Seth Brundle's gradual discovery of becoming-fly is a cry of not being able to control invisible forces. There is no literal crying and screaming, as in traditional horror films. Like Bacon, he could paint the cry in one static moment, and Cronenberg films it in the duration of the becoming.

In *The Fly*, Seth Brundle, who is again a scientist who has isolated himself to dedicate his passion to science, has discovered a machine for teletransportation. This teletransportation (in itself also an old fantasy) can be achieved by means of molecular breakdown and recreation. Very directly, this indicates the molecular level on which all becomings take place and on which the becoming-fly specifically is situated. When Seth shows his invention for the first time to journalist Veronica, the machine still does not know how to teletransport living material. Seth discovers that this is because he (and therefore the computer that is programmed by him) does not understand enough about "the flesh." This discovery is mediated by one of the most "fleshy" experiences human beings can have, namely, making love (again the importance of sexuality is emphasized). It is Veronica who gives him the understanding of the flesh when she says after making love that she would like to eat him: "Now I understand why grannies like to pinch baby-cheeks: the flesh makes them crazy."

Like for Bacon and Fassbinder, the flesh is important; but before Cronenberg shows how the flesh degenerates, he shows how "new flesh" is created:

The most accessible version of the new flesh would be that you can actually change what it means to be a human being in a physical way. We have certainly changed in a psychological way since the beginning of mankind. And we have in fact changed in a physical way as well. We are different physically from our forefathers, partly because of what we take into our bodies and partly because of things like glasses and surgery and so on. But there is a further step that could happen, which would be that you could grow another arm, that you could actually physically change the way you look, mutate, all of these things.[56]

In the next passage of the interview with Cronenberg from which these words are taken, Cronenberg also stresses the importance of sexuality and the wish to "swap organs" or "develop different kinds of organs" or "have no (sexual) organs per se" to diminish sexual polarity. For *The Fly*, the polarity between human and insectile "organs" is diminished. The Fly presents us a BwO.

As soon as Brundle manages to keep the flesh in teletransportation (again a diminisher of distances between bodies and spaces), he is able to transport living beings. After a baboon comes out alive, Seth experiments on himself. Unfortunately, he does not act carefully enough (he is drunk and sad) and does not notice that a fly is transported with him and that on a genetic and molecular level (DNA) their bodies are combined; so Seth is becoming-insect. In the beginning, this has a positive effect on him. Like Randall in *Wolf*, Seth feels strong, liberated, and powerful with a lot of physical energy. Both his bodily movements and his perceptions change. There is an interesting shot in the film that shows Brundle's studio seen from above. It turns out to be the point-of-view shot of Seth who, like a fly, is hanging on the ceiling and looking down on the world below. This is clearly a literal change of perception, which was anticipated by the very first image of the film, which is also a shot from above the scene in which

Seth and Veronica meet each other at a reception. This crane shot, or bird's-eye view, is an "inhuman" perception that is made possible by technology. Cinema in this respect is also a "machine of becoming."

Like Randall, Brundle has experiences that are similar to taking drugs. Brundle even thinks he has discovered the "pure drug" (the drug without being a drug) as promoted by Deleuze and Guattari. Unfortunately, Brundle becomes a "junkie" nevertheless; he feels great and strong but starts looking worse and worse. He eats only chocolate and ice cream ("junkfood"); he no longer bothers about his bodily and spatial hygiene (degeneration); he wants to teletransport himself over and over again (addiction); and he also wants to transmit his experience to other people (contamination). Cronenberg himself acknowledges that creating new flesh is a risky business, which he compares to drug addiction: "It's dangerous. You think you know what is going on, . . . but you're never really sure what you're going to get out of it. I suppose it's like taking a drug. You've heard that this drug is addictive. You think that you are not an addictive personality. You will try this drug, but you don't really know what will happen. You don't know that you will not end up like everybody else or worse, or will you? I mean you just don't know."[57] In the same way, Seth did not know what would happen if he teletransported himself. He did not send the transported baboon to the laboratory for a check-up, and he did not take enough precautions. Even if he had done so, he would not have known what would happen. In this case, the experiment fails in a terrible way. Seth cannot accept his becoming-fly because he loses control of all his movements and actions.[58] This desperate feeling of losing control is the cry we see. In his last desperate teletransportation, he fuses with the telepod machine itself, and even then the thing ("Brundlefly machine") expresses a cry. The new flesh cannot contain all the explosions that take place on the level of immanence; one could say that Brundlefly dies of an overdose of transformation.

Luckily, not all experimentations go wrong (Deleuze and Guattari's only advice is to be cautious in experimenting). The world of bizarre creatures that is created by fine artist Matthew Barney in his video film and related exhibition with sculptures, objects, and photos in *Cremaster 4* (1994) could be seen as an aesthetic experiment that nevertheless is inspired by becomings of all sorts. In this project, Barney is the "Loughton man," who combines human with Loughton ram characteristics. Throughout his work, he has created many BwOs, bodies that make connections that defy many borders.[59] His fascination for the American football player Jim Otto, who has a plastic knee, is significant in this respect. Also, the magician Harry Houdini is important for him. Actually, Barney himself is a magician (or a sorcerer, as Deleuze and Guattari say in their piece on becoming-animal) who transforms his models into fauns (*Drawing Restraint 7*, 1993), androgynous Graces, or race-car drivers whose leather race suits seem to be penetrated by a slimy substance (the first time, except in horror cinema, that the male body is associated with soft and stringy matter—it is not even flesh). In his latest work from the *Cremaster* series, *Cremaster 5* (1997, shot on film) Barney himself is indeed announced as a magician.[60] His world is so incredibly strange and beautiful that he stretches the limits of imagination and the limits of the body. In any case, Matthew Barney wants to free the body from its organic constraints. Like in popular culture, in visual arts, more and more expressions of becomings can be observed.

The last "successful experiment" that I want to mention here is Rachel Talalay's film *Tank Girl* (1995). Here the new image of women (strong, tough, and not innocent, without fear and needy for connections, in short a cyborg) is related to a new sort of "manimals." These creatures are the result of a DNA experiment that combined the genes of humans with those of kangaroos.[61] Tank Girl and her friend Jet Girl first have prejudices about these creatures. Like everybody, they think that the Rippers are demonic monsters; however, they turn out to be gentle and democratic (!) and to possess a great sense of natural justice (the law of the jungle). *Tank Girl* is a sign of the times, showing in a funny and inventive way the fears and hopes of a young generation that will soon be entering the third millennium.[62] The biggest fear, of course, is an ecologic disaster and that a small group of people will make a profit from it. The events in the film take place in 2033, a time by which the earth has changed into a desert and the little water that remains is appropriated by the Department of Water and Power, ruled by a truly sadistic dictator.[63] It is a *1984*-ish nightmare situation; but whereas Big Brother kept watching you, and no escape was possible, this time there is hope for revolution, transformation, and change. This hope comes from the margins, the little parts that are not kept by the system, either literally (like the Rippers, who have their own underground hiding places) or figuratively (like Tank Girl's indestructible fighting spirit for freedom). From this very small group, the war with the system starts:

the war machine or the line of flight. As Deleuze and Guattari explained, the war machine never starts within a state; it always enters from the outside. I will not elaborate on that aspect of the film here, but this possibility of a war machine is certainly part of the utopian side of this film and world vision. The other aspect that is utopian relates to the acceptance of the manimals as complete and respect-worthy beings. Both Tank Girl and the Rippers are cyborgs in the way that Donna Haraway intended them: inappropriate/d others that embody the "promise of monsters" that might change the maps of the world. One might say that this is all fiction and fantasy and nonsense, but this would be a misunderstanding of the world we live in today: "Tank Girls" exist; DNA research is undergoing incredible development, and ecologic disasters are hanging like "swords of Damocles" above the earth.[64]

There is one other aspect in which this film relates to contemporary culture: music. The film's soundtrack is composed in the spirit of MTV.[65] In one scene, the kangaroo-men dance wildly to this music, which for them is a religious dance for the freedom of living and thinking. I think these creatures, which are in a real and permanent state of becoming, are proposing an ethics in the spirit of Spinoza. If he had been alive today, he would have joined the Rippers in their dance. Now they are joined by Tank Girl and Jet Girl. From becoming-animal, they are becoming-music, which is explored more extensively in the next chapter. Concerning the concept of the subject, it is now possible to conclude that its borders have become extremely flexible. In recognizing a zone of proximity between human subject and animals, becomings-animal are finding their own consistencies in various images and practices. Becoming-animal is one of the many possible becomings that open the subject to the invisible forces that can cause powerful effects and affects of change. Becoming-animal and other forms of (techno)mutations seen as a "philosophical teratology" then no longer need be regarded as a threat to humanity but as new ways of increasing powers and affects. Like in *X-Men*, the struggle then is no longer between humans and animals/monsters, but between all kinds of new forces that can be destructive as well as empowering.

6

(De)Territorializing Forces of
the Sound Machine

In the previous chapters, I looked at the various ways in which subjectivity as a process can be constructed within an audiovisual world, a universe as metacinema. I discussed aspects of subjectivity in movement-images and time-images and collective "identities" in political fabulations. Identities are mobile, a *becoming* rather than a *being*; becoming-woman and becoming-animal are particular aspects of becoming that were discussed in the two previous chapters. In contemporary culture, however, music has gained increasing importance, not only because, like images, music seems to be everywhere around us (on the radio, in the shopping mall, as soundtracks of films, on the Internet) but also because it seems to offer a key to identity. This is not because music represents certain groups but because, like in perceiving certain images and telling and listening to stories, in perfoming and listening to music, certain identities are being formed. In his article "Music and Identity," Simon Frith proposes a view on the role of music that is similar to Deleuze's transcendental empiricism in respect of culture in general. In examining the aesthetic of popular music, Frith wants to reverse the usual academic and critical argument: "The issue is not how a particular piece of music or a performance reflects a people, but how it produces them, how it creates and constructs an experience—a musical experience, an aesthetic experience—that we can only make sense of by *taking on* both a subjective and collective identity. The aesthetic, to put this another way, describes the quality of an experience (not the quality of an object); it means experiencing *ourselves* (not just the world) in a different way."[1]

Frith has two premises for his argument. First, like Deleuze and Guattari, he argues that identity is mobile, a becoming and not a being. Second, he argues that the experience of music (both performing and listening) is best understood as this mobile self-in-process. Furthermore, Frith argues that music is at the same time both an aesthetic and an ethic experience: when we like certain music, this also immediately implies an evaluation of that music, an aesthetic response is an ethical agreement. He says, "We need to rethink the usual sociologic approach to aesthetic expression. My point is not that a social group has beliefs which it then articulates in its music, but that music, an aesthetic practice, articulates *in itself* an understanding of both group relations and individuality, on the basis of which ethical codes and social ideologies are understood. . . . Social groups . . . only get to know themselves as *groups* . . . through cultural activity, through aesthetic judgement."[2]

In arguing that music is not a reflection of certain group identities, but that identities are formed through musical practice and experience, Frith is a "transcendental empiricist," like Deleuze and Guattari. His views on popular music in relation to social identity are therefore complementary to the conceptual thoughts on music of Deleuze and Guattari in *A Thousand Plateaus*. Deleuze and Guattari speak about territorial and deterritorial forces of music on a conceptual level. "Flags can do nothing without trumpets," claim Deleuze and Guattari.[3] They think music, which is a temporal form of art *par excellence*, as an aesthetic form with strong spatial (territorial and deterritorial) forces. In Chapter 4, I indicated the ways in which Björk's performance in *Dancer in the Dark* is a form of becoming-music with territorial and deterritorial forces. In a more "down to earth" but nevertheless similar way, Frith concludes his article on music and identity as follows:

What makes music special—what makes it special for identity—is that it defines a space without boundaries (a game without frontiers). Music is thus the cultural form best able to cross borders—sounds carry across fences and walls and oceans, across classes, races and nations—and to define places; in clubs, scenes, and raves, listening on headphones, radio and in the concert hall, we are only where the music takes us.[4]

From the preceding quotes, it is clear that Frith takes sociology as his frame of reference. In music theory, much of the work on popular music is done mainly from a sociologic perspective. Deleuze and Guattari, however, take psychoanalysis as their counterreference. In film theory, too, sound and music often have been discussed in psychoanalytic terms. There are a few other sound theories, but, as in previous chapters, I focus on the psychoanalytic interpretations of music to compare them with the view of Deleuze and Guattari. To see how the power of music and becoming-music works in relation to the image and in film theory, I start with a more traditional and psychoanalytic take on music and sound; then I proceed with the insights provided by Deleuze and Guattari and see how these insights can be related to questions of Frith's social "mobile selves" in the matrix of audiovisual culture.

Acoustic Mirrors and Fantasmatic Structures

Sound in Film: An Acoustic Mirror

Although cinema was born in silence, sound has always been part of the film performance. Live music accompanied most silent films, and sometimes the voice of an *explicateur* narrated or commented on the story. Nevertheless, until recently film theory has concentrated largely on the image, on the ocular, and on the spectacle. As Walter Murch explains in the foreword to Michel Chion's *Audio-Vision*:[5]

We begin to hear before we are born, four-and-a-half months after conception. From then on, we develop in a continuous and luxurious bath of sounds: the song of our mother's voice, the swash of her breathing, the trumpeting of her intestines, the timpani of her heart. Throughout the second four-and-a-half months, Sound rules as solitary Queen of our senses: the close and liquid world of uterine darkness makes Sight and Smell impossible, Taste monochromatic, and Touch a dim and generalized hint of what is to come. Birth brings with it the sudden and simultaneous ignition of the other four senses, and an intense competition for the throne that Sound had claimed as hers. The most notable pretender is the darting and insistent Sight, who dubs himself King as if the throne had been standing vacant, waiting for him. Ever discreet, Sound pulls a veil of oblivion across her reign and withdraws into the shadows, keeping a watchful eye on the braggart Sight. If she gives up her throne, it is doubtful that she gives up her crown. In a mechanistic reversal of this biological sequence, Cinema spent its youth (1892–1927) wandering in a mirrored hall of voiceless images, a thirty-five year bachelorhood over which Sight ruled as self-satisfied, solipsistic King—never suspecting that destiny was preparing an arranged marriage with the Queen he thought he had deposed at birth.[6]

Obviously these words can be explained psychoanalytically, which I will do in a moment. With his comparison between mighty King Sight and veiled Queen Sound, Murch wanted to emphasize in the first instance the unobtrusive role of sound in cinema. Unless something goes wrong, sound is often used in the service of the image, at most a sort of reflecting or emphasizing mirror of the image. Historically, sound is seen as an "afterthought," something of secondary importance. Michel Chion is one of the first to develop a theory of sound that does justice to its complex and diverse relation to the image. He offers a vocabulary and tools to describe and analyze the effects of sound. To gain access to these tools, I first highlight some of Chion's terminology.

The first (and very important) step that Chion makes is to assume that there is no "natural and preexisting harmony between image and sound."[7] We relate images and sounds with our brain, and filmmakers can experiment with these relations, but there is no law that makes images and sounds go naturally together. As filmmaker Robert Bresson once said, images and sounds are like strangers that meet and then cannot separate anymore. Nevertheless, since the official introduction of sound film, the soundtrack has been constructed largely as a function of the representative realism effect. The dialogues between the characters on screen have been a central preoccupation of the sound engineers: the *talkies*. Chion calls this the *vococentrism* of cinema. Related to this is what Chion calls the phenomenon of *synchresis*, the forging of an immediate and necessary relationship between something one sees and something one hears at the same time.[8] The dialogue exchange by characters on the screen produces *theatrical speech*.[9] Clearly, all these terms that Chion invents put the emphasis on sound but also underline the mirroring function that has been assigned to sound.

In *La toile trouée*, Michel Chion describes the sound film as "a place of images with sounds."[10] He explains what he means by this apparently simple definition. First, the sound film is a place of images with sounds. All images are framed and contained within that frame. Of course, this refers to the classic film situation; multiple screens, video, and multimedia installations can have more places. One could say that the image functions as a container, with the frame indicating the edges of this container. Sound, on the contrary, is contained by the image. Sound escapes the frame but has traditionally been "held in place" by the image. Second, the sound film is a *place* of images with sounds. Place is closely connected to the concept of space and is always a construction. We discriminate different spaces, different relations between bodies and spaces (distances and proximities), differences between bodies, the different spaces of a body, and the differences between inside and outside of bodies. The place of images is, according to Chion, clearly concentrated on the (human) body. Mary Ann Doane confirms this in her article "The Voice in Cinema," when she talks about the *somatography* of cinema: "Just as the voice must be anchored in a given body, the body must be anchored in a given space."[11] The connection between place, body, and voice is an important one that will be elaborated in the following pages herein.

The third aspect of the sound film is that it is a place of *images* with sounds. Even if there are no bodies, even if the image is just a black (framed) screen, there is still an image in relation to the sound. Fourth, the sound film is a place of images *with* sounds. The conjunction *with* indicates that different relations between the sound and the image are possible. Sound can be directly related to the image. For instance, the sound of a voice related to a character in the image or music with a visible source in the image, what Chion calls *screen music*, is also termed *diegetic music*. Sounds also come from just outside the frame: the *voice-off* or other sounds that go beyond the frame. In this case, the place and space of the image are enlarged by sounds. Chion calls this phenomenon *extension* of the sound space.[12] Another relation of sound to the image is the sound that transcends the images, for example, the *voice-over* of a narrator and nondiegetic or *pit music*. A voice-over can narrate, comment on, or contradict the images. In some cases, as for instance in Marguerite Duras's *India Song*, the soundtrack gains complete autonomy in respect to the images (which it nevertheless affects).

Sound that does not have a visible source is called *acousmatic sound*. *Acousmatic* is an old Greek term used by Pythagoras to indicate that masters were hidden behind a curtain when teaching their pupils. They were not visible; only their voice was audible, which increased their power (as if they were speaking with the voice of God). Chion has a special term for filmic characters that create power by presenting themselves acousmatically: the *acousmêtre* (a contraction of *acousmatic* and *être en maître*). The most famous examples are the wizard in *The Wizard of Oz* and Dr. Baum/ Dr. Mabuse in *The Testament of Dr. Mabuse*. The power of acousmatic voices and sound is enormous, as I explain later.[13]

Here I need to raise the fifth and last aspect of Chion's definition of the sound film, which is that it is a place of images with *sounds*. Sounds can be diverse, and Chion distinguishes, besides the categories of music already mentioned (such as screen music and pit music), other different sounds, like *ambient sound* (for example, traffic, footsteps, running water), *internal sounds* (bodily noises), *mental sounds* (thoughts, parts of sentences, a melody) and *on-the-air sounds* of radios, telephones, televisions, and computers. A last kind of special sound is of course voices: voices that speak, sing, murmur, whisper, or scream.

The Female Voice as Acoustic Mirror

It is the sound of the voice, especially the female voice, that is the central focus of *The Acoustic Mirror*, Kaja Silverman's important work on sound in cinema.[14] In this book, Silverman gives a psychoanalytic interpretation of the voice in cinema. Walter Murch's quote about the importance of sound before birth and its dethroning after birth is reminiscent of a psychoanalytic interpretation: it is the voice of the mother, which soon after birth is silenced by the law-and-order word of the father. Silverman argues, and many other feminists with her, that classic cinema "has the potential to reactivate the trauma of symbolic castration in the viewer, and that it puts sexual difference in place as a partial defense against that trauma."[15] Silverman says *partial* because the protection is only for the male viewer, not for the female. Laura Mulvey and other feminist theorists demonstrated how this trauma is visually overcome, for instance, by voyeuristic sadism and scopophilic fetishism. In *The Acoustic Mirror*, Silverman makes reference to Chion and argues that the body in relation to the voice often functions as a prison of sexual difference. She demonstrates that Chion's work, despite its descriptive "neutral" appearance, is heavily inspired by castration anxiety, especially when it comes to the voice. Chion compares the embodiment of a voice to a striptease performance:

In much the same way that the feminine sex is the ultimate point in the deshabille (the point after which it is no longer possible to deny the absence of the penis), there is an ultimate point in the embodiment of the voice, and that is the *mouth* from which the voice issues. . . . As long as the face and mouth have not been revealed, and the eye of the spectator has not "verified" the coincidence of the voice with the mouth . . . the vocal embodiment is incomplete, and the voice conserves an aura of invulnerability and of magic power.[16]

This invulnerability and magic power are of course comparable to the voice of Chion's acousmêtre. As Silverman demonstrates, such a voice is almost never designated to a woman. In classic cinema, the all-knowing voice-over is reserved mostly for male characters. If there is a female voice-over, it is an embodied one, the voice of an actress whom we can see in the image, while she is speaking in voice-over.[17] Silverman demonstrates, still following Chion's arguments, that the only disembodied female voice in cinema is a terrifying voice, like the voice of "the mother" (Mrs. Bates) in *Psycho*. The power of the acousmatic voice, then, is related to the omnipotent maternal voice. Again, Chion is caught in a castration panic: he expresses his fear of the voice of the mother, which is woven around a child like a horrible umbilical cobweb. The maternal voice is negatively opposed to the paternal *word*, and it is mostly the word, the discursive and signifying power, that wins this battle in classic cinema.

A last point that strikes Silverman in the work of Chion is his statement that cinema is "a machine made in order to deliver a cry from the female voice." What is demanded from women, Silverman concludes, is an involuntary sound: the scream, the cry, or possibly a (nondiscursive) melody. Ranging from Fay Wray's scream in *King Kong* to the "perfect" scream in *Blow Out*, cinema has indeed produced a whole range of female screams. Male screams are hard to find in classic Hollywood cinema, even in recent horror cinema, which, as we have seen, has some transgendered characteristics. The female voice is embodied within the diegetic world, far from the site where discursive (disembodied) power takes shape in the form of language. In a psychoanalytic mind/body split, the embodied voice utters pure sounds, without symbolic meaning. As Silverman quotes Chion, the female voice "must occupy an unthinkable point at the interior of thought, an inexpressible [point] at the interior of the enunciation, an unrepresentable [point] at the interior of representation."[18]

Silverman also discusses Francis Ford Coppola's film *The Conversation* (1974), a film that could be seen as paradigmatic for the use of sound in cinema (like *Peeping Tom* was for the visual aspects of the cinematographic apparatus). The main character of the film, Harry Caul, is a surveillance expert, who one day makes the big mistake of becoming too involved in a case, and as a result gets caught in a web of intrigue and murder. Caul has a paradoxic attitude toward his job. On the one hand, he is a professional eavesdropper, who is good at his job of stealing conversations. The opening scene of the film shows a crowded Union Square in San Francisco. There is certainly cinematographic voyeurism involved in this scene: a young woman and her apparent boyfriend are being photographed from a rooftop; but the emphasis is on the soundtrack, the private conversation between the two lovers, which is being taped by Harry and his colleagues. On the other hand, Harry is completely paranoid of being surveilled himself. He does not want anyone to enter his apartment, he cannot appreciate the joke a colleague plays on him by secretly listening in on him, and by the end of the film, he ruins his apartment in search of surveillance equipment.

Silverman also looks at the contradictory attitude Harry Caul has toward sounds and voices. On the one hand, he is obsessed by a desire for complete control over sounds emitted by others. On the other, Silverman states, "He is strongly and irrationally attracted by the female voice, which activates in him the desire to be folded in a blanket of sound."[19] Silverman convincingly demonstrates how Caul's obsession with the lovers' conversation is related to a desire for the maternal voice (the voice functions here as an umbilical cord), which during the film becomes stronger than his male discursive and symbolic position of control. He has "a desire to be restored to the 'uterine night' of a presymbolic wholeness—to be enclosed once again in an envelope of pure sonorousness—and his desire to hold back that night by establishing his control over (and exteriority to) sound. Depending upon which definition is activated at any given moment, the female voice assumes the status of an object (of a beloved part of himself which Harry seeks to incorporate), or of the abject (of that which defiles, and which must consequently be jettisoned)."[20]

Silverman justifies her arguments by pointing out moments in the conversation that evoke the mother/child dyad. When the woman notices a drunk asleep on a bench, she says that when she sees somebody like this, she always thinks that once he was somebody's baby boy. Her maternal affect is also noticeable in a children's song she sings: "When the red, red robin comes bob, bob, bobbin' along" (clearly the preoedipal nonsymbolic language associated with the female voice). Caul hears these passages over and again before he discovers a line that is initially obscured by other sounds. It is a line expressed by the man, who says "He'd kill us if he had the chance." Every time we hear this sentence, its meaning shifts. First, we hear with Harry "He'd *kill* us if he had the chance." By the end of the film, when not the couple are killed but the husband of the woman, the emphasis shifts to "*He'd* kill us if *he* had the chance." These words, covered over by the female voice, are inaudible, hidden in the "night of the world," the female principle. It is the confrontation with death. Seen like this, *The Conversation* is an oedipal story in which the mother is the beloved and abjected object (Harry not only wants to prevent the murder of the woman, but he also wants to hear her scream) but in which the father is killed. The female voice is the impossible object of desire and at the same time an object that needs to be controlled discursively. Seen this way, *The Conversation* is paradigmatic for the position of the female voice in all classic Hollywood.

Silverman demonstrates how in most classic Hollywood films this psychoanalytic trauma is connected to women's embodied and discursive powerless positions. The female voice then becomes an acoustic mirror for male anxiety. So, also in psychoanalytic interpretation, sound—especially the female voice—is considered an acoustic mirror for the image. Nondiscursive physical and embodied sounds like screams, cries, and pure sounds are considered negative but fascinating at the same time. The perfect scream or the perfect voice of a diva is thus the impossible object of desire, the *objet petit a*, the impossible signifier of *jouissance*.

The Fantasmatic Powers of the Voice

Slavoj Žižek also argues that the voice, especially the female scream, is an impossible object of desire. Žižek sees this *objet petit a* as a trace of the Real. For instance, he explains the status of the voice in the cinema of David Lynch as such a trace: the voice breaks through the skin surface to cut directly into the raw flesh (which in psychoanalysis has, as mentioned before, the status of abject femininity and the Real). The voice as sound can be "repaired" into comprehensible language only with the help of the big Other (the symbolic order). As Žižek puts it:

In *Twin Peaks* also, the dwarf in the Red Lodge speaks an incomprehensible, distorted English, rendered intelligible only by the help of subtitles, which assume here the role of the microphone—that is the role of the medium of the big Other. This delay—the process by which the inarticulate sounds we utter become speech only through the intervention of the external, mechanical, symbolic order—is usually concealed. It is rendered visible only when the relationship between surface and its beyond is perturbed. What we have here, therefore, is the hidden reverse of the Derridian critique of logocentrism, in which the voice functions as the medium of illusory self-transparency and self-presence: instead, we have the obscene, cruel, superegotistical, incomprehensible, impenetrable, traumatic dimension of the Voice, which functions as a kind of foreign body perturbing the balances of our lives.[21]

The voice as such (without speaking comprehensible language) is seen in connection to the trauma of the Real.

In his article "'I Hear you with my Eyes,' or The Invisible Master" Žižek explains how the gaze and the voice are two *objets petit a* that can give us the uncanny impression of the Real.[22] He warns us, however, that "hearing with one's eyes" is not the same as "seeing with one's ears." The gaze is far more mortifying than the voice. Voice and gaze relate to each other as life and death: voice vivifies, whereas gaze mortifies, says Žižek. He gives the example of Munch's "silent scream," which is an ultimate expression of an encounter with the Real. When even the voice fails, death is nearby. As Žižek puts it, "Far more horrifying than to see with our ears— to hear vibrating life substance beyond visual representations, this blind spot in the field of the visible—is to hear with our eyes, that is, to see the absolute silence that marks the suspension of life, as in Caravaggio's *Testa di Medusa*: Is not the scream of Medusa by definition 'stuck in the throat?'"[23]

The voice is nevertheless still uncanny, according to Žižek, because the voice can threaten the established order. For that reason, it must be brought under control, subordinated to the rational word of meaningful language. Here Žižek joins Silverman in assigning the female voice to the concept of *jouissance*. Talking about the voice, Žižek states: "In order to designate the danger that lurks here, Lacan coined the neologism jouis-sense, enjoyment-in-meaning—the moment at which the singing voice cuts loose from its anchoring in meaning and accelerates into consuming self-enjoyment. The problem is thus always the same: how are we to prevent the voice from sliding into a consuming self-enjoyment that 'effeminates' the reliable masculine Word?"[24]

Žižek demonstrates clearly that all these ideas about the voice, *jouissance/jouis-sense* are *fantasmatic* constructions. We are haunted by nonexisting castration anxiety, by horrifying ideas about the Other (who seems to possess something we do not have and therefore must be destroyed). Žižek calls this "the illusory search for some kernel of the real beyond public mandate ('I want to be loved not for my public titles, but for what I really am as an individual, beneath my titles'), whereas a woman is far more aware of the unsettling fact that *there is nothing, no hidden treasure, beneath the symbolic mandate.*"[25] Women, according to Žižek, are potentially less bound to the fantasmatic structure of our being. Nevertheless, as demonstrated repeatedly, the "effemination" of the masculine world has often put women, and the female voice, in powerless positions: the power of fantasy is much bigger.

The only solution that Lacan/Žižek offers is to go through the fantasm (*la traversée du fantasme*) to "gain the minimum of distance toward the fantasmatic frame that organizes one's enjoyment, . . . to suspend its efficiency."[26] This is crucial not only for the psychoanalytic cure and its conclusion. Žižek demonstrates that in our era of renewed racist tensions and universalized anti-Semitism, it is perhaps foremost a *political* question. We have to break the fantasmatic spell on us, which means to unhook jouissance from its fantasmatic frame. I consider this remark extremely important, and I completely agree with Žižek and Lacan about the importance of *la traversée du fantasme*. Neither Lacan nor Žižek talks about what happens after we have gone through the fantasm, however. We will have to learn to think differently, and one of the possibilities for thinking differently is proposed by Deleuze and Guattari. Let us look now at what they have to say about sounds, music, and the voice.

Rhythm, the Refrain, and (De)Territorialization

So far, sound in cinema has been conceived in a representational or psychoanalytic way. Michel Chion has given some useful tools for describing acoustic phenomena, but as soon as the voice becomes involved, psychoanalysis takes over all interpretational power. In his book on popular music, *Performing Rites*, Simon Frith talks about the function of film music. He, too, in referring to Chion, mentions that sound is contained by the image and is strongly dependent on that image as a sort of acoustic mirror; however, he also emphasizes the internal power and force of music. Music evokes images and gives meaning to certain scenes. Frith gives the example of an experiment in which a silent image is shown: a woman walking down some stairs, quite a neutral image without narrative or dramatic charges. If you show the same clip with music, according to the nature of the music, the image takes on different meanings. With "suspense" music, we know that something is going to happen (a killer down the stairs), melodramatic music tells us something has already happened (a mother died, a lover no longer is down the stairs). Frith also distinguishes five broad functions for music in film: "creating atmosphere, underlining the psychological states of characters, providing background filler, building a sense of continuity, sustaining tension and then rounding it off with a sense of closure."[27] The fact that music can create an atmosphere has led to the phenomenon of mood music.

According to Frith, these "moods" are internal qualities of the music, but they are learned and signified through emotional, cultural, and dramatic codes (qualities of "matter" and "mind" go together).[28] In the same spirit, Frith argues against the mind/body split thinking in music that has led to the split between, for instance, "brainless, physical and sexy" pop music and "serious intellectual brain" music of the avant garde and classical music, between the rhythmic "primitive" music of the body and the harmonic Western music of the mind. Frith counters this current idea about music, which he calls racist. As he puts it:

Musical rhythm is as much a mental as a physical matter; deciding *when* to play a note is as much a matter of thought as deciding *what* note to play (and, in practice, such decisions are anyway not separable). In analyzing the differences between African and European music, then, we can't start from a distinction between body and mind; that distinction, while now an important aspect of musical meaning, is ideological, not musicological.[29]

According to Frith, feeling music (often associated with rhythmic pop music) is a physical as much as a mental experience. He strongly argues against the explanation of (pop) music in terms of *jouissance*. If popular music has something to do with sexuality, his argument is rather that this relates to the following:

The tension between the (fluid) coding of the body in the voice (in the instrumental voice) and the (disciplined) coding of the body in the beat—hence the classic disco (and rave) sound of the soul diva mixed over electronic machines. In the end, music is "sexy" not because it makes us move, but because (through that movement) it makes us feel; makes us feel (like sex itself) intensely present. Rhythm in short is "sexual" in that it isn't just about the experience of the body but also (the two things are inseparable) about the experience of time.[30]

The question of rhythm and the bodily experience combined with the experience of time brings us back to Deleuze and Guattari's concept of becoming. In the previous chapter, Deleuze's remark about rhythm through sensations was raised. According to Deleuze, rhythm (movements, vibrations on a molecular level) is expressed on a visual level in painting and, as I have argued, in affection-images in cinema. On the level of audition, rhythm is of course expressed in music.[31] In *A Thousand Plateaus*, Deleuze and Guattari write extensively about sounds, music, and the voice. The tenth plateau, "Becoming-Intense, Becoming-Animal, Becoming-Imperceptible," ends with becoming-music. The next plateau is called "Of the Refrain." Before going back to the soundtrack of film, I raise a few aspects of becoming-music and the refrain to clarify the position of Deleuze and Guattari.

First, they state that musical expression always involves a becoming-woman, a becoming-child, or a becoming-animal that constitutes its content. They call the refrain the proper content of music:

A child comforts itself in the dark or claps its hands or invents a way of walking, adapting it to the cracks in the sidewalks, or chants "Fort-Da" (psychoanalysts deal with the Fort-Da very poorly when they treat it as a phonological opposition or a symbolic component of the language-unconscious, when in fact it is a refrain). Tra la la. A woman sings to herself, "I heard her softly singing a tune to herself under her breath." A bird launches into its refrain. All music is pervaded by bird songs, in a thousand different ways, from Jannequin to Messiaen. Frr, Frr. Music is pervaded by childhood blocks, by blocks of femininity. Music is pervaded by every minority, and yet composes an immense power. Children's, women's, ethnic, and territorial refrains, refrains of love and destruction: the birth of rhythm. . . . The motif of the refrain may be anxiety, fear, joy, love, work, walking, territory . . . but the refrain itself is the content of music.[32]

Not surprisingly, Deleuze and Guattari do not consider the voice in a psychoanalytic way. According to them, the voice (or sounds and music in general) does not simply go back to a prebirth space of the womb; in any case, sound has nothing to do with castration-anxiety, *jouissance*, or an encounter with the Real. They consider sound in its potential force to engender all kinds of molecular becomings. Furthermore, an important aspect of music is its power to create territories and, by the same token, its power to deterritorialize. As seen in the analyses of several assemblages in previous chapters, territorialization and deterritorialization are concepts that are related to the line of flight: deterritorialization is the movement by which "one" leaves the territory. Deleuze and Guattari distinguish several types of deterritorialization (that can be correlated to reterritorialization) on which I will not elaborate here.[33] What is important is to see that sound has much stronger capacities to (de)territorialize than sight. As Deleuze and Guattari concisely put it, "Flags can do nothing without trumpets." Sound becomes more and more refined; it tends to dissolve and connects with other elements easily in a machinic way: "Sound invades us, impels us, drags us, transpierces us. It takes leave of the earth, as much in order to drop us into a black hole as to open us up to a cosmos. It makes us want to die. Since its force of deterritorialization is the strongest, it also affects the most massive reterritorializations, the most numbing, the most redundant. Ecstasy and hypnosis."[34]

Clearly, Deleuze and Guattari attach great importance to sound: becoming-music might even be the last stage before becoming-imperceptible, although it must be noted that all kinds of becomings can exist parallel to each other (it is not a matter of a teleologic evolution). The refrain, sounds, voices, and music relate to territorializing and deterritorializing forces. Deterritorializing forces allow music and sound to become great lines of flight, but the equally great territorializing force also allows sound easily to become fascistic. Deleuze and Guattari emphasized more than once that the greater the force of flight, the more imminent the danger of the black hole of (self-)destruction. Walter Murch, in his foreword to *Audio-Vision*, makes a similar remark about the potential dangers of sound: "There were of course many more significant reasons for the rise of the Great Dictators in the twenties and thirties, and it is true that the silent film had sometimes been used to rally people around the flag, but it is nonetheless chilling to recall that Hitler's ascension to power marched in lockstep with the successful development of the talking film."[35] The power of sound is, of course, even more obvious when we think of the power of Hitler's voice through the radio. Chion's concept of the acousmêtre now can be explained in terms of territorializing forces of sound. In the 1920s and 1930s, political masses were created around the radio, through the hypnotic power of the disembodied voices of dictators that incited them to become subjects through strict identity politics and exclusion of everything foreign to the self-same identity (Jews, homosexuals, and all other minorities).

Not only the disembodied voice on the radio but also music was highly controlled, regulated, and repressed in Hitler's Germany. As Keith Negus demonstrates in his book *Popular Music in Theory*, the Reich Culture Chamber (*Reichskulturkammer*) coordinated and selected all cultural expressions, especially music.[36] There was a great concern for the preservation of German music culture, which seemed consistently to be "endangered" by foreign influences. Especially American jazz was considered "degenerate music." It was seen as Jewish or Negro music and was to be excluded. In a Lacanian/Žižekian perspective, one could say that here the fantasmatic identity construction is at work and has ideologic and political implications. Deleuze and Guattari would argue that the fear of foreign influences in music demonstrates once more the potential deterritorializing forces of music.[37]

Territorial and deterritorial forces go hand in hand and need each other. According to Deleuze and Guattari, the refrain is territorial and has the function of creating "safe havens" in the chaos of the world. They distinguish three aspects of the refrain, which alternate in various ways. First, they distinguish the refrain as a way to create a stable center, a fragile point in the enormous black hole of chaos: a child comforts itself in the dark by singing softly a nursery rhyme; or the lover's refrain that territorializes the sexuality of the loved one. In respect to cinema, one then could say that film music is not just a commentary on or a reflection of the image but rather has the function of calming the audience, the same way that a child whistles in the dark. In *Composing for the Films*, Theodor Adorno and Hans Eisler already saw this function of musical accompaniment of early cinema.[38] The first aspect of the refrain could therefore be related to this lulling function of film sound.

Deleuze and Guattari continue their list of aspects, stating that at other times the refrain organizes around that stable point a calm "pace" (rather than a form). This is what we call "home." Every household is an aurally marked territory. Homes are created by sound walls: a radio that is playing, singing, and speaking voices; the sound of the washing machine; and other sounds. Also, in cinema, music can have this function of creating a "home" or at least a recognizable environment, for instance, the ambient sounds and music of an urban space. In her article "Forty Acres and a Mule Filmworks," Laleen Jayamanne demonstrates the ways in which Spike Lee uses these territorial forces of music through his use of Public Enemy's "Fight the Power" in his film *Do the Right Thing*. She argues that the song is like a "rhythmic character" or a "territorial motif": "'Fight the Power' as refrain has marked a block, created territorial motifs and counterpoints to it; gathered a rhythmic force of hatred and absolute devotion, LOVE and HATE, shattering the block, plunging it into a black hole called 'Race Riot' by white media and politics."[39] By the end of the film, among the chaos of the final riots, in the rhythmic dialogue between two of the characters, very subtly a new sort of pacing, a new "home" is hesitantly being created.

The third aspect of the refrain is when the "home" is invaded, opened: "One opens the circle a crack, opens it all the way, lets someone in, calls someone, or else goes out oneself, launches forth. . . . This time, it is in order to join with the forces of the future, cosmic forces. One launches forth, hazards an improvisation. But to improvise is to join with the World, or melt with it."[40] In cinema, when the sound takes over from the image, this opening is created, an opening to something beyond the image, a connection with the earth or even the cosmos. These three aspects of the refrain coexist. Deleuze and Guattari call them forces of *chaos, terrestrial forces, and cosmic forces*.

During different (historical) periods, one particular aspect of the refrain can be privileged without the other forces of the refrain being completely excluded. In this way, Deleuze and Guattari distinguish three historical periods, each with its preferred aspect of the refrain. In *Classicism*, the (musical) artist confronts chaos directly: the forces of a raw and untamed matter on which forms must be imposed to make substances. The task of the classic artist is God's own, that of organizing chaos: Creation! Deleuze and Guattari quote Proust to make their point clear: "At first the piano complained alone, like a bird deserted by its mate; the violin heard and answered it, as from a neighboring tree. It was at the beginning of the world, as if there was as yet only the two of them on earth, or *rather* in this world closed to all the rest, fashioned by the logic of the creator, in which there would never be more then the two of them: this sonata."[41]

The next musical period distinguished by Deleuze and Guattari is the period of *romanticism*. In this period, the artist abandons his status as creator and enters a "territorial assemblage." The earth becomes the center of all forces. The artist is no longer in the position of God, but he is the one who defies God: "Found, Found, instead of Create." The little tune, the bird's refrain, is no longer the beginning of a world, as in classicism, but draws a territorial assemblage on the earth. Each refrain has something of an Ur refrain in it that speaks of the deepest forces of the earth. As examples of romantic exponents, Deleuze and Guattari mention Mahler and the German *Lied*, which simultaneously has territorial forces, sings of the lost territory, and sings of the earth. Typical of the German/Northern romantic period is the fact that there is no people: "The territory is haunted by a solitary voice. . . . The hero is a hero of the earth; he is mythic, rather than being a hero of the people and historical. . . . As in the *Lied*, everything in the territory occurs in relation to the One-Alone of the soul and the One-All of the earth."[42] In Latin and Slavic countries, romanticism is different in respect to the people: there is a people; the refrain of the territory is here connected to the one-crowd and the one-all. A cry of the earth and a cry of the people are two exponents of the romantic voice and music.

The final period that Deleuze and Guattari distinguish is the *modern age*. This age, our age, is the age of the cosmic, corresponding to the third aspect of the refrain. The refrain is now in a direct relation with molecularized forces; these forces are necessarily forces of the cosmos, assert Deleuze and Guattari:

The visual material must now capture non-visible forces. *Render visible*, Klee said; not render or reproduce the visible. . . . The forces to be captured are no longer those of the earth . . . but those of an immaterial, nonformal, energetic Cosmos. . . . The essential thing is no longer forms and matters, or themes, but forces, densities, intensities. . . . Music molecularizes sound matter and in so doing becomes capable of harnessing nonsonorous forces such as Duration and Intensity.[43]

Deleuze and Guattari talk about a *sound machine*, a machine that molecularizes and atomizes sound matter and harnesses a cosmic energy. They see the synthesizer and pop music as the exemplary assemblage for this music machine. In the last section of this chapter, I return to the modern age and the function of the sound machine. To find out how a territorial conception of sound works, I first return to sound and the voice in Coppola's *The Conversation*.

As demonstrated in the first section, Kaja Silverman has shown that *The Conversation* can be seen as an example of how the maternal voice functions as an acoustic mirror and fantasmatic structure in classic Hollywood. Coppola's film, however, is no longer a typical classic Hollywood film (which is undeniably based largely on oedipal structures). Would that not also have implications for the voice, sound, and music?

Deleuze mentions at the end of *The Movement-Image* a few characteristics of a new kind of image that was born in post-war European cinema: in Italian Neo-Realism, in French Nouvelle Vague, and in German New Cinema. In the United States, it was not until the late 1960s and 1970s (during and after the Vietnam War) that this kind of new images came to the cinema. One of the characteristics of this American postwar cinema that Deleuze mentions is the growing presence of the idea of a conspiracy through media such as radio, television, microphones, and other surveillance systems. Characters become less and less goal oriented within a structured plot and become persons who have weak links to the dispersive and chaotic situations in which they find themselves.

The Conversation is a typical film showing this conspiracy phobia, related to the possibilities of technical equipment. The film is also aware of the many aural and visual clichés that are around (another characteristic of the new image), and it reworks the cliché of a conversation between two lovers into something new and dynamic (as the meaning of the conversation changes). There is no longer a distinction between private and public spaces, which makes the film very different from classic Hollywood, where there are always clearly defined spaces. We enter the any-space-whatevers of the new image in Deleuzian terminology. Although the voyeuristic aspects of the cinematic apparatus are still present, the emphasis has shifted to sound: the sound track is no longer strictly contained by the image track. Sound (not only the voice) gains prominence and even independence at some points, and in this way *The Conversation* seems to indicate a new paradigm for cinema to come.[44]

If we now listen once more to the soundtrack, we can add another dimension of sound to Silverman's psychoanalytic interpretation, which is related to its (de)territorial forces. First, Caul enters the territorial space of the couple by stealing their voices. He himself is extremely protective about his own territory, especially in respect to sounds: he even hides his phone and does not give anyone his phone number. It is therefore all the more eerie when the telephone does ring: someone found out how to reach him, how to invade his territory with their voice. First, it is his landlady; later, he receives phone calls from the company that instructed him to eavesdrop and finally from the couple he had been watching.

Both the public space (the square in San Francisco) and the private space (Caul's apartment) are invaded by sound forces: these aural invasions are frightening because they remind one of chaos and confusion. Both the children's song the woman sings and Harry Caul's saxophone playing while at home therefore could be seen as the comforting singing of a child in the dark: the creation of a fixed and stable place in the chaos (the first aspect of the refrain). No wonder Caul feels attracted to the refrain the woman sings. He has his own territorial refrain as well, maybe as an aspect of his becoming-child or becoming-woman. *The Conversation* could be seen as the story of a man who thought he had created a home (not only a space but also a "pace") around the stable force of his saxophone music, but this turns out not to be so safe as he hoped. His home is deterritorialized by the invasion of sound. In the end, all he has left is his saxophone, which remains the only stable point in his destroyed apartment.

Another question raised by the film is the question of guilt and responsibility. One could, of course, argue that man is guilty by definition because of original sin (the killing of the father, the mother as love object/abject), as psychoanalysis wants us to believe. This scenario of guilt is repeated in the scenario of the film, but it is also possible to think of guilt that is related to specific circumstances. In that case, Caul is not a priori guilty, but he feels responsible for what he has done in the past. In a previous case, two people were murdered because of the evidence he delivered. He is now afraid that the couple also might be killed because of his sound tapes. The irony and strength of the film, of course, is that it demonstrates so clearly that what is in a man's mind influences what he sees and even more what he hears: the shift from "He'd *kill* us" to "*He'*d kill *us*" shows how his aural perception is influenced by his state of mind. He could not think of the option (which virtually has always been there) that the couple were planning a murder instead of being afraid of being murdered themselves. Seen and listened to in the perspective of new Hollywood and connected to the territorial forces of sound, *The Conversation* is more about the sound bridges between public and private space (mediated by technology) and about the consequences of and individual responsibilities for crossing those spaces than about the guilty desire for the maternal voice. The female (singing) voice, seen in a negative (lethal) although fascinating way by psychoanalysis, is, however, a recurrent aural phenomenon in cinema. It is therefore worthwhile listening to those voices a little longer.

The (Female) Voice: Back on the Throne?

The Music of Animated Images

In Disney's *Little Mermaid*, the female voice plays an important role: teenage mermaid Ariel has a beautiful singing voice, which she swaps for a pair of legs to have access to the (patriarchal) world of the land. She gives her voice to the sea witch Ursula, who certainly uses the seductive and dangerous powers of the female voice to seduce Prince Eric, leaving Ariel voiceless, with "empty hands" and painful legs (until the witch is unmasked as the utmost form of feminine monstrosity and is killed, and Ariel nevertheless finds her place in marriage/the symbolic order). A psychoanalytic interpretation of the voice gives, in this respect, certainly, an adequate explanation of the powers of the female voice. Because of the fluid and molecular quality of both the sound of the voice and the animation of the images, it is useful to consider where there is more to see, hear, and learn from Ariel's adventures.

In the 1940s, Sergei Eisenstein wrote several essays on Walt Disney.[45] Eisenstein was full of admiration for Disney and called his work the greatest contribution to art in the twentieth century. What he liked most was the fact that Disney knew how to relate the rational and the sensual, a problem that the founder of "intellectual cinema" considered increasingly important toward the end of his life. Eisenstein was fascinated by the protoplasmatic qualities of Disney films, which he saw as the basis of life itself. He felt an ecstasy before Disney films: "It is *beyond* any image, *without* any image, *beyond* tangibility—like a pure sensation. . . . [it] is music!"[46] We see here how Eisenstein relates the cartoon, with all its potential qualities of all kinds of becomings, to sensation, to what can be directly felt. Disney's images have a musical quality and a molecular fluidity that can be related to a becoming-child, a becoming-woman, and a becoming-animal.

Eisenstein also made a link between the animal tales of La Fontaine in the seventeenth century, the fairy tales of Andersen in the eighteenth century, Lewis Carroll's *Alice in Wonderland* in the nineteenth century, and Disney in the twentieth century. Hence, according to Eisenstein, it is no coincidence that Disney's world is full of animals and that both Andersen's *Little Mermaid* and Carroll's *Alice* have been transformed into Disney celluloid. The concept of becoming-woman related to the figure of *Alice in Wonderland* was discussed in Chapter 4. Here I want to look at the becoming-music of Disney cartoons, especially at the role of the voice in Disney's *Little Mermaid*.[47]

As Laura Sells demonstrates in her article "Where do the Mermaids Stand?" Disney's *Little Mermaid* has been criticized by several feminists.[48] Ariel's lack of ambition beyond marrying her prince, of course, has met feminist objections. The "matricide" (of Ursula) also has been criticized. Sells, however, also sees some liberating forces in Disney's version of *The Little Mermaid*, precisely because of the figure of the Sea Witch and because in the end Ariel has access to both the human world and to a voice.[49] According to Sells, Ursula (modeled after the drag queen "Divine") teaches Ariel that performance and voice can be used as manifestations and liberations of gender, and she sees Ariel as a potentially subversive character.[50] It is basically in the songs that this performative side and her desire for liberation are expressed and formed. Sells's argument is that, when Ursula is in the end destroyed, Ariel has learned something that she can use for her own ends (so the symbolic integration in marriage is not so stable as it seems). The voice could be seen even more positively as a liberating force: not by opposing the symbolic order but by valuing it in the freedom of becoming-music.

Disney continued to make new stories with Ariel. In Disney's new Princess Series, there is a *Little Mermaid* episode entitled "Ariel and the Dreamwish Starfish."[51] In this episode Ariel, as a rebellious and fearless girl who does not obey the orders of her father, King Triton, finds a music box with a ballerina on it. Ariel wishes to dance like the ballerina. Her girlfriend, mermaid Gabrielle, wishes to sing: she is deaf and dumb and longs for a voice "to express feelings like happiness, sorrow and love." Together, they go to the Dreamwish Starfish to have their wishes fulfilled. The journey is dangerous, but the girls are not afraid. When the starfish does not succeed in giving Ariel legs and Gabrielle a voice, they start to sing and dance together, so that they nevertheless express everything they want—

Ariel through her voice and Gabrielle through her body. The connection between voice and body (both can express the same things) is judged positively here. The two mermaids remain happily in the underwater world, not longing anymore for the world of the land.

The underwater world in the little mermaid's adventures is set up in opposition to the world of dry land. Sells compares the underwater world to the (feminine) Third World, as opposed to the (patriarchal) First World: many sea-world characters do indeed have voices with "foreign accents," and they often perform exotic dances. Of course, this is a classic binary opposition, subscribing to dominant ideology when in the film Ariel desires to leave this "Third World." In the stories of the Princess Series, however, this "minority world" is seen more positively for its own qualities. In "Ariel and the Dreamwish Starfish," she is happy to stay; also, in the episode "In Harmony," the sea world is sung about and celebrated as a beautiful place, but not in an exotic way. In this episode, an awful false stingray—not even gendered as female—tries to set all the fish against each other: crabs should not play with goldfish, octopuses have to stick to octopuses, and swordfish should remain with their own kind. This episode shows clearly how identity and categorization, so very human and territorial, create war.

It is Ariel who saves the harmony of the sea world with her singing voice, making mutual becomings and encounters between different categories possible again. Significantly, the stingray cannot stand the music and disappears in anger.[52] It could be argued that Ariel is another cyborg Alice, who has molecular forces of becoming, which are expressed mostly through her voice: "Long before cyborgs [*sic*] dreamed of electric sheep, Disney artists created 'cyborg' women."[53] As Eisenstein demonstrated a long time ago, the extremely fluid and plasmatic character of the animated image gives musical qualities to the images themselves that match Ariel's singing voice. There is a becoming-music of the image in animation and a positive appreciation of the voice that in singing can territorialize and deterritorialize.

This becoming-music has something to do not only with the quality of animated images but also with the sea world. The voice and the sea share a molecular potentiality. As Deleuze and Guattari state:

The becoming-child and the becoming-woman . . . are intense but are . . . inseparable from a molecularization of the motif, a veritable "chemistry" achieved through orchestration. The child and the woman are now inseparable from the sea and the water molecule (*Sirens*, precisely, represents one of the first complete attempts to integrate the voice with the orchestra). Already Wagner was reproached for the "elementary" character of his music, for its aquaticism, in its "atomization" of the motif, "a subdivision into infinitely small units."[54]

I return later to the orchestration of the voice. Here I want to stress the logical relation between the singing voice, music, water world, and animation: all aspects have forces of molecular becomings that can penetrate at the finest level and subvert all the traditional boundaries that have been set, including the boundary of the female voice as seductive but deadly.

The Undoing of Woman or Deterritorializing Machines

No other voice has been more fascinating than the voice of the opera diva for its functioning as a classic *objet petit a* in psychoanalytic film theory. Therefore, another domain of interest with respect to the female voice is the opera film. In Jean-Jacques Beineix's film *Diva* (1982), the opera singer Cynthia Hawkins (played and performed by Wilhelminia Wiggins Fernandez) refuses to have her voice recorded. The opening of the film stages Hawkins's performance of Catalani's *La Wally*. We not only listen to her beautiful voice, but we also see that her voice is being recorded by one of her fans, the postman Jules. The film has several plot lines, which come together in a complex way around two recorded voices of women: the illegally recorded voice of the opera singer and the voice of a prostitute who, before being killed by accomplices of her pimp, gives a compromising testimony that unmasks the chief of the police as the leader of a criminal network. In *The Acoustic Mirror*, Kaja Silverman discusses the film in respect to the diva's voice and considers it a fantasy of the maternal voice as inaccessible object of desire: "The moment where Jules sinks into a chair, listening to her voice and covering himself with the (also stolen) dress of the Diva, is in this way surely as close as cinema has come to an evocation of *jouissance*."[55]

The Diva's voice is indeed presented as extremely embodied; her refusal to record her voice reinforces her voice as object of desire (instead of a subjective agent). If we listen to the other female voice in the film, the voice of the prostitute on a tape recorder, there is also an increasing disembodiment of the voice, culminating in the unmasking of the police officer (and thus a voice having extreme agency without being an object of desire). We see that through technology the female voice can gain acousmatic power. Here I agree with Silverman that in Beineix's film the voice has a lot to do with a psychoanalytic mother-son dyad, as emphasized by the last image, where the Diva and Jules stand close to each other in the theater, both listening to her (now) technologically transmitted voice; but her body is closer than ever to Jules. By stealing her voice, he seems to have come as close as possible to his ("incestuous") object of desire.

In *Opera, or the Undoing of Women*, Cathérine Clément analyzes how in nineteenth-century opera, women are always killed in the narrative of the opera. As a musicologic equivalent of Laura Mulvey's "Visual Pleasure in Narrative Cinema," Clément concentrates on the objectification and powerlessness of women and the enforcement of male power. According to Clément, women in opera are undone, defeated, and put in a powerless position, as they often are in cinema; their voices are embodied and limited in their discursive access.

Carolyn Abbate, however, in her rich article "Opera, or the Envoicing of Women" does not (always) agree with this feminist position.[56] First, she demonstrates how in Patrick Conrad's film *Mascara* (1978), through the operatic voice, gender is conceived as a performance. Much like the Sea Witch Ursula in *Little Mermaid*, in *Mascara* it is the performance of a transvestite who borrows the (recorded) voice of a female opera singer and demonstrates how much gender is performance. At the same time, the female voice gains authority. As Abbate states, "Female voices make the sound-text that sets biologically male puppets spinning in an interpretive dance. In this sound-text, the women's singing voices themselves have an explicitly authorial force, and these strange lip-synching scenes represent women as the *makers* of musical sonority in opera."[57]

Abbate discusses the authorial forces of women, who traditionally have been seen as "just" performers of the work of male composers. With the help of Barthes's texts, "The Death of the Author" and "The Grain of the Voice," she finds a different appreciation of the female singing voice: a rebirth of the author inside the artwork.[58] Related to the authorial force of the female singing voice is appreciation of the nondiscursiveness of the bodily voice. According to Silverman, who also raises Roland Barthes's authorial feminine singing voice, this authority still depends on negativity and castration: "Insofar as the female voice speaks authorially, it does so at the expense of a system of projection and disavowal."[59] La Zambinella, a character from Barthes's *Sarrasine* is a castrato who embodies for Barthes this female authority and agency. Silverman sees this as a negative appreciation. Abbate wonders if this is so bad—if we can see a castrato (or maybe by extension the performance of a transvestite) as a constructed female singer, not necessarily monstrous. The nonappreciation of femininity and "castration" is implicit in psychoanalytic discourse, and it is difficult to find ways out of this negativity without destroying all pleasure. So would it not be possible, as Abbate seems to suggest as well, to revalue bodily and nondiscursive forces?

Antonin Artaud, who inspired Deleuze and Guattari with his idea of the Body without Organs, has repeatedly expressed such a different valuation of physical and nondiscursive language. In *Pour en finir avec le jugement de Dieu*, he proposes, for instance:

To make language express what it usually does not express: this is to make use of it in a new, exceptional, and unaccustomed fashion; to reveal its possibilities of physical shock; to actively divide and distribute it in space; to handle intonations in an absolutely concrete manner, restoring their power to tear asunder and to really manifest something; to turn against language and its basely utilitarian, one could even say alimentary sources, against its hunted beast origins.[60]

Contrary to psychoanalytic feminist theory, where screams, rhythm, harmony, cacophony, glossolalia, and the materiality (breathing, swallowing, groaning) of the grain of the voice are seen as powerless expressions, they are appreciated positively by Artaud.

Deleuze and Guattari also have a different appreciation of the materiality of the voice. For them, the voice is related to music, and it has the capacity to become music: "Music is a deterritorialization of the voice, which becomes less and less tied to language."[61] They (like Artaud implicitly) do not relate the voice when it becomes-music to a specific molar or segmental gender, although it still can be erotic. The voice, however, is related to a molecular becoming-woman, becoming-child, becoming-animal (becoming-bird). When the voice becomes-music, a "machining" of the voice takes place. The voice enters a machinic assemblage of becoming. Deleuze and Guattari give the examples of the head voice of the countertenor and the stomach voice of the castrati as such machinations of the voice. *Castrati* (or the performed variant of transvestites singing with a woman's voice) do not relate to psychoanalytically negative castration but refer to a musical problem of the machinery of the voice, which implies necessarily the abolition of the overall dualism machine, the molar formation of assigning voices to a "man" or a "woman." Being a man or a woman no longer exists in music, state Deleuze and Guattari. It is a question of real becoming, not a question of imitating a woman, a child, or a bird: "The human musician is deterritorialized in the bird, but it is a bird that is itself deterritorialized, 'transfigured,' a celestial bird . . . purely sonorous."[62] Deleuze and Guattari do acknowledge that sometimes the voice can be reterritorialized, resexualized, but in general something else happens in the becoming-music of the voice.

Finally, I return to the aspect of the technologic possibilities for recording voices and music. Over the last hundred years, audio equipment has become increasingly sophisticated. Technologic equipment, such as microphones, has given tremendous possibilities to the voice. A microphone enables a singer, for instance, to sing quietly against a full orchestra. This intimacy of a voice and a microphone can make the eroticism and the grain of the voice much more explicit. One could even speak of "techno-glosso-lalia," to remain close to Artaud.[63] The voice also can be transformed electronically, thus stretching, for instance, the gender of the voice, as Laurie Anderson has demonstrated in much of her work. The recorded and acousmatic voice of the radio, record player, or telephone has strange and incredible powers, as shown by Michel Chion.

Another aspect of technologic recording possibilities is that one's own voice can return as the voice of another; or, as Allen Weiss says with respect to the work of Artaud:

Recording the voice poses an ontological risk: the recorded voice is the stolen voice that returns to me as the hallucinatory presence of the voice of another. This other's voice may be the voice of God, as is often the case in paranoid experiences, and as was the case for Artaud during the periods of his madness. In paranoid projections, one's own voice is hallucinated as coming from without, as a divine or diabolic presence speaking the forbidden thoughts of unspeakable desires or unbearable prohibitions.[64]

In *Diva*, Cynthia Hawkins's voice comes back as a divine message. She expresses her astonishment about her own voice that comes back as the voice of another: "But . . . I've never heard myself sing," she says to Jules. In this case, "hearing oneself sing" certainly has the uncanny effect that Žižek talks about in "'I Hear you with my Eyes'": the voice is here returned as the voice of another, alienating the subject from itself and making it confront the Real. The technologically disembodied voice also offers other possibilities, however. In *Mascara*, the recorded voice of a female singer is used for a transvestite performance. As Abbate has demonstrated, this shifts the fixed gender roles in music between authorial and performing voices. There is one more filmic example of the deterritorializing power of the singing voice and becoming-music that I want to mention. The fact that the voices are recorded (and acousmatic) is again important.

Frank Darabout's Hollywood film *The Shawshank Redemption* (1994) is a prison film about the wrongly convicted Andy Dufresne, who finally manages to escape. The story is told in a voice-over by another prisoner, "Red" Redding, who becomes his friend. The Shawshank prison is, like all prisons, an extremely closed territory in which there is almost no room for escape. Nevertheless, there is a moment of strong deterritorialization in the film, which is significantly related to acousmatic sounds. Dufresne has managed to set up a library and receives second-hand books. One day, he also receives some records. He puts "The Marriage of Figaro" by Mozart on the record player and then connects it to all the loudspeakers in the whole prison. Everywhere the voices of two divas are audible, and everybody listens in amazement. Then we hear another acousmatic voice, Red's voice, recounting in retrospect what happened. His words are telling for the deterritorializing force of the (acousmatic) voice:

I have no idea until these days what these two Italian ladies were singing about. The truth is, I don't wanna know. Some things are best unsaid. I like to think they were singing about something so beautiful it can't be expressed in words—and make your heart ache because of it. I tell you, those voices soared lighter and farther than anybody in a great place dares to dream. It was like some beautiful bird flapped into our trap-built cage and made those walls dissolve away. And for the briefest of moments every last man at Shawshank felt free.

It is difficult to say that these voices are an *objet petit a*, or a trace of the Real, the nonsymbolizable (a confrontation with death) or, in another psychoanalytic reading, that all the men have been reminded of the voice of their mother, making them long for a safe regression back into the uterine world. This might have been the case if these voices had the comforting effect of the first aspect of the refrain. These voices are not regressive, however, but reach into the future, having intense power to deterritorialize: they express an ultimate line of flight and freedom. If Dufresne had opened the doors of the prison, probably nobody would have dared to walk out (they would have been shot immediately). Through these singing voices, however, Dufresne gave everybody an escape from the prison, a deterritorializing deed for which he is punished with two weeks in the isolation cell, which is literally intended to reterritorialize him again.

The voice that becomes-music in singing has deterritorializing powers. Although the power of the acousmatic voice as it is analyzed by Michel Chion still can be authoritative (the voice also can territorialize as argued before in respect to the voice of dictators on the radio), we now see that it also has affirmative and deterritorializing powers. Whereas Chion saw the acousmatic female voice only in respect of the omnipotent castrating mother or the unattainable object of desire, it is clear that the voice also can be seen differently, as a liberating force, opening up to the future.

Oceans of Sounds

I just mentioned that, with respect to *Little Mermaid*, the singing voice is related not only to the fluid quality of animation but also to the sea world. In this section, I return to the aquatic qualities of the voice in Luc Besson's films *The Big Blue* (1988), *Atlantis* (1991), and *The Fifth Element* (1997).[65] These three films express, albeit in different ways, an aquatic becoming-music.

The Big Blue is based on a true story of the diver Jacques Mayol, which is published in his book *Homo Delphinus*.[66] In this book, Mayol reports on his sporting and later scientific experiences of free diving (diving without oxygen bottles). From 1960 onward, Mayol enters into free diving competition with Enzo Maiorca, who dies during a dive in 1974 when he reaches a depth of eighty-seven meters. Mayol continues with scientific experiments and reaches a depth of a hundred meters without breathing. Scientific observations have proven that, during his dives, Mayol's blood gathers in his heart, liver, and brain, as is the case with dolphins. An actual case of becoming-dolphin (parts of the diver's body enter into the same relation of speed and slowness as the dolphin's body) is transformed by Besson into a fiction film. The contradiction between the earth and the sea is emphasized by two people who are important to Jacques Mayol. On the one hand, there is Johanna, the American woman who is in love with Jacques and who is expecting a child by him. She asks him repeatedly to come back to dry land. On the other hand, there is Enzo, who asks him again and again to dive deeper and deeper but who dives on his human bodily forces, which one fatal day will not be enough to survive the depths of the ocean. Neither Johanna nor Enzo is in a permanent state of becoming, unlike Jacques, who is neither human nor animal. In the film, it is not so much the images that express his becoming, although the underwater scenes of course have this fluid quality. It is mostly in the sounds of the ocean, the sounds of the dolphins and the water that the becoming-dolphin of Jacques and the becoming-music of the ocean are expressed. The film's ending also indicates that the powers of becoming-music can be so great that Jacques is forever deterritorialized and drawn into the depths of the sea.[67] In contrast to Enzo, who was very atttached to the land and who drowns, Jacques chooses to become one with the ocean.

After *The Big Blue*, Besson returns to the sea with his underwater film *Atlantis*. In this, Besson films the sea world, ranging from the white sharks of the Great Barrier Reef to the dancing dolphins of the Bahamas and all other forms of sea life in between. The images are accompanied by a soundtrack composed by Eric Serra, which makes *Atlantis* a sort of "marine opera." Serra also included a piece of an existing opera. Somewhere halfway through the film, a large, impressive stingray swims into the image, all alone, and we hear the voice of Maria Callas singing "La Sonnanbula" of Bellini. Unlike the stingray in *Little Mermaid*'s adventure described in the preceding, the stingray here is not an opposition-creating territorializing machine. The image of the stingray here melts with the voice and in the deep blue, almost black water, all becomes-music, atomized, molecular, aquatic.

In *The Movement-Image*, Deleuze mentions the liquid tradition of French cinema. Of course, one must think here of Jean Vigo's *L'Atalante* (1934), in which there is an opposition between terrestrial and aquatic movements. Deleuze speaks here of the liquid perception-image, which has strong affective powers. In *L'Atalante*, it is in the water that the loved one who has disappeared is revealed. Deleuze remarks, "What the French school found in water was the promise or implication of another state of perception: a more than human perception, a perception not tailored to solids, which no longer had the solid as object, as condition, as milieu. A more delicate and vaster perception, a molecular perception, peculiar to a 'cine-eye.'"[68] In the 1970s, the cinema of Marguerite Duras, with its vast seasides and liquid quality of the flow of images and the flow of sounds, continues this French cinematographic tradition, as Deleuze demonstrates in *The Time-Image*. Besson could be seen as an heir to this liquid tradition in French cinema.

Even with *The Fifth Element*, which was promoted as the European answer to big-budget Hollywood action cinema, Besson is at some times faithful to his fascination for aquatic becomings. In terms of its plot, the film has little more to offer than a traditional science-fiction plot: In the twenty-third century, the earth is threatened by awful alien forces and has to be saved by the hero Korben Dallas and the heroine Leeloo. Leeloo is the "fifth element" that can save the earth. To do so, she also needs to have the four stones that represent the other four elements. Of course, many good and evil people chase these stones, which leads them all to a paradise island far from the chaotic city of New York, where the rest of the film takes place. On the basis of this plot, the film can be dismissed easily; but, if we consider the film as an assemblage, the form of content and form of expression make the film an affective, even spiritual movie. As Deleuze has argued, the affection-image can open up to the fourth dimension of time and the fifth dimension of spiritual choices.[69] The affective qualities in this film are caused by the overabundance of space, where any clear orientation is no longer possible and that works directly on our nervous system. The choices that are to be made in the film vary from a very pragmatic choice between getting caught by the police or jumping from a building to the spiritual choice of Leeloo between saving the earth or letting it be destroyed. Elsewhere, I have elaborated these points more extensively.[70] Here in the otherwise overflowing spatial virtuality of this film, the only big space that is recognizable and confined is a "perfect replica of the old opera house" in which the concert takes place. It is a moment of rest in the film, apparently a territorializing moment, because everything is for once in place and identifiable. Yet it is precisely here that the greatest moment of deterritorialization also takes place.

On the opera stage, a diva appears; however, she is not a "normal" diva: she is a tall aqua-blue creature, with a terribly beautiful voice. When she starts to sing (the voice is that of soprano Inva Mulla Tchacho) a piece from the opera *Lucia di Lammermoor* of Donizetti, everyone is silent and in complete ecstasy.[71] Her voice that is becoming-bird makes the action stop for a moment and makes everything molecular. When the Blue Diva starts to sing, it is as though her body is actualizing some of the virtual potential of the "ocean of sounds" in which we are living. As Deleuze says in *The Time-Image*, the synchronizing of her voice with the image becomes part of the creative function of a mythical tale. Deleuze quotes Chion, who says about synchronization, "Through it the image says to the sound: stop floating everywhere and come and live in me: the body opens to welcome the voice."[72]

The voice is now not so much an acoustic mirror but is the expression of a received (and actualized) virtuality. The blue color of her body here does not have the cold association with death as in the colors in the images of the flesh discussed before. Although related to death, blue is also the color of infinity. Blue is the color of transparency; it has the quality of the empty sky, the transparence of water, the translucence of crystal. The *Dictionary of Symbols* says about the color blue that entering into the blue is like the experience of Alice in Wonderland passing through the mirror.[73] We know by now what happens with Alice when she enters Wonderland: she enters into the world of becomings. The voice of the diva and the blue color of her body are moments of actualization in a virtual field of possible images and sounds; but the liquid and molecular quality of both her voice and her body make it so that this actualization is the actualization of a line of flight that opens to the future.

After the opera song, there is a change in the rhythm and melody of the orchestra. The Blue Diva starts to dance while her voice becomes one with the orchestra and Eric Serra's composition "Diva Dance" takes over. Here we find a complete orchestration of the voice, as mentioned earlier by Deleuze and Guattari. The bird becomes an insect, which will become increasingly important in becoming-music. As Deleuze and Guattari state, birds are vocal, insects are instrumental. We are entering the age of insects, "with its much more molecular vibrations, chirring, rustling, buzzing, clicking, scratching and scraping."[74] It is also during this Diva Dance that one senses literally that the voice is an instrument that goes beyond gender: this Diva's voice ranges from very low "masculine" pitch to very high "feminine" pitch.

The scene of the diva dance is alternated, to the rhythm of the music, with scenes of Leeloo fighting on her own a whole regiment of alien enemies. One could say that both on a molecular musical level and on a more solid action level, planet earth is here defended by two "women" or, better still, by these two cyborg Alices. Soon chaos takes over again.

Leeloo is temporarily defeated. The diva is accidentally shot and dies in the arms of Korben Dallas, to whom she can just whisper that the four stones representing the four elements are hidden inside her body and that he has to help Leeloo with his love. When he "fishes" the precious stones from her bleeding blue body ("the blood of sensibility is blue"[75]), we still hear her aquatic voice in our heads, as if she had made clear that the world can only be saved by a changing perception, a becoming-music of the world. Of course, one could criticize Besson here for letting a "female" opera singer die in a traditional way, and there are indeed many stereo-typical images in Besson's work. His characters are often "flat," like car-toon characters. This effect is reinforced by the fact that Besson collabo-rated for this film with the famous French cartoonists Moebius and Jean-Claude Mézières.

Characters in the new cinema are no longer psychologically moti-vated, however. As Deleuze demonstrated at the end of *The Time-Image*, characters have become like "automata" and "puppets" that perform speech-acts.[76] In this way, they participate in the creation of new myths, myths of a world that is increasingly like an overloaded brain. Besson's "cartoon characters" are precisely such new actors of the new type that Deleuze describes. Their flatness does not necessarily imply that they are meaningless. There is also always a spiritually affective quality to Besson's spectacular images, such that his "stereotypes" can never just be dismissed as naive or simple.[77]

Finally, Leeloo, purely through love and cosmic energy (which is closely connected), saves the world from destruction. It is as though Besson wants to express audiovisually the final words of the plateau on be-coming-intense in *A Thousand Plateaus*:

It is necessary to reach that point, it is necessary for the nonmusical sound of the human being to form a block with the becoming-music of sound, for them to con-front and embrace each other like two wrestlers who can no longer break free from each other's grasp, and slide down a sloping line: "Let the choirs represent the sur-vivors . . . Faintly, one hears the sound of the cicadas. Then the notes of a lark, fol-lowed by the mockingbird. Someone laughs. . . . A woman sobs. . . . From a male a great shout: WE ARE LOST! A woman's voice: WE ARE SAVED! Lost! Saved! Lost! Saved!"[78]

Although the soundtrack is becoming increasingly important in all action cinema, Besson has added a few more blue liquid notes that make even the hard action genre more fluid and susceptible to becomings and change.[79] Literally, Leeloo and Korben Dallas finally embrace in a watertank. As Derek Jarman expresses in a very different way on the soundtrack of *Blue*:

> Salt lips touching
> In submarine gardens
> [. . .]
> Blue is the universal love in which man bathes
> —it is the terrestrial paradise.

The voice of the Blue Diva, opening to cosmic forces, sings a "terrestrial paradise" as well. The voice, with its aquatic and atomic qualities, seems indeed to be back on a throne, though it does not pretend to be above anything else. It is not necessarily a female voice, however, because in the machining of the voice, there is no sexuality. Each voice can become-woman, become-animal, become-music and receive the energy that is floating around. It simply needs to actualize (capture by an *nth* will to art, to creation, to life) the virtual in specific images and sounds.

Cosmic Forces: Becoming in Music

Electronic Music: Creating a New "Home"

As mentioned, Deleuze and Guattari see the modern age as the age of the cosmic, of cosmic energy. In this respect, *The Fifth Element* is a film that belongs very much to the modern age: the film speaks about the cosmos and deals ultimately with pure cosmic energy, as expressed in the character of Leeloo. Another aspect of our age, again as already indicated, is that becoming-animal in music is transforming more and more from birds (voices) into insects (instruments/orchestrated voices). This does not mean, of course, that there are no longer any becomings-bird or that these are no longer important. It only indicates that there is an increasing multiplicity in becomings-animal, "more molecular vibrations, chirring, rustling, buzzing, clicking, scratching, and scraping." According to Deleuze and Guattari, insects are better able to make audible the truth that all becomings are molecular: "The molecular has the capacity to make the *elementary* communicate with the *cosmic*: precisely because it effects a dissolution of form that connects the most diverse longitudes and latitudes, the most varied speeds and slownesses, which guarantees a continuum by stretching variation far beyond its formal limits."[80]

The synthesizer is the assembling machine of this age, say Deleuze and Guattari in the late 1970s and early 1980s. In the late 1990s, it is becoming increasingly evident that in electronic music, various sound machines and sound events indicate the increasingly molecular forces of sound. "Making audible the inaudible." Queen Sound's whispers grow louder and louder, penetrating our culture on several levels: in the music scene, in film and in (youth) culture in general.

After the death of Gilles Deleuze in November 1995, the record label Mille Plateaux was founded and released a compact disc (CD) in honor of the philosopher.[81] Musicians and disc jockeys (DJs), such as Scanner, Mouse on Mars, David Shea, Beequeen, and DJ Spooky the Subliminal Kid, created a "music-machine" that expressed in electronic sounds their affinity with the work of Deleuze and Guattari. There is a great deal of music in their philosophy. Apart from the explicit musical concepts they introduce, *A Thousand Plateaus* as a whole could be read as a piece of music with different layers and variations on the same refrains coming back again and again. The music label Sub Rosa expresses its affinity with Deleuze and Guattari:

> from the beginning, we wanted to be more than a label; a machine perhaps, composed of rhizomes, of peaks and troughs, of tranquility and doubt. that's the way things go: the miracle of an epiphany, under the rose, the intimate utterance of friendship; something beautiful, that grows, that changes, that passes and then comes back in another form, the pack that breaks up and re-forms in the shadow of a wood, the dryness of a desert. with that, we refashioned something else, with the text we made sound. the sound went off we know not where (no doubt things will come back one day in other forms) a deep breath. we set out once again. . . .

Sounds are scanned, transformed, and reworked digitally in such a way that it becomes unclear who actually composes the music: the sound designer, the instruments and machines, or the user. The traditional composer is replaced by a machine–human, a cyborg, one could say. In *The Last Angel of History*, a science fiction documentary about black music, cyberculture, and African-American history by John Akomfrah, one of the interviewed musicians/DJs, Darek May, says that contemporary techno-music expresses this intertwinement of man and machine. *The Last Angel of History* actually creates a minority history of what Deleuze and Guattari call a "war machine," a resisting force: the history and future of black music that goes from the blues to jazz to soul to hiphop and techno music. The film talks about a blues legend that sold his soul to the devil in exchange for the gift of playing the blues. In the same way, "a thief from the future, a Data Thief, gives up his right to belong to his time in order to come to our time to find the 'mothership connection'."

Much like Benjamin's angel of history, who looks at the past while being blown into the future, the thief becomes an angel of history that cannot be part of either the past or the future. The mothership connection, referring obviously to George Clinton's famous album from the 1970s with the same title, indicates the link between music and the cosmic. Many black musicians and DJs in the film talk about the function and effects of technological music. Their words clearly demonstrate the way in which through music and language, gestures, bodily significations, and desires, a social group forms itself as "the outcome of a practical activity."[82] Besides the fact that the synthesizer can make noise into music, this assemblage–machine is seen as the first breakthrough that created the ability to make futuristic space sounds. *The Mothership Connection* and the space music of Sun Ra, the science fiction stories of Samuel Delany and Octavia Butler, as well as the technomusic and jungle/drum'n' base music of the 1990s all are related to the same desire to connect with cosmic energy.

A similar connection between electronic music and cosmic energy is found on the *In Memoriam Gilles Deleuze* album:

Electronic sound machines: it depends on the problem and the question that one asks. What does it mean—making electronic music? That mathematics is the basis of music, a mathematics solution rule, the algorithm? That music happens in the universe of synthesizers, monitors, midis, computer science, computer, etc.? Or ask a second question. How does electronic music function? This question shows that the electronic music can not be sent back to the first question, it follows rather more a paradoxical model: making audible the inaudible. It is made up of a teeming throng of sound materials that represent different intensities (slowness, speed, layering, delay, condensation) and functions (synthesis of sound components, synthesis of sound and rhythm, etc.). . . . The caught forces are now no more forces of the earth, which constitute a large expressive form, but today they are forces of a formless, immaterial energy cosmos. The cosmic forces, jumps, silences, duration, ensembles that go from and include very small to very large, for their part fold the material again and again. The sound machines make music and its being is being of the event. . . . The event is pure becoming.

One can find here several aspects of Deleuzian philosophy: not asking questions about meanings but about functions and effects; thinking in intensities, speed, and slowness; talking about music as an event of pure becoming. The musicians on the CD have expressed the same sensibilities in their music.

One repeated phrase the Data Thief in *The Last Angel of History* finds is "the line between social reality and science fiction is an optical illusion." The film demonstrates that there is a tight connection between black minority existence and science fiction: the rewriting of African-American history in light of alien abduction and genetic transformation is not just metaphorical. "How more alien can you get than slave migrations?" is the rhetorical question. DJ Spooky the Subliminal Kid refers to the history of slavery, the disowning of their own language and the rise of black music to find a new way of expression.[83] The ear seems to be less susceptible to optical illusions. DJ Spooky is one of the young contemporary DJs/musicians who express a molecular becoming in music. He also calls himself a spatial engineer of the invisible city: "Gimme two records and I'll make you a universe," he says in an interview.[84] Electronic music and soundscapes have deterritorializing cosmic powers, and at the same time, they have spatial qualities, they are compositions "to live in," giving expression to territorial forces and to the creation of "identities" or "homes."

A People of a New Kind?

Many of the DJs, sound designers, and musicians I have mentioned work in avant garde or underground circuits. The movement is not limited to these circles, however. In his book *Ocean of Sound*, musician David Toop gives a historical account of ambient music and sound, which also has entered popularity extensively. His account starts in 1889 at the Paris Exposition, when Debussy first heard Javanese music performed. Describing in the introduction first his own sound environment in which he reads and writes, Toop also goes back to the synesthetic experiences of Des Esseintes in Huysmans. Toop seeks "to explore the path by which sound and music has come to express the disorienting and inspiring openness through which all that is solid melts into aether."[85] The becoming-aether of solid things is, of course, another way to say becoming-molecular and even becoming-imperceptible. Toop gives a rich, detailed account of ambient music, attributing an important role to Brian Eno, who invented the term *ambient music.* Eno embraced the notion that all devices used to create music (through a synthesizer, the sound machine), including the environment itself, are musical instruments. So ambient sound now becomes ambient music through the mediation of technical equipment.[86] Toop explains the birth of ambient as music that, rather than standing out from its environment like a ship on an ocean, now has become part of that ocean alongside all the other transient effects of light, shade, color, scent, taste, and sound. Toop describes ambient as follows: "Music that we hear but don't hear; sounds which exist to enable us better to hear silence; sound which rests us from our intense compulsion to focus, to analyze, to frame, to categorize, to isolate. . . . A swarm of butterflies encountered on the ocean."[87]

Ambient music demonstrates that all sounds and noises can become-music: falling rain, footsteps on a wet street, the blowing of the wind, breaking waves of the ocean, whispering voices, and so on. Inversely, music becomes environmental, again, a double becoming to a point where they become indistinguishable. In Amsterdam, there is an outdoor café ("De Ijsbreker") where in summer a sound system (that reacts to the energy of the sun) makes bird songs come from the trees, as if one is in the middle of the forest. But for the signs that explain the sound system, one would not have known about the machinic interference. The calming effect of the bird sounds is nevertheless the same.

Ambient is now part of the technomusic culture, and many DJs work with ambient sounds. In clubs, on raves, and at dance parties, ambient is present. Dancing is a way of becoming-music of the body. Simon Frith refers to dance in his book on popular music in the following way:

Dance matters not just as a way of expressing music but as a way of listening to it, a way into the music *in its unfolding*—which is why dancing music is both a way of losing oneself in it, physically, and a way of thinking about it, hearing it with a degree of concentration that is clearly not "brainless": One who "hears" the music "understands" it with a dance, and the participation of the dancer is therefore the rhythmic interpretation which we have described as the aesthetic foundation of appreciation, the essential foothold on the music so to speak. In short, it is through rhythm, through decisions regarding when to move, at what pace, with what sort of regularity and repetition, that we most easily participate in a piece of music, if only by tapping our feet, clapping our hands or just jigging our heads up and down. And in terms of live performance this is certainly experienced both as collective participation, our movements tied in with those of other people, and as musical participation, our response (as in the African classic call-and-response tradition) a necessary part of the music itself.[88]

Again, it is clear that the classic mind/body opposition is no longer tenable. Bodies and minds become-music at raves and in clubs. The increasing size of clubs, raves, and other dance and music events makes clear that the cosmic music of the last decade is not just restricted to some difficult electronic avant-garde music scene, but that it stretches out into popular culture with which it regularly fuses. Given the scale and collectivity of such events, the becoming-music of the world might even imply a political dimension, in the sense that a new kind of people (not defined by national borders) is invented through music. As Deleuze and Guattari predict in a visionary way:

Finally, it is clear that the relation to the earth and the people has changed and is no longer of the romantic type. The earth is now at its most deterritorialized: not only a point in a galaxy, but one galaxy among others. The people is now at its most molecularized, a molecular population, a people of oscillators as so many forces of interaction. . . . [It] may be that the sound molecules of pop music are at this very moment implanting here and there a people of a new type, singularly indifferent to the orders of the radio, to computer safeguards, to the threat of the atomic bomb. In this respect, the relation of the artist to the people has changed significantly: the artist has ceased to be the One-Alone withdrawn into him- or herself, but has also ceased to address the people, to invoke the people as a constituted force. Never has the artist been more in need of a people, while stating most firmly that the people is lacking. Thus the problem of the artist is that the modern depopulation of the people results in an open earth. (. . .) Instead of being bombarded from all sides in a limiting cosmos, the people and the earth must be like the vectors of a cosmos that carries them off; then the cosmos itself will be art. From depopulation, make a cosmic people; from deterritorialization, a cosmic earth—that is the wish of the artisan-artist, here, there, locally.[89]

The people who go to dance events, festivals, and love parades could be an indication toward such a new people that Deleuze and Guattari see.[90] These masses are different from the masses that collected around the acousmatic territorializing radio voices of the dictators in the 1920s and 1930s: they are not looking for one identity that always leads to fascistic exclusion of many "others." The Second World War shattered that dream of one nation and one identity. Still, in *Anti-Oedipus*, Deleuze and Guattari wonder, "How could the masses be made to desire their own oppression?"[91] The fact that many identity wars and ethnic cleansings continue to exist proves that the identity politics of the traditional conception of the subject is still strong; but the deterritorializing cosmic forces of technomusic are much too molecular to incite consolidated subjects. This music breaks boundaries instead of setting them. There is not one God (dictator, leader) that tells everybody what to do. In these scenes, everybody is in a perpetual state of becoming, finding their utmost expression in a becoming-invisible. It is not clear whether Deleuze and Guattari mean by this a literal disappearance. More likely, it is a molecular becoming that is to be related to the freedom of anonymous multiplicity. In any case, becoming-imperceptible is related to an imperceptibility from the horrible judging Gaze.[92] If there is a "people of a new kind," it is possibly inventing itself through musical experiences and becoming-music.

A short ten-minute film by Jason Spingarn-Koff, *Abducted* (1996), makes all these points very clear. The film shows how we are "walking around" in a rhizomatic network of virtual and actual audiovisual products. In *Abducted*, we follow a girl who is "abducted" from the beginning of the century to contemporary Berlin. First, we see a television screen with images of the city as it is today. An intense underground technosound beat puts the images in the present. Then we leave the television frame and see a girl who leaves her room and enters the world. She is literally walking in (often synthesized) images. All this indicates a very contemporary setting, but the girl's silent amazement and the appearance of intertitles bring us back to the beginning of the century. The girl arrives at a large building. The intertitles say, "At the Reich Air Force Ministry"—"What happened here? Perhaps something terrible." The girl starts to run through the images, and a few minutes later she arrives in a crowd of dancing people: "400,000 youths at the Berlin Love Parade," the intertitle explains now. The girl still does not know what to think of it all. Her face in close-up tells how she is wondering about all these images, sounds, and people. Then the intertitle announces "A mysterious force pulls Maria away." Maria enters a huge building. It takes her some time to recognize that she has arrived in a club where people are dancing. She nevertheless finds it difficult to distinguish the images. Then a smile breaks through on her face in close-up, and the intertitle says, "It's an angel." In the last images, Maria reaches with her arms into the sky to the angel. The film ends.

In a concise way, this short film demonstrates how we are surrounded by images of the past and future, how we literally find ourselves in a matrix of audiovisual culture. It demonstrates the "fog of virtual images" that accompanies the actual images. It is the film's soundtrack that "actualizes," that puts us in the present, the present of contemporary Berlin. The intertitles and the expressionistic shadows and lights bring us back to the 1920s. The Reich Air Force Ministry recalls the Second World War (and maybe many other wars as well). When we read that the girl's name is Maria, the virtuality of that other film about the big city, Fritz Lang's *Metropolis* (1927), becomes stronger. In this film, the good Maria (who joins the heads of the bosses with the hands of the workers and keeps the status quo of patriarchy and fixed identities intact) is opposed to her bad double, the evil Robot Maria (who represents dangerous female sexuality, obscene dancing, and chaos). The "abducted" Maria of the 1990s is beyond this opposition between good and bad. Therefore, she, too, is a cyborg, but a cyborg of a different kind. In her time travel, robot Maria has turned into a cyborg Alice. She stretches her arms (is she going through the fantasm?), she is learning to dance, maybe becoming "people of a new kind" (in this case, the Berlin Love Parade). Soon she will feel and understand the rhythm and become-music in dancing in an audiovisual world. While becoming, she will open up to many encounters that prevent her from being put in one single and imprisoning category and that will lead to the creation and actualization of her new sense of self.

People at raves and concerts find themselves on a line of flight into the future. They are singularities in a multiple collectivity. They do not want to change the world like the hippies wanted to do in the 1960s. They are not opposing the world in the way the punk movement did. They want to develop new sensibilities, new ways of thinking, creating spaces and moments where this is possible and from which this new attitude (that is strongly connected to a new way of conceiving the subject) can be taken into the rest of the world. This process of becoming works by contamination; however, "nobody can do it for another—it is a private affair which is best done collectively."[93] Of course, it is quite necessary to stay alert. As Deleuze and Guattari indicate, we must stay alert for the black holes of microfascism and self-destruction; but staying alert is also a form of becoming-animal.[94] In the ocean of sounds and images that surround us, staying alert also means evaluating virtual and actual audiovisual events for their good and bad effects. In this "virtual sea," the traditional hierarchy of language over nonlinguistic sounds is no longer valid. Language exists next to other "sound matters," and it is not only accessible to privileged subjects. Equally, in the case of images, it is no longer the question of good or bad representations, true or false images. All images have to be evaluated on their internal qualities and in relation to the contexts in which they appear. There is no general recipe or prescription. Only a few tools, like affects and concepts, can help us. Becoming-woman, becoming-animal, and becoming-music are such concepts. Becomings furthermore make us realize that we are witnessing a becoming-cinema of the world and the becoming-life of the cinema. The virtual and the actual form ever-growing and ever-changing crystals in which it is sometimes difficult to distinguish between the two. In any case, all images and sounds are virtual in this world. Every image contains the virtuality of a thousand sounds, and every sound evokes many images. Which ones are actualized depends on our creative will to power. It also depends on our will to "desubjectify" and enter into all kinds of becomings. In this, becoming-music is one of the most molecularizing ways of deterritorializing and at the same time a possibility of empirically creating "transcendental" mobile selves and collective identities through music.

Conclusion

Deleuze always preferred anonymity. While the great French philosophers of his generation were finding success in the international academic
world, he professed his philosophic journeys at home by the fireside or in
the classrooms of Vincennes. After the shock of *Anti-Oedipus*, his and
Guattari's concepts spread slowly further at the margins. Since Deleuze's
death, however, interest in his work seems to have exploded. Over the past
few years, several special issues, critical readers, books, and articles have appeared.[1] Most striking, and at the same time significant of the current popularity of Deleuze, is the multitude of people who find his ideas inspiring:
not only philosophers but also musicians, filmmakers, writers, painters, ar-
chitects, and even economists and managers.[2] Of course, one could say
that it is quite logical for this to occur now that he is no longer literally
among us (it happens all the time); but I think something else is at work as
well. After all the years of critique, deconstruction, cynicism, and negativity in theory and philosophy, there is now clearly a search for more affirmative views. The intensity and liberating forces of Deleuze and Guattari's
work seem to offer "a breath of fresh air, a relationship with the outside
world." It is also an *air du temps*.[3]

With respect to film theory, I hope to have shown concretely that
with Deleuze a new wind is blowing (maybe a *vent de sorcière* indeed), al-
lowing new possibilities.[4] Deleuze's conception of cinema as a pure semiotics
of movement, sound, and images offers an alternative for the traditional

conception of images as representations or as language systems. The increasing digitalization of the audiovisual seriously jeopardizes the ontologic argument of photographic analogy. Actually, digital images have more to do with animation. As I argued in the last chapter, Deleuze's (film) philosophy has much in common with Eisenstein's views on the "plasmaticness" of the animate form. The fluid forms of matter changing in time appear to offer a conception of the image that is useful for reflections about digital technologies as well, and classic animation could be seen as morphing *avant-la-lettre*. The confusion about the status of images (is it a representation or is it fake?) is caused by the fact that it is becoming increasingly difficult to recognize that photorealistic images are animations.[5] In traditional representational thinking, this confusion leads to panic: there are no more criteria for judging whether what we see is real. Deleuze's Bergsonian/Peircian semiotics demonstrates that there is no reason to panic. We just need to ask different questions. We should no longer ask, "What is it?" but rather, "What effect does it have?" "How does it work?" or "What forces (always multiple) are in play?" and "Who wants this to be a true image and for what reason?"

By looking at the specific assemblages that certain images constitute, I hope to have been able to demonstrate, despite Robert Stam's doubts about the usefulness of Deleuze's cinema books for the analysis of cinematographic images, in what ways it is possible to work with Deleuze in film theory. Looking at the horizontal axis of form of content and form of expression, Deleuze's formal concepts of his film books are useful in determining the specific effects and affects that are obtained by certain images. The effects of action-images differ from those of affection-images, and a cinema of the body is different in style from a cinema of the brain. They constitute different types of stories and create different kinds of signs (indexes, icons, gestures, and thoughts), all of which can have emotional, intellectual, and political force. These forces constitute the vertical axis of the assemblage, where questions of territorialization and deterritorialization are important. It is noteworthy that these concepts are not specifically cinematographic ones. Deleuze and Guattari developed various forms of territorialization and deterritorialization in *Anti-Oedipus* and *A Thousand Plateaus*. I have tried to work with some forms of these "moving concepts" by looking at specific images or problems. I have not always followed an "auteurist" approach, as Deleuze did in his cinema books. This is because I think Deleuze's concepts, to be productive, should be "applicable" to a wide range of audiovisual images. Therefore, I have chosen not to make any hierarchical distinctions between art and images of popular culture. The difference between different images resides not in their status as belonging to "high" or "low" culture, but in the different machinic assemblages into which they enter. In Chapter 2, for instance, I tried to look at the connection between different image-types of the flesh in Hollywood, European art cinema, and African cinema and to establish the way in which these images present different territorializing segments on the molar line and deterritorializing movements on the line of flight in relation to the formation of a material kind of subjectivity. In Chapter 3, I discussed how violence in cinema can be a deterritorializing and reterritorializing force and how these violent images can be part of the fabulation of a "people to come." All kinds of becomings always imply deterritorialization as well. In the last three chapters, I concentrated on three different types of becoming (becoming-woman, becoming-animal, and becoming-music) as they can be observed in cinema and audiovisual culture. Music, specifically the refrain, is in this the most powerful force to invite territorial or deterritorial movements and becomings.

Deterritorializing movements do not imply that we take off into a transcendental "other" realm, because all assemblages are formed just as much as other kinds of images: both virtually (in memory) and actually (moving our senses in the present) they affect us. As I argued in Chapter 1, Deleuze showed us how we have come to live in a universe as metacinema. This universe is a fundamentally immanent one[6]—and here Deleuze's conception of cinema and images in general differs strongly from the traditional and transcendental conceptions of the cinematographic apparatus as an illusion machine, which are very much connected to psychoanalytic interpretations of cinema. My aim was not to demonstrate that these interpretations of cinema are incorrect. Rather, it was to find out what other things one can see when one works with Deleuze. If we work with Deleuze's concepts (both his film concepts and the concepts he developed with Guattari), it becomes clear that a camera consciousness has entered our "normal" perception, making it easier to jump between layers of time and to become confused in time. It is a kind of consciousness that is nonpersonal and "detached" from a preconceived idea of the subject. It forms material and temporal aspects of subjectivity. Images surround us; we live in images and images live in us. The forces, energy, and virtualities of the images on the plane of immanence are not always visible; but they can be sensed, experienced, and evaluated in the sense that they are constructive of our subjectivities.

Even narration (traditionally conceived in spatial structures) obtains this energetic and temporal dimension. Narration thus receives the status of an event. Not only in video games, but also in the increasing stimulation of all senses, cinema becomes more an event than a text.[7] That this does not entail that everything becomes "brainless" spectacle can be understood only by letting go of the persistent opposition between mind and body. This classic opposition is to be related to the classic view of images as representations that are directly accessible to the mind via a disembodied eye. Deleuze proposes an alternative model of the brain, which he sees as rhizomatically structured. In the vast rhizomatic network of images, sounds, ideas, concepts, and affects, I hope to have constituted some "planes of consistency," some "plateaus" that put aspects of the model of the brain to work. I do realize that many other virtual images and sounds surround the planes that I have constructed and that other connections could have been made. In any case, it should be clear that, from a Deleuzian perspective, images (cinema included) are realities in their own right, not something of a second order. The brain is itself an image. The brain is the screen. We live in brain cities; the screen is a brain, our bodies are brains, and our brain is part of our body. Therefore, as Deleuze asserts repeatedly, the neurologic reference to the brain, which he and Guattari call the *rhizome*, seems to be an adequate way of conceiving both how we think and how the world (including all its images) is structured. Compared with the brain, the eye as referent is much more tied to representation, although it has been "denigrated" in twentieth-century philosophy, as demonstrated by Martin Jay, Christian Metz, Jacques Lacan, and many feminist film theorists.[8] At the start of the twenty-first century, the eye has found its place among the other senses and consequently given them more room. Especially the ear has come to the fore: sound and music have gained importance in the brain model and are penetrating at the finest levels, "molecularizing" everything. As Deleuze said, "We are all molecules."[9] There is a becoming-molecular and a becoming-music of the image and of the world infusing it with energy.

Support for such a Deleuzian view also comes from an unexpected quarter. In his article "A Semio-Pragmatic Approach to the Documentary," Roger Odin recognizes (not without regret) the "energetics of the flux" of images that for Deleuze is so important. He states:

This energetic positioning does not only exist in relation to television: an ever increasing number of films function according to this principle (the *Mad Max*, *Rambo*, and *Rocky* series, etc.). All videoclips also pertain to this positioning (and we know the success of the music stations that diffuse these products). Finally, it is evident that the popularity of discos and huge spectacular concerts goes in the same direction. It is therefore not absurd to formulate the hypothesis of a modification in the demand of the social space itself. Perhaps we are witnessing the end of the domination of the fictionalizing Desire, and simultaneously the disappearance of the distinction between fictions and documentaries. If this mutation proves to be true, the whole functioning of the field of the audio-visual world would find itself in confusion, and furthermore, in all probability, that of the unity of social space. Because when the conscious awareness of the distinction between the real Enunciator and the fictitious Enunciator disappears, it is the social body itself that is in danger. The "uncivil" man who functions only by way of emotional contact replaces the "public" man who functions by way of contract. The demise of the documentary and of fiction would therefore announce the "end of the social," but luckily the "Cassandras" are not always right.[10]

The developments that Odin describes are undeniably true. I hope to have shown that "fictionalizing desire" is strongly related to psychoanalytic interpretations of the image and of the concept of the subject. Feminist film theory and revisionists of psychoanalysis in the 1990s have demonstrated the imprisoning implications of such an idea of the subject; however, these critiques have offered no real alternatives: what happens after everything has been deconstructed, after we have "gone through the phantasm"?

One possible solution is given by Kaja Silverman, who has indicated how within psychoanalysis a "resisting," liberating, and productive look can be constructed in returning the "impossible gaze" that is so strongly present in Žižek's work. However, Silverman's conception of desire still is based on lack and absence, on negativity. I have proposed a Deleuzian conception of desire that is not based on a fundamental lack but functions as a factory, as an assembly line where all kinds of things are connected and fabricated into something new. This machinic definition of desire (without sublimation) seems important for a new conception of the subject. The BwO is a "subject," or rather a "mobile self," that is full of desire, intensities, energy, movements, and speed.

I also hope to have shown that if Odin's "Cassandras" are not to be proved right, we have to stop seeing the emotional man who functions by contact and the public man who functions by contract as mutually exclusive agents. If so many wars and fights are going on, it is not because "uncivil" emotional men have contact. On the contrary, as I have proposed, violence is either a political option of the line of flight, or it is related to a molar and segmental defense of dominating categories and "civil" contracts. Most importantly, we should stop subordinating "emotional contact" (often equated with the body) to "rational contract" (reason). During the course of this work, I hope to have indicated how such a philosophic body/mind split can be overcome, with a "becoming-woman" as a starting point. Then we can only hope and search for more contact, more connections between people to become-other, multiplied and "richer."

Paradoxical as it may seem, we can only become "richer" if we let go of our traditional conception of what it means to be a subject (with a stable identity based on comparison with something or somebody "other"). We have to "depersonalize" and to "desubjectivize." As Deleuze puts it:

> It's a strange business, speaking for yourself, in your own name, because it doesn't at all come with seeing yourself as an ego or a person or a subject. Individuals find a real name for themselves, rather, only through the harshest exercise in depersonalization, by opening themselves up to the multiplicities everywhere within them, to the intensities running through them. A name as the direct awareness of such intensive multiplicity is the opposite of the depersonalization effected by the history of philosophy; it's depersonalization through love rather than subjection.[11]

With his call for multiplicity and heterogeneous rhizomatic connections and assemblages, Deleuze is in many respects calling for a cyborg subjectivity as conceived by Donna Haraway. The rhizomatic or cyborg subject is aware of its historical situation, its relation to others, its complicity with technology and the dangers of the black holes of old structures. Contrary to a common belief about cyborgs and Bodies without Organs (BwO), the "new" subject does not want to leave this earth, nor does it ignore the political dilemmas pointed at by, for instance, Odin or Žižek. As Deleuze puts it, it just wants a "subtle way out"; and "the subtle way out," then, is not based on believing in a different world. This could only be a transcendental or Platonic world, which restores the system of judgment and, in its incapacity to achieve anything on this earth, only produces a psychology of resentment. To believe in a transcendental world is to believe in an ignoble utopia, but this does not mean that we relinquish either belief or a utopian aspiration. The subtle way out is to believe "not in a different world, but in a link between humanity and the world, in love or life, to believe in this as in the impossible, the unthinkable, which nonetheless cannot but be thought."[12]

It should be clear that a consciousness of unthinkable time is changing fundamentally the concept of the subject. Time has put everything in motion. Everything occurs in time; everything changes in time. According to Deleuze, the personal (the "subjectivizing") is composed of experiences. As Ian Buchanan makes clear in his introduction to *A Deleuzian Century?* we are made of experiences. Experience is not the property of a person, but is nonpersonal. Following Duns Scotus, Spinoza, and Hume, Deleuze redefines experience in terms of effects and relations or in terms of haecceities: experience is individuating. Deleuze has a practical, empirical conception of subjectivity.[13] There is nothing outside the empiric world; but how, then, can we speak at all of the constitution of a subject? Or, in Deleuze's words, "How can a subject transcending the given be constituted in the given?"[14] Buchanan has introduced the paradoxical notion of the "transcendental empirical subject," which is as much the product of self-invention as it is the consequence of conforming to an existing structure, and habit is a very constitutive root of the subject.

It should be emphasized once more, however, that the fact that the subject has to transcend itself does not mean it is a transcendental subject with some preconceived ideas of an "I" or that it is formed by an impossible transcendental entity. As Buchanan formulates it clearly:

The subject does not stand outside what it organizes or makes coherent; rather, organization and coherence—made possible by principles of association—take place in the subject, which is why the subject is fragmented. As the site of the instance of coherence referred to as subjectivity, the subject is not the principle of a totalization that would supply that coherence. "Empirical subjectivity is constituted in the mind under the influence of principles affecting it; the mind therefore does not have the characteristics of a preexisting subject. It transcends itself to the extent that the mind becomes a subject."[15]

The "transcendental moment" takes place within the subject, on the plane of immanence. It is the mind that organizes the rhizomatic structures of the brain into "planes of consistency," one of which could be called "subject," and it is never fixed, changing through new experiences, new affects, new thoughts, new encounters, new images and sounds.

I have tried to put Deleuze to work. What this has allowed me to do is to see cinema as a part of the world instead of a reflection about the world. In talking about cinema, I have been talking about life as well; however, I do not want to make too many claims. I am not arguing that this perspective offers in some sense a better view of the world (there is no hierarchy). I simply want to indicate that some mutations are taking place, both in the image and in the world.[16] Developments in science, art and philosophy all indicate changes in perception and changes in our relation to the world. It may well be that this involves a generational shift. We articulate the world, and the world expresses itself in us (it is enfolded in our brain). Consequently, a different, more immanent way of conceiving the image, the world, and the subject seems necessary and even unavoidable. Ultimately, we have no choice but to change.

It may well be that it is no longer possible or necessary to speak of "subjects." In any case, Deleuze and Guattari doubted whether they still could be seen as separate subjects. They consider themselves more like two streams coming together to make a third stream.[17] In *A Thousand Plateaus*, they start the first plateau "Rhizome" in the following way:

The two of us wrote Anti-Oedipus together. Since each was several, there was already quite a crowd. Here we have made use of everything that came within range that was closest as well as farther away. We have assigned clever pseudonyms to prevent recognition. Why have we kept our names? Out of habit, purely out of habit. To make ourselves unrecognizable in turn. To render imperceptible, not ourselves, but what makes us act, feel, and think. Also because it's nice to talk like everybody else, to say the sun rises, when everybody knows it's only a manner of speaking. To reach, not the point where one no longer says I, but the point where it is no longer of any importance whether one says I. We are no longer ourselves. Each will know his own. We have been aided, inspired, multiplied.[18]

Deleuze and Guattari have kept their names out of habit. They have reached the point where it is no longer important for them to be separate subjects. If I have kept using the term subject in this work, that may well be out of habit as well and also because sometimes it is still important to say "I," if only to "mime the strata" as Deleuze and Guattari invite us to do. The Deleuzian model is a political utopian one. Because many aspects of the world are stratified and organized in molar structures, it is not always possible to let go of the subject grounded in a traditional sense of identity and the subject. As I hope to have demonstrated in concrete filmic examples, however, more important are the break lines that can best be perceived in cinematic perception and with a camera consciousness. In many instances, we might choose to refer to ourselves and others as BwOs, cyborg Alices, melodies, rivers, or just winds or even twisters. Because habit is a strong individuating and depersonalizing force, I think the term subject still can be used, albeit in a refigured and reconceptualized way: it is no longer necessarily tied to one identity in opposition to the other and governed by the Eye and the Gaze of representational thinking and psychoanalysis. The refigured subject refers to a mobile self, an individuated field of energy, a desiring machine that makes rhizomatic assemblages. Multiple forces, movements and rests, powers and affects constitute it. It is fundamentally related to an immanent world, surrounded by virtual and actual images and sounds of all kinds. In that rhizomatic brain world, the mind tries to create planes of consistency, actualized in concrete body; everything being contained in "a life." The mobile self is individual but related, traversed by multiplicities, changing in time and informed by a camera consciousness. It lives and continuously constitutes itself in the matrix of visual culture that is its plane of immanence, where the virtual and actual, memory and the present constantly exchange forces.

REFERENCE MATTER

Appendix A

Deleuze's "Toolbox" of *Cinema 1* and *Cinema 2*

Cinema 1: The Movement-Image
Indirect Time
    Montage > How are images linked (to perception / affection / action)

Category (Bergson)	Sign (Peirce)	Activity	Form	Space	Examples
Perception-image a. Semisubjectivity (free indirect discourse) b. Liquid perception c. Gaseous perception	*Zeroness* a. Dicisign b. Reume c. Gramme	Look	Long-shot	General	a. (Theory of) Pasolini b. French school (Vigo, Renoir) c. Ciné-eye (Vertov); American experimental cinema (Brakhage)
Affection-image a. Face (quality / power) b. Any-space-whatever (quality / power) c. Between social + individual	*Firstness* a. Icon b. Qualisign / potisign c. Dividual	Emotion Affect	Close-up	Empty or any-space-whatevers	a. Von Sternberg / Bergman / Dreyer b. Bresson / Ivens / Antonioni c. Eisenstein
Impulse-image	a. Symptoms b. Fetish / idols				Von Stroheim / Bunuel / Losey

Action-image
a. Large form: SAS' (Situation-Action-New Situation)
b. Small form: ASA' (Action-Situation-New Action)
	Secondness
	a. Synsign
	  Binôme
	  Imprint
	b. Index
	  Vector
		Action
		Behavior
			Medium-shot	Determined	a. Genres: docu (Flaherty) / psycho-social / film noir / nation + historical films / actors studio / burlesque (Keaton) / western
					b. Genres: docu (Grierson) / direct-cinema / police films / comedy / burlesque (Chaplin) / neo-western

Reflection-Image	a. Figure b. Discursive				Eisenstein / Herzog Kurosawa / Mizoguchi
Relation-image	*Thirdness* a. Mark / demark b. Symbol	Mental activity	Tropes		Marx Brothers Hitchcock

Beyond the movement-image:
    Break with sensory-motor link
    No more distinction real / fiction > virtual / actual form crystals
    Autonomy of image and sound

Cinema 2: The Time-Image
Direct Time
    Montage > Montrage
        (What does the image show; what does it relate to if not to a
        perception / affection / action: to memory, time + thought)

Actualization of past / imaginary:

Memory / Dream	Sign	Comment
Recollection-image	Mnemosign	Flashback
Dream-image	Onirosign	Metamorphosis of the real

Opsigns + Sonsigns + Tactisigns >
    Pure optical, sonar + tactile situations

Actual and virtual become indiscernible (crystals):

Direct Time-Images	Sign	Aspect	Comments
Crystal-image (real / imaginary)	Hyalosign	Perfect (Ophüls) Cracked (Renoir) In formation (Fellini) Decomposing (Visconti)	World is shown as a crystal trapped in endless mirror reflections
Chronosign (true / false: powers of the false)	a. Aspect b. Accent c. Gensign	a. Sheets of past (Resnais) b. Peeks of present (Robbe-Grillet) c. Becoming (Welles / Rouch / Godard)	a + b: Memory (Bergson) c. Bodily forces (Nietzsche / Spinoza)
Noosign (what forces to think: noochoc)		a. Godard / Antonioni / Akerman b. Resnais / Kubrick / Antonioni c. Third world cinema / political cinema	Free indirect speech / the irrational a. "Give me a body" b. "Give me a brain" c. "The people are missing"
Lectosign (the readability of the image)		Straubs / Duras	Autonomy of components of image (words, sound, music)

Appendix B

Glossary to *Cinema 1* and *Cinema 2*

From *Cinema 1: The Movement-Image* (London: Athlone Press, 1986) pp. 217–18; and *Cinema 2: The Time-Image* (London: Athlone Press, 1989) p. 335.

Movement-Image

The acentered set (*ensemble*) of variable elements that act on and react to each other.

Image Center

The gap between a received movement and an executed movement; an action and a reaction (*interval*).

Perception-Image (the Thing)

A set (*ensemble*) of elements that act on a center and that vary in relation to it.

> *Dicisign*: A term created by Peirce to designate principally the sign of the proposition in general. It is used here in relation to the special case of "free indirect proposition" (Pasolini). It is a perception in the *frame* of another perception. This is the status of solid, geometric, and physical perception.
>
> *Reume*: Not to be confused with Peirce's *rheme* ("word"). It is the

perception of that which crosses the frame or flows out, the liquid status of perception itself.

Gramme (engramme or photogramme): Not to be confused with a photo, it is the genetic element of the perception-image, inseparable as such from certain dynamisms (immobilization, vibration, flickering, sweep, repetition, acceleration, deceleration, etc.), the gaseous state of a molecular perception.

Affection-Image (Quality or Power)

That which occupies the gap between an action and a reaction, that which absorbs an external action and reacts on the inside.

Icon: Used by Peirce to designate a sign that refers to its object by internal characteristics (resemblance). Used here to designate the affect as *expressed* by a face or a facial equivalent.

Qualisign (or potisign): A term used by Peirce to designate a quality which is a sign. Used here to designate the affect as expressed (or exposed) in an *any-space-whatever*. An any-space-whatever is sometimes an emptied space, sometimes a space the linking up of whose parts is not immutable or fixed.

Dividual: That which is neither indivisible nor divisible but is divided (or brought together) by changing qualitatively. This is the state of the entity, that is to say, of that expressed in an expression.

Impulse-Image (Energy)

Symptom: Designates the qualities or powers related to an *originary world* (defined by impulses).

Fetish: Fragment torn away by the impulse from a real milieu, and corresponding to the originary world.

Action-Image (the Force or Act)

A reaction to the center to the set (*ensemble*)

Synsign (or *encompasser*): Corresponds to Peirce's "sinsign." A set of qualities and powers as actualized in a state of things, thus constituting a real milieu around a center, a situation in relation to a subject: spiral. Belongs to the large form of the action image where we go from the situation to the transformed situation via the intermediatry of the action (SAS').

Impression: Internal link between situation and action.

Index: Used by Peirce to designate a sign that refers to its object by a material link. Used here to designate the link of an action (or of an effect of action) to a situation that is not given, but merely inferred or that remains equivocal and reversible. There are *indices of lack* and *indices of equivocity*: the two senses of the French word *ellipse* (ellipse and ellipsis). Belongs to the small form of the action-image where the action that discloses the situation triggers of a new action (ASA').

Vector (or *line of the universe*): A broken line that brings together singular points or remarkable moments at the peak of their intensity. Vectorial space is distinguished from encompassing space.

Transformation-Image (Reflection)

Figure: A sign that, instead of referring to its object, reflects another (*scenographic* or *plastic image*) or that directly reflects its object (*discursive image*).

Mental-Image (Relation)

Mark: Designates natural relations, that is, the aspect under which images are linked by a habit which takes [*fait passer*] us from one to the other. The *demark* designates an image torn from its natural relations.

Symbol: Used by Peirce to designate a sign that refers to its object by virtue of a law. Used here to designate the support of *abstract relations*, that is to say, of a comparison of terms independently of their natural relations.

Opsign and Sonsign: Pure optical and sound image that breaks the sensory-motor links, overwhelms relations, and no longer lets itself be expressed in terms of movement but opens directly to time.

Time-Image

Chronosign (point and sheet): An image in which time ceases to be subordinate to movement and appears for itself.

Lectosign: A visual image that must be "read" as much as seen.

Noosign: An image that goes beyond itself toward something which can only be thought.

Crystal-Image

> *Hyalosign*: The uniting of an actual image and a virtual image to the point where they can no longer be distinguished.

Dream-Image

> *Onirosign*: An image where a movement of world replaces action.

Recollection-Image

> *Mnemosign*: A virtual image that enters into a relationship with the actual image and extends it.

Filmography

100% Arabica (FR, 1997)

dir: Mahmoud Zemmouri; sc: Mahmoud Zemmouri; ph: Noel Very and Jean-Claude Vicquery; music: Khaled, Cheb Mami, et al.; cast: Khaled, Cheb Mami, Mouss, Farid Fedjer, Najim Laouriga, et al.

Abducted (G, 1997)

dir: Jason Spingarn-Koff; sc: Jason Spingarn-Koff; video: Jason Spingarn-Koff; music: DJ French Blend; cast: Mary Campbell

Alice in the Cities/Alice in den Städten (G, 1974)

dir: Wim Wenders; sc: Wim Wenders; ph: Robby Müller; ed: Peter Prygodda; music: Irmin Schmid; cast: Yella Rottländer, Rüdiger Vogler, Elisabeth Kreuzer, et al.

American Beauty (USA, 1999)

dir: Sam Mendes; sc: Alan Ball; ph: Conrad L. Hall; ed: Tariq Anwar; prod: Bruce Cohen and Dan Jinks; cast: Kevin Spacey, Annette Benning, Thora Birch, Wes Bentley, Mena Suvari, et al.

Angel of Vengeance/MS. 45 (USA, 1980)

dir: Abel Ferrara; sc: Nicholas St. John; cast: Zoe Tamerlis, Jimmy Laine, Peter Yellem, Vincent Gruppi, et al.

Atalante, L'/Le Chaland Qui Passe (FR, 1934)

dir: Jean Vigo; sc: Albert Riéra and Jean Vigo; ph: Boris Kaufman and Louis Berger; music: Maurice Jaubert; cast: Michel Simon, Dita Parlo, Jean Dasté, Jaques Prévert, et al.

Atlantis (FR, 1992)

dir: Luc Besson; ph: Christian Petron; ed: Luc Besson; music: Eric Serra; locations: North Pole, Red Sea, Great Barrier Reef, Bahamas

Aurélia Steiner Melbourne/Aurélia Steiner Vancouver (FR, 1979)

dir: Marguerite Duras; text: Marguerite Duras; voice: Marguerite Duras; ph: Pierre Lhomme; ed: Geneviève Dufour.

Big Blue, The/Le Grand Bleu (FR, 1988)

dir: Luc Besson; sc: Roger Garland and Luc Besson; ph: Carlo Varini; prod: Patrice Ledoux; music: Eric Serra; cast: Roseanna Arquette, Jean Reno, Jean-Marc Barre, et al.

Blade Runner (USA, 1982)

dir: Ridley Scott; sc: Hampton Fancher and David Peoples; sp. eff: Douglas Trumbull; ph: Jordan Cronenweth; prod: Michael Deeley; music: Vangelis; cast: Harrison Ford, Rutger Hauer, Sean Young, et al.

Blow Out (USA, 1981)

dir: Brian de Palma; sc: Brian de Palma; ph: Vilmos Zsigmond; prod: Paul Sylbert; music: Pino Donaggio; cast: John Travolta, Nancy Allen, John Lithgow, et al.

Blue (GB, 1993)

dir: Derek Jarman; music and sound: Simon Fisher Turner; voices: John Quentin, Nigel Terry, Tilda Swinton, and Derek Jarman

Brainstorm (USA, 1983)

dir: Douglas Trumbull; sc: Robert Stitzel and Frank Massina; ph: Richard Yurich; cast: Christopher Walken, Nathalie Wood, Louise Fletcher, et al.

Bram Stoker's Dracula (USA, 1992)

dir: Francis Ford Coppola; based on the novel by Bram Stoker; sc: James Hart; ph: Michael Ballhaus; ed: Nicholas Smith, etc.; prod: Thomas Sanders; music: Wojciech Kilar; cast: Keanu Reeves, Winona Ryder, Gary Oldman, Anthony Hopkins, et al.

Breaking the Waves (D/NL, 1996)

dir: Lars von Trier; sc: Lars von Trier; ph: Robby Müller; ed: Anders Refn; music: Joachim Holbeck; cast: Emily Watson, Stellan Skarsgard, Jean-Marc Barre, et al.

Brothers/Frères, La Roulette Rouge (FR, 1994)

dir: Olivier Dahan; sc: Olivier Dahan, et al.; ph: Alex Lamark; ed: Zofia Mennet; sound: Louis Foropon; music: Yarol; cast: El Bouhairi, Véronique Octon, Samy Naceri, Saïd Taghmaoui, et al.

Carrie (USA, 1976)

dir: Brian de Palma; sc: Lawrence D. Cohen, based on the novel by Stephen King;

ph: Mario Tosi; music: Pino Donaggio; cast: Sissy Spacek, Piper Laurie, William Katt, John Travolta, Amy Irving, et al.

City of Lost Children, The/La Cité des Enfants Perdus (FR/G/SP, 1995)
dir: Jean-Pierre Jeunet and Marc Caro; ph: Darius Khondji; ed: Hervé Schneid; music: Angelo Badalamenti; cast: Ron Perlman, Daniël Emilfork, Judith Vittet, Dominique Pinon, et al.

Coma (USA, 1978)
dir: Michael Crichton; sc: Michael Crichton, based on the novel by Robin Cook; ph: Victor Kemper; prod: Albert Brenner; music: Jerry Goldsmith; cast: Geneviève Bujold, Michael Douglas, Elizabeth Ashley, Rip Torn, Tom Selleck, et al.

Company of Wolves, The (GB, 1984)
dir: Neil Jordan; sc: Angela Carter and Neil Jordan; ph: Bryan Loftus; cast: Angela Lansbury, David Warner, Sarah Patterson, Stephen Rea, et al.

Conversation, The (USA, 1974)
dir: Francis Ford Coppola; sc: Francis Ford Coppola; ph: Bill Butler; sound: Walter Murch; music: David Shire; cast: Gene Hackman, John Cazale, Allen Garfield, Cindy Williams, et al.

Cremaster 4 (USA, 1994)
dir: Matthew Barney; video: Peter Strietman; ph: Michael James O'Brian and Larry Lame; makeup and spec. eff.: Gabe Z. Bartalos; cast: Dave and Graham Molyneux, Steve and Karl Sinnot, Matthew Barney, et al.

Dancer in the Dark (D/NL, 2000)
dir: Lars von Trier; sc: Lars von Trier; music: Björk; ph: Robby Müller; ed: Molly Malene Stensgaard and Françoise Gedigier; prod; Vibeke Windelov; cast: Björk, Catherine Deneuve, David Morse, Peter Stormare, et al.

Discreet Charm of the Bourgeoisie, The/Le charme Discret de la Bourgeoisie (FR/I/SP, 1972)
dir: Luis Buñuel; sc: Luis Buñuel and Jean-Claude Carrière; ph: Edmond Richard; cast: Fernando Rey, Stéphane Audran, Delphine Seyrig, Bulle Ogier, Michel Piccoli, et al.

Diva (FR, 1980)
dir: Jean-Jacques Beineix; sc: Jean van Hamme and Jean-Jacques Beineix, based on a novel by Delacorta; ph: Philippe Rousselot; prod: Hilton McConnic; music: Vladimir Cosma; cast: Wilhelminia Wiggins Fernandez, Frédéric Andréi, Richard Bohringer, Thuy An Luu, et al.

Dr. Jekyll and Mr. Hyde (USA, 1931)

dir: Rouben Mamoulian; sc: Samuel Hoffenstein and Percy Heath, based on the novel by R. L. Stevenson; ph: Karl Struss; cast: Fredric March, Miriam Hopkins, Rose Hobart, Holmes Herbert, et al.

Dracula (USA, 1931)

dir: Tod Browning; ph: Karl Freund; music: Tchaikovsky; cast: Bela Lugosi; David Manners; Helen Chandler, et al.

Eyes Wide Shut (USA, 2000)

dir: Stanley Kubrick; sc: Stanley Kubrick and Frederic Raphael, inspired by *Traumnovelle* by Arthur Schnitzler; ph: Larry Smith; ed: Nigel Galt; prod: Stanley Kubrick; cast: Nicole Kidman and Tom Cruise.

F for Fake/Nothing but the Truth (FR/IR/G, 1973)

dir: Orson Welles and François Reichenbach (for the dramatizations); with: Orson Welles, Oja Kodar, Elmy de Hory, Clifford Irving, et al.

The Fantome of Liberty/Le Fantôme de la Liberté (FR/I, 1974)

dir: Luis Buñuel; sc: Jean-Claude Carrière and Luis Buñuel; ph: Edmond Richard; ed: Hélène Plemiannikov; cast: Michel Lonsdale, Michel Piccoli, Marie-France Pisier, Jean Rochefort, et al.

Fifth Element, The/Le Cinquième Elément (FR, 1997)

dir: Luc Besson; sc: Luc Besson and Robert Kamen; prod: Patrice Ledoux; ph: Thierry Arbogast; ed: Sylvie Landra; music: Eric Serra; costume: Jean-Paul Gaultier; spec. eff: Mark Stetson and Stella Bruzzi; set design: Moebius and Jean-Claude Mézières; cast: Milla Jovovich, Bruce Willis, Gary Oldman, Chris Tucker, Ian Holm, et al.

Fight Club (USA, 1999)

dir: David Fincher; sc: Jim Uhls, based on the novel by Chuck Pajahnuick; ph: Jeff Cronenweth; sound: Ren Klyce; music: The Dust Brothers; prod: Art Linson; cast: Edward Norton, Brad Pitt, Helena Bonham Carter, Meat Loaf, et al.

Fly, The (USA, 1986)

dir: David Cronenberg; sc: Edward Pogue and David Cronenberg; ph: Mark Irwin; prod: Carol Spier; ed: Ronald Sanders; cast: Jeff Goldblum, Geena Davis, John Getz, et al.

Fourth Man, The/De Vierde Man (NL, 1983)

dir: Paul Verhoeven; sc: Gerard Soeteman; ph: Jan de Bont; ed: Ine Schenkkan; music: Loek Dikker; cast: Renée Soutendijk, Jeroen Krabbé, Thom Hoffman, et al.

Frankenstein (USA, 1931)

dir: James Whale; sc: Garret Fort and Francis Edwards Faragoh; ph: Arthur Edeson; makeup: Jack Pierce; music: David Broekman; cast: Boris Karloff, Mae Clarke, Colin Clive, John Boles, et al.

Hiroshima Mon Amour (FR, 1959)

dir: Alain Resnais; sc: Marguerite Duras; ph: Sacha Vierny and Takahashi Michio; ed: Henri Colpi and Jasmine Chasney; prod: Sacha Kamenenka and Shirakawa Takeo; music: Georges Delerue and Giovanni Fusco; cast: Emmanuelle Riva, Eiji Okada, Stella Dassas, Pierre Barbaud, and Bernard Fresson

I Can't Sleep/J'ai Pas Sommeil (FR, 1994)

dir: Claire Denis; sc: Claire Denis and Jean-Paul Fargeau; ph: Agnes Godard; ed: Nelly Quettier; cast: Katherine Golubeva, Richard Courcet, Line Renaud, Beatrice Dalle, et al.

I Spit on your Grave/Day of the Woman (USA, 1978)

dir: Meir Zarchi; cast: Camile Keaton, Eron Tabor, Richard Pace, et al.

Idiots, The (D, 1998)

dir: Lars von Trier; sc: Lars von Trier; ph: Lars von Trier; cast: Bodil Jorgensen, Jens Albinus, Anne Louise Hassing, et al.

In a Year of 13 Moons/In Einem Jahr mit 13 Monden (G, 1978)

dir: Rainer Werner Fassbinder; sc: Rainer Werner Fassbinder; prod: Rainer Werner Fassbinder; photo: Rainer Werner Fassbinder; ed: Juliane Lorenz; music: Peer Raben; cast: Volker Spengler, Ingrid Caven, Gottfried John, Elisabeth Trissenaar, et al.

Interview with the Vampire (USA, 1994)

dir: Neil Jordan; sc: Anne Rice; ph: Philippe Rousselot; cast: Brad Pitt, Tom Cruise, Antonio Banderas, Stephen Rea, et al.

Island of Dr. Moreau, The (USA, 1977)

dir: Don Taylor; sc: John Hermann Shaner and Al Ramus, based on the novel by H. G. Wells; ph: Garry Fisher; music: Laurence Rosenthal; cast: Burt Lancaster, Michael York, Nigel Davenport, Barbara Carrera, et al.

Jungle Book, The (USA, 1942)

dir: Zoltan Korda; sc: Laurence Stallings, based on the novel by Rudyard Kipling; ph: Lee Garmes; cast: Sabu, André De Toth, Rosemary DeCamp, Ralph Byrd, et al.

King Kong (USA, 1933)

dir: Merian Cooper and Ernest Schoedsack; sc: James Creelman and Ruth Rose;

prod: Merian Cooper and Ernest Schoedsack; music: Max Steiner; cast: Fay Wray, Bruce Cabot, Robert Armstrong, et al.

Last Angel of History, The (GB, 1996)

dir: John Akomfrah; prod: Black Audio Film Collective; sound: Trevor Mathison; music: Trevor Mathison, Sun Ra and Kraftwerk; with: George Clinton, Sun Ra, Goldie, Octavia Butler, Darek May, DJ Spooky, et al.

Little Mermaid (USA, 1989)

dir: John Musker and Ron Clements; based on the fairy tale by Hans Christian Andersen; prod: Disney Studios; voices: Jodi Benson, Pat Carroll, Samuel E. Wright, Kenneth Mars, et al.

Lost Highway (USA, 1996)

dir: David Lynch; sc: David Lynch and Barry Gifford; ph: Peter Deming; ed: Mark Sweeney; music: Angelo Badalamenti; cast: Bill Pullman, Patricia Arquette, Balthazar Getty, et al.

The Matrix (USA, 1999)

dir: The Wachowski Brothers; sc: The Wachowski Brothers; ph: Bill Pope; ed: Zach Steanberg; prod: Joel Silver; music: Don Davis; cast: Keanu Reeves, Laurence Fishburn, Carrie-Ann Moss, et al.

Metropolis (G, 1927)

dir: Fritz Lang; sc: Fritz Lang and Thea von Harbu; ph: Eugen Schüfftan; cast: Alfred Abel, Gustav Frölich, Brigitte Helm, et al.

Mondo, un Diverso E' Possibile (I, 2001)

dir: Franscesco Maselli and 30 other directors (Etore Scola et. al.); music: Manu Chao, et al.

Nathalie Granger (FR, 1972)

dir: Marguerite Duras; sc: Marguerite Duras; prod: Luc Moulet & Cie; cast: Lucia Bosé, Jeanne Moreau, Gérard Dépardieu, Nathalie Bourgeois

Nosferatu, Phantom der Nacht (G/FR, 1979)

dir: Werner Herzog; inspired by *Nosferatu, Eine Symphony des Grauens*; cast: Klaus Kinski, Isabelle Adjani, Bruno Ganz, Roland Topor, Rijk de Gooyer

Nosferatu, Eine Symphony des Grauens (G, 1922)

dir: F. W. Murnau; inspired by the novel *Dracula* by Bram Stoker; cast: Max Schrenk, Alexander Granach, Gustav von Wangenheim, Greta Schröder

Orlando (GB/NL/SU/I/FR, 1992)

dir: Sally Potter; sc: Sally Potter, based on the novel by Virginia Woolf; ph: Alexei Rodionov; cast: Tilda Swinton, Billy Zane, John Wood, Quentin Crisp, et al.

Pandora's Box/Büchse der Pandora, Die (G, 1929)

dir: Georg Wilhelm Pabst; based on the plays *Der Erdgeist* and *Die Büchse de Pandora* by Frank Wedekind; cast: Louise Brooks, Fritz Kortner, Franz Lederer, et al.

Peeping Tom (GB, 1960)

dir: Michael Powell; sc: Leo Marks; ph: Otto Heller; music: Brian Easdale; cast: Karl-Heinz Boehm, Moira Shearer, Anna Massey, Maxine Audley, et al.

Pickpocket (FR, 1959)

dir: Robert Bresson; cast: Martin Lassalle, Pierre Leymarie, Pierre Etaix, Marika Green, Jean Pelegri, Kassagi and Pierre Etaix

Pulp Fiction (USA, 1994)

dir: Quentin Tarantino; sc: Quentin Tarantino; prod: Lawrence Bender; ph: Andrzej Sekula; ed: Sally Menke; cast: Samuel L. Jackson, John Travolta, Uma Thurman, Bruce Willis, Roseanna Arquette, et al.

Rear Window (USA, 1954)

dir: Alfred Hitchcock; sc: John Michael Hayes, based on the short story by Cornell Woolrich; ph: Robert Burks; sound: Sam Corner and Ray Moyer; ed: George Tomasini; music: Franz Waxman; cast: James Stewart, Grace Kelly, Thelma Ritter, Raymond Burr

Servant, The (GB, 1963)

dir: Joseph Losey; sc: Harold Pinter, based on the novel by Robin Maugham; ph: Douglas Slocombe; music: Johnnie Dankworth; cast: Dirk Bogarde, James Fox, Sarah Miles

Shawshank Redemption, The (USA, 1994)

dir: Frank Darabont; sc: Frank Darabont, based on a story by Stephen King; prod: Niki Marvin; ph: Roger Deakins; ed: Richard Francis-Bruce; music: Thomas Newman; cast: Tim Robbins, Morgan Freeman, Bob Gunton, James Whitmore, et al.

Strange Days (USA, 1995)

dir: Kathryn Bigelow; sc: James Cameron and Jay Cocks; prod: James Cameron; ph: Matthew Leonetti; ed: Howard Smith; music: Randy Gerston; spec. eff: Terry Frazee; sound: Gary Rydstrom; art dir: John Warnke; cast: Ralph Fiennes,

Angela Bassett, Juliette Lewis, Tom Sizemore, Michael Wincott, Glenn Plummer, et al.

Sunless/Sans Soleil (FR, 1982)

dir: Chris Marker; sc: Chris Marker and Adrian Miles; ed: Chris Marker; narration: Alexandra Stewart (English version) and Florence Deleay (French version); music: M. Moussorgski, Sebelius and song by Arielle Dombasle; film extracts: *Carnival in Bissau, Vertigo*

Tank Girl (USA, 1995)

dir: Rachel Talalay; sc: Tedi Safarian, based on the comic strip created by Alan Martin and Jamie Hewlett; prod: Richard Lewis, et al.; ph: Gale Tettersal; ed: James Symons; makeup: Stan Winston; music: Grame Revell; cast: Lori Petty, Ice-T, Naomi Watts, Michael McDowell, et al.

Testament of Dr. Mabuse/Das Testament des Dr. Mabuse (G, 1933)

dir: Fritz Lang; sc: Thea von Harbou and Fritz Lang; ph: Fritz Arno Wagner; music: Hans Erdmann; cast: Rudolf Klein-Rogge, Otto Wernicke, Oscar Beregi, et al.

This Obscure Object of Desire/Cet Obscur Objet du Désir (FR/SP, 1977)

dir: Luis Buñuel; sc: Luis Buñuel and Jean-Claude Carrière, based on the novel *La Femme et la Pantin* by Pierre Louys; ph: Edmond Richard; cast: Fernando Rey, Angela Molina, Carole Bouquet, et al.

Total Recall (USA, 1990)

dir: Paul Verhoeven; sc: Gary Goldman, etc.; ph: Jost Vacano; makeup eff: Rob Bottin; ed: Frank Urioste; music: Jerry Goldsmith; prod: Buzz Feitshans and Ronald Shusett; cast: Arnold Schwarzenegger, Sharon Stone, Michael Ironside, Ronny Cox, et al.

Touch of Evil (USA, 1958)

dir: Orson Welles; sc: Orson Welles, based on the novel *Badge of Evil* by Whit Masterson; ph: Russell Metty; cast: Charlton Heston, Janet Leigh, Orson Welles, Joseph Calleia, Marlene Dietrich, et al.

Twelve Monkeys (USA, 1995)

dir: Terry Gilliam; sc: David and Janet Peoples, inspired by *La Jetée* by Chris Marker; prod: Charles Roven; ph: Roger Pratt; ed: Mick Audsley; music: Paul Buckmaster; cast: Bruce Willis, Madeleine Stowe, Brad Pitt, Christopher Plummer, et al.

Vertigo (USA, 1958)

dir: Alfred Hitchcock; sc: Alec Coppel and Samuel Taylor, based on the novel *D'Entre les Morts* by Pierre Boileau and Thomas Narcejac; prod: Alfred Hitchcock;

ph: Robert Burks; ed: George Tomasini; sound: Sam Comer and Frank McKelvey; music: Bernard Herrmann; titles: Saul Bass; cast: James Stewart, Kim Novak, Barbara Bel Geddes, Tom Helmore

Wild Child, The/L'Enfant Sauvage (FR, 1969)
dir: François Truffaut; sc: François Truffaut and Jean Gruault; ph: Nestor Almendros; music: Vivaldi; cast: Jean-Pierre Cargol, François Truffaut, Françoise Seigner

Wolf (USA, 1994)
dir: Mike Nichols; sc: Jim Harrison, etc.; makeup eff: Rick Balar; prod: Douglas Wick; music: Ennio Morricone; cast: Jack Nicholson, Michelle Pfeiffer, James Spader, Christopher Plummer, et al.

X-Men (USA, 2000)
dir: Bryan Singer and Coney Yuen (action); sc: David Hayter; story: Tom DeSanto and Bryan Singer, based on the Marvel comic strips; ph: Tom Sigel; music: Michael Kamen; cast: Hugh Jackman, Patrick Stewart, Ian McKellen, Famke Jansen, et al.

Notes

Notes to Introduction

1. Gilles Deleuze, *Cinema 1: The Movement-Image*. Trans. Hugh Tomlinson and Barbara Habberjam (London: The Athlone Press, 1986) p. 59.

2. G. Deleuze, "The Brain is the Screen." *The Brain is the Screen: Deleuze and the Philosophy of Cinema*. Trans. Marie Therese Guiris. Ed. Gregory Flaxman (Minneapolis and London: University of Minnesota Press, 2000) p. 367.

3. Bastiaan van Werven, *De herinneringsmachine: Godard, Deleuze, Historie(s)*. MA thesis (Amsterdam: University of Amsterdam, 2000), p. 32. Van Werven here quotes an article by the Dutch journalist Bas van Heijne ("Kijk opnieuw: Bernlef, Couperus en American Beauty over de essentie van het leven" in *NRC-Handelsblad* 11-02-00: p. 29). My translation.

4. G. Deleuze and Félix Guattari, *A Thousand Plateaus: Capitalism and Schizophrenia*. Trans. Brian Massumi (London: The Athlone Press, 1988) p. 261.

5. *Movement-Image*, p. 3.

6. Michael Shapiro, *Cinematic Political Thought: Narrating Race, Nation and Gender* (Edinburgh: Edinburgh University Press, 1999) p. 23.

7. G. Deleuze, "L'Actuel et le Virtuel." *Dialogues* (Paris: Flammarion, edition 1996) pp. 179–80. My translation.

8. G. Deleuze, *Cinema 2: The Time-Image*. Trans. Hugh Tomlinson and Robert Galeta (London: The Athlone Press, 1989) p. 68.

9. *Time-Image*, p. 23.

10. G. Deleuze, *Difference and Repetition*. Trans. Paul Patton (London: The Athlone Press, 1994) p. 138.

11. See first chapter of *A Thousand Plateaus*, pp. 3–25.

12. Dorothea Olkowski, *Gilles Deleuze: The Ruins of Representation* (Berkeley, Los Angeles, and London: University of California Press, 1999) p. 26.

13. G. Deleuze, *Negotiations*. Trans. Martin Joughin (New York: Columbia University Press, 1995) p. 60.

14. David N. Rodowick, *Gilles Deleuze's Time Machine* (Durham: Duke University Press, 1997) p. x.

15. Gregory Flaxman, ed., *The Brain is the Screen: Deleuze and the Philosophy of Cinema*. (Minneapolis and London: University of Minnesota Press, 2000).

16. Robert Stam, *Film Theory: An Introduction* (Malden and Oxford: Blackwell, 2000) p. 262.

17. David Rodowick gives, for instance, an analysis of Ousmane Sembene's film *Borom Sarret* (*Gilles Deleuze's Time-Machine*, pp. 162–69); and in *The Brain is the Screen*, Laura Marks looks at the relevance of Deleuze's use of Peirce with respect to Arabian documentaries (pp. 193–214).

18. *Time-Image*, pp. 215–24.

19. Ian Buchanan, *Deleuzism: A Metacommentary* (Edinburgh: Edinburgh University Press, 2000) p. 8. Buchanan gives an interesting Deleuzian analysis of *Blade Runner* and popular music, to which I briefly return in Chapter 1.

20. Brian Massumi quotes Deleuze's own description of the earliest period of his work: "What got me by during that period was conceiving of the history of philosophy as a kind of ass-fuck, or, what amounts to the same thing, an immaculate conception. I imagined myself approaching an author from behind and giving him a child that would indeed be his but would nonetheless be monstrous." Brian Massumi, "Translator's Foreword" in *A Thousand Plateaus*, p. x.

21. *Thousand Plateaus*, p. xv.

22. *Thousand Plateaus*, pp. 43–44.

23. *Thousand Plateaus*, p. 88.

24. In this book, I refer only in passing to the territorializing and deterritorializing powers of capitalism. This is, however, an important aspect of contemporary media culture. For additional discussions on the role of money, media, and Deleuze and Guattari's schizophrenic strategies, see Patricia Pisters, ed., *Micropolitics of Media Culture: Reading the Rhizomes of Deleuze and Guattari* (Amsterdam: Amsterdam University Press, 2001).

25. Slavoj Žižek, "*The Matrix*, The Two Sides of Perversion," <http://www.britannica.com> 2 Dec 1999, 18 pp.

26. Jean-Louis Baudry, "Ideological Effects of the Basic Cinematographic Apparatus" and "The Apparatus: Metapsychological Approaches to the Impression of Reality in the Cinema." *Narrative, Apparatus, Ideology*. Ed. Philip Rosen (New York: Columbia University Press, 1986) pp. 286–98, 299–318.

27. In "*The Matrix*, The Two Sides of Perversion," Žižek gives a Lacanian moebius strip analysis of the interdependence of the matrix and the Real. The matrix is the "big Other," the virtual symbolic order: "The big Other pulls the strings, the subject does not speak. He 'is spoken' by the symbolic structure" (p. 3). The first perversion of *The Matrix* is therefore the belief that reality is reduced to a virtual domain regulated by arbitrary rules that can be suspended; however, one should avoid thinking that the Lacanian Real is "the true reality" behind the virtual simulation, a mistake we could easily make if the film is taken at face value. The Real is much more implicated in the matrix of the big Other; it is the void that makes

reality incomplete/inconsistent (p. 4). Žižek quotes agent Smith's remark in *The Matrix* that the first matrix was perfect, but no one would accept that program as real because there was no misery, to demonstrate that the matrix itself is the Real that distorts our perception of reality. The imperfection of our world is thus at the same time the sign of its virtuality and the sign of its reality, Žižek argues (p. 12). The unique impact of the film thus resides not so much in its central thesis (what we experience is merely an artificial virtual reality) but in its ultimate perverse fantasy: the image of the millions of human beings lying passively in prenatal fluid, serving as instruments of the Matrix's *jouissance*. The second perversion is thus the twist of the film: what is rendered as the scene of our awakening into our true situation is effectively its exact opposition, the very fundamental fantasy of passivity that sustains our being (p. 15). Thus speaks Žižek in cyberspace.

28. G. Deleuze, "Immanence: A Life." Trans. Nick Millet. *Theory, Culture & Society*, Vol. 14(2). (London: Sage, 1997) pp. 3–7.

29. *Deleuzism*, p. 63. The quote is from Gilles Deleuze and Félix Guattari, *What is Philosophy?* Trans. Graham Burchell and Hugh Tomlinson (London and New York: Verso, 1994) p. 213.

Chapter 1: The Universe as Metacinema

1. Hitchcock, during the shooting of *North by Northwest*, quoted in Donald Spoto, *The Dark Side of the Genius: The Life of Alfred Hitchcock* (New York: Ballantine 1984) p. 440.

2. *Movement-Image*, p. 59.

3. *Time-Image*, p. 23.

4. *Movement-Image*, p. 205.

5. Eric Rohmer and Claude Chabrol, *Hitchcock—The First Forty-Four Films* (New York: Frederick Ungar, 1979).

6. Slavoj Žižek, ed., *Everything You Always Wanted to Know about Lacan . . . but Were Afraid to Ask Hitchcock* (London and New York: Verso, 1992) pp. 212–13.

7. *Movement-Image*, p. 202.

8. *Everything You Always Wanted to Know*, p. 254. The Gaze, in contrast to the eye, is related to this impossible realm of the Real. In "The Ideological Sinthome" in *Looking Awry: An Introduction to Jacques Lacan through Popular Culture* (Cambridge, Mass., and London: MIT, 1991), Žižek explains the difference between the eye and the Gaze. The latter marks "the point in the picture from which the subject viewing is already gazed at. Far from assuring the self-presence of the subject (i.e., the gaze as instrument of mastery and control), the Gaze introduces an irreducible split: I can never see the picture at the point from which it is gazing at me" (p. 125). See also note 11.

9. *Everything You Always Wanted to Know*, p. 241.

10. See Joan Copjec, ed., *Shades of Noir* (New York and London: Verso, 1993;

Supposing the Subject. New York and London, Verso, 1994); Joan Copjec, *Read my Desire: Lacan Against the Historicists* (Cambridge, Mass: MIT, 1994).

11. Žižek refers to Racine's *Phaedre*, who misreads her lover's expression and thus brings about her own downfall. "In his Bold Gaze my Ruin is Writ Large" are Phaedre's words, and these are borrowed by Žižek as the title of his main article in *Everything You Always Wanted to Know*; the title reflects Lacan's idea that the Gaze we encounter is not the Gaze of the other, but the Gaze as we imagine it "in the field of the Other" (p. 258). In other words, our desire is constituted by what we think the other desires: "Desire is the desire of the other," according to Lacan. Žižek calls this form of desire "intersubjective": it is only through the other that we can desire. One could argue that in this conception of desire the O/other is always an object of desire, which makes it rather difficult to speak of intersubjectivity. Of course, this should be seen as an exchange of positions: each subject functions as the other's "object of desire." Žižek himself demonstrates how the status of the "object" has changed (both in Lacan and in Hitchcock): "For Lacan in the 1950s the object is reduced to the role of the 'stake' in the intersubjective game of recognition (to desire an object is a means to desire the desire of the other who claims this object, etc.), whereas for the later Lacan, the object is what the subject is looking for in another subject—what bestows upon the subject his/her dignity" (pp. 223–24). Žižek argues with Lacan that we are all haunted subjects desiring something that is by definition impossible.

12. *Everything You Always Wanted to Know*, p. 236.

13. In his film *That Obscure Object of Desire* (1977), Luis Buñuel presents an image of desire related to an object that can well be analyzed psychoanalytically. Mathieu, the protagonist (the subject) desires Concha, the woman-as-object, played by two very different actresses. One could say they represent the virgin and the whore, or one could say they are interchangeable (Mathieu never sees the difference) because they merely represent the object that must fill the fundamental lack in the subject, from which desire is born. Buñuel also provides highly symbolic images, such as the final image in which a woman in a shop window is sewing a bloody gown (a metaphor for the fetishistic "covering up" of the wound; the shop window refers to the commodity aspect of objects of desire). The notion of subject is thus much related to the notion of object, and desire based on lack never can be fulfilled completely by the object of desire. One might actually wonder, however, whether Buñuel is perhaps joking, giving us these images to bring them to the fulfillment of their cliché aspects. It is all too obvious and thus reaches a different dimension. Therefore, Buñuel, like Hitchcock, also can be read differently. According to Deleuze, Buñuel's choice of two actresses to play one person is more connected to a mental image related to time: "It is as if Buñuel's naturalist cosmology, based on the cycle and succession of cycles, gives way to a plurality of simultaneous worlds; to a simultaneity of presents in different worlds. These are not subjective (imaginary) points of view in one and the same world, but one and

the same event in different objective worlds, all implicated in the same, inexplicable universe" (*Time-Image*, p. 103).

14. According to Spinoza, the role of imagination is to think also of what might be good for others. To be joyful also means wanting joy for others, which can mean very different things than for the self; Spinoza believes every person has a singular essence.

15. Genevieve Lloyd, *Spinoza and the Ethics* (London and New York: Routledge, 1996) pp. 96–97.

16. In his book *Cinematic Political Thought: Narrating Race, Nation and Gender* (Edinburgh: Edinburgh University Press, 1999), Michael Shapiro discusses Kant's concept of the subject: "Kant's solution to the aporias of experience is to make the subject larger than the world" (p. 13). He does this with the aim of moving the subject toward creating a common sense. See also Deleuze, *La Philosophie Critique de Kant* (Paris: PUF, 1963).

17. See, for instance, François Truffaut, *Hitchcock/Truffaut* (New York: Simon and Schuster, 1967) p. 160.

18. *Movement-Image*, pp. 141–96. In Chapter 2, Deleuze's image categories from his cinema books are explored more elaborately.

19. When the third dimension of spatial depth and coherence is abandoned, we open up to other dimensions. In his discussion of the affection-image and Dryer's use of the close-up, Deleuze states: "Flattening the third dimension, he puts two-dimensional space into immediate relation with the affect, with a fourth and fifth dimension: Time and Spirit" (*Movement-Image*, p. 107).

20. *Late Review*, BBC television. The critics were Mark Lawson (presentation), Tom Paulin, Tony Parsons, and Suzanne Moore. The most striking masculine objection to the film was (I quote all three critics addressing their female colleague): "If this film had been made by a man, for instance, Brian de Palma, you would have been disgusted" (it sounded almost as though they were jealous). In a similar way at the conference Tender Bodies, Twisted Minds (University of Amsterdam, Department of Film and Television Studies), where this film was discussed, whenever anything positive was said about the film, it was no longer a Katherine Bigelow film but a James Cameron script. In any case, one could say that, in its initial reception, *Strange Days* shared a fate similar to that of *Peeping Tom* and *Vertigo*.

21. SQUIDS (superconducting quantum interference devices), although not as sophisticated as presented in Bigelow's film, are actually used in neurologic research. See, for instance, Louis Bec, "Squids, Elements of Technozoosemiotics—A Lesson in Fabulatory Epistemology of the Scientific Institute for Paranatural Research," Joke Brouwer and Carla Hoekendijk, eds. *Technomorphica* (Amsterdam: De Balie and Idea Books, 1997) pp. 279–314. In the television documentary on *Strange Days* (VPRO-laat, October 1995), neuroscientist Michael Persinger talks about the scientific research on direct brain stimulation.

22. See Jean-Louis Baudry, "Ideological Effects of the Basic Cinematographic Apparatus" (first published 1970) and "The Apparatus: Metapsychological Approaches to the Impression of Reality in Cinema" (first published 1975). Both articles are reprinted in Philip Rosen, ed., *Narrative, Apparatus, Ideology* (New York: Columbia University Press, 1986; references hereafter are to this edition) pp. 286–318; Jean-Louis Commoli, "Machines of the Visible," Teresa de Lauretis and Stephen Heath, eds., *The Cinematic Apparatus* (Houndmills, Basingstoke, and London: Columbia University Press, 1986) pp. 121–42; Christian Metz, "The Imaginary Signifier," *Screen*, vol. 16, no. 2, 1975: 14–76. See also Robert Stam, et al., *New Vocabularies of Film Semiotics: Structuralism, Post-Structuralism and Beyond* (London and New York: Routledge, 1992).

23. "The Apparatus," p. 315.

24. "Ideological Effects," p. 292.

25. "Ideological Effects," p. 292.

26. *Movement-Image*, pp. 58–61.

27. Laura Mulvey, "Visual Pleasure and Narrative Cinema." First published in 1975, reprinted in *Narrative, Apparatus, Ideology*, pp. 198–209.

28. Laura Rascaroli, "Strange Visions: Kathryn Bigelow's MetaFiction" *Enculturation* 2(1), Fall 1998.

29. Joan Smith, "Speaking Up For Corpses," Karl French, ed., *Screen Violence* (London: Bloomsbury Publishing 1996) p. 198. Smith quotes here from James Cameron's screenplay.

30. "Speaking Up For Corpses," p. 204.

31. For a media evaluation of the Rodney King beating, see John Caldwell, *Televisuality: Style, Crisis and Authority in American Television* (New Brunswick, NJ: Rutgers University Press, 1995) pp. 302–35. For a deeper analysis of the King beating and *Strange Days*, see Patricia Pisters, "The War of Images: Appropriation and Fabulation of Missing People," *ASCA Yearbook* (Amsterdam: ASCA Press, 2000) pp. 69–81.

32. *Movement-Image*, p. 74.

33. *Movement-Image*, p. 3.

34. Tania Modleski, "Femininity by Design," *The Woman who Knew Too Much: Hitchcock and Feminist Theory* (New York and London: Methuen 1988) pp. 87–100.

35. Hitchcock quoted in *The Woman who Knew Too Much*, p. 100.

36. *Time-Image*, p. 82.

37. Jean-Pierre Esquenazi, *Image-mouvement et image-temps: une idée du cinéma*. (Paris: Ph.D. diss.) pp. 134–72. See also his book *Film, perception et mémoire* (Paris: L'Harmattan, 1994) pp. 196–201.

38. In his book on Bergson, Deleuze explains that, according to Bergson, we do not go back from the present to the past but rather move from the past to the present, selecting the images from the past that are necessary for the present: "Integral memory responds to the call of the present by two simultaneous movements: one is

a movement of *translation*, by which memory places itself in front of the experience and contracts more or less in respect of the action of the present; the other movement is a rotation of memory around itself, by which it orients itself toward the situation of the moment to present its most useful side. Deleuze, *Le bergsonisme* (Paris: PUF, 1966) p. 60. (My translation from the French.) The rotating movement of Madeleine's profile in close-up could be seen as such a movement from the virtual toward the actual.

39. *Time-Image*, p. 23.

40. The Australian techno-performance artist Stellarc has demonstrated in several performances (e.g., *Stimbod*; *Ping Body*) that not only the brain but also the body can be extended beyond the self-same. For instance, through touch-screen muscle stimulation, a program that enables touching of the muscle sites on a computer model, he has made his body "a host" so that other people (at remote places) can make it move and act. Touch-screen muscle stimulation also makes it possible for two people to touch each other at a distance: "Given tactile and force-feedback, I would feel my touch via another person from another place as a secondary and additional sensation. Or, by feeling my chest I can also feel her breast. An intimacy through interface, an intimacy without proximity" (Stellarc in "Parasite Visions—Alternate, Intimate and Involuntary Experiences," *Technomorphica*, p. 23). See also his website: <http://www.merlin.com.au/stellarc>.

41. Many consider one of the first films to play with the idea of brain stimulation, Douglas Trumbull's *Brainstorm* (1987), to be more successful in showing the possible consequences of such experiments. I disagree. The film does indeed demonstrate the dangers of overdose, but so does *Strange Days*. The difference lies in the context. In *Brainstorm*, the experiments take place in a laboratory, in a scientific context, whereas in *Strange Days* SQUIDS have become a more common (though illegal) use.

42. See also Anke Burger, "Strange Memories—Kathryn Bigelow's Strange Days und 'Erinnerung' in Science-Fiction-Film." *Blimp—Film Magazine* 34, summer 1996.

43. In his book *Terminal Identity: The Virtual Subject in Postmodern Science Fiction* (Durham and London: Duke University Press, 1993), Scott Bukatman emphasizes the spatial dimensions of the cinematic dimension of *Blade Runner*: "The specificity of cinema lies, not in the emphatic dramaturgy of narrative temporality, but rather in a spatial exploration that complexly binds multiple perspectives and scalar shifts" (p. 137). Bukatman adds that the effectiveness of *Blade Runner* lies in the fact that this space finally becomes terminal. See also his monograph on *Blade Runner* in the BFI series Modern Classics (London: BFI, 1997). In this essay, he briefly refers to time as constructed memory (p. 80), which could be seen as an immanent way of constructing subjectivity. In *Screening Space: The American Science Fiction Film* (New Brunswick, NJ, and London: Rutgers University Press, 1987), Vivian Sobchack discusses the problem of time in *Blade Runner* more elaborately.

According to Sobchack, the temporal gets lost in the spatiality of the film, at least the kind of classical chronological kind of temporality: "The New SF tends to conflate past, present, and future—in décor constructed as temporal pastiche and/or in narratives that either temporally turn back on themselves to conflate past, present, and future, or are schizophrenically constituted as a 'series of pure and unrelated presents in time'" (pp. 273–74; Sobchack quotes here from Jameson's "Postmodernism, or The Cultural Logic of Late Capitalism"). With this observation, she describes a Bergsonian conception of time that has entered American science fiction cinema. For an elaborated applied Deleuzian analysis of *Blade Runner*, see Ian Buchanan. *Deleuzism: A Metacommentary* (Edinburgh: Edinburgh University Press, 2000) pp. 127–40. Buchanan is not satisfied with the many psychoanalytic interpretations of *Blade Runner* (such as those from Slavoj Žižek and Kaja Silverman) and argues for an analysis of assemblages, abstract-machines, and "schizzes" or breakflows, intertextuality and finally the plane of composition of the film, where he uses specific concepts from Deleuze's film books.

44. *Twelve Monkeys* is based on Chris Marker's film *La Jetée*; however, the scriptwriters of the film, David and Janet Peoples, must have been influenced by Marker's other film about time and loss of identity, *Sunless*. In this film, Marker also "follows" Scottie and Madeleine, wondering about their relation to time.

45. For a narrative analysis of the "out of jointness" of time in contemporary Hollywood, see Sasha Vojkovic, *Subjectivity in New Hollywood Cinema: Fathers, Sons and Other Ghosts* (Amsterdam: Ph.D. diss. University of Amsterdam, 2001).

46. *Matière et Mémoire*, p. 170.

47. Jorge Louis Borges's short essay "Borges and I" comes to mind here. Borges describes how he conceives of himself as two people: "Years ago I tried to free myself from him and went from the mythologies of the suburbs to the games with time and infinity, but those games belong to Borges now and I shall have to imagine other things. Thus my life is a flight and I lose everything and everything belongs to oblivion, or to him. I don't know which of us has written this page." In *The Mind's I: Fantasies and Reflections on Self and Soul*, composed and arranged by Douglas R. Hofstadter and Daniel C. Dennett (London, New York, etc.: Penguin 1981) p. 20.

48. In "The Cinema as Experience—Kathryn Bigelow and the Cinema of Spectacle," Yvonne Tasker emphasizes the physical and spectacular dimensions of Bigelow's films *Near Dark*, *Blue Steel*, and *Point Break* in her book *Spectacular Bodies—Gender, Genre and the Action Cinema* (London and New York: Routledge, 1993). Steven Shaviro refers to the embodied visual fascination that the images of *Blue Steel* provoke ("Film Theory and Visual Fascination" in *The Cinematic Body* [Minneapolis and London: University of Minnesota Press, 1993]). Although the appeal of the visual spectacle and action in *Strange Days* is undeniable, I have tried to demonstrate that the challenges to the mind are just as important in Bigelow's work.

49. Deleuze says, "The organization of space here loses its privileged directions . . . , in favour of an omni-directional space which constantly varies its angles and co-ordinates" (*The Time-Image*, p. 265).

50. Maybe this is because each person conceives itself in the brain as several other persons as well, as became clear in Borges's story "Borges and I."

51. Peter Canning, "The Imagination of Immanence: An Ethics of Cinema." Gregory Flaxman, ed. *The Brain is the Screen*, pp. 351 and 357.

52. "The Imagination of Immanence," p. 346.

Chapter 2: The Universe as Metacinema

1. *Movement-Image*, p. 61.

2. *Gilles Deleuze's Time Machine*, p. 28.

3. *Gilles Deleuze's Time Machine*, p. 29.

4. Julia Kristeva, *Pouvoirs de l'horreur—essai sur l'abjection* (Paris: Editions du Seuil, 1980).

5. Slavoj Žižek, *The Metastases of Enjoyment: Six Essays on Women and Causality* (London and New York: Verso, 1994) p. 116. As shown in the previous chapter, in other instances, Žižek relates the Real to the Impossible Gaze of God.

6. Barbara Creed, *The Monstrous Feminine—Film, Feminism, Psychoanalysis* (London and New York: Routledge, 1993) p. 9.

7. Until the early 1970s, rape was only a side theme in horror cinema, never explicit. Or, if it was central, the point of view was always from the perspective of the aggressor and women were, as in the classic horror film, victims without any possibility for revenge, as in Hitchcock's *Frenzy*. It was Wes Craven's film *Last House on the Left* (1972) that first aligned rape with female revenge (revenge in itself is of course already an old filmic theme). Influenced by the women's movement, the revenge aspect was joined to the rape theme. Many low-budget cult films have been made in this genre, of which the most stunning and controversial (and really difficult to watch) is *I Spit on Your Grave/Day of the Woman* by Meir Zarchi (1977). One of the main contributions of feminism to the horror genre seems to be the image of an angry woman. As Carol Clover argues, it is very interesting to see that a lot of "exploitation" themes reappear later in a polished version within mainstream cinema: *The Accused* (Jonathan Kaplan, 1988) is in fact basically the same story as *I Spit on Your Grave*: the story of a gang-raped woman hell-bent on revenge (also films like *Extremities* and *Thelma and Louise* are comparable to their low-budget sisters). The difference between *The Accused* and *I Spit on Your Grave* is that the latter shows a perverse simplicity: the woman knows she has been raped and therefore she takes revenge. There is no deep psychology, no law interferes, no difference is made between the men, and it is pure rage. As Clover demonstrates, the cheap horror movie in general is the repressed of American mainstream cinema. In *The Accused* the men are brought to court, and the affair will be settled legally.

8. *Monstrous Feminine*, p. 138.

9. *Metastases of Enjoyment*, p. 122.

10. Catherine Breillat's film *Romance* (1999) presents a psychoanalytic universe from a female point of view, combining elements from Creed's interpretation of Freud and Žižek's reading of Lacan. In the film, the female character loves a man who is actually disgusted by her femininity. She looks for sexual pleasures with other men, but when she finally becomes pregnant by the man she loves, she kills him. Although not a rape–revenge film, it is a "bad treatment"–revenge film.

11. I am here not referring to the very detailed and interesting reworkings of Lacan by, for instance, Kaja Silverman. See her books *The Threshold of the Visible World* (London and New York: Routledge, 1996); and *World Spectators* (Stanford: Stanford University Press, 2000).

12. *Thousand Plateaus*, p. 14.

13. *Thousand Plateaus*, p. 257.

14. Carol Clover, *Men, Women and Chainsaws: Gender in the Modern Horror Film* (Princeton, New Jersey: Princeton University Press, 1992) p. 4.

15. See, for instance, Kaja Silverman, *Male Subjectivity at the Margins* (London and New York: Routledge, 1992).

16. The horror possession plot has even entered the world of soap opera. In *Days of our Lives*, the otherwise nice and good character Marlena is possessed by the devil while her ex-husband (and now priest!) is in crisis.

17. *Men, Women and Chainsaws*, p. 105.

18. *Men, Women and Chainsaws*, pp. 154 and 157. See also Peter Lehman's article "Don't Blame this on the Girl—Female Rape-Revenge Films" in Steven Cohan and Ina Rae Hark, eds., *Screening the Male: Exploring Masculinities in Hollywood Cinema* (London and New York: Routledge, 1993). Concentrating on male identification strategies, Lehman argues that men are not at all invited to identify with the rapists (the scenes are not erotic and are hard to watch). The audience is made to feel disgusted by the rape in order to feel that what follows is justified. Lehman inquires into the nature of those pleasures which are complex, multiple, and fluid in their address of male subjectivity, which is both (heterosexually) masochistic and (homosexually) sadistic.

19. Rosi Braidotti, "Teratologies," *Deleuze and Feminist Theory*. Ed. Ian Buchanan and Claire Colebrook (Edinburgh: Edinburgh University Press, 2000) p. 172.

20. In "The Bodily Ego," Kaja Silverman rereads Freud and Lacan through Paul Schilder and Henri Wallon to restore the body in psychoanalysis (*The Threshold of the Visible World*, pp. 9–37).

21. Spinoza, quoted by Genevieve Lloyd, *Spinoza and the Ethics* (London and New York: Routledge, 1996) p. 79.

22. Edwin Curley, ed., trans., *A Spinoza Reader—The Ethics and Other Works*

(Princeton: Princeton University Press, 1994) xxviii, xix (Curley here quotes Lodewijk Meyer's commentary on Spinoza).

23. In her article "Through a Spinozist Lens: Ethology, Difference, Power" (in Paul Patton, ed., *Deleuze: A Critical Reader* [Oxford and Cambridge, Mass.: Blackwell, 1996]), Moira Gatens discusses Deleuze's Spinozistic reading of Michel Tournier's *Friday*: "There is no form, substance, essence or subject 'underlying' Robinson which 'causes' his humanity. Rather a specific *human* body persists only whilst it exists in extensive and intensive interrelations with those bodies which together constitute a human society" (p. 172).

24. Moira Gatens uses Sharon Marcus's term rape script ("a framework, a grid of comprehensibility which we may feel impelled to use as a way of organizing and interpreting events and actions") to indicate that rape is not an essential feature of male–female (active–passive) relations. In a Spinozist/Deleuzian way, she defines it rather as a "'specific technique' through which sexual difference is created and maintained." Women could try to "rewrite" the script, "perhaps by resisting the physical passivity which it directs us to adopt" ("Through a Spinozist Lens," pp. 180–81). Even though Carol Clover does not speak about possibilities of resisting, her antiessential "sexes that seem up for grabs" is close to a Spinozian reading of the body as well.

25. *Spinoza and the Ethics*, p. 78.

26. See *Spinoza and the Ethics*, especially pp. 83–96, which serve as the basis for my reflections in this section.

27. *Spinoza and the Ethics*, p. 90.

28. *Spinoza and the Ethics*, p. 91.

29. *Thousand Plateaus*, pp. 505–506.

30. *Movement-Image*, pp. 64–65. Deleuze here quotes Bergson. As Deleuze explains, on the plane of immanence, there is a double reference system of images: "The thing and the perception of the thing are one and the same thing, but related to one or other of two systems of reference. The thing is the image as it is in itself, as it is related to all other images to whose action it completely submits and on which it reacts immediately. But the perception of the thing is the same image related to another special image which frames it, and which only retains a partial action from it, and only reacts to it mediately. In perception thus defined, there is never anything else or anything more than there is in the thing: on the contrary, there is 'less.' We perceive the thing, minus that which does not interest us as a function of our needs" (p. 63).

31. Buchanan also proposes a four-step analysis (more or less similar but in a different order to the assemblages I propose), but he concentrates on the whole film, not in the first instance on particular scenes. First, he establishes the limits of the film as an open totality; second, he looks at the schizzes or breakflows; third, this aspect involves the intertextual codes and generic discontinuities; fourth, this

step is a close reading of the plane of composition of the film (*Deleuzism: A Meta-commentary*, pp. 129–30).

32. Elisabeth Cowie, "The Popular Film as a Progressive Text: A Discussion of *Coma*," in Constance Penley, ed., *Feminism and Film Theory* (London: BFI and Routledge 1988).

33. *The Movement-Image*, p. 142. SAS (Situation–Action–New Situation) is the code Deleuze uses for what he calls the large form of the action-image. Deleuze also distinguishes the small form of the action image (ASA, or Action–Situation–New Action) where "a very slight difference in the action, or between two actions, leads to a very great distance between two situations" (p. 162). For instance, when an innocent person is assumed guilty because he is found near a corpse.

34. Elisabeth Cowie demonstrates that Susan Wheeler is not a classic detective who knows from the beginning that a crime has been committed and starts to investigate with this knowledge. On the contrary, she has nothing but an intuitive feeling (traditionally labeled as feminine) that something is wrong.

35. *The Movement-Image*, p. 218. Deleuze explains further: "Everything here is two by itself. Already, in the milieu, we distinguish the power-qualities and the state of things that actualizes them. The situation, and the character or the action, are like two terms which are simultaneously correlative and antagonistic. The action in itself is a duel of forces, a series of duels: duel with the milieu, with the others, with itself. Finally, the new situation which emerges from the action forms a couple with the initial situation" (p. 142).

36. *Movement-Image*, p. 65.

37. *Movement-Image*, pp. 197–205.

38. For a historical and critical analysis of Fassbinder's work, see Thomas Elsaesser, *New German Cinema—A History* (London: BFI, 1989) and *Fassbinder's Germany: History, Identity, Subject* (Amsterdam: Amsterdam University Press, 1995).

39. *Thousand Plateaus*, p. 165.

40. *Thousand Plateaus*, p. 152.

41. Joseph Vogl, "Schöne Gelbe Farbe—Godard mit Deleuze," in Friedrich Balke and Joseph Vogl (eds.), *Gilles Deleuze—Fluchtlinien der Philosophie*. Ed. Friedrich Balke and Joseph Vogl (München: Wilhelm Fink Verlag, 1996).

42. *Movement-Image*, p. 31.

43. See, for instance, *The Movement-Image*, p. 206.

44. See *Le bergsonisme*, pp. 65–66.

45. *Time-Image*, p. 47.

46. For more information, see the Special Issue on Mambety of *African Screen/Ecrans Afrique* 7(24), 1998. For a different Deleuzian take on African cinema, see Dudley Andrew, "The Roots of the Nomadic: Gilles Deleuze and the Cinema of West Africa," in Gregory Flaxman (ed.), *The Brain is the Screen*, pp. 215–49. In

Gilles Deleuze's Time-Machine, David Rodowick discusses the work of another important Senegalese filmmaker, Sembene Ousmane (pp. 162–69).

47. *Time-Image*, p. 256.

48. Deleuze gives the example of Jeff in *Rear Window*, who is paralyzed and therefore opened up to the mental-image and time-image, reduced as it were to a purely optical situation. See *The Movement-Image*, p. 205.

49. *Time-Image*, p. 83.

50. *Time-Image*, pp. 68–97 and 98–125.

51. As horror filmmaker Wes Craven said in a television interview, some of the success of these kinds of images also has to do with a "persistence of being." In many horror films, it is the survival of the main character that fascinates (how to survive in the most horrible of worlds, where—mental—life depends on the extreme fragility of the body?). In *Men, Women and Chainsaws*, Carol Clover called this (transgendered) surviving character in slasher films the "final girl" (cf. Jamie Lee Curtis in *Halloween*). Wes Craven was talking about his latest films *Scream* and *Scream II*, which in their deconstruction of the genre could be considered as *Men, Women and Chainsaws* on celluloid. Although *Scream* explains the rules and mechanisms of the genre, it is still an incredibly scary and exciting movie. (The interview with Craven was broadcast on VPRO television, *Stardust* [film magazine], December 1997.)

52. *Time-Image*, p. 201.

Chapter 3: Cinema's Politics of Violence

1. *Gilles Deleuze's Time-Machine*, p. 139.

2. *Time-Image*, p. 170.

3. I will use the term *political* again in this chapter in a rhizomatic way (the three intersecting political lines discussed in the previous chapter) and not as strictly and only related to ideology, government, and policy plans. For more discussions on politics, philosophy, and cinema, see *Micropolitics of Media Culture*.

4. *Time-Image*, pp. 189–224.

5. *Time-Image*, p. 205.

6. To mention but a few recently published books on the question of violence: Karl French, ed., *Screen Violence* (London: Bloomsbury Publishing, 1996); Stephen Hunter, *Violent Screen* (New York: Dell Publishing, 1995); John Archer, ed., *Male Violence* (London and New York: Routledge, 1994); René Boomkens, *De angstmachine: over geweld in films, literatuur en popmuziek* ("The Fear Machine: On Violence in Films, Literature and Pop Music") (Amsterdam: De Balie, 1996).

7. *Screen Violence*, p. 239. All three of these articles can be found in this book.

8. Deleuze can be seen as a "spider philosopher" who makes webs of connecting lines around a concept. See Jean-Louis Leutrat, "L'Araignée," *Kaleidoscope: Analyses de Films* (Lyon: Presses Universitaires de Lyon, 1988). Leutrat calls

Deleuze "the example of the spider–philosopher." In this respect, Deleuze is again close to Spinoza, who was also such a philosopher; Nietzsche played with the phonetic resemblance between "Spinne" and "Spinoza," remarks Leutrat. Both Nietzsche and Spinoza will be important in this particular web of violence.

9. Apart from these directors, Deleuze also mentions a few others who have made some naturalist impulse-images (although not as consistently or success-fully). For instance, King Vidor's *Duel in the Sun* is a naturalist western, with Jen-nifer Jones as a naturalist woman. Sam Fuller is a director who is obsessed with naturalist violent impulses, but he is too much caught up in the realism of the ac-tion-image to present impulse-images. See *The Movement-Image*, pp. 123–40.

10. *Movement-Image*, p. 133.

11. *Thousand Plateaus*, p. 13.

12. *Time-Image*, p. 7. Deleuze takes neo-realist description in the *nouveau ro-man* as his example: "Since it replaces its own object, on the one hand it erases or destroys its reality which passes into the imaginary, but on the other hand it pow-erfully brings out all the reality which the imaginary or the mental create through speech and vision. The imaginary and the real become indiscernible" (p. 7).

13. *Time-Image*, pp. 126–55.

14. *Time-Image*, p. 133.

15. *Time-Image*, p. 139.

16. *Time-Image*, p. 189. Deleuze discusses, for example, the tiredness of Anto-nioni's everyday bodies and Warhol's six-and-a-half-hour sleeping body. At the op-posite pole, he distinguishes the ceremonial bodies. John Cassavetes, Jean-Luc Go-dard, Chantal Akerman, and Phillipe Garrel are filmmakers of the body *par excellence*, Deleuze argues. In various ways, they show how change takes place and thought can be raised through bodily postures and gestures.

17. As an example of a cinema of the brain, Deleuze mentions the work of Stanley Kubrick, whose work constantly renews the theme of "the initiatory jour-ney because every journey in the world is an exploration of the brain. . . . The identity of world and brain, the automaton, does not form a whole, but rather a limit, a membrane which puts an outside and an inside in contact, makes them present to each other, confronts them or makes them clash" (*Time-Image*, p. 206). In this respect Kubrick's last film, *Eyes Wide Shut*, fits perfectly in Kubrick's brain cinema. The shock in Dr. William Harford's brain when his wife tells him about a sexual fantasy with another man leads to a confrontation between the inside (his wife's fantasy, the doctor's phantasm about this fantasy) and the outside (the ad-ventures he throws himself into after that shock). At the end of the film, Harford and his wife conclude that "reality is not all real" and "a dream is never just a dream." The actual and the virtual have met in a cinema of the brain.

18. For a more detailed analysis of the relationship between Spinoza and Nietz-sche (according to Deleuze), see the article by Pierre Zaoui "La grande identité:

Nietzsche et Spinoza—quelle identité?" *Philosophie* 47 (Paris: Editions de Minuit, 1995).

19. It is useful to recall here that a body, according to Spinoza, has a longitudinal (north–south) kinetic axis, which consists of movement and rest and which functions through extension, and a latitudinal (east–west) dynamic axis, which contains the intensities of affects and power. The two axes are parallel to each other (although not in a causal relation).

20. Constantin Boundas, ed., "Ethics Without Morality," *The Deleuze Reader* (New York: Columbia University Press, 1993) pp. 69–77. This text is translated from Deleuze's *Spinoza: philosophie pratique* (Paris: Editions de Minuit, 1981).

21. Deleuze, *Expressionism in Philosophy: Spinoza*. Trans. Martin Joughin (New York: Zone Books, 1992) p. 247.

22. *Time-Image*, p. 141.

23. Deleuze explains in *Nietzsche and Philosophy*, trans. Hugh Tomlinson (London: Athlone and New York: Columbia University Press, 1983) that the will to power does not mean the desire for power (over others) but the will to do everything to the "*nth* power," as intensively as possible. "The will to power is essentially creative and giving: it does not aspire, it does not seek, it does not desire, above all it does not desire power. It gives" (p. 85). See also Ronald Bogue, *Deleuze and Guattari* (London and New York: Routledge, 1993).

24. *Expressionism in Philosophy*, p. 243.

25. *Expressionism in Philosophy*, p. 244.

26. In "7000 B.C.: Apparatus of Capture" (*A Thousand Plateaus*, pp. 447 ff). See also in the same book, chapter 12 "1227: Treatise on Nomadology: The War Machine" pp. 351–423.

27. Paul Patton, *Deleuze and the Political* (London and New York: Routledge, 2000) pp. 109–15.

28. In 1983, this film was distributed on video together with *La classe de la violence*, an interview with Dominique Nogez (Ministère des relations extérieures).

29. *Time-Image*, p. 215.

30. *Thousand Plateaus*, p. 469.

31. After the terrorist attacks on the World Trade Center and the Pentagon on September 11, 2001, the world seems again to be divided in two camps ("You are either with us or with them"), which would bring back the idea of the classic political film. At the same time, however, it is evident that such an easy division into good and bad is not possible. There are many differences within each minority that are not recognized in simply opposing "the West" against "terrorism." On the other hand, fundamentalism (and terrorism) could be seen as an "invention of a people" that is a reaction to the structure of binary oppositions. These aspects of recent political developments, however, are beyond the scope of this book.

32. The series was called *Tous les garçons et les filles de leur age* ("All the Boys and

Girls of Their Age"), completed in 1994. Some of the other directors in the series were Olivier Assayas, Patricia Deleuze, and André Téchiné.

33. Deleuze, "L'Epuisé," *Samuel Beckett. Quad et autres pièces pour la télévision* (Paris: Editions de Minuit, 1992) p. 57. My translation from the French.

34. *Time-Image*, p. 222.

35. *Gilles Deleuze's Time Machine*, pp. 159–60. Rodowick explains that Deleuze uses the term *légender*, which means "to make up stories, mythmaking, but also to comment on or caption an image" (p. 149). In this sense, the term refers both to the storytelling potential of the modern political film and to the way the image is infused with another dimension by the soundtrack, producing "ambiguous land-scapes" where "there is produced a whole 'coalescence' of the perceived with the remembered, the imagined, the known. . . . [A] perception which does not grasp perception without also grasping its reverse, imagination, memory, or knowledge" (Rodowick quoting Deleuze from *The Time-Image*, pp. 245, 319). In this way, fab-ulation is one of the terms of a "new analytic of the image."

36. *Gilles Deleuze's Time Machine*, p. 151.

37. *Gilles Deleuze's Time Machine*, p. 151.

38. *Gilles Deleuze's Time-Machine*, p. 165.

39. At the screening of the film during the Rotterdam Film Festival, the direc-tor was asked if he had written the monologues for the interviewed boys, which was not the case; but it shows clearly the double fabulatic movement between the director and the people as well as the fading away of the border between reality and fiction.

40. For an elaboration on the fabulating effect of *Strange Days* and its free in-direct relation to the Rodney King beating, see Patricia Pisters, "The War of Im-ages: Appropriation and Fabulation of Missing People," *ASCA Brief Privacies*. Ed. Beate Roessler (Amsterdam: ASCA Press, 2000) pp. 69–81.

41. bell hooks, for instance, called *Pulp Fiction* a cynical and fascist film. See bell hooks, "Cool Cynicism—Pulp Fiction," *Reel to Real: Race, Sex and Class at the Movies* (London and New York: Routledge, 1996). Susan Granger describes *Fight Club* as "socially irresponsible and repellent in its graphic depictions of extreme vi-olence and brutality" <http://www.all-reviews.com/videos/fight-club.htm>.

42. For an elaborated analysis of the differences between Marx and Deleuze and Guattari, see Malene Busk, "Micropolitics: A Political Philosophy from Marx and Beyond," *Micropolitics of Media Culture*, pp. 105–25.

43. *Anti-Oedipus*, p. 227.

44. Jonathan Beller, "Capital/Cinema," in Eleanor Kaufman and Kevin Jon Heller (eds.), *Deleuze and Guattari: New Mappings in Politics, Philosophy, and Cul-ture*. Ed. Eleanor Kaufman and Kevin Jon Heller (Minneapolis and London: Uni-versity of Minnesota Press, 1988) pp. 82–83.

45. See also Eugene Holland, *Deleuze and Guattari's Anti-Oedipus: Introduc-tions to Schizoanalysis* (London and New York: Routledge, 1999).

46. For a more elaborate analysis of *Fight Club*'s schizophrenia in relation to the paranoia ("the opposite pole of capitalism") of Bret Easton Ellis's novel *Glamorama*, see Patricia Pisters, "Glamour and Glycerin: Surplus and Residual of the Network Society from *Glamorama* to *Fight Club*," *Micropolitics of Media Culture*, pp. 127–43.

47. *Anti-Oedipus*, p. xvi.

48. For more on the problem of freedom and unfreedom, see Aden Evens, et al., "Another Always Thinks in Me," *New Mappings in Politics, Philosophy, and Culture*, pp. 270–80.

49. See, for instance, David Putman's review: "The twist is admittedly surprising, but also preposterous and a frustrating gimmick" <http://www.all-reviews.com/videos/fight-club,htm>.

50. Jennifer Heusen, "The Duration of Oblivion: Deleuze and Forgetting in *Fight Club* and *Lost Highway*." MA thesis, Dept. of Film and Television Studies, Amsterdam University, 2000: p. 8. *Lost Highway* is not a movement-image of thought but a time-image of thought where the characters Pete/Fred never find themselves in the same spatial-temporal layer. In this film, it is impossible to distinguish the actual from the virtual. Pete/Fred is a crystal image.

51. Perhaps this creation of their own counterimage has to do with the absence of father figures in *Fight Club*. At one point in the film, Tyler and Jack discuss the fact that they have never known their fathers and were raised only by women, but I have not elaborated this thought here.

52. A good example of these two positions can be read in film magazine *Skrien* 199 (Dec. 1994/Jan. 1995) and 201 (April/May 1995). The three formalistic pieces of the editors met with violent moral critiques, which were debated in a round-table discussion with filmmakers, writers, critics, and philosophers.

53. Dana Polan, *Pulp Fiction* (London: British Film Insitute, 2000) p. 7.

54. The BBC's cult program *Mondo Rosso* brought on a "Tarantino gimp" (accompanied by the music from the film) in each episode as a sort of assistant to the presenter Jonathan Ross.

55. In her interesting article "The Fathers Watch the Boys' Room" (in *Camera Obscura* 32, May 1995:41–73), Sharon Willis takes the fact that Tarantino's characters are so often (literally) caught with their pants down as a central metaphor for the reading of the film: the spectators are also "caught with their pants down." This shameful feeling does indeed translate the ambiguous reactions people often have toward Tarantino's films.

56. See, for instance, Stan Lapinski's article "Een Hecht Doortimmerde Structuur," *Skrien* 199 (1994) for a formal analysis of the narrative structure.

57. *Time-Image*, p. 266.

58. See also Dana Polan, *Pulp Fiction*, pp. 58–63.

59. Sharon Willis remarks in "The Fathers Watch the Boys' Room" that the strongest character is actually the black wife of Jim (Tarantino) in "The Bonnie

Situation": in all her absence she has even more power than the boss Marsellus when everything is done to prevent her coming home and finding blood-smeared gangsters in her house and a car with a body minus head in the garage. Willis sees this as a compensation for misusing all kinds of racist remarks (cf. "Did you see a sign 'dead nigger storage' outside?"). Probably that is true, just as much as it is true that Tarantino appropriates all the "cool" aspects of black men and their (film) history (cf. "blaxploitation" in *Jackie Brown*); but he does it in a self-aware, affirmative way.

60. "Cool Cynicism," p. 48.

61. In *Dialogues*, Deleuze talks about (English, Jewish, Stoic, Zen) humor as "the art of the surfaces" and "the art of consequences and effects" ("On the Superiority of English-American literature"). In *Difference and Repetition*, he states in relation to Nietzsche's ideas on theater that humor as an indispensable operation is needed.

62. Zarathustra expresses Nietzsche's ideas on the superman (übermensch). In *The Time-Image*, Deleuze talks about the Nietzschean concepts of the veracious (righteous) man, the superior man, and the superman in relation to the films of Orson Welles, Vargas, Quinlan, and Falstaff (see also Chapter 3).

63. John Lippitt, "Nietzsche, Zarathustra and the status of Laughter," *British Journal of Aesthetics* 32(1), 1992. Lippitt quotes Thomas Nagel to explain the absurd: "What makes everyone's life absurd is the collision between the seriousness with which we take our lives and the perpetual possibility of regarding everything about which we are serious as arbitrary, or open to doubt. We cannot live human lives without energy and attention, nor without making choices, which show that we take some things more seriously than others. Yet we have always available a point of view outside the particular forms of our lives, from which the seriousness appears gratuitous. These two inescapable viewpoints collide in us, and that is what makes life absurd. It is absurd because we ignore the doubts that we know cannot be settled, continuing to live with nearly undiminished seriousness in spite of them" (p. 46).

64. Marguerite Duras expressed this idea, for instance, in an interview with Michelle Porte, published together with *Le Camion* (Editions de Minuit 1977:107).

65. It should be noted that the eternal recurrence of Nietzsche goes beyond the cyclic eternal recurrence of the impulse-image, as Deleuze has shown in respect of Buñuel.

66. Dana Polan, *Pulp Fiction*, p. 47.

67. "Nietzsche, Zarathustra, . . . ", p. 44. According to Bergson, we laugh about things that are "something mechanical encrusted on the living." See Bergson, *Le rire: essai sur la signification du comique* (Paris: Quadrige/Presses Universitaires de France, 1990, orig. publ. 1899). Bergson considered laughing as a social correction of automatic behavior. Bergson gives a beautiful analysis of the mechanisms of the comical, but in his conclusion he states that there is something bitter about the foamy liveliness of the comic. Actually, laughing, according to Bergson,

is what Nietzsche calls "the laughing of the herd," a laughing of the group (often at the expense of others) as opposed to a "laughing of the height" of the superman.

68. "Nietzsche, Zarathustra, . . . ", p. 48.

69. *Reservoir Dogs* did not provoke so many confused reactions because the film was more unambiguously unrealistic, full of symbolic "white boys fucking each other over" (to use bell hook's phrase). People either love or hate it.

Chapter 4: Conceptual Personae and Aesthetic Figures of Becoming-Woman

1. *Thousand Plateaus*, p. 291.

2. *Thousand Plateaus*, pp. 232–309.

3. For instance, Jerry Aline Flieger, Catherine Driscoll, and Dorothea Olkowski in Ian Buchanan and Claire Colebrook, eds., *Deleuze and Feminist Theory* (Edinburgh: Edinburgh University Press, 2000); and Lorraine Code, *Irigaray and Deleuze: Experiments in Visceral Philosophy* (New York: Cornell University Press, 1999).

4. *Thousand Plateaus*, p. 293.

5. Ian Buchanan, *Deleuzism: A Metacommentary* (Edinburgh: Edinburgh University Press, 2000) p. 94.

6. *Deleuzism*, pp. 94–95.

7. *What is Philosophy?*, pp. 64–66.

8. Verena Andermatt Conley, "Becoming-Woman Now," *Deleuze and Feminist Theory*, p. 18. Conley draws a parallel between Deleuze's ideas on becoming-woman and the Body without Organs (BwO) and Hélène Cixous's Newly Born Woman (NBW); in the second part of her article, she discusses how in *The Time-Image* Deleuze relates becomings in terms of bodily attitudes and poses. Conley elaborates on the work of Chantal Akerman, which is mentioned by Deleuze as an example of such cinema of becoming.

9. An earlier and shorter version of this chapter appeared in David Rodowick. "Gilles Deleuze, Philosopher of Cinema." *IRIS* 23, Spring 1997:147–64.

10. Gilles Deleuze, *The Logic of Sense*. Trans. Mark Lester and Charles Stivale, Ed. Constantin V. Boundas (New York: Columbia University Press, 1990; orig. publ. Paris: Editions de Minuit, 1969); Lewis Carroll, *Alice's Adventures in Wonderland* and *Through the Looking Glass* (London: Penguin, 1994; orig. publ. 1865 and 1872).

11. *Logic of Sense*, pp. 2–3.

12. *Expressionism in Philosophy: Spinoza*, p. 222.

13. *Thousand Plateaus*, p. 159.

14. *Thousand Plateaus*, p. 276.

15. See also Marianna Fraaij. "Figures of Childhood: Alice, a Writer's 'Dream-Child'," *Encounter/Infraction/Contagion*. Conference papers collected by Joost de Bloois (Utrecht: University of Utrecht, 2000).

16. Félix Guattari, "A Liberation of Desire," in Gary Genosko, ed. *The Guattari Reader* (Oxford: Blackwell Publishers, 1996) p. 206. In the same interview, Guattari also explains once more his (and Deleuze's) position toward psychoanalysis and desire: "I was Lacan's student, I was analyzed by Lacan, and I practiced psychoanalysis for twelve years; and now I have broken with that practice. Psychoanalysis transforms and deforms the unconscious by forcing it to pass through the grid of its system of inscription and representation. For psychoanalysis the unconscious is always *already there*, genetically programmed, structured, finalized on objectives of conformity to social norms. For schizoanalysis it is a question of constructing an unconscious, not only with phrases but with all possible semiotic means, and not only with individuals or relations between individuals, but also with groups, with physiological and perceptual systems, with machines, struggles, and arrangements of every nature. There is no question here of transference, interpretation, or delegation of power to a specialist."

17. Moira Gatens, *Imaginary Bodies: Ethics, Power and Corporeality* (London and New York: Routledge, 1996) p. 206.

18. *Gilles Deleuze and the Ruin of Representation*, pp. 32–58. See also her article "Body, Knowledge and Becoming-Woman: Morpho-logic in Deleuze and Irigaray," *Deleuze and Feminist Theory*, pp. 86–109.

19. Rosi Braidotti, "Towards a New Nomadism: Feminist Deleuzian Tracks; or, Metaphysics and Metabolism," *Gilles Deleuze and the Theater of Philosophy*, ed. Constantin Boundas and Dorothea Olkowski (New York and London: Routledge, 1994) p. 169. See also Braidotti's *Patterns of Dissonance: a Study of Women and Contemporary Philosophy* (Cambridge: Polity Press, 1991); and her "Discontinuous Becomings: Deleuze on the Becoming-Woman of Philosophy," in *JBSP: The Journal of the British Society for Phenomenology* 24(1), 1993. Elisabeth Grosz writes about Deleuze in *Volatile Bodies: Toward a Corporeal Feminism* (Bloomington: Indiana University Press, 1994) and in "A Thousand Tiny Sexes: Feminism and Rhizomatics," *Gilles Deleuze and the Theater of Philosophy*. Both Braidotti and Grosz summarize the several critiques of Deleuze made by feminists such as Luce Irigaray and Alice Jardine before mapping Deleuzian thoughts that can be useful for feminists. Irigaray, for instance, remarks that women have always been seen as BwOs (at least without the essential organ); so, according to her, it would not help them to go on creating such bodies. This demonstrates clearly the confusion about the concept of the BwO. Moira Gatens, whose work is discussed later in this chapter, therefore proposes the less misleading term BwOO (Body without Organized Organs). In her book *Becoming-Woman* (Minneapolis and London: University of Minnesota Press, 1997), Camille Griggers works with the concept of becoming-woman, putting it in a lesbian perspective. The anthology *Deleuze and Feminism* contains a few articles on becoming-woman (see note 2). Dorothea Olkowski ("Body, Knowledge and Becoming-Woman: Morpho-logic in Deleuze and Irigaray") and Lorrain Code (*Irigaray and Deleuze*) revise the relationship between Deleuze and Irigaray,

suggesting that their ideas on the fluidity of the body have more in common than Irigaray's criticism of Deleuze appears to allow.

20. *Gilles Deleuze and the Theater of Philosophy*, pp. 182 and 208–209.

21. Rosi Braidotti, for instance, confesses she is in doubt about this point in Deleuzian philosophy: "[W]e are left with two options. One consists of saying that our culture is not Deleuzean yet and that we need to put more effort into exploring radical forms of molecular becoming. . . . The second option consists in saying that Deleuze's scheme of becoming is faulty and it needs to be revised in the sense of multiple but not undifferentiated becomings. Between the two my heart lingers, and I shall not be pushed to choose." ("Meta(l)morphoses" in *Theory, Culture & Society* 14(2) May 1997:77).

22. From *Dialogues*, quoted from *The Deleuze Reader*, p. 114.

23. *Thousand Plateaus*, pp. 277 and 276.

24. Teresa de Lauretis, *Alice Doesn't: Feminism, Semiotics, Cinema* (Bloomington: Indiana University Press, 1984). Another "constructionist" feminist critique of Deleuze comes from Judith Butler, who objects to Deleuze's positive conception of desire as the basis of a nonhistoricized ontology. For a discussion of Butler's position against Deleuze, see Dorothea Olkowski, *Gilles Deleuze and the Ruins of Representaion*, pp. 40–47.

25. See *The Logic of Sense*, pp. 82–93. Deleuze compares Antonin Artaud (who invented the term BwO) with Lewis Carroll and Humpty Dumpty. Although Artaud did not like Carroll's surface writing, Deleuze sees many similarities between the two authors. Furthermore, Deleuze and Guattari have described the BwO as a zero-degree or egg: "We treat the BwO as the full egg before the extension of the organism and the organization of the organs, before the formation of the strata . . .," *A Thousand Plateaus*, p. 153.

26. Gatens sees the work of Hélène Cixous and Luce Irigaray, who propose a similar recognition of at least two sexes, not as essentialist but as an important contribution to the understanding of different bodily experiences (which are not fixed and essential to all women). Besides, the biological determination of bodies is not so straightforwardly clear, and Gatens suggests "sex as a continuum and bodies as multiple." "Normal"-looking women, for instance, can carry the male XY-code. Some people have the hermaphrodite XXXY code.

27. *Imaginary Bodies*, p. 16.

28. Deleuze says this in his *Abécédaire* with Claire Parnet (letter "G" for *Gauche*, ARTE television, 1995; also distributed on videocassette, Vidéo Editions Montparnasse 1996). Deleuze talks here about minority politics, which involve molecular movements; minorities are not to be measured by numbers.

29. Moira Gatens, "Through a Spinozist Lens: Ethology, Difference, Power," *Deleuze: a Critical Reader*. Ed. Paul Patton (Oxford: Blackwell Publishers, 1996) p. 178. Don Ihde speaks in a similar way about both microperceptions (which he relates to bodily sensory dimensions of perception) and macroperception (related to

a cultural hermeneutic dimension): "There is no bare or isolated microperception except in its field of a hermeneutic or macroperceptual surrounding; nor may macroperception have any focus without its fulfillment in microperceptual (bodily-sensory) experience." (Don Ihde, *Postphenomenology—Essays in the Postmodern Context* [Evanston, Ill.: Northwestern University Press, 1993]).

30. "Through a Spinozist Lens."

31. "Through a Spinozist Lens," p. 181. Gatens here quotes Sharon Marcuse.

32. Donna Haraway, "A Cyborg Manifesto," *Simians, Cyborgs, and Women: The Reinvention of Nature* (London: Free Association Books, 1991). In her article "Towards a New Nomadism," Rosi Braidotti also notes a certain affinity between Haraway and Deleuze. Braidotti sees the limits of this comparison to be precisely when the question of feminist politics is raised.

33. Moira Gatens also refers to Haraway in this respect. According to her, Haraway's work demonstrates that the borders which the cyborg defies are not monstrous or scary from an ethologic point of view: "The distinction between artifice and nature, human and non-human, will not be of interest on an ethological view since these terms too will be analyzable only on an immanent plane where distinctions between one thing and the next amount to kinetic or dynamic differences" ("Through a Spinozist Lens," p. 167).

34. "A Cyborg Manifesto," p. 180. See also the interview with Haraway by Constance Penley and Andrew Ross, "Cyborgs at Large" in *Social Text* 25/6, 1990.

35. "A Cyborg Manifesto," p. 154.

36. "A Cyborg Manifesto," p. 154. See for an overview of the tendencies in cyborg culture that try to transcend the limits of the body and matter (in a Cartesian spirit) Mark Dery's book *Escape Velocity: Cyber Culture at the End of the Century* (New York: Grove Press, 1996).

37. Deleuze has rethought Foucault's disciplinary society into a more contemporary concept of control society. See Deleuze, *Negotiations*. Trans. Martin Joughin (New York: Columbia University Press, 1995) pp. 177–82. Haraway talks about new scary networks that form the "informatics of domination." See the "Cyborg Manifesto," pp. 161–65.

38. Jerry Aline Flieger. "Becoming-Woman: Deleuze, Schreber and Molecular Identification," *Deleuze and Feminist Theory*, p. 62. The orchid and the wasp are the examples Deleuze and Guattari give when they discuss the rhizome; it also is an example of becoming: "The orchid deterritorializes by forming an image, a tracing of a wasp, but the wasp reterritorializes on that image. The wasp is nevertheless deterritorialized, becoming a piece in the orchid's reproductive apparatus. But it reterritorializes the orchid by transporting its pollen. Wasp and orchid, as heterogeneous elements, form a rhizome. . . . [A] becoming-wasp of the orchid and a becoming-orchid of the wasp" (*Thousand Plateaus*, p. 10).

39. *Movement-Image*, p. 271.

40. *Time-Image*, p. 257.

41. The famous ball scene in *India Song* creates an extreme confusion between actual and virtual images. The mirror wall in the ballroom makes it almost impossible to distinguish between the "real" Anne Marie Stretter and her image (which in the film also relates to the fact that everything actually takes place after her death).

42. Marguerite Duras, *Le navire night et autres textes* (Paris: Mercure de France, 1979; 1986 edition for my references).

43. "Becoming-Woman: Deleuze, Schreber and Molecular Identifcations," p. 47. The quote from Deleuze and Guattari is from *A Thousand Plateaus*, p. 293.

44. In *Les Yeux Verts* (Paris: Cahiers du Cinéma and Gallimard, 1980, p. 75; my translation). Duras tells how she lived with Aurélia Steiner, how it took her six weeks of isolation to write the thirteen pages of *Aurélia Steiner (Vancouver)*. She saw with the eyes of Aurélia, she saw the sea through her eyes, with her "history" in mind, she saw Vancouver and Melbourne (neutral cities where many Jews found their escape from deportation), she saw that "the sea cried or slept the cries or sleep of Aurélia" (p. 90, my translation). Duras becomes Aurélia, Aurélia becomes Duras. One could say that in this work, Duras (as a non-Jew) becomes Jewish. In any case, *Aurélia Steiner* demonstrates the double becoming of modern political cinema as described by Deleuze. Clearly, this does not mean Duras is Aurélia (or Jewish). As Duras herself explains, again in paradoxic terms: "It is true that she is separate from me and that it is she who speaks in my films. All I did was listen and translate her voice, each word, every second" (*Les Yeux Verts*, p. 66, my translation). On the back cover of the written texts of *Aurélia Steiner*, Duras invites the lecturer to enter into a similar process of becoming (triple becoming): "Try when you are alone in your room, free, to call or respond beyond the abyss. To mingle with the vertigo of the enormous sea of calls. That first word, that first cry one does not know how to cry. One could just as well call God. It is impossible. And yet it happens" (my translation).

45. *Les Yeux Verts*, p. 66. For *Aurélia Steiner (Paris)*, it was really impossible for Duras to accompany this Aurélia with images.

46. Catherine Driscoll, "The Woman in Process: Deleuze, Kristeva and Feminism," *Deleuze and Feminist Theory*, pp. 78 and 81. Although Kristeva is much more in favor of psychoanalysis than Deleuze, Driscoll demonstrates how they both theorize "the girl" as a position to escape the norm of the (molar) majority/ the symbolic order. Both Kristeva and Deleuze emphasize that "the feminine" or "becoming-woman" escapes, undermines, or transgresses for both sexes.

47. See also Patricia Mellencamp, "What Virginia Woolf did tell Sally Potter," *A Fine Romance: Five Ages of Film Feminism* (Philadelphia: Temple University Press, 1995). Mellencamp here puts *Orlando* in the perspective of economic feminism. In "Five Ages of Film Feminism" (in Laleen Jayamanne, ed., *Kiss me Deadly: Feminism and Cinema for the Moment*. Sydney: Power Institute, 1995:18–76), Patricia Mellencamp regularly makes references to the possible significance of Deleuze for

feminism. For instance, when she discusses the affective and emotional levels of Tracey Moffat's films that create new sensations: "'Emotional fusion' involves 'some *new quality*.' This 'qualitative leap' is enabled by feminism and, perhaps, Deleuze" (p. 58).

48. *The Logic of Sense*, p. 165.

49. Virginia Woolf, *Orlando* (London: The Hogarth Press, 1928). All quotes refer to the annotated edition by Penguin, 1993. This quote is on p. 174.

50. *Orlando*, pp. 175, 179. In the film the dialogue is as follows: Orlando: "If I were a man, I might not choose to risk my life for an uncertain cause, I might think that freedom won by death is not worth having. In fact . . . " Shelmerdine: "You might not choose to be a real man at all. If I were a woman, I might choose not to sacrifice my life caring for my children and my children's children or to drown anonymously in the milk of female kindness but instead say, to go abroad. Would I then be . . . " Orlando: "A real woman?"

51. *Orlando*, p. 223.

52. It is of course no accident that all the singing voices in the film are very high-pitched although they are coming from a male body. The opening and closing songs of the film are performed by Jimmy Sommerville (in Isaac Julien's film *Looking for Langston*, he again performs as a singing angel).

53. See also *Spinoza and the Ethics*, pp. 98–107.

54. See for neurologic references to Alice, for instance, Douglas Hofstadter, *Gödel, Esher, Bach: An Eternal Golden Braid* (New York: Vintage Books, 1979; and Daniel Dennett, *Consciousness Explained* (London: Penguin, 1991). Other references: Robert Gilmore. *Alice in Quantumland: An Allegory of Quantum Physics* (New York: Springer-Verlag, 1995); and Jeff Noon, *Automated Alice* (New York: Crown Publishers, 1996). Alice now also has a digital sister in the computer game *American McGee's Alice* (Electronic Arts, 2000). This Alice is also equipped with a lot of weapons, called "toys." About her knife it is said: "Alice has an instinctive affinity for this toy. As Alice gains experience with the blade, she is able to master some highly advanced chops."

55. It is clear that *The City of Lost Children* is a European co-production made for an international (and largely English-speaking) audience.

56. See Tom Gunning, "The Cinema of Attractions: Early Film, its Spectator and the Avant-Garde," *Space, Frame, Narrative*. Ed. Thomas Elsaesser (London: BFI and Bloomington University Press, 1990) pp. 56–62. I am grateful to my colleague Gerwin van der Pol for bringing this aspect of the film to my attention.

57. In his article "Taking Shape," Scott Bukatman relates morphing to the experience of time and duration in a Bergsonian perspective (my reference is to the Dutch translation in *Andere Sinema*, no. 142, Nov./Dec. 1997).

58. For Alice's Victorian context, see, for instance, Nicolaas Matsier, *Alice in Verbazië* (Amsterdam: De Bezige Bij, 1996) or the *Victorian Website* <http://www.stg.brown.edu/projects/hypertext/landow/victorian/cbronte/cb&lc.html>.

59. Jeff Noon presents *Automated Alice* as the third (yet only recently discovered) part of Lewis Carroll's work. It takes place in 1998.

60. Michelle Langford, "Film Figures: Rainer Werner Fassbinder's, *The Marriage of Maria Braun*; and Alexander Kluge's *The Female Patriot*," Laleen Jayamanne, ed., *Kiss Me Deadly*, p. 147. The quote is from Kluge's film *Occasional Work of a Female Slave* (1977).

61. For this information on Lars von Trier and his films, see the website <http://intimate.org/bjork/special/ditd/articles/bibel/index.htm>. This is the translation of an article from Swedish fashion and trend magazine *Bibel* 11, October 1999.

62. See S. Kierkegaard, *Concluding Unscientific Postscript to Philosophical Fragments I-II*. Trans. Howard Hong and Edna Hong (Princeton, NJ: Princeton University Press, 1992). In "A Life of Pure Immanence: Deleuze's Critique et Clinique Project," Daniel Smith explains the pathos in the affective film: "For Deleuze, the affective film par excellence is Carl Dreyer's *The Passion of Joan of Arc*, which is made up almost exclusively of short close-ups. Joan of Arc's trial is an event actualized in a historical situation, with the affections of these characters and roles (Joan, the bishop, and the judges), with the affections of these characters (the bishop's anger, Joan's martyrdom). The ambition of Dreyer's film is to extract the 'passion' from the trial: All that will be preserved from the roles and situations will be what is needed for the affect to be extracted and to carry out its conjunctions— this 'power' of anger or of ruse, this 'quality' of victim or martyrdom" (Introduction to *Essays Critical and Clinical*, p. xxxiii). In a similar way, von Trier wants to extract the "passion" from his films.

63. Bodil Marie Thomsen, "Idiocy, Foolishness, and Spastic Jesting," Richard Raskin (ed.), *P.O.V.—A Danish Journal of Film Studies* 10, December 2000:57 (special issue on dogma cinema). Thomsen relates Kierkegaard's pathos to von Trier's movies and suggests that besides "suffering" and "impassioned emotion," Kierkegaard's pathos can also mean "enthusiastic passion" and "the solemnly stirred or earnestly elevated in esthetics" (p. 47).

64. Frans-Willem Korsten. "Is Bess a Bike? Gender, Capitalism and the Politics of a BwO," Patricia Pisters, ed., *Micropolitics of Media Culture*, pp. 143–57.

65. *Essays Critical and Clinical*, pp. 134 and 133.

66. "Is Bess a Bike?", p. 157.

67. Richard Dyer, "Entertainment and Utopia," *Movies and Methods*, Vol II. Ed. Bill Nichols (Berkeley and Los Angeles: University of California Press, 1985), pp. 220–232.

68. *Time-Image*, pp. 60–67.

69. *Time-Image*, p. 62.

70. *Time-Image*, p. 61.

71. See on melodrama, for instance, Christine Gledhill, ed., *Home is Where the Heart Is: Studies in Melodrama and the Woman's Film* (London: BFI, 1987).

72. *Movement-Image*, p. 35. Deleuze talks about the changed dimension and function of the close-up in Eisenstein; I refer here to the change of style—montage—
and "temperature"—colors—of the image.

73. *What is Philosophy?*, p. 218.

74. *Thousand Plateaus*, p. 348.

75. Selma is poor and saves every penny for her son's operation. Selma's neighbor Bill steals her money because he has debts and does not dare tell his wife he
has no more money to afford her luxurious lifestyle. The law sentences her to
death, but she is actually the victim and not the perpetrator, even though she eventually killed Bill.

Chapter 5: Logic of Sensations in Becoming-Animal

1. Rosi Braidotti, "Teratologies," *Deleuze and Femininist Theory*, p. 165.
Braidotti gives the example of cannibalism to indicate the move of monstous
imaginary to mainstream: "Cannibalism, made visible by Romero in *Night of the
Living Dead* in the 1960s, became eroticised by Greenaway in the 1980s and made
it into the mainstream by the 1990s, with *Silence of the Lambs*" (p. 156). One only
needs to think, for instance, of the *Terminator* films and the *Alien* films to realize
the popularity of this type of image.

2. "Teratologies," p. 170. Braidotti writes *figurations* instead of *figures*. I have
chosen to use Deleuze's term *figure* to mark the opposition to *representation*. See
also notes 18 and 19.

3. Many stories are not discussed here, such as the numerous stories on cat
people, as presented in films like *Cat People* (Jacques Tourneur, 1942, and Paul
Schrader, 1982) and, more specifically, the myth of the cat woman (Michelle Pfeiffer in *Batman Returns*, Tim Burton, 1992). See for "feline-becomings," for instance, James Roberts, "Becoming-Cat, Becoming Irena: Deleuze, Guattari, and
Cat People," *Enculturation* 1(1), 1997. The relationship between humans and pri-
mates is equally not elaborated, although it has many cinematographic variations
(cf. *King Kong*, Merian Cooper, 1933; *Planet of the Apes*, Franklin Schaffner, 1968;
Max mon Amour, Nagisa Oshima, 1986; *Project X*, Jonathan Kaplan, 1987; *Goril-
las in the Mist*, Michael Apted, 1988). Nor have I taken into consideration a lesbian
perspective on "becoming-horse" as proposed by Elspeth Probyn in her book *Outside Belongings* (New York and London: Routledge, 1996).

4. Stoker was also inspired by Polidori's *The Vampyre* (1819), based on a story
by Lord Byron (created at the same time and place as Mary Shelley's *Frankenstein*),
which is seen as the real basis of the modern vampire. See also Gordon Melton,
The Vampire Book—the Encyclopedia of the Undead (Detroit: Visible Ink Press,
1994).

5. Batman is, of course, the other popular figure associated with the bat; but
mostly he represents the good side and is not so much considered as a monster.

6. There are also many female vampires, often based on the legend of Countess Elizabeth Bathory (cf. Delphine Seyrig in Harry Kumel's *Daughters of Darkness*, 1971) or as represented by Catherine Deneuve in Tony Scott's *The Hunger* (1983). One of the most recent vampire films is Abel Ferrara's *The Addiction* (1994). Ferrara here explicitly relates vampirism to the addiction to heroin. Furthermore, he relates all kinds of philosophic questions (such as Nietzschian nihilism and the power of the will) to vampirism by connecting it to the horrors of the Second World War and other awful "human" experiences.

7. *Thousand Plateaus*, pp. 233–37. The term *inappropriate/d other* is from Trinh T. Minh-ha (*Woman, Native, Other: Writing Postcoloniality and Feminism*). Bloomington: Indiana University Press, 1989). Donna Haraway borrowed the term for her essay "The Promise of Monsters: A Regenerative Politics for Inappropriated Others" (L. Nelson and P. Treichler, eds. *Cultural Studies*. New York: Routledge, 1992) and uses it sometimes to address cyborgs.

8. *Thousand Plateaus*, pp. 237–38.

9. *Thousand Plateaus*, p. 275.

10. Anne Rice, *Interview with the Vampire* (Book I of the Vampire Chronicles) (New York: Ballantine Books, 1979). In 1994, Neil Jordan turned this vampire story into a movie of the same title.

11. Robert Louis Stevenson, *The Strange Case of Dr. Jekyll and Mr. Hyde* (London: Penguin, 1994; first published in 1886).

12. Another famous version is Victor Fleming's *Dr. Jekyll and Mr. Hyde* (1941), with Spencer Tracy, Lana Turner, and Ingrid Bergman. A comic version of the Jekyll and Hyde theme is presented in *The Nutty Professor* (1963), directed and acted by Jerry Lewis.

13. See *Movement-Image*, pp. 87–101.

14. In *Becoming-Woman*, Camille Griggers demonstrates how the face normally is a means to construct the normative subject ("The Despotic Face of White Femininity," pp. 1–35).

15. G. Deleuze, *Francis Bacon: logique de la sensation* (Paris: Editions de la Différence, 1981) p. 28.

16. Deleuze writes *Figures* systematically with a capital. Except in quotations, I will use a lower case "f" to indicate this concept.

17. Although Deleuze has distanced himself in several instances from phenomenology, I think there are certainly some connections to be made between his work and the phenomenologic work of Merleau-Ponty. Like Deleuze, Merleau-Ponty has expressed his fascination for painters who tried to paint sensations. His *L'oeil et l'esprit* (Paris: Editions Gallimard, 1964) starts with a quote from Cézanne: "What I will try to translate for you is much more mysterious, entangled in the roots of being, at the imperceptible source of sensations" (my translation). Like Deleuze, Merleau-Ponty states that these sensations are not reached through figuration; he calls figuration "the suspicious relation of resemblance"

("le louche rapport de ressemblance," p. 38). On the contrary, it is again through nonrepresentative deformation that essential sensations can escape (p. 39).

18. Significantly there is not just one word to translate this term; the French verb *sentir* is translated as "to feel, to perceive, to become conscious of" or "to smell" or "to taste" or "to understand" (Van Dale: French-Dutch/Dutch-English).

19. *Francis Bacon*, p. 31. My translation.

20. *Francis Bacon*, p. 31. My translation.

21. See *Francis Bacon*, p. 30.

22. See also Merleau-Ponty. *Phénoménologie de la perception* (Paris: Gallimard, 1945) p. 256.

23. *Francis Bacon*, p. 78. My translation. In his reflections on Cézanne, Merleau-Ponty expresses the same idea as follows: "What is mysterious, is the connection between things; I see each thing at its own place, precisely because they block each other—they are rivals for my perception, precisely because they each occupy their own space. . . . Seen this way, spatial depth can no longer be understood in 'three dimensions.' Seen this way, spatial depth is rather the experience of the reversibility of dimensions that is of a global 'locality' where everything is at the same time, where height, width and distance are abstract. . . ." (*L'oeil et l'esprit*, p. 65. My translation.)

24. In his book on Francis Bacon, Ernst van Alphen also speaks about the deformations and the "fluid selves" (especially of the male figures) in Bacon's paintings and sees them as liberating forces. Ernst van Alphen, *Francis Bacon and the Loss of Self* (London: Reaktion Books, 1992).

25. Of course, they are not the only painters who work in this way. Paul Klee, Vincent van Gogh, Paul Gauguin, and Henri Matisse, for instance, also reach the senses by remaining on the surface and by expressing in this way a perpetual becoming.

26. In *Phénoménologie de la perception*, Merleau-Ponty describes the specific internal forces of certain colours. For instance, red and yellow favor sliding movements, whereas blue and green prefer shaking movements. Outward movements are accelerated by green and slowed down by red (maybe traffic lights are not so arbitrary and conventional after all . . .). He provides a whole list of different experiences of colors that have different motor qualities and invoke different movements (p. 242).

27. *Thousand Plateaus*, p. 255.

28. *Thousand Plateaus*, p. 257.

29. *Expressionism in Philosophy*, pp. 262–63.

30. *Expressionism in Philosophy*, p. 264.

31. Walt Disney's animation version of 1969, directed by Wolfgang Reitherman, is of course very famous. In Disney's version, Mowgli decides at the end to give up his becoming-animal, when he makes the step to enter the human world. One might see this as a sort of "domestication" or "becoming-pet." Stephen Sommers

directed *Rudyard Kipling's Jungle Book*, with Sam Neill and John Cleese. The phenomenon of going back to the original novel to film a myth yet another time (the last time?) was common in the 1990s. Cf. *Bram Stoker's Dracula* (Coppola, 1992) and *Mary Shelley's Frankenstein* (Branagh, 1994).

32. *Francis Bacon*, p. 21. My translation.

33. Crucifixions do, of course, have a long "tradition."

34. Thomas Elsaesser has demonstrated how history can challenge the purely psychoanalytic interpretations of Fassbinder's masochism. Elsaesser states that what is needed is a critique of the critique of victimhood in Fassbinder's cinema. Fassbinder's work needs not only to be explained around the false symmetry of sex and class or the difference between a sadistic gaze and masochistic ecstasy but also to be situated in a historical perspective. In his book *Fassbinder's Germany: History, Identity, Subject* he gives such a historical perspective of Fassbinder's work. Kaja Silverman also extends libidinal strategies to a wider context (although she does not do this explicitly in the case of Fassbinder). Instead of "historicizing the subject," she wants to "subjectivize history." For Silverman sadomasochism has political consequences, whereas for Elsaesser history explains (partly) the (perverted) behavior of subjects. This comes close to the Deleuzian idea of history as the condition for specific actualizations.

35. Gilles Deleuze and Leopold von Sacher-Masoch, *Presentation de Sacher-Masoch avec le texte integrale de la Venus à la fourure* (Paris: Editions de Minuit, 1967).

36. Deleuze's study on Sacher-Masoch is an early work. Although he is already inspired by the idea of multiplicity (he distinguishes several mothers instead of one oedipal mother) and he also takes some distance from Freud (by disconnecting sadism and masochism), this work is inspired by Freud as well. Later, in his collaboration with Félix Guattari, he will emphasize the relation of becoming-animal and masochism. I nevertheless make some references to Deleuze's early study on masochism, combining it with his later findings.

37. *Presentation de Sacher-Masoch*, p. 55. I agree with Kaja Silverman's criticism of Gaylyn Studlar's conflation of the oral mother with the preoedipal mother, which would lead to an a-political reading. See *Male Subjectivity at the Margins*, p. 417, and Studlar's article "Masochism and the Perverse Pleasures of the Cinema," *Movies and Methods*, vol I. Ed. Bill Nichols (Berkeley: University of California Press, 1976).

38. Deleuze does not agree with Theodor Reik's version of Christian masochism, which sticks to the sadomasochistic union (Reik, *Masochism and Sex in Society*. Trans. Margaret H. Beigel and Gertrud M. Kurth [New York, Grove Press, 1963]).

39. *Francis Bacon*, pp. 20–21. My translation. In *What is Philosophy?* Deleuze and Guattari say: "The agony of a rat or the slaughter of a calf remains present in thought not through pity but as the zone of exchange between man and animal in which something of one passes into the other" (p. 109).

40. "All this superfluous flesh! It's because you don't have your own will. You're just passive." A short experimental film by Robert Sanders, called *Bacon* (1991), shows in penetrating images how man and animal, flesh, and meat are cruelly one. The last images show the head of a man alternated with the head of a pig and slices of bacon coming out of a slicer. Little argumentation is needed to see that *Bacon* (the film) and Bacon (the painter) and bacon (the meat) have too much in common to go unnoticed.

41. Marianne herself is even compared to food by Elvira: the child served as a binding agent (a thickener) between Irene and Erwin/Elvira, "wie eine Suppe die zu flüssig ist, dann braucht mann auch Mehl, diese zutate war Marianne auch."

42. *Thousand Plateaus*, p. 239. Interestingly, in the plateau on becoming-animal, Deleuze and Guattari create three "planes of consistency" around the sorcerer ("Memories of a Sorcerer I, II, and III"). They talk about writers who are sorcerers in that they "become-animal" (or become-other) in writing. Besides, they explain, "becoming is an affair of sorcery because (1) it implies an initial relation of alliance with a demon; (2) the demon functions as the borderline of an animal pack, into which the human being passes or in which his or her becoming takes place, by contagion; (3) this becoming itself implies a second alliance, with another human group; (4) this new borderline between the two groups guides the contagion of animal and human being with the pack" (p. 247). Deleuze and Guattari are sorcerers as well; at least their becomings are contagious. With my emphasis on certain films, I hope to create some planes of consistency and demonstrate how filmmakers with their audiovisual creations can express becoming-animal as well.

43. *Thousand Plateaus*, p. 28.

44. Traditionally, they have an even greater understanding of the passive becoming-animal; but, as we saw in previous chapters, women are learning more and more to transform their passive affects into active ones.

45. Actually, three short stories are interwoven and visually elaborated: "The Werewolf," "The Company of Wolves," and "Wolf-Alice." For more analyses of her work, see Lorna Sage, ed., *Flesh and the Mirror—Essays on the Art of Angela Carter* (London, Virago Press, 1994).

46. The term *mise-en-abîme* is a technical term to indicate the way in which an artwork refers to itself. More loosely, it is also used to refer to a narrative structure in which a story is told within a story.

47. Bruno Bettelheim. *Psychoanalyse des Contes de Fée* (1976). In *Politically Correct Bedtime Stories* (New York: Macmillan, 1994), James Finn Garner gives an exaggerated although funny feminist interpretation of "Little Red Riding Hood" in which the forester is killed in the end. These bedtime stories demonstrate that politically correct interpretations of fairy tales lead to role reversals that do not bring any solution (although it can be satisfyingly hilarious to reverse roles).

48. *Thousand Plateaus*, p. 243.

49. "Cinema Magic and the Old Monsters," *Flesh and the Mirror*, p. 240.

50. "A Cyborg Manifesto," p. 155.

51. *Thousand Plateaus*, pp. 282–84.

52. *Thousand Plateuas*, p. 251.

53. In Wayne Drew, ed., *David Cronenberg* (London: BFI dossier No. 21, 1984).

54. For an extended analysis of Cronenberg's work in relation to Deleuze and Guattari, see Eva Jørholt, "The Metaphor Made Flesh: A Philosophy of the Body Disguised as Biological Horror Film," *Micropolitics of Media Culture*, pp. 75–100.

55. *Francis Bacon*, p. 41. As a personal note, I might add that *The Fly* was my first "experiment" with horror films that I could fully watch. In any case, it opened a whole new range of perceptions: from that moment on, I could watch and like horror movies by relating them to other levels of experience (seeing them as re-zoning projects, for instance). *The Fly* remains a personal "classic," even more than Cronenberg's other cult classic *Videodrome* (1982).

56. Cronenberg, in an interview with Piers Handling and William Beard in *The Shape of Rage*, ed. by Piers Handling (Toronto, 1983).

57. *Shape of Rage*.

58. According to Shaviro in *The Cinematic Body*, Brundle also transforms into a monster because he tries to adapt to social norms. I agree with this, although I would also like to turn Shaviro's statement around: because social norms, society, do not (yet) accept any becomings, aberrations from the norm take monstrous proportions.

59. See also my article about BwOs in video art, "Het Orgaanloze Lichaam—Filmische Effecten in de Videokunst," *Skrien* 205 Dec. 1995/Jan 1996. Here I relate the concept of BwO to the work of Matthew Barney, Tony Oursler, Pippilotti Rist, and Douglas Gordon.

60. *Cremaster 5* is situated in Budapest (the State Opera and the Thermal Baths of Gellert). Barney plays the roles of Diva, Magician, and Giant, next to Ursula Andress in her role as Queen of Chain. The film is completely sung and contains incomprehensibly beautiful images (such as underwater scenes with strange "nymphs" that tie silk ribbons to Barney's "cremaster muscles." Cremaster muscles are the muscles that belong to the male sexual organ (they make the testicles move up). In Barney's *Cremaster* series, these "organs" (unrecognizable as a traditional male organ) come back in different forms.

61. This is stressed even more by the fact that the film is regularly taken over by animation; *Tank Girl* is in fact based on an Australian cartoon (hence the kangaroos).

62. One inventive (but cruel) device is a new weapon, invented by Water and Power: a cylinder. On one side, it has sharp tubes that first suck blood and then water out of the victim; the other end consists of two containers on top of each other (one to absorb the blood, the other looks like a plastic bottle for mineral water and receives the water). No water can be lost in this world in which water is no longer abundantly available for everybody.

63. In the original cartoon, there is no plot at all, but this would be too big a leap for Hollywood. The water-shortage plot is reminiscent of a Japanese film called *Wicked City* (1993), produced by Manga Studios (although without animation).

64. *Blvd.*, a Dutch magazine for "culture, music, fashion, media and cyberspace," recently photographed real Tank Girls.

65. The soundtrack was compiled by Courtney Love and contains music of among others Portishead, Björk, Hole, and Ice-T (who also plays one of the kangaroo-men, who is the "reincarnation" of Jack Kerouac).

Chapter 6: (De)Territorializing Forces of the Sound Machine

1. Simon Frith, "Music and Identity," *Questions of Cultural Identity*. Eds. Stuart Hall and Paul du Gay (London: Sage, 1996) p. 109.

2. "Music and Identity," pp. 110–11.

3. *Thousand Plateaus*, p. 348.

4. "Music and Identity," p. 125.

5. Walter Murch is a Hollywood sound specialist who is famous for (among other things) the sound effects in *The Godfather*, *The Conversation*, and *Apocalypse Now*. See also Michel Chion's French publications *La voix au cinéma* (Paris: Editions de l'Etoile, 1982); *Le son au cinéma* (Paris: Editions de l'Etoile, 1986); *La toile trouée—la parole au cinéma* (Paris: Editions de l'Etoile, 1988).

6. Walter Murch in Michel Chion, *Audio-Vision: Sound on Screen*. Trans. Claudia Gorbman (New York: Columbia University Press, 1994) pp. vii/viii.

7. *Audio-Vision*, p. xvii.

8. *Synchresis* is a combination of *synthesis* and *synchronism*. Another term, related to this one, which Chion introduces, is *magnetization*: the psychological process (in monaural film viewing) of locating a sound's source in the space of the image, no matter what the real point of origin of the sound in the viewing space is (*Audio-Vision*, p. 224).

9. Chion also distinguishes *textual speech* (speech in a film having the power to make visible the images that it evokes—not often used and usually limited to one character) and *emanation speech* (a use of speech found infrequently in films in which the words are not completely heard or understood. Speech becomes a sort of emanation of the characters, not essential for understanding significant action or meaning, cf. the "speech" in the films of Jacques Tati).

10. *La toile trouée*, pp. 153–54 ("un lieux d'images avec des sons").

11. Mary Ann Doane. "The Voice in the Cinema—The Articulation of Body and Space," *Narrative, Apparatus, Ideology*. Ed. Philip Rosen, pp. 335–48.

12. In *null extension*, the sonic universe is shrunken to the sounds heard by a single character; in vast extension, the sonic space is widely stretched (*Audio-Vision*, p. 222). In the previous chapter, it was remarked (in respect to the different

dimensions of the senses) that the sound space can be different from the visual space.

13. In his *Phénoménologie de la perception*, Merleau-Ponty demonstrates that this "magic power" is created by addressing only one of the senses: "When a phenomenon—for instance a soft breeze—offers itself to only one of my senses, it's a phantom, and it will become only real if, by accident, it will speak to my other senses, for instance when there is a strong wind that shows itself in the movements of the landscape" (p. 368; my translation). In the same way the acousmêtre is "phantomatic" and therefore powerful as long as he is not embodied and invisible.

14. Kaja Silverman, *The Acoustic Mirror: The Female Voice in Psychoanalysis and Cinema* (Bloomington and Indianapolis: Indiana University Press, 1988).

15. *Acoustic Mirror*, p. 1.

16. Chion in Silverman, *The Acoustic Mirror*, p. 50.

17. See also Leslie C. Dunn and Nancy A. Jones, eds., *Embodied Voices—Representing Female Vocality in Western Culture* (Cambridge: Cambridge University Press, 1994).

18. *Acoustic Mirror*, p.78.

19. *Acoustic Mirror*, p. 87.

20. *Acoustic Mirror*, p. 95.

21. *Metastases of Enjoyment*, p. 117.

22. Slavoj Žižek, "'I Hear You with My Eyes' or The Invisible Master," *Gaze and Voice as Love Objects*. Eds. Slavoj Žižek and Renata Salect (Durham and London: Duke University Press, 1996) pp. 91–126.

23. "I Hear You with My Eyes," p. 94.

24. It should be noted that this does not entail only that the word means discipline and power, whereas the voice means transgression and liberation. As Žižek demonstrates, the U.S. Marine Corps uses mesmerizing and nonsensical "marching chants" in the service of power and authority. ("I Hear You with My Eyes," p. 104). Although the voice is labeled as "feminine," it can be used in the service of "masculine" power as well.

25. "I Hear You with My Eyes," p. 112.

26. "I Hear You with My Eyes," p. 117.

27. Simon Frith, *Performing Rites—On the Value of Popular Music* (Oxford and New York: Oxford University Press, 1996) p. 115. Frith is here quoting Aaron Copeland.

28. See also Joseph Lanza, *Elevator Music: A Surreal History of Muzak, Easy-Listening, and Other Moodsongs* (New York: Picador, 1994). In the chapter entitled "Elevator Noir," he states "Bernard Herrmann's Psycho soundtrack, for example, is sufficient to turn any dwelling into the Bates Motel." (Hitchcock, very conscious of this mood effect, had an album released in the 1960s: *Music to be Murdered By*.) See also Claudia Gorbman, *Unheard Melodies* (Bloomington and London: Indiana University Press and BFI, 1987).

29. *Performing Rites*, p. 132.

30. *Performing Rites*, p. 144.

31. In the introduction to *Sound Theory, Sound Practice*, Rick Altman proposes another model of cinema: instead of considering films as texts (which makes each film appear as self-contained, centered, and structured around the image), he proposes that films should be seen as events. Altman proposes the term to make room for sound theory, which is becoming decreasingly able to be contained by the image: "In opposition to the notion of film as text, I have found it helpful to conceive of *cinema as event*. Viewed as macro-event, cinema is still seen as centered on the individual film, but according to a new type of geometry. Floating in a gravity-free world like doughnut-shaped spaceships, cinema events offer no clean-cut or stable separation between inside and outside or top and bottom. . . . The event that is cinema cannot be identified as privileging one particular aspect of the system. Instead, the cinema event is constituted by a continuing interchange, neither beginning nor ending at any specific point." By proposing cinema as event, Altman includes not only sound but also production and reception circumstances, of which sound is an important aspect. He emphasizes the heterogeneous and material aspects of film sounds and prefers not to interpret sounds in a psychoanalytic way, considering this to be an ontologic fallacy. The notion of event, and the idea of cinema as event, is conceptualized by Deleuze as well. If we now concentrate on sound, it can be argued that sound can create events, namely, events of becoming-music. See Rick Altman, ed., *Sound Theory, Sound Practice* (New York and London: Routledge, 1992) pp. 3–4.

32. *Thousand Plateaus*, pp. 299–300.

33. See *Thousand Plateaus*, pp. 508–10.

34. *Thousand Plateaus*, p. 348.

35. *Audio-Vision*, p. xi.

36. Keith Negus, *Popular Music in Theory: An Introduction* (Cambridge and Oxford: Polity Press and Blackwell, 1996) pp.190–224.

37. In *The Time-Image*, Deleuze talks about the end-product (not the moment of transition as in the cinema of Hitchcock) of the movement-image that is Leni Riefenstahl's cinema: " . . . the masses, state direction, politics become 'art': Hitler as film-maker. . . . And it is true that up to the end Nazism thinks of itself in competition with Hollywood. The revolutionary courtship of the movement-image and an art of the masses become subject was broken off, giving way to the masses subjected as psychological automaton, and to their leader as great spiritual automaton. This is what compels Syberberg to say that the end-product of the movement-image is Leni Riefenstahl, and if Hitler is to be put on trial by cinema, it must be inside cinema, against Hitler the film-maker, in order to 'defeat' him cinematographically, turning his weapon against him' . . ." (p. 264). So here we see another reason (again related to the traumas of the Second World War) for the emergence of the time-image, for the changes in the image, and for the necessity to challenge pure information and "order-words" of the control society.

38. See the article "Whistling in the Dark" by Max Bruinsma and Petra Pijnappels, *Mediamatic* 6(4) (special issue, "The Ear") (Amsterdam, 1992:258–62). For more recent research on the musical accompaniment of early cinema, see Rick Altman, "The Silence of the Silents," *The Musical Quarterly*, Winter 1997. Claudia Gorbman's remark in *Unheard Melodies* about easy-listening music also indicates this calming function of music: "Easy-listening music (at least in theory) helps the consumer buy, the patient relax, the worker work." In the same way, it is common practice in airplanes to put on "everything-is-fine-music" to soothe passengers' fear of flying when they enter the aircraft.

39. Laleen Jayamanne, "'Forty Acres and a Mule Filmworks'—Do the Right Thing—'A Spike Lee Joint': Blocking and Unblocking the Block," in *Micropolitics of Media Culture*, pp. 235–49.

40. *Thousand Plateaus*, p. 311.

41. *Thousand Plateaus*, p. 338.

42. *Thousand Plateaus*, p. 340.

43. *Thousand Plateaus*, pp. 342–43. It should be noted that Deleuze and Guattari see these developments in music parallel to developments in philosophy: "Philosophy follows the same movements as the other activities; whereas romantic philosophy still appealed to a formal synthetic identity ensuring a continuous intelligibility of matter (a priori synthesis), modern philosophy tends to elaborate a material thought in order to capture forces that are not thinkable in themselves. This is Cosmic philosophy, after the manner of Nietzsche" (p. 342).

44. In the 1970s, several films gave prominence to the soundtrack. See, for instance, Alan Pakula's *Klute* (1971), in which recording devices and surveillance play an equally important part; *India Song* by Marguerite Duras (1975) (with the same soundtrack she made another film a year later, *Son Nom de Vénise dans Calcutta Desert* [1976]); *Apocalypse Now* (1979) by Francis Ford Coppola, with Walter Murch again (like for *The Conversation*) as sound designer; this film is famous for its soundtrack. See also Thomas Elsaesser and Michael Wedel, "The Hollow Heart of Hollywood: *Apocalypse Now* and the New Sound Scape," Kene Moore, ed., *Conrad on Film* (Cambridge: Cambridge University Press, 1997).

45. See Jay Leyda, ed. *Eisenstein on Disney*. Trans. Alan Upchurch (London: Methuen, 1988).

46. *Eisenstein on Disney*, p. 46.

47. For an elaboration on "becoming," see Deleuze's film philosophy and Eisenstein's ideas about Disney, Keith Clancy, "Prester—The T(r)opology of Pyromania" and Keith Broadfoot and Rex Butler, "The Illusion of Illusion," *The Illusion of Life: Essays on Animation*. Ed. Alan Cholodenko (Sydney: Power Publications, 1991).

48. Laura Sells, "Where do the Mermaids Stand? Voice and Body in *The Little Mermaid*," *From Mouse to Mermaid: the Politics of Film, Gender, and Culture*. Ed. Elisabeth Bell, et al. (Bloomington and Indianapolis: Indiana University Press, 1995). Although a lot could be said about the institutional, political, and ideological

contexts and implications of Disney, I will not elaborate on those aspects. See also Eric Smoodin, ed. *Disney Discourses: Producing the Magic Kingdom* (New York and London: Routledge, 1994).

49. In Andersen's tale, the story does not have such a happy ending: the mermaid has terrible pain when she walks on her feet, she loses her voice forever, and she has no access to the prince. "Passing" into the white male system is, in Andersen's world, still impossible.

50. Elisabeth Bell looks at the subversive elements of female Disney characters through their body language: "Disney artists have created a somatic mixed message. While the characterizations of Disney heroines adhere to fairy-tale templates of passivity and victimage, their bodies are portraits of strength, discipline, and control, performing the dancing roles of princesses" (from "Somatexts at the Disney Shop: Constructing the Pentimentos of Women's Animated Bodies," *From Mouse to Mermaid*, p. 112).

51. In the Princess Series, new adventures of Little Mermaid Ariel and Aladdin's Jasmin are brought to the video screen.

52. In a way, this little Disney animation recalls another recent partly animated film, Tim Burton's *Mars Attacks!* (1996). In this film, not even the strongest nuclear bomb is effective against the invasion of evil aliens; but a little song, a little refrain from the radio makes them explode and disappear for ever. . . . . A more hilarious and yet powerful example of the (de)territorial forces of the refrain cannot be given.

53. Elisabeth Bell, *From Mouse to Mermaid*, p. 108.

54. *Thousand Plateaus*, p. 308.

55. *Acoustic Mirror*, p. 87.

56. Carolyn Abbate, "Opera, or the Envoicing of Women," *Musicology and Difference: Gender and Sexuality in Music Scolarship.* Ed. Ruth A. Scoly (Berkeley, Los Angeles, and London: University of California Press, 1993) pp. 225–58. See also Abbate's book *Unsung Voices—Opera and Musical Narrative in the Nineteenth Century* (Princeton, NJ: Princeton University Press, 1991).

57. "Opera, or the Envoicing of Women," p. 228. The opera film generally is associated with the work of Werner Schroeter, who has been filming and recording the voices of opera divas for many years. In his latest film *Poussières d'Amour* (1996), he invited his favororite singers to perform a few opera pieces and to talk about their voices, about love, tragedy, life, and death. There is one diva in the film for whom Schroeter has been looking for more than thirty years: Anita Cerquetti. This Italian opera singer was as famous as Maria Callas when she was in her twenties, but at the age of twenty-nine she lost her voice. *Poussières d'Amour* ends with Anita Cerquetti listening and lip-synching to her own voice, recorded in 1958 when she gave a chillingly beautiful performance of "Casta Diva" from Bellini's *Norma*. Past and present coincide in this touching scene where Anita Cerquetti "performs" her own voice.

58. Both of the texts by Roland Barthes can be found in *Image—Music—Text*. Trans. Stephen Heath (New York: Hill and Wang, 1977).

59. *Acoustic Mirror*, p. 193. This passage is also quoted by Abbate.

60. Artaud cited in "Radio, Death, and the Devil-Artaud's Pour en Finir avec le Jugement de Dieu," by Allen S. Weiss, in Dougles Kahn and Gregory White-head, eds., *Wireless Imagination: Sound, Radio, and the Avant-Garde* (Cambridge and London: MIT Press, 1992).

61. *Thousand Plateaus*, p. 302.

62. *Thousand Plateaus*, p. 304.

63. See David Toop, *Ocean of Sound—Aether Talk, Ambient Sound, Imaginary Worlds* (London: Serpent's Tail, 1995) pp. 106–107. I will return to Toop's book in the last section of this chapter.

64. "Radio, Death and the Devil."

65. Besson is also known for his films *Subway* (1982) and *La Femme Nikita* (1990). As a French filmmaker, he has always worked between Hollywood and Europe. His films are mostly action films combined with some European art cinema sensibilities. Maybe this ambiguity of his productions is a first indication for his sensibility for in-between states, border zones, and states of becoming. In *Subway*, he shows the underground world of people living in subways, a borderzone by definition. In *Nikita*, the main character shifts between her status as a performing beautiful woman and a trained fighter.

66. See also Florence Dupont's chapter "Vu d'Homère: Le Grand Bleu" in *Homère et Dallas* (Paris: Les Essais du XX-ième siècle, Hachette, 1991) pp. 85–91.

67. James Cameron's underwater science fiction film *The Abyss* (1989) is filmed almost completely underwater. A research team in an underwater boat tries to dismantle a nuclear bomb that has created an abyss in the sea bottom. Here they encounter a benign alien species that, composing themselves from seawater, can take any shape. This is an instance where digital morphing has the same protoplasmatic characteristics as animation film.

68. *Movement-Image*, p. 80.

69. See *Movement-Image*, pp. 107–11.

70. See Patricia Pisters. "The Fifth Element and the Fifth Dimension of the Affection-Image," *Cinema Studies into Visual Theory?* Ed. Anu Koivunen and Astrid Söderberg (Turku: University of Turku, 1998) pp. 93–107.

71. Here it is possible to make a sidestep to Fassbinder's work again. For Fassbinder and his composer, Peer Raben, music was also important and often used for its deterritorializing and reterritorializing effects. In *Martha*, the main character, Martha, loves Donizetti's *Lucia de Lammermoor*, but her sadistic husband forbids her to listen to it. *Lili Marleen* is a film about the territorializing forces of a song. See also Caryl Flinn's forthcoming book on music in New German Cinema.

72. *Time-Image*, p. 332.

73. See Jean Cavalier and Alain Gheerbrandt, *Dictionnaire des Symboles* (Paris:

Robert Lafont/Jupiter, 1982; first published in 1969). See also Jacques Aumont, *Introduction à la couleur: des discours aux images* (Paris: Armand Colin, 1994).

74. *Thousand Plateaus*, p. 308.

75. From *Blue*, a film/soundtrack written by Derek Jarman and composed by Simon Fisher Turner (London: Mute Record, 1993).

76. *Time-Image*, p. 266.

77. See also Susan Hayward, *Luc Besson* (Manchester and New York: Manchester University Press, 1998). Hayward argues, for instance, that in all Besson's films, his characters construct their "subjectivity" in the absence of their fathers and mothers (outside the oedipal family). According to Hayward, Besson's films have a bardic function in the sense that they talk about the human condition (especially of youth) in modern society. Besson's bardic function emphasizes once more the fact that we have here a case of "modern mythmaking."

78. *Thousand Plateaus*, p. 309. *The Fifth Element* is probably also the first action film in which a scream is uttered by a man (by the cross-gendered, trans-ethnic Ruby Rod, the television "talk show" presenter; on the soundtrack of the film, his words are also presented as music). Again, this might be seen as a French tradition, given the screams of Artaud, and the heart-aching scream of the vice-consul in Duras's *India Song*. In a big-budget action film, however, this is unprecedented.

79. In music, a *blue note* is a "microtonally lowered third, seventh or (less commonly) fifth degree of the diatonic scale, common in blues, jazz, and related music. The pitch or intonation of blue notes is not fixed precisely but varies according to the performer's instinct and expression. Together with other, noninflected, pitches they make up the blues scale." (Barry Kernfeld, ed., *The New Grove Dictionary of Jazz*. [London: Macmillan Press, 1988]). The Blue Note is also the name of several nightclubs.

80. *Thousand Plateaus*, p. 309. Once again, in this respect, Deleuze mentions drugs: "If the experimentation with drugs has left its mark on everyone, even nonusers, it is because it changed the perceptive coordinates of space-time and introduced us to a universe of microperceptions in which becomings-molecular take over where becomings-animal leave off" (p. 248).

81. *In Memoriam Gilles Deleuze*, released by Mille Plateaux, Frankfurt, 1996. The Belgian label Sub Rosa had already released *Folds and Rhizomes for Gilles Deleuze*, Brussels, 1995. In 1997, the tracks of this album were remixed as *Double Articulation: Another Plateau*.

82. Simon Frith, "Music and Identity," p. 123. Frith here quotes Paul Gilroy.

83. DJ Spooky is part of the New York underground club The Knitting Factory. As a writer, he publishes under the name Paul D. Miller.

84. See *Andere Sinema*, nos. 137/138/139, 1997, for a series of interviews with musicians and DJs influenced by Deleuze and Guattari and on the phenomenon of "imaginary soundtracks."

85. *Ocean of Sound*, p. 11.

86. Chion, who speaks about ambient sound, is (as a musician) influenced by the *music concrète*, which could also be seen as a precursor of ambient music.

87. *Ocean of Sound*, pp. 140 and 179.

88. *Performing Rites*, p. 142.

89. *Thousand Plateaus*, pp. 345–46.

90. On a more directly political level, the Anti-Globalist movement (or better the "Alternative Globalization" movement) that came into existence in the late 1990s can be aligned with the "organization" of "Love Paraders." Although the media tried to label this very heterogeneous group of people as a violent and anarchistic movement (especially around the G8 summit in Genoa in 2001), this movement does strive for a "people of a new kind" that is not organized according to old binary structures. It is a utopian movement in the sense that it tries to imagine a different world from the one that currently exists. In their book *Empire* (Harvard University Press, 2001), Michael Hardt and Toni Negri explore such a different world. Hardt and Negri are inspired by Spinoza and Deleuze. In an interview about the book, Hardt states: "We had the impression that the left had lost the utopian thinking. Utopia, not in the sense of an impossible world, but the ability to imagine a different and better world. Rather than just criticizing the present, which is often accompanied by a nostalgic longing for the past, we prefer to express a belief in the future" (*De Groene Amsterdammer*, September 1st, 2001, p. 11. My translation from the Dutch). In a similar spirit, Francesco Maselli, together with thirty other Italian directors, among whom Etore Scola composed an alternative report on the "Anti-globalist" demonstrations in Genoa in the film *Un Mondo Diverso E' Possibile* (2001; "A Different World is Possible").

91. Deleuze and Guattari, *Anti-Oedipus—Capitalism and Schizophrenia*. Trans. Robert Hurley, Mark Seem, and Helen R. Lane (London: The Athlone Press, 1984) p. xvi.

92. In *100% Arabica* (*Do the Rai Thing*), a film by Mahmoud Zemmouri from 1987, music plays a crucial role. In a multiethnic suburb of Paris, rai singers Cheb Mami and Khaled regularly give illegal street concerts that make many people come together and create a sense of community. The local Islamic fundamentalists try everything possible to prevent these events and to reestablish their power by blackmail and corruption. In a light way, the problems of fundamentalism and the power of music for the creation of a community are pictured here.

93. Henry Miller quoted by Mark Seem in his introduction to *Anti-Oedipus*, p. xxi.

94. Cf. Deleuze in his *Abécédaire*, letter "A" for Animal.

Conclusion

1. See, for instance, Ian Buchanan, ed. *A Deleuzian Century? South Atlantic Quarterly* 93:3, Summer 1997 (Durham: Duke University Press). The bibliography contains additional references.

2. In October 1997, Dutch television broadcast a program called *Mille Gilles* (VPRO television). The program gave an overview of the different disciplines that show an interest in Deleuze's work.

3. From the introduction to *Anti-Oedipus*. Ian Pindar recalls Deleuze's comparison of himself and Guattari to Laurel and Hardy. See "A Very Long Scream with the Odd Couple—Deleuze and Guattari as the Laurel and Hardy of French Thought" in *Times Literary Supplement* 4944, Jan. 1998. In *Negotiations*, Deleuze and Guattari emphasize the idea of an *air du temps*: "We need allies. And we think these allies are already out there, that they've gone ahead without us, that there are lots of people who've had enough and are thinking, feeling, and working into similar directions: it's not a question of fashion but of a deeper 'spirit of the age' informing converging projects in a wide range of fields" (p. 22).

4. As also indicated in the introduction, David Rodowick's *Gilles Deleuze's Time Machine* presents a metareflection on the philosophic implications of Deleuze's film books. Gregory Flaxman in *The Brain is the Screen* has collected various interesting articles on the cinema books that sometimes discuss specific films but in general remain on a philosophic and theoretic level as well. I have tried to work more in the mode Ian Buchanan characterizes as "applied Deleuzism" in his book *Deleuzism: A Metacommentary*.

5. For the "realism" of computer-generated images (CGI), see Lev Manovich, "Reality Effects in Computer Animation," *A Reader in Animation Studies*. Ed. Jayne Pilling (London, Paris, Rome, and Sydney: John Libbey and Company, 1997). See also Thomas Elsaesser and Kay Hoffmann, eds. *Cinema Futures: Cain, Able or Cable—Media Kinship in the Digital Age* (Amsterdam: Amsterdam University Press, 1998).

6. Gilles Deleuze, "Immanence: A Life . . . " Nick Millet. *Theory, Culture & Society—Explorations in Critical Social Science* 14(2). Trans. Nick Millet (London: Sage, May 1997:5). See also Gilles Deleuze, *Pure Immanence: Essays on A Life*. Introd. John Rajchman. Trans. Anne Boyman (New York: Zone Books, 2001).

7. In his book *Towards a Postmodern Theory of Narrative* (Edinburgh: Edinburgh University Press, 1996), Andrew Gibson proposes to look at narrative force by a "Deleuzian energetics": "Force is a certain pure and infinite equivocality which gives signified meaning no respite, no rest, but engages in its own economy so that it always signifies again and differs" (p. 33; Gibson here discusses a connection between Deleuze and Derrida). Gibson also refers to the virtual: "the shadow of excluded possibilities of the development of narratives" (especially in interactive narratives), which becomes part of the narrative. Multiple spaces, different time zones, parallel worlds, all form this virtual field of potential that accompanies the actualization of each narrative form, and in which each actualization becomes a narrative event.

8. See Martin Jay, *Downcast Eyes: The Denigration of Vision in Twentieth Century French Thought* (Berkeley and London: University of California Press, 1993).

9. "On est tous des molecules," claims Deleuze in the *Abécédaire*.

10. Roger Odin, "A Semio-Pragmatic Approach to the Documentary Film," in Warren Buckland (ed.), *The Film Spectator—From Sign to Mind* (Amsterdam: Amsterdam University Press, 1995) p. 233.

11. *Negotiations*, p. 6.

12. Deleuze quoted in *Gilles Deleuze's Time Machine*, p. 192 (from *Time-Image*).

13. *A Deleuzian Century?*, p. 386. We here see a different conception of the relation between the personal, the individual and the subject than is commonly assumed. In a common (bourgeois) conception of the subject, there is a close relation between the individual and the personal; in the psychoanalytic paradigm, the subject never coincides with the individual or the personal (there is always something lacking or missing); in a Deleuzian view, the "subject" is individuated by the nonpersonal.

14. From *Empiricism and Subjectivity*, quoted by Ian Buchanan in "Deleuze and Cultural Studies," in *A Deleuzian Century?*, p. 484.

15. *A Deleuzian Century?*, pp. 486–87.

16. This can be compared to Deleuze's nonhierarchical explanation about the change from the movement-image to the time-image: "The new image would therefore not be a bringing to completion of the cinema, but a mutation of it" (*Movement-Image*, p. 215). See also pp. 205–11 on "the crisis of the movement-image" and *Time-Image*, p. 264, about the relation between Hitler and Hollywood.

17. *Negotiations*, p. 136.

18. *Thousand Plateaus*, p. 3.

Bibliography

Abbate, C. "Opera; or, the Envoicing of Women." *Musicology and Difference: Gender and Sexuality in Music Scholarship*. Ed. R. Solie. Berkeley, Los Angeles, and London: University of California Press, 1993. 225–58.

Alliez, E. *Deleuze: Philosophie Virtuelle*. Le Plessis-Robinson: Synthélabo, 1996.

——., ed. *Gilles Deleuze: une vie philosophique* (Rencontres Internationales Rio de Janeiro–Sao Paulo juin 1996). Le Plessis-Robinson: Synthélabo, 1998.

Alphen, E. *Francis Bacon and the Loss of Self*. London: Reaktion Books, 1992.

Altman, R., ed. *Sound Theory—Sound Practice*. New York and London: Routledge, 1992.

Andrew, D. "The Roots of the Nomadic: Gilles Deleuze and the Cinema of West Africa." *The Brain is the Screen: Deleuze and the Philosophy of Cinema*. Ed. G. Flaxman. Minneapolis and London: University of Minnesota Press, 2000. 215–49.

Ansell Pearson, K., ed. *Deleuze and Philosophy: the Difference Engineer*. London and New York: Routledge, 1997.

Aumont, J. *Introduction à la couleur: des discours aux images*. Paris: Armand Colin, 1994.

Asselberghs, H. "De Mille Plateaux Remix." *Andere Sinema*, no. 138, Antwerp: Harry Eysakkers, 1997.

Balke, F., and J. Vogl, eds. *Gilles Deleuze: Fluchtlinien der Philosophie*. München: Wilhelm Fink Verlag, 1996.

Balsamo, A. *Technologies of the Gendered Body: Reading Cyborg Women*. Durham and London: Duke University Press, 1996.

Baudry, J. "The Apparatus: Metapsychological Approaches to the Impression of Reality in the Cinema." *Narrative, Apparatus, Ideology*. Ed. P. Rosen. New York: Columbia University Press, 1986. 299–318.

——. "Ideological Effects of the Basic Cinematographic Apparatus." *Narrative, Apparatus, Ideology*. Ed. P. Rosen. New York: Columbia University Press, 1986. 286–98.

Bell, E. "Somatexts at the Disney Shop: Constructing the Pentimentos of

Women's Animated Bodies." From *Mouse to Mermaid: The Politcs of Film, Gender and Culture*. Bloomington and Indianapolis: Indiana University Press, 1995. 107–24.

Bell, E., et al., eds. *From Mouse to Mermaid: The Politics of Film, Gender and Culture*. Bloomington and Indianapolis: Indiana University Press, 1995.

Beller, J. "Capital/Cinema." *Deleuze and Guattari: New Mappings in Politics, Philosophy and Culture*. Ed. E. Kaufman and K. J. Heller. Minneapolis and London: University of Minnesota Press, 1998. 77–95.

Bellour, R., ed. "Gilles Deleuze." *Magazine Littéraire* (Special Issue) 257 September 1988.

———. "Penser, raconter. Le cinéma de Gilles Deleuze," *Der Film bei Deleuze*. Ed. O. Fahle and L. Engel. Weimar and Paris: Verlag der Bauhaus Universität and Presses de la Sorbonne Nouvelle, 1997. 22–40.

Benjamin, W. "Thesis on the Philosophy of History." Trans. H. Zohn. New York: Schocken Books, 1969. Reprinted in H. Adams and L. Searle, eds. *Critical Theory Since 1965*. Tallahassee: University Presses of Florida, 1986. 680–85.

Bergson, H. *Matière et mémoire: essai sur la relation du corps à l'esprit*. Paris: PUF, 1993 (first publ. 1896); *Matter and Memory*. Trans. N. M. Paul and W. S. Palmer. New York: Zone Books, 1988.

———. *Le rire: essai sur la signification du comique*. Paris: PUF, 1990 (first publ. 1899).

Bernard, J. *Quentin Tarantino: The Man and his Movies*. London: HarperCollins, 1995.

Bogue, R. *Deleuze and Guattari*. London and New York: Routledge, 1989.

Boundas, C. *The Deleuze Reader*. New York: Columbia University Press, 1993.

Boundas, C., and D. Olkowski, eds. *Gilles Deleuze and the Theater of Philosophy*. New York: Routledge, 1994.

Braidotti, R. *Patterns of Dissonance: a Study of Woman and Contemporary Philosophy*. Cambridge: Polity Press, 1991.

———., ed. *Post-restante: feministische berichten aan het postmoderne*. Kampen: Kok Agora, 1994.

———. Nomadic Subjects: *Embodiment and Sexual Difference in Contemporary Feminist Theory*. New York: Columbia University Press, 1994.

———. "Teratologies." *Deleuze and Feminist Theory*. Ed. I. Buchanan and C. Colebrook. Edinburgh: Edinburgh University Press, 2000. 156–72.

Brenez, N. "Le voyage absolu: remarques sur la theorie contemporaine." *Art Press, un second siècle pour le cinéma*, no. 14, 1993; "The Ultimate Journey: remarks on contemporary theory." Trans. W. Routt, et al. *Screening the Past*. <http://www.latrobe.edu.au/www/screeningthepast/>.

Buchanan, I., ed. *A Deleuzian Century? South Atlantic Quarterly* (Special issue) 96 (no. 3) Summer 1997.

————. *Deleuzism: A Metacommentary.* Edinburgh: Edinburgh University Press, 2000.

Buchanan, I., and C. Colebrook, eds. *Deleuze and Feminist Theory.* Edinburgh: Edinburgh University Press, 2000.

Buckland, W., ed. *The Film Spectator: From Sign to Mind.* Amsterdam: Amsterdam University Press, 1995.

Bukatman, S. *Terminal Identity: The Virtual Subject in Post-Modern Science Fiction.* Durham: Duke University Press, 1993.

————. *Blade Runner.* London: BFI, 1997.

Butler, J. *Bodies that Matter: on the Discursive Limits of "Sex."* New York and London: Routledge, 1993.

————. *Gender Trouble: Feminism and the Subversion of Identity.* New York and London: Routledge, 1990.

Caldwell, J. *Televisuality: Style, Crisis and Authority in American Television.* New Brunswick, NJ: Rutgers University Press, 1995.

Canning, P. "The Imagination of Immanence: An Ethics of Cinema." *The Brain is the Screen: Deleuze and the Philosophy of Cinema.* Ed. G. Flaxman. Minneapolis and London: University of Minnesota Press, 2000. 327–62.

Chabrol, C., and E. Rohmer. *Hitchcock: the First Forty-Four Films.* New York: Frederick Ungar, 1979.

Chion, M. *Audio-Visions: Sound on Screen.* Ed. and Trans. C. Gorgman. New York: Columbia University Press, 1994.

————. *La parole au cinéma.* Paris: Editions de L'Etoile, 1985.

————. *La toile trouée.* Paris: Editions de L'Etoile, 1988.

————. *La voix au cinéma.* Paris: Editions de L'Etoile, 1982.

Cholodenko, A., ed. *The Illusion of Life: Essays on Animation.* Sydney: Power Publications, 1991.

Clover, C. *Men, Women and Chain Saws: Gender in the Modern Horror Film.* Princeton: Princeton University Press, 1992.

Cohan, S., and I. Rae Hark, eds. *Screening the Male: Exploring Masculinities in Hollywood Cinema.* London and New York: Routledge, 1993.

Colebrook, C. *Gilles Deleuze.* London and New York: Routledge, 2002.

Collins, J., et al., eds. *Film Theory Goes to the Movies.* London and New York: Routledge, 1993.

Comolli, J. "Machines of the Visible." *The Cinematic Apparatus.* Ed. T. de Lauretis and S. Heath. Houndmills, Basingstoke, and London: Macmillan, 1980. 121–42.

————. "Technique and Ideology: Camera, Perspective, Depth of Field." *Narrative, Apparatus, Ideology.* Ed. P. Rosen. New York: Columbia University Press, 1986. 421–43.

Cook, P., and P. Dudd, eds. *Women and Film: A Sight and Sound Reader.* London: Temple University Press, 1993.

Copjec, J. *Read my Desire: Lacan Against the Historicists.* Cambridge: MIT Press, 1994.

————., ed. *Shades of Noir.* London: Verso, 1993.

————., ed. *Supposing the Subject.* London: Verso, 1994.

Corrigan, T. *A Cinema without Walls. Movies and Culture after Vietnam.* London: Routledge, 1991.

Curley, E., ed. *A Spinoza Reader.* Princeton: Princeton University Press, 1994.

Creed, B. *The Monstrous Feminine: Film, Feminism, Psychoanalysis.* London: Routledge, 1993.

De Lauretis, T. *Alice Doesn't: Feminism, Semiotics, Cinema.* Bloomington: Indiana University Press, 1984.

————. *Technologies of Gender: Essay on Theory, Film and Fiction.* Bloomington: Indiana University Press, 1987.

Deleuze, G. "L'actuel et le virtuel," in *Dialogues.* Paris: Flammarion, edition 1997. 179–85.

————. "Avoir une idée en cinéma." *Hölderlin Cézanne.* Ed. Jean-Marie Straub and Danièle Huillet. Paris: Editions Antigone, 1990.

————. *Le bergsonisme.* Paris: PUF, 1966.

————. *Cinéma 1: L'image-mouvement.* Paris: Editions de Minuit, 1983; *Cinema 1: The Movement-Image.* Trans. H. Tomlinson and B. Habberjam. London: The Athlone Press, 1986.

————. *Cinéma 2: L'image-temps.* Paris: Editions de Minuit, 1985; *Cinema 2: The Time-Image.* Trans. H. Tomlinson and R. Galeta. London: The Athlone Press, 1989.

————. "Le cerveau, c'est l'écran." *Cahiers du Cinéma.* 1986; "The Brain is the Screen." Trans. M. T. Guiris; Ed. G. Flaxman. *The Brain is the Screen: Deleuze and the Philosophy of Cinema.* Minneapolis and London: University of Minnesota Press, 2000. 365–73.

————. *Critique et clinique.* Paris: Editions de Minuit, 1993; *Essays Critical and Clinical.* Trans. D. W. Smith and M. A. Greco. London and New York: Verso, 1998.

————. *Différence et répétition.* Paris: PUF, 1968; *Difference and Repetition.* Trans. P. Patton. London: The Athlone Press, 1994.

————. *Empirisme et subjectivité: essai sur la nature humaine selon Hume.* Paris: PUF, 1953; *Empiricism and Subjectivity.* Trans. C. Boundas. New York: Columbia University Press, 1991.

————. *L'épuisé.* Paris: Editions de Minuit, 1992 (published with *Quad et autres pièces pour la télévision* by Samuel Becket).

————. *Foucault.* Paris: Editions de Minuit, 1986.

————. *Francis Bacon: logique de la sensation.* Paris: Editions de la Différence, 1981.

————. "L'immanence: une vie . . . ," in *Philosophie*, no. 47. Paris: Editions de

Minuit, 1995; "Immanence, A Life." Trans. N. Millet. *Theory, Culture and Society: Explorations in Critical Social Science.* Vol. 14, no. 2. London, Thousand Oaks, and New Delhi: Sage 1997. 3–7.

————. *Logique du sens.* Paris: Editions de Minuit, 1969; The *Logic of Sense.* Trans. M. Lester and C. Stivale. New York: Columbia University Press, 1990.

————. *Nietzsche et la philosophie.* Paris: PUF, 1962.

————. "Optimisme, pessimisme et voyage—lettre à Serge Daney." *Serge Daney, Cinéjournal 1981–1986.* Paris: Editions du Cinéma, 1986.

————. *La philosophie critique de Kant.* Paris: PUF, 1963.

————. *Le pli: Leibniz et le baroque.* Paris: Editions de Minuit, 1988; *The Fold: Leibniz and the Baroque.* Trans. T. Conley. Minneapolis and London: University of Minnesota Press, 1993.

————. *Pourparlers.* Paris: Editions de Minuit, 1990; *Negotiations.* Trans. M. Joughin. New York: Columbia University Press, 1995.

————. *Présentation de Sacher Masoch.* Paris: Editions de Minuit, 1967.

————. *Proust et les signes.* Paris: PUF, 1964.

————. *Pure Immanence. Essays on A Life.* Introd. J. Rajchman; Trans. Anne Boyman. New York: Zone Books, 2001.

————. *Spinoza et le problème de l'expression.* Paris: Editons de Minuit, 1968; *Expressionism in Philosophy: Spinoza.* Trans. M. Joughin. New York: Zone Books, 1992.

————. *Spinoza: philosophie pratique.* Paris: Editions de Minuit, 1981; *Spinoza: Practical Philosophy.* Trans. R. Herley. San Francisco: City Lights, 1988.

————. "Trois questions sur six fois deux." *Cahiers du Cinéma* 271. November 1976.

Deleuze, G., and C. Bene. *Superpositions.* Paris: Editions de Minuit, 1979.

Deleuze, G., and F. Guattari. *Anti-oedipe: capitalisme et schizophrénie.* Paris: Editions de Minuit, 1972; *Anti-Oedipus: Capitalism and Schizophrenia.* Trans. R. Hurley, et al. London: The Athlone Press, 1984.

————. *Kafka: pour une littérature mineure.* Paris: Editions de Minuit, 1975.

————. *Mille plateaux: capitalisme et schizophrénie.* Paris: Editions de Minuit, 1980; *A Thousand Plateaus: Capitalism and Schizophrenia.* Trans. B. Massumi. London: The Athlone Press, 1988.

————. *Qu'est-ce que la philosophie?* Paris: Editions de Minuit, 1991; *What is Philosophy?* Trans. G. Burchell and H. Tomlinson. London and New York: Verso, 1994.

Deleuze, G., and C. Parnet. *Dialogues.* Paris: Flammarion, 1977; *Dialogues.* Trans. H. Tomlinson and B. Habberjam. New York: Columbia University Press, 1987.

Dery, M., ed. *Escape Velocity: Cyberculture at the End of the Century.* New York: Grove Press, 1996.

————. *Flame Wars: The Discourse of Cyberculture.* Durham: Duke University Press, 1994.

Doane, M. *The Desire to Desire: The Woman's Film of the 1940s*. Bloomington and Indianapolis: Indiana University Press, 1987.

———. *Femmes Fatales: Feminism, Film Theory, Psychoanalysis*. New York and London: Routledge, 1991.

———. "The Voice in the Cinema: the Articulation of Body and Space." *Yale French Studies* 60, 1980. Reprinted in P. Rosen, ed. *Narrative, Apparatus, Ideology*. New York: Columbia University Press, 1986. 335–48.

Drew, W. *David Cronenberg*. London: BFI dossier no. 21, 1984.

Dunn, L., and N. Jones, eds. *Embodied Voices: Representing Female Vocality in Western Culture*. Cambridge: Cambridge University Press, 1994.

Duras, Marguerite. *Le navire night et autres texts*. Paris: Mercure de France, 1979.

———. *Les Yeux Verts*. Paris: Cahiers du Cinéma and Gallimard, 1980.

Eisenstein, S. *Film Form. Essays in Film Theory*. Trans. J. Leyda. New York: Harvest Books, 1949.

Elsaesser, T. *Fassbinder's Germany: History, Identity, Subject*. Amsterdam: Amsterdam University Press, 1995.

———. *New German Cinema: A History*. Houndmills, Basingstoke, Hampshire, and London: Macmillan Press, 1989.

———., ed. *Space, Frame, Narrative*. London: BFI and Bloomington University Press, 1990.

Elsaesser, T., and K. Hoffmann, eds. *Cinema Futures: Cain and Able or Cable? Media Kinship in the Digital Age*. Amsterdam: Amsterdam University Press, 1998.

Elsaesser, T., and M. Wedel. "The Hollow Heart of Hollywood: *Apocalypse Now* and the New Sound Space." *Conrad on Film*. Ed. K. Moore. Cambridge: Cambridge University Press, 1997.

Esquenazi, J. *Film, perception et mémoire*. Paris: L'Harmattan, 1994.

Evens A., et al. "Another Always Thinks in Me." *Deleuze and Guattari: New Mappings in Politics, Philosophy and Culture*. Ed. E. Kaufman and K. J. Heler. Minneapolis and London: University of Minnesota Press, 1998. 270–80.

Fahle, O., and L. Engell, eds. *Der Film bei Deleuze/Le cinéma selon Deleuze*. Weimar and Paris: Verlag der Bauhaus-Universität and Presses de la Sorbonne Nouvelle, 1997.

Flaxman, G., ed. *The Brain is the Screen: Deleuze and the Philosophy of Cinema*. Minneapolis and London: University of Minnesota Press, 2000.

Flieger, J. A. "Becoming-Woman: Deleuze, Schreber and Molecular Identification." *Deleuze and Feminist Theory*. Ed. I. Buchanan and C. Colebrook. Minneapolis and London: University of Minnesota Press, 2000. 38–63.

Foucault, M. "Theatrum philosophicum." *Language, Counter-Memory, Practice*. Trans. D. Bouchard and S. Simon. Ithaca: Cornell University Press, 1977.

French, K., ed. *Screen Violence*. London: Bloomsbury, 1996.

Friedberg, A. *Window Shopping: Cinema and the Postmodern*. Berkeley: University of California Press, 1993.

Frith, S. *Performing Rites: On the Value of Popular Music.* Oxford and New York: Oxford University Press, 1996.

———. "Music and Identity." *Questions of Cultural Identity.* Ed. S. Hall and P. du Gay, eds. London: Sage, 1996. 108–27.

Gatens, M. *Feminism and Philosophy: Perspectives on Difference and Equality.* Cambridge: Polity Press, 1990.

———. *Imaginary Bodies: Ethics, Power and Corporeality.* London and New York: Routledge, 1996.

———. "Through a Spinozist Lens: Ethology, Difference, Power." *Deleuze: A Critical Reader.* Ed. P. Patton. Oxford and Cambridge: Blackwell, 1996. 162–87.

Genosko, G., ed. *The Guattari Reader.* Oxford and Cambridge: Blackwell, 1996.

Gibson, A. *Towards a Postmodern Theory of Narrative.* Edinburgh: Edinburgh University Press, 1996.

Gilmore, R. *Alice in Quantumland: An Allegory of Quantum Physics.* New York: Springer Verlag, 1995.

Gledhill, C. *Home is Where the Heart is: Studies in Melodrama and the Woman's Film.* London: BFI, 1987.

Goodchild, P. *Deleuze and Guattari: An Introduction to the Politics of Desire.* London: Thousand Oaks and New Delhi: Sage Publications, 1996.

Goodwin, A. *Dancing in the Distraction Factory: Music Television and Popular Culture.* London: Routledge, 1993.

Griggers, C. *Becoming-Woman.* Minneapolis and London: University of Minnesota Press, 1997.

Grosz, E. *Volatile Bodies, Toward a Corporeal Feminism.* Bloomington and Indianapolis: Indiana University Press, 1994.

Guattari, F. *Chaosophy.* New York: Semiotext[e], 1995.

———. *La révolution moléculaire.* Fontenay-sous-Bois: Editions Recherches, 1977.

Hables Gray, C., et al., eds. *The Cyborg Handbook.* New York and London: Routledge, 1995.

Haraway, D. *Modest_Witness@Second_Millennium.FemaleMan©_Meets_OncoMouse^{TM}: Feminism and Technoscience.* New York and London: Routledge, 1997.

———. "The Promise of Monsters: a Regenerative Politics for Inappropriated Others." *Cultural Studies.* Ed. L. Nelson and P. Treichler. New York: Routledge. 1992. 295–337.

———. *Simians, Cyborgs and Woman: The Reinvention of Nature.* London: Free Association Books, 1991.

Hardt, M. *Gilles Deleuze: An Apprenticeship in Philosophy.* London: UCL Press, 1993.

Hardt, M., and T. Negri. *Empire.* Harvard University Press, 2001.

Hayward, S. *Luc Besson.* Manchester and New York: Manchester University Press, 1998.

Heath, S., and T. de Lauretis, eds. *The Cinematic Apparatus*. London: Macmillan Press, 1980.

Heusen, J. *The Duration of Oblivion: Deleuze and Forgetting in Fight Club and Lost Highway*. M.A. thesis. Amsterdam: University of Amsterdam, 2000.

Hofstadter, D., and Dennett, D. *The Mind's I: Fantasies and Reflections on Self and Soul*. London, New York: Penguin, 1981.

Holland, E. *Deleuze and Guattari's Anti-Oedipus: Introduction to Schizoanalysis*. London and New York: Routledge, 1999.

hooks, b. *Black Looks: Race and Representation*. Boston: South End Press, 1992.

———. *Reel to Real: Race, Sex and Class at the Movies*. New York and London: Routledge, 1996.

Hunter, S. *Violent Screen*. New York: Delta Books, 1995.

Jay, M. *Downcast Eyes: The Denigration of Vision in Twentieth Century French Thought*. Berkeley and London: University of California Press, 1993.

Jayamanne, L., ed. *Kiss Me Deadly: Feminism and Cinema for the Moment*. Sydney: Power Publications, 1995.

Kahn, D., and G. Whitehead, eds. *Wireless Imagination: Sound, Radio and the Avant Garde*. Cambridge and London: MIT Press, 1992.

Kaufman, E., and K. J. Heller, eds. *Deleuze and Guattari: New Mapping in Politics, Philosophy and Culture*. Minneapolis and London: University of Minnesota Press, 1998.

Kristeva, J. *Pouvoirs de l'horreur*. Paris: Editions du Seuil, 1980.

Kuhn, A., ed. *Alien Zone—Cultural Theory and Contemporary Science Fiction Cinema*. London and New York: Verso, 1990.

Lanford, M. "Film Figures: Rainer Werner Fassbinder's *The Marriage of Maria Braun* and Alexander Kluge's *The Female Patriot*." *Kiss Me Deadly: Feminism and Cinema for the Moment*. Ed. Laleen Jayamanne. Sydney: Power Publications, 1995. 147–79.

Lanza, J. *Elevator Music—A Surreal History of Muzak, Easy Listening, and Other Moodsongs*. New York: Picador, 1994.

Leutrat, J. *Kaleidoscope: analyses de films*. Lyon: Presses Universitaires de Lyon, 1988.

Leyda, J., ed. *Eisenstein on Disney*. Trans. A. Upchurch. London: Methuen, 1988.

Lindon, G., ed. "Gilles Deleuze." *Philosophie* (Special Issue) 47, September 1995.

Lippitt, J. "Nietzsche, Zarathustra and the Status of Laughter." *British Journal of Aesthetics* 32(1), 39–49, 1992.

Lloyd, G. *Being in Time: Selves and Narrators in Philosophy and Literature*. London and New York: Routledge, 1993.

———. *Spinoza and the Ethics*. London and New York: Routledge, 1996.

Lykke, N., and R. Braidotti, eds. *Between Monsters, Goddesses and Cyborgs. Feminist Confrontations with Science, Medicine and Cyberspace*. London and New Jersey: Zed Books, 1996.

Lynn, G., ed. *Folding in Architecture*. London: Academy Editions, 1993.

Manovich, L. "'Reality' Effects in Computer Animation," in J. Pilling, ed. *A Reader in Animation Studies*. Sydney: John Libbey and Company, 1997. 5–15.

Marks, L. *The Skin of Film: Intercultural Cinema, Embodiment and the Senses*. Durham and London: Duke University Press, 2000.

Massumi, B. *A User's Guide to Capitalism and Schizophrenia: Deviations from Deleuze and Guattari*. Cambridge and London: MIT Press, 1992.

———. "Too-Blue Colour-Patch for an Expanded Empiricism." *Cultural Studies* 14(2). London: Routledge, April 2000. 177–226.

Mellencamp, P. *A Fine Romance: Five Ages of Film Feminism*. Philadelphia: Temple University Press, 1995.

Merck, M., ed. *The Sexual Subject—A Screen Reader in Sexuality*. London and New York: Routledge, 1992.

Merleau-Ponty, M. *L'oeil et L'esprit*. Paris: Gallimard, 1964.

———. *Phénoménologie de la perception*. Paris: Gallimard, 1945.

Metz, C. *Film Language: A Semiotics of Cinema*. Trans. M. Taylor. New York: Oxford University Press, 1974.

———. "The Imaginary Signifier." *Screen* 16(2), 14–76, Summer 1975.

Modleski, T. *The Woman Who Knew Too Much: Hitchcock and Feminist Theory*. New York and London: Methuen, 1988.

Moore, F. *Bergson: Thinking Backwards*. Cambridge: Cambridge University Press, 1996.

Mulvey, L. *Visual and Other Pleasures*. Bloomington: Indiana University Press, 1989.

Negua, K. *Popular Music in Theory: An Introduction*. Cambridge and Oxford: Polity Press, 1996.

Nichols, B., ed. *Movies and Methods*, Volume I and Volume II. Berkeley: University of California Press, 1976 and 1985.

Noon, J. *Automated Alice*. New York: Crown Publishers, 1996.

Odin, R. "A Semio-Pragmatic Approach to the Documentary Film." *The Film Spectator*. Ed. W. Buckland. 1995. 227–35.

Olkowski, D. *Gilles Deleuze and the Ruin of Representation*. Berkeley, Los Angeles and London: University of California Press, 1998.

Patton, P. ed. *Deleuze: A Critical Reader*. Oxford and Cambridge: Blackwell, 1996.

———. *Deleuze and the Political*. London and New York: Routledge, 2000.

Penley, C., ed. *Feminism and Film Theory*. New York: Routledge, 1988.

———. *Future of an Illusion—Film, Feminism and Psychoanalysis*. London: Routledge, 1989.

Penley, C., et al., eds. *Close Encounters—Film, Feminism and Science Fiction*. Minneapolis: University of Minnesota Press, 1991.

Penley, C., and A. Ross. "Cyborgs at Large: Interview with Donna Haraway." *Technoculture*. Minneapolis: University of Minnesota Press, 1991.

Pindar, I. "A Very Long Scream with the Odd Couple: Deleuze and Guattari as the Laurel and Hardy of French Thought." *Times Literary Supplement* 4944, January 1998.

Pisters, P. "Cyborg Alice; or, Becoming-Woman in an Audiovisual World." *IRIS* 23, 147–64, 1997.

———., ed. *Micropolitics of Media Culture—Reading the Rhizomes of Deleuze and Guattari*. Amsterdam: Amsterdam University Press, 2001.

———. "The War of Images: Appropriation and Fabulation of Missing People." *ASCA Brief: Privacies*. Ed. B. Roessler. Amsterdam: ASCA Press, 2000. 69–81.

Polan, D. *Pulp Fiction*. London: British Film Institute, 2000.

Probyn, E. *Outside Belongings*. London and New York: Routledge, 1996.

Rajchman, J. *The Deleuze Connections*. Cambridge, Mass. and London: The MIT Press, 2001.

Rodowick, D. *The Difficulty of Difference: Psychoanalysis, Sexual Difference and Film Theory*. New York and London: Routledge, 1991.

———. *Gilles Deleuze's Time Machine*. Durham: Duke University Press, 1997.

———., ed. "Gilles Deleuze, Philosopher of Cinema/Gilles Deleuze, philosophe du cinéma." *IRIS* 23, Spring 1997.

Rosen, P., ed. *Narrative, Apparatus, Ideology*. New York: Columbia University Press, 1986.

Sage, L., ed. *Flesh and the Mirror. Essays on the Art of Angela Carter*. London: Virago, 1994.

Shapiro, M. *Cinematic Thought: Narrating Race, Nation and Gender*. Edinburgh: Edinburgh University Press, 1999.

Shaviro, S. *The Cinematic Body*. Minneapolis and London: University of Minnesota Press, 1993.

Silverman, K. *The Acoustic Mirror: the Female Voice in Psychoanalysis and Cinema*. Bloomington and Indianapolis: Indiana University Press, 1988.

———. *Male Subjectivity at the Margins*. London and New York: Routledge, 1992.

———. *The Subject of Semiotics*. New York: Oxford University Press, 1987.

———. *The Threshold of the Visible World*. London and New York: Routledge, 1996.

———. *World Spectators*. Stanford: Stanford University Press, 2000.

Smith, J. "Speaking Up for Corpses." *Screen Violence*. Ed. K. French. London: Bloomsbury Publishing, 1996. 196–204.

Sobchack, V. *The Address of the Eye: a Phenomenology of Film Experience*. New Jersey: Princeton University Press, 1992.

———. *Screening Space: The American Science Fiction Film*. New York: Ungar Press, 1987.

———. "Towards a Phenomenology of Cinematic and Electronic Presence: The Scene of the Screen." *Post-Script* 10, 1990.

Spoto, D. *The Dark Side of Genius: The Life of Alfred Hitchcock.* New York: Ballantine, 1984.

Stam, R. *Film Theory: An Introduction.* Malden and Oxford: Blackwell, 2000.

Stam, R., and S. Flitterman-Lewis, eds. *New Vocabularies in Film Semiotics, Structuralism, Post-Structuralism and Beyond.* London and New York: Routledge, 1992.

Stivale, C. *The Two-Fold Thought of Deleuze and Guattari.* New York and London: The Guilford Press, 1998.

Studlar, G. "De-Territorial Imperative." *Quarterly Review of Film and Video* 12(3), 1990.

———. "Masochism and the Perverse Pleasure of Cinema." *Movies and Methods,* Vol. II. Ed. B. Nichols. Berkeley and Los Angeles: University of California Press, 1985. 602–21.

Tapsoba, C., ed. *Tribute to Djibril Diop Mambety. African Screen,* vol. 7, no. 24, 1998.

Tarkovski, A. *Sculpting in Time: Reflections on the Cinema.* New York: Alfred Knopf, 1987.

Tasker, Y. *Spectacular Bodies: Gender, Genre and the Action Cinema.* London: Routledge, 1993.

Thompson, B. M. "Idiocy, Foolishness, and Spastic Jesting" in *P.O.V., A Danish Journal of Film Studies* 10, 47–60, December 2000.

Thornton, S. *Club Cultures: Music, Media and Subcultural Capital.* Cambridge and Oxford: Polity Press, 1995.

Toop, D. *Ocean of Sound. Aether Talk, Ambient Sound and Imaginary Worlds.* London and New York: Serpent Tail, 1995.

Toubiana, S. "Le cinéma est Deleuzien." *Cahiers du Cinéma* 497, 1995.

Truffaut, F. *Hitchcock/Truffaut.* New York: Simon and Schuster, 1967.

Turim, M. *Flashbacks in Film: Memory and History.* New York and London: Routledge, 1989.

Vojkovic, S. *Subjectivity in the New Hollywood Cinema: Fathers, Sons and Other Ghosts.* Amsterdam: ASCA Press, 2001.

Werven, van, B. *De Herinneringsmachine: Godard, Deleuze, Histoire(s).* Amsterdam: M.A. thesis, University of Amsterdam, 2000.

Williams, L. *Hardcore: Power, Pleasure and The Frenzy of the Visible.* London: Pandora, 1987.

———. "The Body in Horror, Science Fiction and Melodrama." *Film Quarterly* 44, 1991.

Willis, S. "The Fathers Watch The Boys' Room." Camera *Obscura* 32, 1994.

Woolf, V. *Orlando.* London: The Hogarth Press, 1928 and Penguin, 1993.

Zaoui, P. "La grande identité: Nietzsche et Spinoza—quelle identité?" in *Philosophie.* No. 47. Paris: Editions de Minuit, 1995.

Žižek, S. *Enjoy Your Symptom! Jacques Lacan in Hollywood and Out*. London and New York: Routledge, 1992.

————., ed. *Everything You Always Wanted to Know about Lacan . . . But Were Afraid to Ask Hitchcock*. London and New York: Verso, 1992.

————. *For They Know Not What They Do: Enjoyment as Political Factor*. London: Verso, 1991.

————. *Looking Awry: an Introduction to Jaques Lacan through Popular Culture*. Cambridge and Massachusetts: MIT Press, 1991.

————. "Grimaces of the Real, or When the Phallus Appears," *October* 56, 44–68, 1992.

————. "The Lamella of David Lynch." *Reading Seminar XI: Lacan's Four Fundamental Concepts of Psychoanalysis*. Ed. R. Feldskin et al. New York: State University of New York Press, 1995. 205–20.

————. "The Matrix, the Two Sides of Perversion." <http://www.britannica.com.>.

————. *The Metastases of Enjoyment: Six Essays on Women and Causality*. London and New York: Verso, 1994.

————. *The Plague of Fantasies*. London and New York: Verso, 1997.

————. *The Sublime Object of Ideology*. London: Verso, 1989.

————. *Tarrying with the Negative—Kant, Hegel and the Critique of Ideology*. Durham: Duke University Press, 1993.

Žižek, S., and R. Salect, eds. *Gaze and Voice as Love Objects*. Durham and London: Duke University Press, 1996.

Zohar, D. *The Quantum Self*. London: HarperCollins, 1991.

Zourbichvilli, F. *Deleuze, une philosophie de l'événement*. Paris: PUF, 1994.

Index

100% Arabica, 281*n*92

Abbate, Carolyn, 198, 199, 201
Abducted, 213, 214
abject, the, 47, 48, 50, 52, 55, 75, 142, 182
abject femininity, 5, 47–49, 53, 56, 142,
   183, 193
acousmatic sound, 179–81, 198, 200–
   202, 212
acoustic mirror, 5, 177, 180, 183, 186, 192,
   197, 205
action-image, 12, 42, 78, 97, 100, 101,
   104, 217, 227, 230, 254*n*33; and
   material aspects of subjectivity, 46,
   58–63, 65, 71, 74, 75; and time-image,
   79, 83, 99, 102; and violence, 80, 82,
   95. *See also* assemblage
actual and virtual, 3, 4, 33, 36, 38, 75, 83,
   121, 213, 214, 224, 228, 265*n*41
actualization, 114, 151, 205, 214, 228,
   271*n*34, 282*n*7
Adorno, Theodor, 189
aesthetic figures, 10, 106–8, 120, 122, 123,
   131–33, 140
affection, 70, 73, 144, 145, 148, 227, 228
affection-image, 46, 58, 60, 66, 68, 70–
   72, 74, 75, 80, 127, 187, 204, 217, 227,
   230, 247*n*19; and becoming-animal,
   10, 69, 70, 75, 142, 145–48, 151, 153

African cinema, 10, 72, 92, 218, 254*n*46
Aion, 120, 123–27, 131
Alice: as aesthetic figure, 120–23, 127–
   32, 134, 140; as conceptual persona, 10,
   107, 205; and becoming-woman, 108,
   109, 111, 112, 120, 127, 151, 165, 195,
   205; cyborg, 117–20, 128–30, 196, 205,
   214, 224; and feminism, 112, 115
Alice in the Cities, 121, 123
American Beauty, 1, 2
Angel of Vengeance/Ms. 45, 51
Anti-Oedipus, 9, 96, 212, 216, 217, 223
any-space-whatever, 122, 151, 192, 227,
   230
Artaud, Antonin, 199, 200, 263*n*25
assemblage, 4–7, 9, 10, 47, 58–61, 75–
   77, 80, 95–97, 114, 117, 142, 144, 148,
   153, 168, 204, 217, 218, 221; and action-
   image, 61, 63, 59; and affection-image,
   68, 69; and becoming-woman, 131–33,
   139; and (de)territorialization, 58, 188,
   191; machinic, 1, 9, 10, 52, 152, 199,
   209, 218; rhizomatic, 7, 60, 224; and
   sound, 191, 199, 209; tetravalence of,
   10, 58–60; and time-image, 72, 75
Atalante, L', 203
Atlantis, 202, 203
audiovisual culture, 11, 14, 96, 141, 142,
   177, 214, 218. *See also* visual culture

Cultural Memory | *in the Present*

Ian Balfour, *The Rhetoric of Romantic Prophecy*

Martin Stokhof, *World and Life as One: Ethics and Ontology in Wittgenstein's Early Thought*

Gianni Vattimo, *Nietzsche: An Introduction*

Jacques Derrida, *Negotiations: Interventions and Interviews, 1971-1998*, ed. Elizabeth Rottenberg

Brett Levinson, *The Ends of Literature: Post-transition and Neoliberalism in the Wake of the "Boom"*

Timothy J. Reiss, *Against Autonomy: Global Dialectics of Cultural Exchange*

Hent de Vries and Samuel Weber, eds., *Religion and Media*

Niklas Luhmann, *Theories of Distinction: Re-Describing the Descriptions of Modernity*, ed. and introd. William Rasch

Johannes Fabian, *Anthropology with an Attitude: Critical Essays*

Michel Henry, *I am the Truth: Toward a Philosophy of Christianity*

Gil Anidjar, *"Our Place in Al-Andalus": Kabbalah, Philosophy, Literature in Arab-Jewish Letters*

Hélène Cixous and Jacques Derrida, *Veils*

F. R. Ankersmit, *Historical Representation*

F. R. Ankersmit, *Political Representation*

Elissa Marder, *Dead Time: Temporal Disorders in the Wake of Modernity (Baudelaire and Flaubert)*

Reinhart Koselleck, *The Practice of Conceptual History: Timing History, Spacing Concepts*

Niklas Luhmann, *The Reality of the Mass Media*

Hubert Damisch, *A Childhood Memory by Piero della Francesca*

Hubert Damisch, *A Theory of /Cloud/: Toward a History of Painting*

Jean-Luc Nancy, *The Speculative Remark (One of Hegel's bon mots)*